INSIGHT GUIDES

Korea

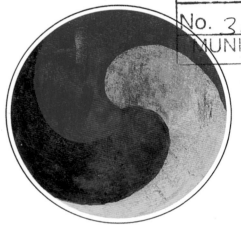

Discovery
CHANNEL

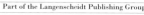
APA PUBLICATIONS L
Part of the Langenscheidt Publishing Group

INSIGHT GUIDES
Korea

ABOUT THIS BOOK

Editorial

Editor
Tom Le Bas
Editorial Director
Brian Bell

Distribution

UK & Ireland
GeoCenter International Ltd
The Viables Centre, Harrow Way
Basingstoke, Hants RG22 4BJ
Fax: (44) 1256 817988

United States
Langenscheidt Publishers, Inc.
46–35 54th Road, Maspeth, NY 11378
Fax: 1 (718) 784 0640

Canada
Thomas Allen & Son Ltd
390 Steelcase Road East
Markham, Ontario L3R 1G2
Fax: (1) 905 475 6747

Australia
Universal Publishers
1 Waterloo Road
Macquarie Park, NSW 2113
Fax: (61) 2 9888 9074

New Zealand
Hema Maps New Zealand Ltd (HNZ)
Unit D, 24 Ra ORA Drive
East Tamaki, Auckland
Fax: (64) 9 273 6479

Worldwide
Apa Publications GmbH & Co.
Verlag KG (Singapore branch)
38 Joo Koon Road, Singapore 628990
Tel: (65) 6865 1600. Fax: (65) 6861 6438

Printing

Insight Print Services (Pte) Ltd
38 Joo Koon Road, Singapore 628990
Tel: (65) 6865 1600. Fax: (65) 6861 6438

© 2005 Apa Publications GmbH & Co.
Verlag KG (Singapore branch)
All Rights Reserved
First Edition 1981
Eighth Edition 2001
Updated 2005

This guidebook combines the interests and enthusiasms of two of the world's best known information providers: Insight Guides, whose titles have set the standard for visual travel guides since 1970, and Discovery Channel, the world's premier source of nonfiction television programming.

The editors of Insight Guides provide both practical advice and general understanding about a destination's history, culture, institutions and people. Discovery Channel and its Web site, www.discovery.com, help millions of viewers explore their world from the comfort of their own home and also encourage them to explore it first hand.

This fully updated edition of

Insight: Korea is structured to convey an understanding of Korea and its culture as well as to guide readers through its sights and activities:

◆ The **Features** section, indicated by a yellow bar at the top of each page, covers the history and culture of the country in a series of informative essays.

◆ The main **Places** section, indicated by a blue bar, is a guide to the sights and areas worth visiting. Places of special interest are coordinated by number with the maps.

◆ The **Travel Tips** listings section, with an orange bar, provides a handy point of reference for information on travel, hotels, shops, restaurants and more. An index to the section is on the back flap of the book.

The contributors

This edition of *Insight Guide: Korea* was co-ordinated and edited by **Tom Le Bas** at Insight Guides' London office. The book has been fully updated with the invaluable help of a team of specialists.

The Places section and the Travel Tips were updated by **Craig Brown**, an American photo-journalist who has been resident in Korea for several years. Brown also worked on the Geography chapter, the Insight on... essays about Korean Festivals and Mountain Temples, and the new essays on North-South Relations, Korean Script and Hard Times for Shopkeepers.

The chapters on Korean History, The Koreans, Performing Arts, and Architecture were comprehensively revised by **Keith Howard**, a leading authority on Korean culture and head of the Department of Korean Studies and Music at London's prestigious School of Oriental and African Studies (SOAS). Howard also wrote the essay on the Korean Diaspora. **Beth McKillop**, curator of the Chinese and Korean section of the British Library in London, worked on the Arts and Crafts chapter and the Insight on... Korean Costume photo essay. The chapter on Korean Religion was provided by **James Grayson**, who served as an educational missionary with the Methodist Church of Korea for 16 years and is currently head of the School of East Asian Studies at the University of Sheffield. **Professor An Sonjae** (a.k.a. Brother Anthony), who has been a resident in Korea for the past 20 years, wrote the Insight on... Korean Tea Culture photo essay.

The current edition builds on the excellent foundations created by the editors and writers of previous editions of the book, including **Leonard Lueras, Nedra Chung, Michael Breen, John Gustaveson, Barbara Mintz, Norman Thorpe, James Wade, Jon Carter Covell, Gary Clay Rector, Laurel Kendall, Norman Sibley, Gertrude Ferrar, Michael E. Macmillan, Tom Coyner and Ken Kaliher**.

Principal photographers for this new edition of the book were **Blaine Harrington, Craig Brown, Leonard Lueras, Bill Wassman, Andreas M. Gross** and **Catherine Karnow**.

This latest edition of the book was proofread by **Alison Copland** and indexed by **Peter Gunn**. Thanks go to the **Korean National Tourism Organization** for their valuable help. The book was thoroughly updated in 2005 by **Youngkyung Hahn**.

Map Legend

▬▬ ▬ ▬	International Boundary
▬ ▬ ▬	Province Boundary
▬ ● ▬	National Park/Reserve
▬ ▬ ▬	Ferry Route
Ⓜ	Subway
✈ ✈	Airport: International/ Regional
🚌	Bus Station
❶	Tourist Information
✉	Post Office
✝ ✝ ✝	Church/Ruins
✝	Monastery
☾	Mosque
✡	Synagogue
🏰	Castle/Ruins
∴	Archeological Site
∩	Cave
⚊	Statue/Monument
★	Place of Interest

The main places of interest in the Places section are coordinated by number with a full-color map (e.g. ❶), and a symbol at the top of every right-hand page tells you where to find the map.

INSIGHT GUIDES
Korea

CONTENTS

Maps

Introduction

History

Features

Peaceful Songgwang
Temple, Jeollanam-do

THE LAND OF MORNING CALM

Ancient and modern casually co-exist in this fascinating country, which remains blessedly free of mass tourism

Surrounded by the less-than-gentle giants of Japan, China and the former Soviet Union, the Korean peninsula has long been the "shrimp between whales", as it is referred to in a Korean proverb. But today it is a significant shrimp. South Korea's remarkable economic achievements are well known, yet this is also a land rich in cultural heritage and natural beauty that has somehow remained far removed from the Asian tourist trail.

The haunting beauty of this mountainous and forested land, with its innumerable offshore islands, creates an unspoilt haven for the world-weary traveler. Far from being a new country, as often perceived in the West, Korea is one of the globe's oldest-known land areas, tilting westwards into the Yellow Sea, the granite and limestone foundations tough and tenacious like its long-suffering people.

Contrasting with all this, of course, is the teeming, high-rise conurbation of Seoul with its frantic pace of life and 11 million inhabitants. Despite superficial similarities with other vast cities such as Tokyo and New York, this 600-year-old capital has a rich history, the traditions of the old Joseon dynasties surviving amid the clamor of a rapidly evolving metropolis.

Still fiercely independent after centuries of invasions and wars – the bitter memories of Japanese colonization still strong in the minds of its people – Korea combines Confucian and Buddhist traditions with a maddening modernity. Monks and fortune tellers wander among the fashionable young, shrines and temples sit quietly beneath towering office blocks. Gigantic factories churn out their goods beneath hills of misted forest.

You can expect a friendly, humorous reception from the proud and spontaneous people of this rapidly changing country. Even in the capital, you will be regarded with curiosity and hospitality. With a penchant for drinking and entertainment, for song and dance and traditional theater, the Koreans are boisterous and joyous hosts.

Since 1988, when the Olympic Games put Seoul on the international map, South Korea's profile has steadily grown. The co-hosting of the 2002 soccer World Cup has accelerated this process, yet somehow the "Hermit Kingdom" remains one of Asia's unexplored gems. And the ongoing thaw in diplomatic relations between communist North and capitalist South makes this a particularly fascinating time to visit. ❏

PRECEDING PAGES: guardian figures on a temple doorway; two generations at a mountain temple; traditional *Hanbok* costume; mask dancers.
LEFT: The Land of Morning Calm – pine-covered mountain ridges swathed in mist.

GEOGRAPHY

The compact, mountainous peninsula of Korea is urbanized, industrialized
and over-populated, yet many areas of natural beauty remain

Wherever the traveler walks, drives or flies in Korea, he or she will see hills, mountains, "…the distant peaks." Whether in the joyous lyricism of the great *sijo* poet Yun, or in the many paintings of Korea's Geumgangsan (Diamond Mountains), the majestic peaks of this lovely country are depicted time and again.

From Manchuria south to Jeju Island in the East China Sea, the entire Korean landscape is ribbed by forested, rocky mountain ridges. In fact only about 20 percent of the peninsula's total land area is flatland. Yet the mountains do not reach any great elevation; the highest point on the peninsula, Baekdusan on the North Korean border with China, reaches 2,744 meters (9,002 ft). Mainland South Korea's loftiest peak is Jirisan, in Jeollanam Province, at 1,915 meters (6,283 ft); the summit of volcanic Hallasan, on Jeju island, reaches 1,950 meters (6,400 ft).

The Korean peninsula is relatively small – about the size of Romania or New Zealand – approximately 1,000 km (620 miles) long and 215 km (134 miles) wide at its narrowest points. Seoul is, as the crow flies, approximately 1,100 km (680 miles) east of Beijing and approximately 1,400 km (870 miles) west of Tokyo.

This is one of the world's oldest land areas, dating back to the pre-Cambrian period (1,600 to 2,700 million years ago). The basic foundation of granite and limestone is old and tough. As you travel up and down this peninsula, take note that you are crossing an ancient land bridge that is tilted toward the west and into the Yellow Sea. This tipping, caused by volcanic pressure on the peninsula in ancient geological times, has left the offshore area of Korea's west coast dotted with hundreds of islands. Also, in concert with the Yellow Sea's tremendously wide tide changes, this west-side sinking produced far-reaching, shallow inlets which look like huge, placid, sky blue lakes at high tide.

On the east coast fronting the East Sea (which is better known as the Japan Sea to foreigners), the mountains march right down to a coastline marked by tiny coves. These eastern waters, cooled by the Japan current which flows south from the Siberian coast, produce an abundance of cuttlefish and salmon, while

the warmer, shallower Yellow Sea supplies clams, oysters, shrimp, sea snails and abalone.

Migratory pit stop

Where the water is shallow enough, there are great expanses of sedge to play host to a variety of water birds – the most notable of which is the Manchurian crane. This bird was assumed to be virtually extinct, but in 1977 Dr George Archibald, head of the International Crane Foundation, found a large colony in Korea's Demilitarized Zone (DMZ).

The shallow waters and inlets of the western side of the country are home to the white-napped crane and many different species of

LEFT: the spectacular view from the cable car on Bisondae, Seoraksan National Park.
RIGHT: fish drying in the sun.

ducks, geese and swans. The country has a large population of storks, their huge unwieldy nests seeming to occupy almost every tree in the land. Korea also acts as a part-time home for birds that follow migration routes cutting across the country.

The avian population has been rising in recent years as government regulations crack down on shooting. As the result of a bird-killing ban, the sparrow population has increased so much that sparrow netting is now permitted for a limited period every autumn and, where only a few years ago the pheasant seemed on its way to extermination, it is now common.

problem today, is the common perception that wild animals are considered to have special medicinal properties – few of the larger mammals and reptiles have managed to escape the Korean stew pot.

The Korean tiger is still celebrated in art, but is now extinct. Local leopards are another popular subject, but all that remains of them is speculation that that they may still be roaming the forests in the remote north of Korea.

One of life's ironies is that the DMZ between North and South Korea has provided a peaceful place where wildlife can proliferate. One creature which has benefitted from this DMZ refuge

Even so, there are several seriously endangered bird species in Korea. The aforementioned Manchurian crane has been greatly reduced in numbers and the Tristram's woodpecker population is way down, although it is now recovering. There are now more than 20 rare species thriving in the protected woodland area of the Gwangneung National Arboretum.

Mammals and snakes

Mammals have not fared so well as birds, for two reasons. Firstly, the wholesale deforestation that occurred during the Japanese occupation destroyed animal habitats that were already under stress. Secondly, and still a

is a small wildcat, which has all but completely disappeared in mountains south of the 38th parallel. Some of the small native Korean bears, which are now protected, have been found on Jirisan. They had almost disappeared, as the eating of bear meat has long been considered good for the health. Also, an entire community of otters – about 100 of them – was found along the Nakdong River at about the same time the bears were discovered.

Korea used to have a large indigenous snake population, but they are now rarely seen. You are more likely to see snakes in the Oriental medicine market than slithering across the trails of Seoraksan.

Jeju Island is famous for its horses, which are allowed to roam freely. The island's subtropical climate provides ample forage for grazing throughout the year.

Korea also boasts a unique breed of dog, the *Jindotgae*. This is a medium-sized, short-haired canine with a moderately pointed snout, heavy shoulders, and a coloring that varies from cream to off-brown. The breed seemed in danger of extinction a few years ago, but now appears well on its way to recovery.

URBAN FLORA

City streets in Korea are often edged with gingkos, ailanthus, plane trees, sumac and paulownia, and most villages have an ancient zelkova or persimmon tree.

clearings without trampling them. Wild weigela, spiraea, viburnums (Wayfaring trees), holly, hydrangeas, boxwood, daphne, and a host of other plants are all viewed as "weeds," but it is now against the law to dig up such plants in the wild or cut down a tree without government permission (at least in theory). The woody plants have become common as a result of reforestation programs.

Korean roadsides in the autumn are iced with a beautiful floral froth of lavender, pink, white and deep red cosmos.

Fruits of the forest

Korea's forest flora is closely related to that of neighboring China and Japan. The peninsula's indigenous plants are most likely to be preserved in temple gardens where, for centuries, Buddhist monks tended Korea's flora and fauna with loving care. It is here that the finest specimens of gingko trees, a variety of maple, and herbaceous plants thrive.

Korea has such a large population of azaleas that it is quite often impossible to cross forest

Oddly enough, the azalea that covers almost every mountainside and fills every untilled field is not the national flower. That official honor has been bestowed on the Rose of Sharon (Mugunghwa), which supposedly symbolizes the resilient spirit of the Korean people.

The rural landscape

Until a few generations ago, Korea was a land of farmers. While the vast majority of young people have abandoned the countryside for factory jobs and city life, they dutifully pack into their new cars and head back to their rural homes whenever an opportunity arises. Farms and country villages still have strong

FAR LEFT: a pair of dancing Manchurian cranes.
LEFT: Korean fir cones.
ABOVE: planting rice in Jeollanam-do.

sentimental appeal for Koreans, even though they avoid physically demanding, low-paying farm jobs as they would the plague.

Drive through the countryside and 80 percent of those working the fields are elderly. While the rest of the economy has modernized, agriculture has been left behind, stuck with farming methods from a bygone era. You can still see farmers (though becoming rarer every day) plowing with oxen, or harvesting rice by hand.

Largely because of their older populations, Korean villages are bastions of tradition and conservatism, where change comes slowly. The majority of village homes are traditional in style, with sliding *hanji* doors (made of mulberry tree paper), surrounded by a clay and rock wall. These dwellings huddle together in tight hillside clusters, their roofs tiled in matching colors. There is some irony that there are so many made-for-tourists "folk villages," when all you have to do is drive a half-hour out of the city and walk around almost any rural village to get a glimpse of traditional Korean life.

Yet changes are coming to the countryside. Small, (formally) subsistence farms are being consolidated into larger, more profitable units. Also, though Koreans hate to hear this, the hilly terrain is not especially well suited to commercial rice production. In a global economy, Korean farmers may find that they have to become more specialized in crop production if they want to survive.

The urban landscape

The contrasts between farm and city life are great. While the villages are peaceful and slow-paced, the South Korean cities are full of energy. The streets are crowded, there are neon lights plastered on every wall, and youths on scooters swerve in and out of pedestrian traffic. The city is where it's happening, and the draw for young people is undeniable. The concentration of industry in and around the cities has only exacerbated their phenomenal growth. On the outskirts, islands of apartment complexes are gobbling up green space, extending the cities inexorably outward.

Urbanization has come at a price. There are far too few green spaces in the cities among the honking horns and blaring loudspeakers, and the ever-increasing sale of cars has given South Korea one of the worst air pollution problems in the world.

There is some good news for the human landscape, though. Urbanization and economic development have curtailed population growth, and increased affluence has allowed the government to turn its attention to the worst environmental problems. It has done a good job of limiting development in mountain regions – South Korea has one of the best National Park systems in Asia, providing temporary escape from the hustle and bustle of modern urban life. ❑

SATELLITE CITIES

South Korea faces a major problem in that only 20–30 percent of its land area is habitable. There are simply too many people living in such a small, mountainous country, especially in the main urban areas. Concerned with the rapid urban growth, particularly in the Seoul area, the Korean government came up with the idea of building satellite cities to encourage decentralization. The new cities (and they are called "new cities") of Gwacheon, Ilsan, Bucheon, and Bundang were built almost overnight. These planned communities are graced with wide avenues, pleasant parks and mile after mile of high-rise apartments.

LEFT: traditional rural housing.
RIGHT: wild cosmos blossoms.

天下圖

封淵
深目国
大澤
無腸国
比肩国
係民山
始州国
大人国
勞民国
玄股国
廣野
拘纓国
衡天山
毛民国
龜山
姑射山
中國
朝鮮
日本国
龍伯国
扶桑
流波山
甘淵
天台
衡山
方丈
蓬萊
瀛洲
琉球国
真臘
暹羅
安南国
廣桑山
夏州国
君子国
女人国
中容国
大人国
長沙国
倚天山

Decisive Dates

PREHISTORIC PERIOD

circa 30,000 BC Evidence of early settlement is provided by various Paleolithic sites discovered in the 1960s.

circa 4000–800 BC Neolithic man settles on the peninsula, forming Walled-Town states and leaving behind dolmen burial tombs.

GOJOSEON PERIOD

circa 2333 BC The mythical founder of the nation, Dangun, is said to have begun his reign.

800–400 BC Korea's Bronze Age. The merging of the Walled-Town states into confederations.

THE THREE KINGDOMS PERIOD

57 BC Foundation of Saro state (renamed Silla).
37 BC The state of Goguryeo in Manchuria emerges.
18 BC The Baekje tribe arises in central Korea.
AD 372 Buddhism is introduced to Goguryeo and a school is established for Confucian studies.
400–500 Silla is transformed from a tribal league to a kingdom. Another tribal federation, the Kaya league, occupies the southern coast.
660–668 Joining forces with China, Silla defeat the Baekje in 660 and the Goguryeo in 668.

UNITED SILLA DYNASTY

668 The Silla Kingdom is able to repel Chinese forces and unifies the peninsula for the first time – beginning a cultural, artistic and religious golden age centered in Gyeongju.
Mid 700s Buddhist texts are printed.
751 Silla is at the height of its glory, and the building of Seokguram and Korea's most famous temple, Bulguk-sa, begins.

GORYEO KINGDOM

918 The Kingdom of Goryeo is founded by Wang Geon, finally overthrowing Silla in 935.
958 A competitive civil examination system is created, filling the highest offices with members of the ruling class most highly schooled in Chinese literature and Confucian classics.
1018 Invasions of the Khitans.
1231 Mongols overrun most of northern Korea and force the government to surrender.
1251 Hoping for divine intervention in forcing out the Mongols, Buddhist sutras are carved on to wood blocks (the Koreana Tripitaka).
1271 The Mongols adopt the dynastic name Yuan and proceed to take over the rest of China. Korea becomes a tributary state to China.

JOSEON DYNASTY

1392 Yi Seonggye ousts the Goryeo king, becoming the founder of his own dynasty.
1446 Under King Sejong's direction, the Korean alphabet (Hangeul) is created.
1592–98 The Imjin War: hoping to gain a foothold for an invasion of China, Japan invades Korea and lays waste to the peninsula.
1598 Yi Sun-sin, Admiral of the Korean Navy, dies a hero having outwitted the Japanese. Under pressure from Chinese troops, the Japanese withdraw.
1627 First Manchu invasion.

THE WESTERNERS ARRIVE

1780s Catholicism is introduced.
1811, 1862 Rebellions occur after decades of social unrest and popular agitation.
1839 Religious persecution results in the deaths of 130 Christians.
1860 The Donghak ("Eastern learning") movement is founded, beginning as a religious society.
1866 Nine French Catholic priests and some 8,000 Korean converts are executed.
1871 Americans try to establish trade links, occupying Ganghwa island; 350 Koreans and three Americans are killed before the mission is aborted.

1876 The rise of Japanese influence spurs the Chinese to preserve their traditional influence, leading to a series of confrontations.

1894 The Donghak uprising begins, followed by the outbreak of the Sino-Japanese War.

RUSSO-JAPANESE WAR

1895 Russia weakens the Japanese position. Queen Min, the real power behind the throne, is murdered.

1902 Alliance between Japan and Great Britain begins to turn the situation in Japan's favor.

JAPANESE CONTROL

1905 Japan's control of Korea is officially recognized, ending a brief war with China.

1910 Japanese control the justice system and have complete police power, but Korean resistance is unflagging. Official end of the Joseon dynasty.

1919 Independence Movement of March 1, with provisional governments formed outside of Korea.

1937 Colonial policy turns toward a complete "Japanization of Korea".

1939–42 Hundreds of thousands of Korean workers are conscripted to the Japanese army.

INDEPENDENCE AND THE KOREAN WAR

1945 Despite bitter opposition from the Koreans, the Allied foreign ministers agree to go ahead with an international trusteeship, which is to direct Korean affairs through a provisional government, staffed by Koreans, for at least five years.

1946 Communists begin to dominate politics under the leadership of Soviet-backed Kim Il Sung.

1948 The Republic of Korea is recognized by the UN and Syngman Rhee is sworn in as president. A formidable North Korean army is created with Russian help. The stage is set for civil war.

1950 On June 25, North Korean troops pour across the 38th parallel. US forces, backed by further troops from the UN, are ordered into battle by President Truman.

1953 An armistice agreement is reached, but not before Korea has been reduced to ruins.

MODERN HISTORY

1948–60 A period of heavy-handed military rule under President Rhee; economic stagnation.

PRECEDING PAGES: an old Chinese-Korean map identifies China as the "Middle Kingdom".
LEFT: a 5th-century Goguryeo wall painting.
RIGHT: a United States Marine searches a captured Chinese Communist for concealed weapons, 1950.

1960 Yun Po-son is elected.

1962 The Yun government falls. Military government is formed under Major General Park Chung-hee, who retains control for 18 years until his assassination in 1979. Industrialization gathers momentum.

1980 Major General Chun Doo-hwan is president.

1980 Citizens' democratic movement in Gwangju threatens government. Military crushes uprising.

1987 Roh Tae-woo becomes the first "democratically" elected president. Roh's ruling party merges with opposition forces of Kim Young-sam ("YS").

1988 South Korea hosts the Olympic Games.

1993 "YS" takes office as the first civilian president in over 30 years, promising democratic reform.

1996 Former presidents Roh and Chun go on trial for corruption, sedition and treason.

1997 Korea's economy is swamped by the crisis that sweeps through Asia.

1998 Opposition leader Kim Dae-jung is elected president and inherits an economy in disarray.

1999–2000 Steady recovery in the economy.

2000 On June 13, Kim Dae-jung visits his counterpart Kim Jong-il in Pyongyang, marking an unprecedented thaw in North-South relations. Relatives, separated for decades, are reunited.

2002 South Korea co-hosts soccer World Cup.

2003 Arson attack on an underground train in Daegu kills 125. Roh Moo-hyun becomes president, amid rising tension between North Korea and the US. ❑

EARLY KINGDOMS AND DYNASTIES

Koreans are proud of their five millennia of history. Despite numerous invasions and attacks, they have developed and preserved a unique identity

A Korean proverb describes the country as "a shrimp between whales". Located at a strategic crossroads in northeast Asia, the Korean peninsula has been overrun by armies of Chinese and Japanese, Mongols and Manchus and, more recently, Russians and Americans. Yet, although often overshadowed by the political might of China, and the economic power of Japan, the Koreans have managed to maintain a distinct political and cultural identity. They have borrowed much from Chinese civilization and then, in turn, transmitted elements of this to Japan. The ability of Koreans to assimilate yet preserve a unique identity while enduring the depredations of intruders is a striking theme in modern history. Koreans proudly contest that, among other inventions, they designed movable type in 1234 (some 200 years before the Germans), and iron-clad ships in the 1590s (centuries before the Americans).

The Korean peninsula was first settled some 30,000 years ago by wandering tribes from Central and Northern Asia. Some Paleolithic stone tools from this early period have been found on the peninsula. Waves of migration followed, pushing earlier settlers deeper into the mountains, and creating rival states and tribal federations. The oldest evidence of a Neolithic society has been assigned a date of 4270 BC.

By around 300 BC, various tribes had established loosely-affiliated organized states in the peninsula. These were the earliest to be mentioned in Chinese records. The most powerful was the Gojoseon, in the north. Skirmishes with the Chinese Han dynasty (206 BC to AD 220) resulted in invasion by the Han in 108 BC, who established four military commanderies, one of which, at Nangnang near present-day Pyeongyang, survived as a military and trading post until AD 313.

LEFT: the now-extinct Korean tiger, once worshipped as a messenger of the mountain gods.
RIGHT: dating from the 1st century AD, this lacquered basket was discovered at the Han military post of Nangnang, near present-day Pyeongyang.

The Three Kingdoms

The Chinese were eventually ousted by the Goguryeo kingdom (traditional dates, 37 BC to AD 668) which, starting as a tribal alliance of nomadic people in southeastern Manchuria, grew into a kingdom that, by the 5th century, dominated the northern half of the peninsula,

and Manchuria to the Amur, Sungari and Liao rivers. Further south, a number of related tribes had, by the 3rd century, formed three weak tribal confederations: Mahan, Jinhan, and Byeonhan. From these, Baekje (18 BC to AD 660) and Silla (57 BC to AD 668) arose to form, with Goguryeo, the Three Kingdoms. Baekje evolved from the Mahan in the southwest, and initially ruled from the vicinity of modern Gongju. Silla, based in the southeast, was transformed from tribal league to kingdom in the late 4th century, annexing neighboring territories such as those of the Gaya league in 562. Gaya, and subsequently Silla, was an important point of contact between the Korean peninsula and Japan.

The next few centuries were unsettled, but in 660 Tang China joined with Silla to defeat Baekje. Realizing the Chinese had ambitions to control the peninsula, Silla then marched northwards, defeating Goguryeo in 668 and expanding to the Daedong River by 676. The Chinese withdrew, leaving a unified peninsula under Silla. The unification, albeit at times tenuous, lasted 1,300 years until 1945.

Scholars and monks

Buddhism, Confucianism, art, architecture, a written language, and bureaucratic organizational principles were all introduced from

China during the Three Kingdoms Period. Under Unified Silla, Buddhism flourished as rulers lavished funds on temples and images, and dispatched monks to China and India to study the religion. The epitome of Silla Buddhist art can still be seen in the Seokguram stone grotto near the former capital of Gyeongju (*see page 235*), which was begun, along with the nearby temple of Bulguk-sa, in 751.

Silla maintained a tributary relationship with the Tang, preventing Chinese domination. The Tang administrative system became the model for Silla's state structure.

By the late 8th century, the growth of the royal clan led to intense internal rivalries, as the aristocracy came under increasing attack from lower echelons who felt that they were being excluded from power. Large landowners refused to pay taxes and some farmers turned to banditry to survive, while wealthy merchants added a further disaffected element. The Silla government became ever more weak. Major revolts broke out as early as 768, and in 780 the king, Hyegong, was assassinated. From this chaos, rebel chieftains rose up and struggled for position until the appearance of Wang Geon. Supported by the landlord and merchant class from which he sprang, Wang Geon's power grew until 935 when, after the ruler, Gyonhwon,

sent him to the northern border to face Song Chinese forces, he turned around, reunited the peninsula, and founded his own dynasty, Goryeo, which lasted for more than 450 years.

Korean influence on Japan

There were frequent migrations of Koreans to Japan from the 4th to the 7th centuries, with Korean and Chinese technological, intellectual and cultural practices exported. The exchange may be even older, since many archaeological remains in the Gaya area are superficially similar to those found in and around Nara in Japan.

In the 6th century, monks from Baekje and Goguryeo staffed the first Buddhist monastery in Japan and were active in a great burst of temple construction. Other Koreans brought their expertise in calendrics, while the importation of Chinese embroidery has been attributed to Goguryeo women at the Japanese court. Zen Buddhism was passed on to Japan from China via Korea, and the Japanese tea ceremony is likely to have descended from Baekje practice. A millennium later, during the Hideyoshi invasion of Korea in the 1590s, Korean potters were abducted and taken to Japan.

KOREAN INFLUENCE

Koreans became the tutors of Japan's Prince Shotoku, and nearly one third of the nobles in the 815 Japanese family register were of Korean descent.

the 12th century a network of schools was in place to train boys in the Chinese classics required for the top exam. However, Wang Geon invoked the Chinese notion of the "mandate of Heaven" as his justification for assuming the throne. He claimed moral superiority, and he and his successors developed a centralized system of government that outwardly resembled Chinese practice.

There was an abrupt change in August 1170, when a military escort conveying the king,

Wang Geon's mandate of Heaven

Wang Geon moved his capital to Gaeseong, just north of today's demilitarized zone. The power base of the Goryeo dynasty (which is the origin of the Western name for the country) was a partially non-aristocratic élite of literati who gained office through a state examination system set up in 958. To prepare candidates, a national university was created in 992, and by

FAR LEFT: Confucius is *Gongja* to Koreans.
LEFT: Silla crown from the 6th century AD.
ABOVE: serene Buddhas of Silla.
RIGHT: an early portrait of the 8th-century Sokkuram Buddha at Gyeongju.

Uijong, and his party revolted and killed every man except the king himself. The king was banished to Geoje Island, where he was murdered. The coup is normally interpreted as a revolt against discrimination by civilian officials and against the debauchery of the royal court. After a confused period, a soldier, Choe Chungheon, managed to seize power in 1196. He suppressed all opposition and, in a gesture that marked the beginning of the end of Buddhist dominance, banished monks and clergy from the capital. He soon induced scholar-officials to join him in reviving the dynasty, but other powers were looking to expand into Korea.

The Khitan, ruling around the Yalu River

basin as the Liao, had launched three attacks against Goryeo between 993 and 1018; in the last attack they were heavily defeated. The Jurchen, who set themselves up as the Jin dynasty in northern China, then came into conflict with Goryeo.

A century later, in 1231, Goryeo faced an invasion by a Mongol army. Initially, Goryeo assistance was sought to overrun the Song Chinese, and the Koreans agreed in order to subvert other border threats. From 1219 until 1224, Goryeo reluctantly met demands for large tribute payments in return for Mongol help. Relations were broken off after the murder of a

Mongol envoy to Korea, and the reckoning came in 1231, when the Mongols quickly overran most of northern Korea, laid siege to Gaeseong and forced the government to surrender.

As the Mongols relaxed their grip a year later, the Goryeo government fled from Gaeseong with most of its people, and took refuge on Ganghwa Island at the mouth of the Han River. This led to a full invasion, in which all major towns were sacked, yet the Mongols failed to cross the narrow channel separating Ganghwa from the mainland. In 1259 a truce was struck, but military officials who dominated the government refused to capitulate, and the government remained on Ganghwa.

Extracting female quotas

The situation worsened under King Wonjong who ruled from 1259 to 1274. He went in person to the Mongols and offered submission in return for aid against the military clique in his court. He even agreed to marry the crown prince to a Mongol princess to seal the bargain. When he returned to Goryeo with a Mongol army, many among the military faction still refused to capitulate. As the *Sambyeolcho*, they boarded boats and set up a rival government on islands off the southwest coast. It took four years to restore the civilian bureaucracy.

The Mongols, who from 1279 ruled as the Yuan dynasty in China, then allowed the Goryeo government to retain control, but required that Goryeo princes continue marrying Mongol princesses, thus effectively subjugating the peninsula. They also extracted a large annual tribute – gold, silver, horses, ginseng, hawks for hunting, artisans, eunuchs, and women. An office was set up to select girls and young widows to fill the annual quotas. In addition, Korea had to build hundreds of ships and furnish soldiers for ill-fated Mongol expeditions to Japan in 1274 and 1281. On the positive side, Koreans gained Mongol knowledge of astrology, medicine, artistic skills and cotton cultivation.

By the mid-14th century, rebellions in China were undermining the Mongol regime, culminating in the founding of the Ming dynasty in 1368. A revival in Korean independence began after the enthronement of King Gongmin in 1351. Gongmin reorganized his government and army. Landholders proved so powerful, however, that he was forced to compromise when he tried to return appropriated slaves to their rightful owners. In 1374, he was assassinated, and his 10-year-old son was made king.

Chinese brigands and Japanese pirates had by this time increased their attacks on the country, and disagreement on how to control Goryeo raged among military leaders, until one of them, Yi Seonggye (Taejo), seized power in 1388. Yi proclaimed a new dynasty, Joseon, four years later. The distinguished dynasty was to be Korea's last, retaining power until 1910 – East Asia's longest-lasting dynasty.

The Joseon dynasty

The new kingdom moved its capital to Hanyang, today's Seoul, and promptly went about resuming tributary relations with Ming China. Reformers around Yi embraced the ideas of Chinese neo-Confucianism. The new doctrines gave the traditional political system metaphysical underpinnings, and imbued its followers with a zealous reforming spirit. Reforms attempted to break the power of the landlords and reduce the influence of the Buddhist establishment; land was confiscated and temples closed. Reformers toiled to impose Confucian norms on Korean life, and the changes reached into the very fabric of society.

The third king of the dynasty, Taejong, who came to power in 1401 after killing his youngest brother, the heir-apparent, reorganized the government to strengthen the throne.

his uncle, imprisoned, and finally strangled. His uncle took the throne as the tyrannical King Sejo (r. 1456–68). He intimidated and executed critics, instituted banishments, and seized property. When his reign ended, a backlash began, diminishing the power of the monarchy and initiating a long period of decline.

Admiral Yi and the turtle ships

The threat of foreign invasion was never far away, and in April 1592 a newly reunified Japan under Toyotomi Hideyoshi began an invasion of Korea. The Koreans had little military expertise on land, but their navy presented

King Taejong's successor was called Sejong (r. 1418–1450). Intelligent and scholarly, he presided over the creation of the remarkable Korean alphabet, Hangeul, and, indeed, over the flourishing of cultural activity. As an administrator, he was meticulous and indefatigable, and initiated a thorough revision of all state practices; but he was succeeded by men of lesser capacity, Munjong (r. 1450–1452) and the ill-fated boy-king Danjong (r. 1452–1455). This unfortunate boy was forced to abdicate by

LEFT: the "Floating Rock" at Buseok-sa.
ABOVE: *Korean Chief and Attendants*, a lithograph sketched in 1817.

CONFUCIANISM CHANGES KOREAN LIFE

In the late 14th century, reformers embraced the ideas of Chinese neo-Confucianism, bringing about many changes in Korean society. Koreans had long practiced burial rituals that were an amalgam of local and Buddhist traditions. Now these customs, including cremation, were thrust aside in favor of Confucian ancestor worship and its related rituals. Until the end of Goryeo times, endogamy, polygamy and remarriage of widows had been allowed. The Joseon court, however, broadened the circle of kin with whom marriage was prohibited. They also forbade the practice of giving equal social status to multiple wives, as well as discouraging remarriage.

a very different proposition. Korea's naval hero, Admiral Yi Sun-sin, commanded a force based at Yeosu on the south coast. Among his ships were several "turtle ships," which were used to foil the Japanese invasion by choking off supply lines and preventing troop reinforcements from arriving. The "turtle ships" averaged 30 meters (100 ft) in length, and used oars to ensure they were faster and more maneuverable than the Japanese vessels. Iron jackets studded with pointed rivets made them invulnerable to projectiles, and each vessel was heavily armed. The bow of each ship was decorated with a large turtle's head.

the mainland and the island of Jindo. There, Yi had assembled women on local hilltops to give the illusion of a massive force waiting to engage the enemy and, not knowing the tides, the Japanese were caught and fled in disarray. Fate, though, failed to smile on the admiral: in the final battle of the war, in 1598, he was killed by a bullet as he stood on his flagship.

The "Hermit Kingdom"

Threats also came from the north, where Jurchen tribes had united in the Manchurian mountains. Attacks began in 1583, and by the 1590s Ming Chinese outposts in Manchuria

From May to July 1592, the Korean fleet sank more than 250 Japanese vessels in eight major engagements. They attacked the Japanese base at Busan, sinking more than half the vessels there. Negotiations led to the withdrawal of the bulk of Japan's troops, but in January 1597 the Japanese renewed their attack, sending 100,000 men to Korea. This time, they met stiff resistance in ferocious land battles, and the invasion was confined to the southern provinces. According to Japanese history, Hideyoshi's death in September 1598 prompted a final withdrawal. Local Korean belief differs, however, and remembers how Yi Sun-sin led the pursuing Japanese fleet into a strait between

were under pressure. Joseon, under King Injo (reigned 1623–49), sided with the Ming and this led to invasions in 1627 and 1636. In the first, Pyongyang fell, and the court fled once more to Ganghwa Island. The king signed a peace treaty that committed Joseon to a Confucian-style, elder-younger brother relationship with the Manchus. Dissatisfied, in 1632 the Manchus demanded annual tribute, and the Koreans reacted with a declaration of war. This time the capital, Hanyang, was taken, before the Manchus captured Ganghwa and took 200 hostages, including the queen. They extracted a heavy price: tributes, severance of ties with the Ming court and the submission of two princes as hostages. Soon, the Manchus established themselves in Beijing, ruling from 1644 as the Qing dynasty. The suzerain relationship allowed the Joseon court to retain control, but from this point onwards Joseon controlled all border access, treating China as a superior state and keeping its distance from Japan as a trading neighbor. In this way, Korea became the "Hermit Kingdom".

In the 18th century, Joseon recovered some vitality. The reigns of Yeongjo (1724–76) and Jeongjo (1776–1800) are re-

SILHAK EXPRESSION

The ideas of the *silhak* "practical learning" school are reflected in the landscapes by artists such as Jeong Seon (1676–1759) and the genre paintings of Kim Hongdo (b. 1745) and Shin Yunbok (b. 1758).

Korean scholars of the *silhak* or "practical learning" school. *Silhak* thinkers embraced various ideas, but shared a common concern to find pragmatic solutions to Korea's problems.

Their acceptance of reality was reflected in art and in the growing body of literature written in the Hangeul script. Yet *silhak* also led to conflict, notably in 1801 when a ruthless purge of rivals was carried out.

In 1783, a young Korean, Yi Seunghun, was baptized in Beijing by a Catholic priest; he

membered as periods of relative stability, but these were also times when new intellectual currents stimulated Korean thinkers, beginning a process that would lead to dismissing the speculative metaphysics of the orthodox neo-Confucian tradition.

Western ideas flowing into China reached Korea through traders and envoys, while at the same time a Qing school of empirical studies also appeared, emphasizing critical reasoning. The two currents began to appear among

LEFT: replica of a "turtle ship" at Yeosu.
ABOVE: 18th-century painting showing Westerners at the Korean court.

returned to Korea as the first Christian convert. Others converted, and in 1791, when Yun Jichung failed to perform a Confucian service for his dead mother, he was sentenced to death. He became Korea's first Christian martyr; many more persecutions followed. In 1839, 130 Christians were killed, and some 8,000 perished between 1866 and 1873.

The 19th century was marked by widespread social unrest, including major rebellions in 1811 and 1862, and this left the conservative ruling class even more inward-looking and isolationist. By the second half of the century, Korea was ill prepared to open its doors to an expansion-hungry and technologically superior West. ❏

A CENTURY OF CONFLICT

The hundred years from 1850 saw the Koreans forced to abandon their policy of seclusion, as both Western and Oriental powers sought to gain influence

In 1860, Korean officials were badly shaken by the news that British and French forces had occupied Beijing. The Koreans had looked to China for many centuries, offering tribute to its leaders, and absorbing Chinese culture and civilization. Determined that the same fate should not befall Korea, the exclusionist foreign policy was reinforced when the 12-year-old Gojong (reigned 1864–1907) ascended the throne. The dowager queen was his nominal regent, but actual power was in the hands of his father, Yi Hang. For a decade, Yi effectively ruled as the Daewongun ("Great Prince of the Court").

The Daewongun confronted a second peril, for domestic disputes also seriously threatened the survival of the dynasty. To break up the factions jockeying for power, he began a program of Confucianist reform, banishing many officials, and appointing others on merit rather than lineage. Yi chose a queen for Gojong from a minor aristocratic family, the Min from Yeoheung. He also reconstructed the royal palace – this had been in ruins since the Japanese invasion in the 1590s – and he reformed the tax system.

Western pressure

The outside pressures on Korea did not abate. The Russians demanded coaling rights, trade, and diplomatic relations, but were turned down in 1866. In the same year, nine French Catholic priests and thousands of Korean Christian converts were executed. One priest escaped, and persuaded the French Asiatic Squadron to take punitive action: seven warships were sent to seize Ganghwa Island. In August, the US-owned *General Sherman* sailed up the Daedong River; she ran aground and Koreans set her on fire, killing her crew. In 1871, the American minister to China, Frederick Low, accompanied five warships to Korea to try to open trade links. After a clash, the Americans occupied

Ganghwa, where 350 Koreans and three Americans were killed before the mission withdrew.

In 1875, the Japanese determined to force the Koreans to abandon their policy of seclusion. For several centuries, the Koreans had insisted that trade with Japan should be limited, carried out through a closed quarter in Busan port.

Now, after a clash between Korean shore batteries and a Japanese ship, Japan pressed upon Korea a treaty of friendship and commerce that provided for the opening of three ports and permanent diplomatic offices.

Military coups

Japan itself was modernizing rapidly, and its increased presence in Korea spurred the Chinese to redouble their efforts to preserve their influence. Korea was forced, often unsuccessfully, to balance the desires of its two neighbors. In 1882, Korean soldiers killed their Japanese instructors, burned the Japanese legation, and attacked the residences of the Mins,

LEFT: Yi Gojong (r. 1864–1907) in an 1898 portrait by Hubert Vos.
RIGHT: Queen Min, Gojong's wife.

who were by now the dominant family in government. When the soldiers seized Gojong, the Mins petitioned the Chinese for help. The Chinese sent troops. Following a stand-off, Japan won indemnity, and was granted permission to station a legation guard in Korea.

In December 1884, a further revolt took place, this time led by a faction of Koreans sympathetic to Japan. Known as the Gapshin coup, and beginning on the night when the opening of the first Korean post office was being celebrated, this eventually led to the temporary withdrawal of both Chinese and Japanese troops.

chants. A peasant force marched northwards from Jeolla province, twice defeating government troops. The king appealed to China for assistance. China responded, but the Japanese, feeling their presence in Korea threatened, sent 7,000 men and warships.

The rebellion was quashed, but Japan refused to withdraw its forces, using them to press the Korean government for a program of reform and modernization. In July, the Japanese occupied the royal palace and ousted the administration. They installed a progressive, pro-Japanese cabinet. This, through a deliberative council, began to put in place a series of

The Donghak uprising

The Donghak ("Eastern learning") movement began around 1860 as a mix of Confucian, Buddhist and shamanist ideas, opposing the new philosophies coming from the West. Its founder, Choe Jewoo, had been born into a disenfranchised aristocratic family. He was eventually executed for challenging orthodoxy, but his movement developed both religious and social dimensions, challenging external influences on Korea, and embracing both peasants and discontented upper-class elements. Trouble flared in the spring of 1894, starting as a rebellion caused in part by deepening economic problems and the activities of foreign mer-

reforms. Japan now had ambitions to match the European powers by creating her own East Asian empire, and her actions in Korea proved to be a prelude to conflict. This was to pit the fading Qing empire against the rising imperial power of Meiji Japan in the Sino-Japanese War. In the brief conflict, the Chinese were defeated, and in a treaty signed at Shimonoseki they formally drew to a close the many centuries of the Korean suzerain-vassal relationship.

Koreans, opposed to Japanese dominance, needed a new counterforce, and they found one in Russia. In 1895, Russia forced Japan to restore to China the Liaotung peninsula, which she had seized during the war. In Korea, a pro-Russian faction associated with Queen Min obtained the dismissal of pro-Japanese ministers. Soon, though, Queen Min was murdered, officially by disaffected Korean troops, but clearly in an action planned by Japan. In fear of his life, Gojong slipped out of the palace and took refuge in the Russian legation. He dismissed his cabinet and replaced it with pro-Russian ministers.

Gojong reigned for a year from the legation, his decrees passed through a small group of trusted officials. He returned to the palace only in February 1897, once he was convinced he could do so without fear of Japanese reprisals.

The Russo-Japanese War

Japan and Russia maintained an uneasy truce in Korea. Russian interests were balanced by other Western powers, notably when Britain occupied the southern island of Geomun-do to prevent expansionism, and as American missionaries and traders increased their presence. The showdown came in February 1904, when Japan launched an attack on the Russian fleet at Port Arthur. Korea declared its neutrality, but Japan moved into the peninsula in force, and compelled the Korean government to authorize military occupation. By the end of 1905, Japan's control over Korea was recognized, ending the conflict.

There, he sought to reassert Korea's independence. In October, he took the title of "emperor", by so doing claiming equality with the rulers of both China and Japan; he announced that the name of Korea would be changed, from Joseon to Daehan Jeguk, "Empire of the Great Han".

Gojong's efforts were initially aided by the emergence of the Independence Club, formed by nationalists and by participants in the unsuccessful 1884 coup *(see panel, right)*.

LEFT: lithograph of Japanese troops on the attack in Korea, 1904.
ABOVE: 1880s Presbyterian missionary Reverend Samuel Moffett with new Korean Christians.

THE INDEPENDENCE CLUB

Using public subscriptions, the so-called Independence Club (founded by nationalists and those involved in the failed 1884 coup) built a gate known as the Independence Arch at the entrance to Seoul on the road from Beijing. They founded a newspaper, *The Independent*, published in Korean script, Hangeul (rather than Chinese characters), and in English. The paper proved an important means of popularizing reformist ideas. The club quickly grew, and was recast two years later as a political party, criticizing foreign encroachment and the influence of Russia, and attacking government policies; in November 1898, the government forcibly dissolved it, jailing prominent leaders.

Next, the Japanese moved to gain Korea's formal acceptance of Japan as her protector. Ito Hirobumi arrived in Seoul in November 1905 to persuade Gojong to approve a treaty transferring partial sovereignty to Japan. Gojong and his ministers resisted, but pressure was applied by isolating the emperor from his advisers, and within two weeks a majority of the cabinet had agreed to accept the arrangement. A treaty was signed on 18 November that gave Japan control of Korea's foreign relations and the right to station in Korea a resident-general to manage her external affairs. The treaty was greeted with public protests and demands for the punishment of the "Five Traitors" who had approved it. Japanese gendarmes were called out to suppress the demonstrations, and both the emperor's aide, Min Yonghwan, and his former prime minister, Jo Byeongse, committed suicide.

In June 1907, Gojong sent an envoy to the International Peace Conference at The Hague to generate international pressure for Japan's withdrawal. The Japanese delegation argued that Korea had ceded control of external affairs, and the envoy was refused admission. Japanese retaliation for this was channeled through Gojong's cabinet; announcing he had lost the trust of his people, Gojong was forced to abdicate in favor of his son, Sunjong (reigned 1907–10). Sunjong is widely remembered as being feeble-minded and, to further undermine Korean royalty, he was given a Japanese consort.

In fact, the 1905 treaty had been very broad in its scope. It claimed the right to maintain law and order, the right to intervene in Korea's internal administration, the authority to supervise Japanese officials in Korea, including those employed by the Korean government, and the power to issue ordinances. In December 1907, the treaty was revised to give the resident-general a veto over administrative acts, internal reforms, and the appointment and dismissal of high officials. By mid-1909, the administration of justice was in Japanese hands, and a year later the Japanese had complete police power.

Korean resistance to the treaty erupted in a series of guerrilla actions mounted by the so-called "righteous armies". In October 1909, Ito was assassinated by a Korean patriot. Reprisals were severe. On August 22, 1910, a further treaty finally annexed Korea to Japan, extinguishing Korean hopes for independence. Resistance gradually waned, particularly under the iron-fisted rule of General Terauchi Masatake, the new governor-general. Suppression reflected Japanese confidence, and a belief that they had a divine mission to control Korea. They suppressed Korean opinion and political participation, intending to exploit the new territory.

JAPANESE COLONIZATION

The process of Japanese colonization was a painful one for the independently minded Koreans. In 1937, the Japanese language was made mandatory in schools and public places, and Korean history was dropped from the curriculum. Koreans were compelled to adopt Japanese names and were required to participate in Shinto rituals. The colonial period did, however, prepare Korea for modernization, developing agriculture and industry, installing highways, railroads, ports and communications facilities. Yet all this took place along lines dictated by the needs of Japan's domestic economy, and profits, together with agricultural surplus, went primarily to the Japanese.

The March 1 Movement

In 1919, one of the most celebrated incidents in Korean history took place. Taking as their inspiration the call for the self-determination of subject peoples heard at the Versailles Conference following World War I, a coalition of nationalists planned a non-violent protest. A draft declaration of independence was produced by Korean students in Japan, and in Korea it was distributed by Christians, Buddhists, and members of the Cheondogyo (meaning Heavenly Way) religion, which had emerged from the Donghak movement. Gojong had died, and his funeral was slated for March 3; thousands of people would be in Seoul. It was decided that the declaration should be read out on March 1, in Pagoda Park, Seoul *(see page 132)*. Along the streets near the park shouts of *"Dongnip*

SIBERIAN LINK

In an attempt to refute Japanese cultural domination following the March 1 Movement, Koreans promoted cultural links with Siberia, suggesting that this was where their people originated.

known as "cultural rule". Officials and school teachers stopped wearing swords, and the number of military police was temporarily reduced. Korean publications were permitted, including two newspapers that still survive, the *Donga ilbo* and the *Choson ilbo*. Journals were set up by youth, religious, social and labor organizations, which encouraged a loose grouping of moderate ideologues to emerge. They established an indigenous style of literature, promoted a standardized Korean

manse!" ("Long live independence!") rang out. By the end of May, 1,542 meetings had involved more than 2 million people; 7,500 Koreans had been killed and 50,000 arrested as Japanese repression turned bloody.

The declaration, and the size and ferocity of the meetings that followed it, caught the Japanese by surprise. The result was a new, softer administration promoting what became

LEFT: Prince Yi Un, seventh son of Gojong, became a "puppet" figurehead for the Japanese regime in Korea.
ABOVE: bronze mural at Seoul's Pagoda Park to commemorate the March 1 movement.

alphabet and fought for a Korean university. In an attempt to refute Japanese cultural domination, they popularized the legend of Korea's mythical founder, Dangun. But they argued for gradual reform, displaying a tolerance for Japanese rule that left them outmaneuvered by left-wing groups.

In September 1931, the Japanese army attacked Chinese troops in Manchuria. Korea was the land bridge for this operation, and industrial plants were built along a southeast to northwest corridor to link Japan to Manchuria. Korean workers were drafted to staff Japanese factories, and to work in Manchurian mines. At the same time, students were compelled to join patriotic "volunteer" forces, and women were enlisted to repair roads and maintain the Korean transport infrastructure. As men were drafted into the military, women took their places in factories at home and abroad. By 1945, several million Koreans had been conscripted, with thousands among the victims of the Hiroshima atom bomb. As Japan shifted to a war footing, any hint of tolerance was abandoned: Koreans were to be made Japanese.

Liberation

Many Koreans took it for granted that Japan's surrender at the end of the Pacific War in

Soviet occupation of Korea would harm their security interests in the region. When the Russians entered the Pacific War on August 9, Washington officials hurriedly proposed that a demarcation line be drawn across the peninsula. The Russians were to accept the Japanese surrender north of the line and the Americans south of it. They chose the 38th parallel as the line, a seemingly arbitrary and hurried choice, partly explained in the comment of one of the architects, Dean Rusk, that this "would place the capital city in the American zone". The line left most raw materials, energy sources, and considerable industrial plant in the north. In

August 1945 would mean immediate independence. International politics, however, already had other plans. In 1943, at meetings of the Allies in Cairo and Tehran, the US advanced the idea of a four-power trusteeship for the Korean peninsula. In Cairo, President Roosevelt, conscious that Russian territory touched the Korean border, talked of Korean independence "in due course". The British, French, and Russians were not enthusiastic, but nobody rejected the plan.

The Grand Alliance was already being split by tensions that would soon give rise to the Cold War when Roosevelt died in April 1945. American planners were concerned that a

fact, General Douglas MacArthur, hero of the Pacific campaign, accepted the Japanese surrender on board an American vessel, while only the Russians were present on Korean soil.

The division was not conceived of as permanent, but with world affairs competing for attention, little progress was made towards reunification. Allied foreign ministers met in Moscow in December 1945 and agreed a modified multilateral trusteeship to direct Korean affairs. This envisaged a provisional government, staffed by Koreans, for a minimum of five years. Protracted attempts were made in 1946 and 1947 to implement this agreement, but these were undermined less by the Soviets than by attempts by the American military to practice an early "containment" doctrine. This interpreted the initial resistance to US policy among Koreans in the South as radical and pro-Soviet.

The two armies of occupation began to create the beginnings of two separate Korean states. North of the demarcation line, the Russians moved to establish a regime that would be friendly to them. They recognized the populist people's committees that sprang up immediately after Japanese capitulation, and worked

UNTCOK

To reduce their involvement in Korea in 1947, the US turned to the fledgling UN, and the United Nations' Temporary Commission on Korea (UNTCOK) was set up.

who had returned from China, to create the North Korean Workers Party. Later, as this was merged with equivalent South Korean organizations in 1949, Kim wrested control from Pak.

South of the demarcation line, the US occupation force distrusted local people's committees. General Hodge, in charge, decided to retain many of the authority structures left by the Japanese, and in this way failed to remove collaborators. In September 1945, the Korean People's Republic was formed, with a

through them. Korean Communists, some of whom had been with Mao Zedong in Yan'an, and others who had been in Siberia, returned, jostling for position with those who had stayed in Korea. Pak Heon Yeong, who had established the Korean Communist Party, was the best known within Korea. In December 1945, however, Kim Il Sung became leader of the North Korean Communist Party. In July 1946, he merged his party with the group of Koreans

LEFT: Korean refugees fleeing to the south from advancing armies.
ABOVE: US General Douglas MacArthur makes an inspection tour of the front line.

cabinet joining the nationalist Kim Ku and the right-wing Syngman Rhee. Hodge refused to recognize it, so Kim organized strikes, which Hodge interpreted as a threat to stability. After February 1946, when a right-wing Representative Democratic Council was set up, Hodge sided increasingly with Rhee, particularly as he struggled to cope with the influx of refugees from the Russian zone and with returnees from Japan. When in October Rhee announced an Interim Legislature, his supporters stirred up demonstrations, further undermining the Americans. It was from this weak position that the US began to look for ways to reduce its involvement.

The Republic of Korea

Elections were proposed for a Korean government, with US and Soviet troops to be withdrawn three months later. By the start of 1948, the Russians considered that Communist rule was sufficiently secure in the north to begin a withdrawal. UNTCOK now found itself faced with an impossible task; unable to observe anything north of the demarcation line, it agreed in February 1948 to supervise elections only in the south. In this way, on May 10, just half of Korea chose a constituent assembly to draft a constitution and elect a chief executive.

The assembly picked as chairman, and, on July 15 as president, Syngman Rhee. A month later he was sworn in. A new constitution, approved on July 12, enshrined the claim that the assembly represented "all Korea". In reaction, a constitution was approved in the north in September 1948, partly modeled on the Soviet constitution. This thereby created a separate state, the Democratic People's Republic of Korea. To assist the state to develop, the Soviets supplied arms, creating a formidable army.

The Americans, for their part concerned more with Taiwan and the Communist takeover of mainland China, established a Korean Military Advisory Group. Military manpower was

enhanced, to leave a standing force that in May 1950 numbered 100,000, but the Senate refused to pay for arms, on the grounds that South Korea should develop a policy of self-defense. As a result, weapon stocks were low: South Korea had just 14 obsolete military aircraft.

The Korean War

The stage was set for war. North Korean troops poured across the 38th parallel in strength early Sunday morning, June 25, 1950. Within three days, Seoul had fallen. What began as a civil conflagration soon, however, took on international dimensions. The US was concerned that global communism, directed from Moscow, would soon be on the march. From Washington, President Truman ordered American forces into battle. The first troops arrived on July 5, but by the middle of the month the joint South Korean and US forces had been pushed back to a small pocket around Busan.

The Americans asked the UN for backing, and got it, since the Soviets were boycotting the assembly in protest at the failure to seat the People's Republic of China. Support for Korea was placed under the flag of the UN, and forces from 16 other states followed the US to the peninsula. Overall command was given to Truman, who appointed General MacArthur,

capital, Pyeongyang, fell, and on October 26, US and South Korean troops reached the Yalu River, the border with China. MacArthur proposed using nuclear weapons to press forward. China reacted by sending huge numbers of troops across the border, driving the UN back. The Chinese pushed south, across the 38th parallel, and on January 4, 1951, they took Seoul.

Seoul was recaptured on March 15, and the battlefront gradually stabilized in an area just north of the 38th parallel. Here, small advances required the sacrifice of large numbers of men, and a stalemate prompted the start of truce negotiations in July. These dragged on for two years,

the Commander in Chief in Japan, as Supreme Commander. MacArthur, to relieve the pressure on Busan, planned an amphibious landing at Incheon to the west of Seoul, well behind enemy lines. This took place in September and, meeting little resistance, quickly created a pincer movement. The forces in Busan broke out of the perimeter and began to fight their way north, crossing the 38th parallel by the end of the month. On October 19, the North Korean

LEFT: American GIs watch as British troops arrive in South Korea, September 1950.
ABOVE: a North Korean general arrives for the 1953 peace talks at Panmunjeom on the DMZ.

opposed by Syngman Rhee. The armistice was finally signed, near the village of Panmunjeom, on July 27, 1953, by the Chinese, the North Koreans, and the UN Command; Rhee refused to sign. The armistice created a demilitarized zone (DMZ) to replace the 38th parallel, stretching from coast to coast along the line of stalemate. A Military Armistice Commission was set up, to supervise the implementation of the agreement. Although the signatories were charged with recommending to their governments that a conference be held within three months to settle the issue of Korean reunification, the Commission, never making much progress, has continued to meet periodically at Panmunjeom ever since. ❏

RECOVERY AND PROSPERITY

In East Asian mythology, the phoenix rises from the ashes. After the devastation of the 1950–53 war, this is what has happened in South Korea

The Korean War left the rival capitals, Seoul and Pyongyang, reduced to rubble. Millions were homeless, and millions more were displaced, isolated from families and homes by the Demilitarized Zone (DMZ). Nobody knows how many Koreans died, but North Korean civilian and military casualties alone are estimated at 2 million, while official statistics in the south claim 300,000 civilians wounded, killed, or missing. The UN Command lost nearly 37,000 soldiers, of whom 33,629 were Americans. The war left the DMZ as a 4-km (2½-mile) wide scar etched across the peninsula that neither side would allow to heal: even after both sides simultaneously joined the UN in 1991, there was no peace treaty.

Personality cult

North Korea quickly rebuilt its shattered economy with Soviet aid, skillfully avoiding total dependence on either China or the Soviet Union itself. Kim Il Sung, as the "Great Leader", encouraged a personality cult to grow that allowed him to purge all domestic opposition. He developed his own socialist ideology based on the principles of self-reliance and non-alignment. Inspiration often came from China – Beijing's Great Leap Forward became North Korea's Cheollima (Galloping Horse) Movement, and the Cultural Revolution was reflected in Kim's *juche* philosophy.

As aid declined, barter trade propped up an economy that during the 1960s and 1970s became over-reliant on outdated heavy industry and unmodernized farming methods. Kim's personality cult was such that after a traditional mourning period following his death in 1994 he was elected "Eternal President". The state he founded and ruled has found it difficult to change, and his son and successor, Kim Jong-il, formerly the "Dear Leader", continues with the

same "on the spot guidance" to encourage interminable "revolutionary speed campaigns".

In the 1950s, South Korea stagnated. Despite massive American aid, recovery was slow. The problem was in the administration, where favoritism and corruption were widespread. Syngman Rhee clung to power, engineering a constitutional amendment before elections in 1952 to ensure a narrow victory, and coercing the National Assembly in 1954 to drop a bar from him running for a third term. He was 85 when the next election loomed, in 1960.

By this time, his Liberal Party was deeply unpopular and, even after the execution of his main rival, Cho Pongam, for alleged Communist connections, the election was marred by such blatant fraud that popular demonstrations broke out. On April 19, police fired on a crowd in Seoul, killing 115 people. Rhee promised reforms, but the demonstrations continued. He finally resigned on April 27, and a month later left for exile in Hawaii.

LEFT: General Park Chung-hee, South Korean premier from 1961 to 1979.
RIGHT: monument commemorating those who died in the war, at the National Cemetery.

A fledgling democracy

In July 1960, the constitution was changed to form a government with a cabinet responsible to the legislature. Yun Poson, from the former opposition Democratic Party, was elected to the largely ceremonial role of president to the new Second Republic. Chang Myon, who had served as prime minister and vice-president under Rhee was chosen as prime minister. Rivalry between Yun and Chang compromised the government. On May 16, 1961, after Chang had announced he would cut 30,000 military posts, a junta led by General Park Chung-hee took control. The architect of the coup was Park's

ular demonstrations reminiscent of those that brought down Syngman Rhee. In 1963, Park retired from the army and ran as presidential candidate for a new civilian government. He won, narrowly beating Yun Poson. He was re-elected in 1967, and two years later secured a constitutional amendment to permit him a third term, which he duly won in 1971. A year later, in 1972, he declared martial law, bringing to a close the Third Republic. This allowed him to redraw the constitution in a way that allowed him presidential power for life. The new constitution, named Yusin to indicate that it was to revitalize Korea, came with a glimmer of hope for détente

nephew by marriage, Kim Jongpil. The junta promised to stamp out corruption, build a self-supporting economy, and work for reunification. With a nod to the international community, it announced it would respect the UN charter and seek closer relations with the free world.

Military rule and economic success

Park was a career officer from rural Gyeongsangbuk province. He had trained in Japanese military academies and served the colonial power in Manchuria during the Pacific War. By 1960, he was deputy commander of South Korea's Second Army. He would now rule until assassinated in 1979 as he moved to quell pop-

with North Korea, but this was shattered after infiltrators assassinated Park's wife.

Park's harsh rule is today measured against his remarkable success at developing an export-led economy that laid the foundations for prosperity. Park forged a partnership with industry, effectively encouraging the emergence of today's conglomerates, the *jaebeol*. Tax concessions and favorable loans were provided through state banks. In the first five years, the average annual GNP growth was 8.5 percent and exports increased at an annual 40 percent. The state took on infrastructure projects to develop a transport and communications network. Certainly, the four economic plans unveiled during Park's tenure pulled South Korea from mass poverty into the modern age. His administration built domestic car- and ship-building industries, then gradually moved from labor-intensive heavy industry to skill-intensive electronics and high-technology production.

In 1979, Park was assassinated by his own head of intelligence, Kim Jae Kyu. Kim was later executed, along with six accomplices. The Defense Security Command, the agency investigating the assassination, was led by Major General Chun Doo-hwan. On December 12, 1979, Chun called on the Ninth Army, under General Roh Tae-woo, to enter Seoul and, after arresting a number of senior military officers, it became clear that a bid for power was under way.

In May 1980, Chun declared martial law and ruthlessly put down a revolt in the southwestern city of Gwangju. Local residents claim that more than 2,000 died. In August, Chun resigned from the army and an electoral college declared him president. Chun recycled Park's government style, depriving people of civil and political rights and, through a new economic plan, forcing conglomerates to swap interests.

While GNP figures increased rapidly, so did Korea's international debt. In early 1987, Chun announced that Roh Tae-woo would be his favored successor as president. The public became restless, and when a student was tortured to death by police early in January, demonstrators took to the streets.

Democracy reborn

On June 29, 1987, after months of demonstrations, Roh gave a TV address. He announced an unexpected liberalization of politics and the release of political prisoners, effectively separating himself from Chun. In the elections that autumn, the opposition, led by three Kims – Kim Young-sam, Kim Dae-jung and Kim Jongpil – was split by internal rivalry, and Roh became the first democratically elected president. Roh lifted restrictions on media and unions, allowing bitter labor disputes to erupt. However, his five-year tenure began as South Korea emerged from under the wing of the US, and as the 1988 Olympics brought the world's media to Seoul. As a partner on the world stage,

and keen to find new markets for its exports, South Korea embarked on a diplomatic initiative it called *Nordpolitik*. In part, this would further isolate North Korea, as was apparent when full relations were established with the Soviet Union in 1990 and with China in 1992.

In 1990, to overcome a political stalemate caused after National Assembly elections had left the ruling camp without a majority, Roh merged his party with two opposition parties led by Kim Young-sam and Kim Jongpil. After much wrangling, Kim Young-sam became Roh's presidential candidate. In 1992, he took office as the first civilian president in over 30 years.

Kim Young-sam brought a promise of complete democratic reform. Within days of taking power he launched a sweeping anti-corruption drive, which toppled prominent figures in the military, government and business – including some of his own allies. Although he initially released many prisoners, including some held for decades under the archaic National Security Law, he was intolerant of dissidence. In 1995, he sent police to the Buddhist Jogye sect's headquarters to evict squatting monks.

By the early 1990s, the major conglomerates were responsible for around 75 percent of Korean exports, but Kim Young-sam alienated them, forcing them to sell off land, and accusing

---

LEFT: Syngman Rhee and his wife are greeted at La Guardia airport, New York, in July 1954.
RIGHT: riot police in Seoul.

the head of Hyundai of tax evasion. He soon incurred the wrath of farmers when he agreed in GATT talks to open the local market to rice imports, and his campaign for "globalization" was seen as a sell-out of local industry. The protected local market had been threatened by anti-dumping legislation in the US and elsewhere, and the administration now saw it as inevitable that import tariffs be reduced. Although the process proved painful for small businesses, per capita income continued to rise.

ECONOMIC CRISIS

In the economic turmoil of 1997, the Korean currency collapsed, leading to an appeal to the IMF for loans totalling US$57 billion.

the collapse of a bridge over the Han River in Seoul, and the collapse of the Sampoong department store in which hundreds were killed.

Kim Young-sam tried to distance himself from his former allies as the 1996 National Assembly elections approached. His party managed to secure a slim majority, but some of those who opposed Kim boycotted the Assembly, creating legislative turmoil. The final blow came when the Asian economic turmoil of summer 1997 spread quickly to Korea. Suddenly, the profligate expansionism

The policies, however, gradually unraveled. Incompetence and corruption resurfaced as blame was sought for a series of major disasters. Pressure increased to bring ex-presidents Roh Tae-woo and Chun Doo-hwan to trial. In late 1995, Roh made a tearful televized apology for having amassed a fortune of US$650 million during his term in office, largely from conglomerates in exchange for government contracts and favors. Prosecutors were allowed to probe recent history, and in 1996 Roh and Chun, along with other former military leaders, went on trial for corruption and treason. Their corruption was blamed for a series of disasters including gas explosions in Daegu and Seoul,

of conglomerates, the lack of central control, and the poor debt provision of domestic banks was revealed, and the currency collapsed.

The Sunshine Policy

Enter Kim Dae-jung. In 1971, Kim had stood against Park Chung-hee in the presidential elections. In Tokyo, he had denounced martial law and the imposition of the new Yusin constitution. In August 1973, he was kidnapped and forcibly repatriated to Seoul, where he was placed under house arrest. Kim was arrested again in 1980, when Chun Doo-hwan declared martial law. When Chun moved against the revolt in Gwangju, Kim, who hails from Jeolla province in the southwest, was charged with inciting the revolt and sentenced to death. He was allowed to go to America for medical treatment, but was returned to house arrest when he arrived back in Seoul in 1984. Having been defeated by Roh and Kim Young-sam, Kim stood for president once more in the 1995 elections. This time he was successful. The first opposition candidate to take power, uniquely able to isolate himself from past regimes and present himself as the people's choice, Kim Dae-jung proved himself an able administrator. Within two years, Korea had re-emerged from economic collapse; state support for banks and

1999 – and an international effort to stop the North's nuclear program presented opportunities for renewed relations. In 1995, Seoul donated 150,000 tons of rice, but several incidents, including forcing South Korean vessels to raise North Korean flags when in port, led to a suspension of aid. Rice and fertilizer shipments were sent in subsequent years, while Hyundai was allowed to start a tourist operation from the South to the North in late 1998 *(see page 172)*.

The summer of 2000 saw a sensational breakthrough in North-South relations, when Kim Dae-jung became the first South Korean leader to visit Pyeongyang. This historic meeting was

loss-making companies had been withdrawn, allowing them to be sold off, amalgamated, or to fail. Foreign capital was flowing in, and foreign reserves were healthy.

At the same time, Kim set about rapprochment with North Korea. This was the "Sunshine Policy". North-South relations had ground to a halt after the death of Kim Il Sung in 1994, but the deepening food shortage in the North – mass starvation, with the loss of perhaps 10 percent of the population, occurred between 1995 and

LEFT: at the 1988 Olympic Games in Seoul.
ABOVE: the historic meeting of Kim Jong-il and Kim Dae-jung in Pyeongyang, June 2000.

hailed as a definite step towards reunification, and as a result Kim was awarded the Nobel Peace Prize. The most high-profile result of the thaw saw the first reunions between family members who had been separated by the war.

But five decades of stand-off could not be solved with a handshake, and it was not long before the North was back to its old sabre-rattling tricks. While Koreans north and south of the DMZ still talk fervently about reunification, the divide was emphasized in early 2003 with US/North Korea relations deteriorating rapidly over the issue of the North's refusal to abandon its nuclear weapons programme – a major concern for the new South Korean president Roh Moo-hyun. ❑

KOREA'S VIBRANT FESTIVALS

For short-term visitors to Korea, there's no better way to appreciate the country's true character than to witness one of the many colorful festivals

Spring and autumn are lively seasons in Korea, where almost every weekend there is a festival going on somewhere in the country. Some, such as the Andong International Mask Festival, are large affairs that attract people from all over Korea. Others, such as the Tea Festival in Boseong, are local affairs that you might come across while traveling the countryside. Visiting a festival is a great opportunity to see just how downright sociable Koreans can be. Despite all the pushing and shoving, and those stony Confucian faces encountered in the city, Koreans can party with the best of them. While attending a festival, it's likely you'll be offered a sip of *soju* from some grandfather's bottle, or maybe a brightly dressed *ajumma* will ask you to sit and enjoy a plate of *gimbap*.

LOCAL FLAVOR

Activities at Korean festivals revolve around a theme, usually a product or a cultural activity for which the region is famous. Ginseng, mud baths, mushrooms and Korean liquors all have a weekend set aside to celebrate their attributes. But, invariably, you'll also be treated to continual folk performances – the noisy farmer bands, the softer sounds of *pansori* (traditional song), the local mask dance, and probably some fascinating ceremonies performed by shamans to ensure the community's prosperity. If at all possible, schedule a day for a festival while visiting Korea.

▷ **FARMERS' DANCE**
At many festivals, villages from throughout the region send bands to a competition to see which is the most colorful and noisy.

▷ **GIMCHI FESTIVAL**
Foreigners are encouraged to try their luck at making the ubiquitous Korean staple at Gwangju's Gimchi Festival.

△ **FUN AND GAMES**
Neolttwigi, pictured here at the spring Dano festival, is Korea's version of the seesaw.

◁ **FESTIVE LANTERNS**
Brightly colored lanterns fill the courtyard of a mountain temple during the week-long celebration of Buddha's birthday, Korea's most important Buddhist festival.

△ **ALMS APPRECIATION**
Monks are no longer allowed to beg for alms on Korea's streets, so offerings of rice, fruit and money, as at the Buddha's birthday festival, are much appreciated.

KOREAN KITE FIGHTING

In Korea, kites *(yeon)* aren't just for children. Indeed, you're more likely to find an accountant or college professor holding a kite string than a bright-eyed waif. It's been that way for centuries, as soldiers and the upper class used fighting kites to hone their battle strategies.

The objective of Korean kite fighting is to maneuver your kite so it cuts your opponents kite string, sending their kite floating ignobly to earth. Strings are made of silk, with ceramic filings (or even finely crushed diamonds) along their length – making them deadly when rubbed against an opponent's string.

A favorite location for kite flying is the Hangang Citizen's Park in Seoul. Go on a windy Sunday, and you'll see members of the Seoul Kite Club engaged in good-natured combat, or discussing strategies and admiring each other's kites. The International Kite Festival is held here in the first month of the Lunar Year.

▽ **VILLAGE PARODY**
The Korean mask dance, where every stuffed shirt and village oddball is parodied, is a true folk tradition with roots in Korea's shamanistic past.

△ **MASK FESTIVAL**
A young boy is dwarfed by masks at the Andong International Mask Festival. Korea's best dance groups make this one of the country's liveliest festivals.

▷ **TAKING IN THE SHOW**
No one loves a festival like Korea's senior citizens, who put on their finest clothes, pack a lunch and stock up on *soju* for a day of merry-making.

THE KOREANS

To understand the Koreans and their intriguing society, you need to consider their long and turbulent history

Koreans have long memories. They have learnt to survive in a dangerous neighborhood, surrounded by China, Japan and Russia (with which North Korea today shares a 16-km/10-mile border) and, from the 19th century, threatened by Occidental powers. To survive, they have had to develop patience, flexibility, stubbornness and a robust, satirical, and unabashed sense of humour.

Korean patience does not mean passivity, nor does flexibility imply lack of individuality. Complementing and contrasting these, stubbornness – which might better be referred to as perseverance – has produce a time-tested resilience. These counterpointed national traits can be traced back many centuries. They also echo influences absorbed from outside Korea's borders, namely the patience of the Chinese, Japanese adaptability, and American determination.

The longstanding close relationship with China, and a willingness to accept Chinese notions of governance, ethics and morality, has left indelible marks on the Korean psyche. Japanese colonialism represented a more recent threat to Korean uniqueness, and memories of exploitation and brutality, of being forced to speak Japanese and to take Japanese names, remain painful. More recent still, the devastation of the Korean War, and the influence of America thereafter, forced Koreans to confront the outside world in a new way.

Today, Seoul looks and feels much like any other major international city. When a traveler first meets a Korean, there may seem to be little mystery in his character. With his tailored suit and silk tie, a Korean businessman would not be out of place in London or New York. Mobile phones are everywhere, and on each corner there are shops selling the most up-to-date fashions. In 1988, as an indication that Koreans had joined the international community, the Seoul Olympics adopted the slogan "the world to Seoul, Seoul to the world". Scratch the surface, however, and things are very different. Old ways of thinking and behavior remain remarkably strong in the minds of Korean people, almost regardless of their education and rank.

Gibun and Nunchi

Korean codes of etiquette remain strong, an elaborate system of formalized gestures designed to foster smooth relations. The maintenance of proper *gibun*, by avoiding arguments or any overt display of emotion, is paramount. *Gibun* signifies mood or aura, and literally translates as "personal energy". Koreans also employ a strategy known as *nunchi* to observe and imitate the feelings of others. *Nunchi* means that in conversations Koreans will try to say nothing that could be construed as negative; stating the truth, being scrupulously fair, or quickly settling any contractual agreement are all alien to the face-saving that *nunchi* usually requires.

PRECEDING PAGES: the "thousand Buddhas" at Jikji-sa temple.
LEFT: craftsman at Suwon Folk Village.
RIGHT: train conductors bow to arriving passengers.

Nunchi means that visitors find the Koreans warm, friendly and sympathetic. Foreigners are classless and they are not expected to know how to behave in an appropriate manner. Once they were "non-persons", little different to outcasts. Until reforms in the 1890s, Korean society was very hierarchical, from royalty and aristocracy (the *yangban)* down to commoners *(sangmin)* and below *(cheonmin).* Today, the Korean language still preserves the hierarchy, offering a mass of honorifics that are used to reflect status, education and age. When Koreans first meet, apart from exchanging namecards, they quickly size up a new friend, deciding within a few brief seconds whether to talk up, down, or as an equal.

Much of the Korean psyche stems from deeply-rooted Confucian values. Chinese emperors called the Koreans "the ceremonious people of the East", in effect an admission that the Koreans had outdone Confucius' own people, the Chinese. Confucianism stresses the importance of a strong family structure, the ethic of frugality, hard work (not just for oneself but for the common good), and respect for education. A Korean child is given a two-syllable name chosen by a wise elder, one syllable indicating his or her generation, and one

THE LEGEND OF DANGUN

The Korean peninsula was first settled some 30,000 years ago by wandering tribes from Central and Northern Asia, who brought with them elements of their own cultures, shamanist rituals, and a language. The Korean language is part of the Altaic linguistic group, related to such widely separated tongues as Mongolian, Finnish and Hungarian.

The founder of Korea, according to legend, was Dangun, born on Baekdusan (Changbaishan in Chinese), on the border between present-day North Korea and China, close to where the earliest migrants would have entered the Korean peninsula. The story begins when Hwanung, the son of the Divine Creator, heard the prayers of a bear and

a tiger who wished to become human. He gave them each 20 pieces of garlic and a piece of artemisia, and told them they would be transformed if they ate the plants and avoided sunlight for 100 days. The tiger failed, but the bear remained in a cave for the prescribed period and emerged as a woman. Her wish was to have a son; soon her prayers were answered, and Dangun was born. He ruled from 2333 BC to 1122 BC, then resumed his spirit form and disappeared. The legend was revived in the early 20th century to reassert Korean national identity. In the 1990s the North Koreans claimed to have uncovered his bones: these are now displayed in a mausoleum near Pyeongyang.

predicting his or her character. His or her name is added to the *jokbo*, a book that links families into lineages and clans traced back to founder figures. A child is taught to respect parents and elders; in all things, he or she should behave properly, so as not to bring shame on the family.

Alongside proper etiquette, *mat* and *meot* provide a counterbalance. These concepts signify taste and style, but also give meaning to the sobriquet that the Koreans are "the Irish of the Orient". On one hand, the burden of history has left songs that are sad and poetry that is piercingly nostalgic; there is a common sense of longing and oppression known as *han* that continues to weigh heavily. On the other hand, Koreans grasp any opportunity to sing and dance, to entertain, and be entertained. Of course, good food, drink and entertainment are essential in the building of any friendship.

Life begins at 100 days

In every district of Seoul there is a photography shop that proudly displays pictures of tiny children, some boys naked, and others dressed in fine silk. In villages, one still finds strings of dried red peppers hung across the gateway to a home. Void of all culinary connotations, the peppers proclaim with obvious symbolism the birth of a baby boy a week or less before. Girls are announced by strings of charcoal and pine needles, the significance of which is rather less apparent. Once, the strings conveyed a message: it was taboo for visitors to enter, since it was believed that during the first week the newborn child was vulnerable to bad luck or evil spirits brought by visitors.

After 100 days, it is time to name the child. In the past, when the death of newborn children was common, this was the time to publicly celebrate in a ceremony known as the *baegil janchi*; today, this is when the photographer is called. Next, the first birthday is celebrated with a special rice cake flavored with mugwort. This is the time to predict a child's future. Everyone is invited, and pencils, thread

LEFT: respectful progeny gathers round at a *hwangap*, or 60th birthday party, in 1933.
RIGHT: South Korea's children face a bright future.

ALUMNI GROUPS
Loyalty is prized in alumni groups for students and young soldiers. Both Chun Doo-hwan and Roh Tae-woo, presidents in the 1980s, were members of the secretive military alumni group, Hanahoe.

and other presents are placed before the child. If the child takes the pencils, then they are destined to become a scholar, while the thread indicates a long and full life.

A world away from the small, isolated villages of old Korea, urban children develop alliances beyond the family. Alumni groups feature in most Korean schools and universities. They also play an important part in young men's lives during their compulsory military service.

Within families, as within all social groups, a

hierarchy based on age is still the norm, and Koreans routinely call each other older brother (*hyeongnim*) or older sister (*nuna, eonni*). Within schools, and later in life within the workplace, seniors are *seonbae* and juniors are *hubae*; *seonbae* have a responsibility to guide *hubae*.

The right match

In the past, marriage was a contract between families, and spouses were chosen by parents. Many Koreans now want more say in selecting their own partners. Nightclubs and discos now offer venues for the search to begin, but a more popular method among university students is the "line up", where an equal number of men and women meet in a coffee shop and, through games or ballots, pair off.

Still, roughly half of all Korean marriages begin with a matchmaker. Meetings are arranged, most commonly in the coffee shop of a hotel on a weekend afternoon. Sometimes the matchmaker will be present to smooth the introduction. Before this, though, the mothers will have visited a fortune-teller to check the prospective couple's compatibility *(gunghap)* based on their birth date and time (their *saju*).

As a rule of thumb, women should be married before they reach 28; beyond this they

become "old maids". Men are typically a year or two older than their spouse.

Today, most Korean weddings take place in gaudy *yesikjang* ("wedding halls"). These are like factories, and they provide everything from flowers and dress hire to piped organ music. The ceremony is captured on video; friends and relatives gathered in the pew-like seats struggle to see the couple through lines of photographers. Everyone adjourns to two nearby restaurants, one for the groom's guests and one for the bride's.

Finally, today as in the past, the new couple are required to produce a child – preferably a son to pass on the family name – little more than nine months later.

The final journey

Koreans traditionally retire when they reach 60, and this, the *hwangap* birthday, is a time for great celebration. It marks the completion of one life cycle, based on the Chinese astrological system of 12 earthly animals and 10 heavenly characters. The celebrant sits enthroned on cushions, surrounded by tables piled high with fruit, rice cakes, cookies and candies, receiving respectful kowtows from children and grandchildren.

When Koreans die, they hope to do so at home. Although cremation is encouraged in urban Korea, old customs still survive in the countryside. There, after a party resembling a wake, and a shaman ritual to ensure the soul's safe passage to the other world, the funeral bier is taken to a hillside, where the body is buried. Grave sites are chosen with care, for from here the dead will continue to influence the living as an ancestor.

Seoul, though, seems a very different place in this respect to the rest of the country; but not at lunar new year, *seollal*, or harvest festival, *chuseok*. Suddenly, the city is left virtually deserted. Tickets for buses and trains are sold out months in advance, and the expressways are renamed as "parking lots", as everyone rushes to escape to the countryside. These are the traditional times for tending ancestral graves and visiting family elders, and it is at these times that Koreans, both young and old, return to their roots. ❏

MATCHMAKERS AND PRENUPTIALS

In recent years, professional matchmakers have found new trade working on behalf of overseas Koreans, who will return on the basis of a photograph to meet potential spouses, and also on the behalf of men who find the pressures of building a successful career leaves them little time for social matters.

In the past, pre-pubescent boys were married to older girls. The girl's parents would send her bedding and trousseau chest to the boy's home. On the nuptial day, she would be carried to the house in a palanquin and the couple would pledge their troth, then bow to their parents in a time-honoured ceremony.

LEFT: Korean brides often choose to wear Western-style wedding dresses.

The Korean Diaspora

Today, some 4½ million Koreans live abroad. More than a third of the Koreans in the US have settled in California. Korean-Americans are known for their industriousness – they own and run many of the grocery stores in LA and NYC.

Migration to America began with 7,000 Koreans sent to work on sugar plantations in Hawaii, between 1903 and 1905; many later moved to the mainland. Early exiles from Korea included some who had argued for modernization and change during the late Joseon period. After the Korean War, emigration picked up, and by 1980 there were 357,000 Korean-Americans. Almost 56,000 Korean women had married US servicemen, and many Korean children had been adopted into American families. The 1992 riots in Los Angeles left more than 2,000 Korean-owned businesses in ruins.

A second community of Koreans traces its roots back further. Korean peasant farmers, escaping poverty, began to cross into Manchuria in the 1860s; they were granted land tenancy in the provinces of Liaoning, Jilin and Heilongjiang during the 1880s. Some moved eastwards to what later became the Soviet Far East, and in 1884 were offered Russian citizenship. Korean guerrillas based in China and Russia harried the Japanese during the early colonial period. A Korean provisional government was established in Shanghai in 1919; later, 63,000 Koreans fought with the communists during the Chinese civil war.

During the 1930s, when Japan established its puppet state in Manchuria, it began to draft in Korean labor, and the Korean population peaked at 2,163,115 in 1945. The 1985 Chinese census reported 1,765,000 citizens of Korean descent.

Korean is one of the six recognized languages of China. The first Korean school was opened in 1906, and a Korean university was established in 1949. The Koreans also brought rice cultivation to this cold northern region, and in 1933 one farmer succeeded in growing rice at a latitude of 50° north.

The Koreans in the Soviet Far East fared less well. 168,000 Koreans are recorded in the region in the 1926 census, and Vladivostok had its own Korean quarter. The population came under suspicion as Stalin sought to liquidate his opponents during the next decade, and in 1937 the entire

community was relocated to Central Asia. Around 180,000 resettled in Kazakstan and Uzbekistan. Initially, they continued to plant rice and cultivate cotton. Increasingly, Koreans have utilized their high levels of education to emerge as a distinct urban professional class. Beyond Central Asia, 40,000 Korean laborers were isolated on Sakhalin at the end of the Pacific War, when the island was transferred from Japanese to Soviet control.

Some 700,000 Koreans still live in Japan, forming around 85 percent of Japan's officially recognized "foreigners" and living primarily around Osaka and Fukuoka. In the 16th century, Korean potters and other artisans were taken to Japan; earlier

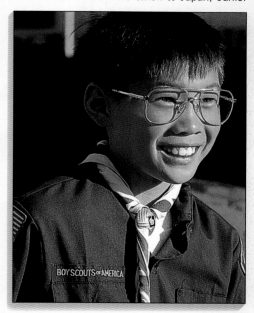

still, there is evidence of Korean royalty living around Nara near Kyoto.

Migration, though, is largely a result of the colonial period. By 1940, some 1,250,000 Koreans, mostly from Korea's southern provinces, had been drafted to work in Japan. Repatriation of around 60 percent to South Korea took place after 1945, and a Red Cross agreement allowed 100,000 more to return to North Korea.

Those who remained in Japan were isolated once South Korea signed a normalization agreement in 1965, and this left the majority of the remainder allied to North Korea and to an educational, financial, and political organization known as Chongnyeon. ❑

RIGHT: the new generation of Korean-Americans, far removed from the land of their ancestors.

RELIGION

*Korea is a country of diverse spiritual traditions and philosophies, where
major belief systems have become established alongside regional folk religions*

There are five strands of religious practice in Korea today: a strand of folk religion, a Buddhist strand, a Confucian strand, a Christian strand, and a strand consisting of the various new syncretic religious traditions which have grown up since the end of the 19th century. It is hard to calculate the numbers of adherents in the different traditions because the understanding of self-identity varies from tradition to tradition. For example, people might only call themselves a Christian if they were baptized or registered members of a church, whereas a person might identify him or herself as a Buddhist if their mother went to a particular temple. Likewise, attitudes toward worship vary greatly. Christians would probably feel that frequent, preferably weekly, attendance was a sign of faithfulness, whereas Buddhists would take a more relaxed attitude towards formal worship, and believers in the folk tradition would view participation in certain important annual festivals as being sufficient.

Even given these difficulties in defining the numerical size of the religious traditions, about one third of the population of South Korea would identify themselves as Buddhist, one quarter as Christian, and the remainder adhere to Confucianism, traditional practices, and the syncretic traditions in various combinations, or have no clear religious identity.

The regional context

Korea is distinct from Japan in that, on the whole, religious adherence tends to be exclusive and to lack the syncretism typical of post-war Japan. This is due, in part, to the way in which Confucianism was adapted in Korea. Likewise, the impact of Confucianism on Korean society historically has been much greater than in Japan, and even China. The result has been a much more "pure" approach to religious practice. Another contrast with

LEFT: descendants of Yi-dynasty royal families honor their ancestors in Confucian rites at Jongmyo Shrine.
RIGHT: statue of Buddha flanked by deities.

China and Japan is that the Confucian policy of the last dynasty (which lasted for over 500 years) was responsible for the suppression of Buddhism, which only revived in the changed political circumstances of the 20th century. Compared with Japan, where they account for less than 1 percent of the whole, Christians

form a very significant part of the population, and are its most articulate and politically aware element. Unlike Japan, the post-war new religious movements have not been a mixture of Buddhism and folk traditions, but of Christianity and folk traditions.

Another interesting comparison with Korea's neighbors is that the folk traditions of Korea did not form themselves into formal, institutionalized traditions such as religious Taoism in China, or Shinto in Japan, but remained amorphous customary practices. Finally, and contrary to much that is mistakenly said, there is no tradition of religious Taoism in contemporary Korea, although there are a few shrines of Chinese origin. Philosophical Taoism (which is very different from the religious traditions calling themselves Taoist) has had a great impact on neo-Confucian thought.

Folk religion

Something which will strike any first-time visitor to Korea is that the indigenous religious traditions of the country have no name. If you query anyone about this, they will tell you that it is "shamanism". Yet this is not a name for the folk religion, but rather a description of it, and an inaccurate one at that. As mentioned above, one curious feature of the folk religious

the other on the practices of the shaman, or *mudang* in Korean. These shamanistic practices are the most colorful, vibrant features of Korean folk religion. The shaman is an intercessor, a person who has been selected by spirits, and often in a trance, to have a special relationship with a particular spirit or group of spirits. Because of this power, the shaman is thought to be able to cure disease by finding the spirit causing the illness, to bring blessing and prosperity on a family or person, and to be able to see that the soul of a deceased person is successfully escorted into the next world. During the *gut* or shamanistic ritual, the

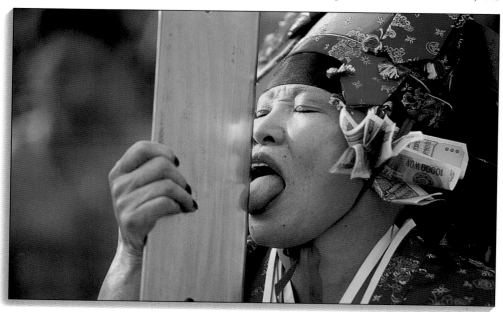

traditions of Korea is that, unlike in China and Japan, they never became a formal religious tradition with ritual buildings, formalized rituals, recognized scriptures, and an organised clerical leadership. Korean folk religion has remained a non-institutional, customary series of practices, the received traditions of the nation. How can you name it? Like any folk tradition, it just *is*. The origins are as ancient as the Korean people themselves reflecting the different traditions of the non-Chinese ethnic groups of Northeast Asia.

There are two principal threads within the folk strand of Korean religious life, one which is focused on village and household rituals, and

shaman's special spirit is believed to descend into her body and to speak through her mouth.

Korean shamans are predominantly women. Whatever their sex, when they perform a *gut* the clothing of the opposite sex is worn. The *gut* are lively and noisy because of the drums and percussion instruments accompanying the actions of the shaman. These features of Korean shamanism point to a link with the practices of the most ancient inhabitants of Siberia, the Palaeo-Siberian tribes of the far northeastern corner of the Asiatic landmass.

In contrast to these colorful rituals are the more restrained village ceremonies. At certain key points in the cycle of the lunar calendar, for example the first or 15th day of the first lunar month, one or more adult male members of a village will be chosen to offer up a sacrifice at the village shrine to *Sansin*, the mountain god, or to the spirits of the founding ancestors of the village. These rituals are short and the leaders are selected for a brief period of time only, unlike the *mudang* who remains a shaman for life.

There are other Korean folk practices ranging from indigenous, non-Confucian ancestral practices – both shamanistic and non-shamanistic

VILLAGE SHRINES

Although some shrines are actual buildings, it's not uncommon to find local shrines that are no more than a large stone in front of a tree in the midst of a grove of trees.

istic practices. Ascending the hill past these shrines you come to the *Guksadang* itself and a strange pock-marked rock which is the center for its own cult.

Buddhism

Buddhism is a missionary religion from India which spread from China into Korea some time during the 4th century, eventually becoming the state religion of all three of the ancient kingdoms of Korea – Goguryeo, Baekje, and Silla. By the time it reached Korea, Buddhism had

– to simple acts of tossing a stone onto a pile of stones, called a *seonghwangdang*, when crossing a mountain pass as an offering to *Sansin*.

The principal shamanistic shrine in Seoul, called the *Guksadang*, is located on the western slope of Muaksan just to the east of the Independence Arch. This is by the Dongnimmun station on the Number 3 underground line. The *Guksadang* is surrounded by a cluster of buildings which proclaim themselves to be Buddhist temples, but which in reality are shrines dedicated to syncretized Buddhist and shaman-

LEFT: a shaman goes into a trance during the *gut* ritual.
ABOVE: the Jindo shaman lures spirits.

altered from its form in India, absorbing elements of the local folk traditions of the countries into which it had spread.

By the 7th century Buddhism was well established, as seen in the numbers of great temples which had been erected throughout the peninsula, the numbers of monks who went to China and India to study, and the important role which Korean monks played in the spread and development of Buddhism in Japan.

By the end of the Silla period in the early 10th century, Buddhism had effectively taken on the form which we see in modern Korea. Monastic Buddhism is predominantly of the meditative *Seon* school (better known by the

Japanese term *Zen)*, whereas popular Buddhism, the Buddhism practiced by the laity, belongs predominantly to the Pure Land traditions. The all-encompassing doctrinal *Dienai* school (*Jeondae* in Korean) remained important for a few more centuries, but the meditation and Pure Land schools came to form the core of Buddhist practice in Korea. The *Seon* school is based on the idea that suffering is caused by attachment to things of this world, and that release from suffering can only come through the abrupt realization of the illusionary nature of all things. Methods of meditation and monastic life are meant to bring the monk or

nun into a state of sudden enlightenment. The Pure Land doctrines, in contrast, teach that there is a great Buddha, *Amita*, who is the ruler of the Western Paradise or Pure Land and who desires the salvation of all people. The teaching of this school has a kind of Lutheran "by faith alone" aspect, as it is believed that anyone who with true faith repeats the name of Amita 10 times will be brought to live in the Pure Land. The figure most closely associated with Amita is *Gwaneum* (Chinese *Guanyin*, Japanese *Gannon*), mistakenly called the Goddess of Mercy.

Buddhism during the Goryeo period (918–1392) flourished, existing in a complementary state of harmony with Confucianism. However, by the end of the 14th century, as Buddhism had been associated with the Mongol overlords of Korea and as recent developments in Confucianism made Buddhism seem superstitious, the neo-Confucian Joseon dynasty (1392–1910) suppressed Buddhism, and on two occasions attempted to eradicate it altogether. By the end of the 19th century the religion was only a shadow of what it had been during the heyday of the Goryeo era.

With the demise of the Joseon dynasty, and the annexation of Korea by Japan, Buddhism's fortunes changed dramatically. The redevelopment and modernization of Buddhism is due to the work of both more traditionalist monks, and to the work of modernizers who looked to the laity as the core of the Buddhist community.

Although temples were banned from the cities during the Joseon dynasty, all major Korean cities now have numerous temples in them. In Seoul, the most important is the Jogyesa temple, head temple of the *Jogyejong*, the largest – by far – of the Buddhist denominations. It is the most untypical of all Korean Buddhist temples, because the structure was originally the central shrine for a provincial syncretic sect which was brought to Seoul in 1935 and reassembled on the present site. The temple ground also lacks many of the other features of a standard Korean temple. Nonetheless, it provides the visitor with a good introduction to Buddhist ritual activity. Other temples which the visitor should seek out are the Haein-sa temple west of Daegu, housing the 80,000 printing blocks of the entire Buddhist canon, the Tongdo-sa temple north of Busan, housing a relic of the Buddha in its central pagoda, and the Bulguk-sa temple just

UPDATING BUDDHISM

Consciously or unconsciously, the modernizers of Korean Buddhism looked to the rapidly growing Protestant Christian community in the country both for inspiration and as a competitor. Many features of contemporary Korean Buddhism reflect Protestant practice, such as the emphasis on lay groups, institutional outreach in the form of schools, universities, print and broadcast media, as well as popular liturgical practices that use Buddhist words to the tunes of well-known Christian hymns. The modernization of Buddhism has allowed its return to an important place on the Korean religious scene.

outside the ancient capital of Silla, Gyeongju, with the associated Seokguram grotto overlooking the East Sea, housing one of the finest Buddhist statues in East Asia.

When visiting a Buddhist temple, you should look for the following buildings and structures, among many others. The *iljumun* using two large tree trunks as pillars is topped by a tiled roof and displays a placard enscribed with the name of the temple and the mountain on which it is located. This gate marks the outer perimeter of the temple grounds. Further along will be the *Sacheonwangmun*, or Gate of the Four Heavenly Kings, guardians of the four cardinal points of the universe, which marks the entrance into the inner area of the temple. Beyond this will be a *beopdang*, or lecture hall. Passing under or by this hall will bring you into the main court of the temple with pagodas containing the cremated remains of eminent monks. In front will be the *daeungjeon*, the principal shrine and dedicated to the Buddha. Nearby will be a *myeongbujeon*, or hall of judgement, with statues of the 10 kings of hell. Behind this main complex, frequently to the left rear of the *daeungjeon*, is the *sansingak*, containing a portrait of the Mountain God seated under a pine tree, with a tiger nearby.

Confucianism

Confucianism is not a religion as such, but a system of socio-political philosophy which has absorbed an extensive ritual system derived from the religious practices of the Zhou dynasty of ancient China (1111–429 BC). Confucius (Kongfuzi; Gongja in Korean, 551–479 BC), the first and greatest philosopher of East Asia, developed a system of political philosophy which was revolutionary in its day, arguing that the ruler of a state should appoint ministers and officials on the basis of merit alone. Confucius saw that society was composed of five sets of relationships – ruler/ruled, parent/child, husband/wife, older/younger sibling, friend/ friend – which were hierarchical and characterized by benevolent actions from above and loyalty from below. These relationships imply a high degree of mutual responsibility, which explains why languages like Korean have so many ways of

indicating social distance or closeness. Confucius felt that the outward expression of filial love was symbolized by the performance of ancestral rituals. The conduct of these rites, listening to the stately music of the day, and the study of classical philosophical literature, all led to moral cultivation. Confucius implied, and subsequent Confucian thinkers stated, that human nature was good in essence and only needed cultivation (education) to refine and develop itself.

With the establishment of the Han dynasty in the 2nd century BC, Confucianism became the state ideology. The bureaucracy was

grounded in Confucian political thought, schools grew up to train the next generation of scholarly bureaucrats, and an examination system was instituted to admit people on the basis of merit. The pattern of Confucian government was set for the next two millennia.

In the 4th century, when the Korean kingdoms were accepting substantial amounts of Chinese civilization, a process called Sinization, Buddhism and Confucianism were accepted as part of a cultural package. As Confucianism spread beyond China, its influence on other nations was three-fold – political, cultural and social. Political influences were on the structure and conduct of

LEFT: celebrating Buddha's birthday at Tongdo-sa temple, north of Busan.
RIGHT: an elderly Confucian gentleman.

government whereas the cultural influences were on education, the keeping of historical records, and the use of a writing system. These were the primary influences of Confucianism on Korea until the late 14th century. Until then, Buddhism and Confucianism existed in a state of complementarity. Buddhism dealt with religious matters and the after-life, Confucianism dealt with the here and now. The rise of neo-Confucianism, a philosophy with a strong interest in issues such as the origin and nature of

BUDDHIST OUTCASTS

Joseon scholars, in their support of Confucianism, classified Buddhist monks as social outcasts, along with prostitutes, pedlars and butchers.

this influence. Christian churches have conformed to the national Confucian culture by instituting memorial rituals for deceased parents and relatives.

The ritual imprint of Confucianism can be seen in the remaining shrines and altars. Just west of the Gyeongbok Palace is the Sajikdan (altar) in the Sajik Park where there are the altars to the spirits of grain and harvest. Ancestral ceremonies for the royal family are still held at the grand Jongmyo shrine on Jongno street.

the universe, created a clash with Buddhism, which came to be viewed as superstitious. The Joseon scholars set about creating a model Confucian society, suppressing all aberrant tendencies, heterodox thoughts and superstitions.

With the Manchu conquest of China in the 17th century, the Korean Confucian élite felt that Korea was the last bastion of orthodox East Asian civilization. This led to attempts to suppress the Catholic Church from the late 18th century.

Today, Confucianism does not have the formal support of the state, but its social influence is very evident. Hierarchial family and social relationships, social distance, and respect for elders, parents and teachers are all symbolic of

Twice-yearly rituals are offered to Confucius and his chief disciples at the Munmyo Shrine in the grounds of the Sungkyunkwan University *(see page 128)*. Every large town will have its *hyanggyo*, the regional Confucian school in traditional times, in the grounds of which will be a shrine dedicated to Confucius and his principal followers.

Likewise there are many local Confucian academies called *seowon* where there are shrines commemorating the founding scholar and his chief followers. These regional shrines are ubiquitous and are the main visible signs of Confucianism's historic influence on the Korean nation.

Christianity

In many ways the history of both Roman Catholic and Protestant Christianity in Korea is different from surrounding countries in that both forms of Christianity were self-evangelized. The origins of the Catholic Church date to 1784 when a young Korean aristocrat who had been baptized in Beijing returned and began to evangelize among his relatives and friends. Within 10 years, by the time of the arrival of the first priest and missionary from China, there was a Christian community of about 2,000 people. From the 1790s, a persecution of the Church began which was to last

seemed to be a moral and political threat, the persecution was severe. Literally thousands of people died, including a number of French missionaries and missionary bishops. When the persecution stopped in the last quarter of the century, the church developed a ghetto mentality and effectively retreated from the world for the better part of a century.

From the end of the 19th century, Protestantism (primarily North American Presbyterianism and Methodism) spread rapidly throughout the peninsula, beginning with the self-dissemination of the Korean translation of the New Testament (using the Korean alphabet) from Manchuria. Before

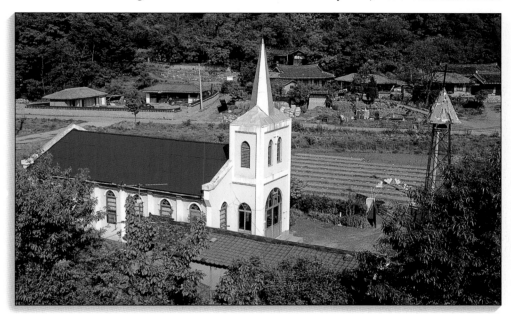

for three-quarters of a century and was over the issue of the refusal of Christians to perform the *jesa*, or ancestral ritual, as it was idolatrous. The élite saw this act as undermining the moral foundations of the nation as the ritual was the outward symbol of filial respect to the ancestors. The aristocratic Catholics hid themselves among the oppressed and outcast social groups where Christianity spread rapidly, as it offered an explanation for their suffering in this life and hope for the next life. Because this movement

LEFT: procession during Confucian rites ceremony.
ABOVE: churches are part of the South Korean landscape, in both urban and rural settings.

missionaries arrived in Korea, there were small Christian communities already formed in parts of northern Korea. By 1910, 1 percent of the population claimed adherence to a Protestant group. Early mission work involved the establishment of hospitals, schools and universities, a work which appealed to Koreans who looked to rebuild their nation intellectually and spiritually. During the era of Japanese colonial occupation (1910–45), a substantial number of Korean independence leaders were Christian. As with the Catholic church in an earlier period, many Koreans died as a result of their opposition to idolatrous worship at Japanese *Sinta* shrines. Even more people were martyred subsequently under the communists, which has given a politically conservative cast to many Protestants.

During the generation of rapid development from the 1960s onward, Catholics and Protestants alike were in the forefront of movements for democracy, social equality, workers' rights, and equality for women. The last two presidents of Korea, Kim Young-sam and Kim Dae-jung, were both opposition leaders during that period, and are devout Christians. Of a total Christian population of over 10 million (out of a national population of 42 million), there are over 2 million Catholics, over 2 million Methodists, and over 5 million Presbyterians.

Christian monuments are, for the Catholics, martyr shrines. Myeongdong Cathedral is built on the site of the home of the first Korean martyr, Kim Bom-woo. Next to the Hapjeong station on the Number 2 underground line is the Jeoldusan Martyrs' Church and Museum, located on the site of the principal execution grounds for Catholics in the Seoul area. There are three other sites outside the walls of the old city. The oldest extant Protestant church in Seoul is the Jeongdong Methodist Church, just behind the Deoksu Palace (City Hall station on the Numbers 1 and 2 underground lines). Other major points of interest in Seoul are Sogang, Yonsei and Ewha women's universities, which

are among the top five institutions in the country and are respectively Catholic, Methodist/Presbyterian, and Methodist in foundation. The modernistic Yonsei chapel is worth a visit. There is also a small Orthodox Christian community from a Russian foundation dating back to the late 19th century. There is a large Orthodox church in the Mapo area of Seoul.

New religion

At the end of the 19th century, various new syncretic religious movements emerged which combined elements of the folk religion with other traditions. The best known of these movements is the Donghak (latterly called Cheondogyo, Religion of the Heavenly Way). Its founder, Choe Jewoo (1824–64), had a shamanistic-type experience of the Ruler of Heaven who gave him a formula to cure disease. He was executed for being a crypto-Catholic. Subsequently his group became a major political movement at the end of the 19th century and a force in the Independence Movement against Japan in the early 20th century.

Another important new religious movement is the Holy Spirit Association for the Unification of World Christianity, or simply the Unification Church (Tongilgyo). Founded in Seoul right after the Korean War, this movement came to prominence in the late 1950s and 1960s. Its doctrines concern the Lord of the Second Advent, a mysterious figure who is to complete the unfinished work of salvation started by Jesus Christ. This movement has not proved highly successful in Korea, but has been extraordinarily successful in spreading throughout many parts of the world.

Islam

In addition to these groups, there is a small Korean Muslim community, numbering around 30,000 persons, which descends from Koreans living in Manchuria in the late 19th century who had converted to Islam. This community has been augmented by Koreans who worked in the Middle East in the 1970s or later and had converted to Islam while there. There is a large mosque in Seoul in the Itaewon area, and mosques in several other cities. ❑

LEFT: nuns out for a stroll in the sunshine.
RIGHT: spirit posts were formerly placed at village entrances to ward off evil.

BUSINESS CULTURE

To understand South Korea's economic miracle, one must look
at national etiquette and the nature of the conglomerate-like "jaebeol"

South Korea's economic growth since the dark days of the 1950s has been nothing short of miraculous. To understand the modern Korea, it is essential to examine this "economic miracle," and its central character – the businessman. Much of the national confidence that is freeing Koreans from a heritage

of being looked down upon by the regional big boys is due to the success of its export machine, which has turned the nation into one of Asia's economic powerhouses. Korea was still a nation of farmers a generation ago, but now, because of its economic success, over two-thirds claim to be members of the urbanized middle class.

The backbone of this astonishing success story has been the *jaebeol* business conglomerates, and the industrial chiefs who run them; they have seen per capita GNP grow from US$100 to US$6,000 in one generation. By the middle of the 1990s, the figure had passed the US$10,000 mark. Although the economy suf-

fered a rather alarming slump in 1997 and 1998, in common with other Asian "tigers", business has recovered strongly into the 21st century.

Korean tycoons have modeled themselves on the Confucian statesmen of the past. Most former chairmen, espousing Confucian ideals, have always regarded their employees as "family." The challenge facing the next generation of *jaebeol* tycoons is to balance Korea's Confucian background with its transition into the modern world. Economic success, and the hosting of the Olympics, have pulled the once-closed doors of the Hermit Kingdom off their hinges.

The role of the *jaebeol*

With the top 30 *jaebeol* accounting for over 50 percent of GNP – and over 70 percent of exports – it is virtually impossible to examine the industrial success without exploring the contribution of the *jaebeol*. Similar in structure to the mighty Japanese conglomerates, the Korean *jaebeol* still retain many of the unique cultural characteristics of Korea.

The first industrial barons were masters of all they surveyed. Now, in line with the winds of change sweeping the country, many of the second-generation chairmen educated in the US tend to be more open to advice. Nowadays, senior executives or "advisers," who often wield more power than MDs of subsidiaries of the *jaebeol*, are often schoolfriends or army colleagues of the chairman. An aide in the chairman's office of Hyundai, although technically not having the same rank as the MD of Hyundai Heavy Industries, may have more influence on the running of the group.

Many of these advisers are major figures in their own right. They tend to work in the chairman's office or secretariat, or are the heads of "think-tanks." This is usually a euphemism for the planning and coordination office (*gijosil*), the chairman's office (*hwoejangsil*), or even the secretaries' office (*biseosil*). These offices are charged with collecting and processing information useful to the business. They have the function of a group intelligence agency.

Business etiquette

The foreign businessman approaching these key conglomerate offices or simply meeting Korean counterparts is advised to seek some guidance on etiquette. The initial meeting is the most important and is taken seriously by a Korean businessman. He may decide to end the relationship there and then on the basis of a poor first impression. Such a setback may be caused by an innocent "mistake" such as arriving unannounced, being introduced by

NAMECARD ETIQUETTE

In Korea, the namecard is to be treated with respect. It should be received with decorum and read, not taken casually and slipped into the pocket. Give your own card to the most senior person first.

Americans, used to a more casual tone, frequently find themselves in difficulty.

You should always bring an interpreter. Just because an executive speaks English, do not assume everything you say is understood. Korean language teaching is not geared towards conversation. One of the great sources of misunderstanding is the Korean use of the word "yes." It may often mean "I heard you" rather than "I agree with you" and sometimes it can even mean "I don't understand

someone the targeted contact does not respect, or failing to produce a namecard.

The foreign businessman should consider whether he has done everything to gain his contact's trust. The best way to ensure this is to have a go-between, such as a consultant or mutual acquaintance. Do not bring your lawyer. It implies lack of trust and, anyway, there will be no detailed business agreed on at the first meeting. These subtleties come naturally to most Asians and even to some Europeans, but

what you're saying but keep talking." The foreigner is advised to speak non-colloquial English slowly and clearly.

Koreans are warm and emotional, but at the same time they are extremely formal. Informality only exists between close friends. Never use first names unless invited to do so. Be prepared for questions about your age, marital status and religion. Your contact is trying to place you socially and characterize your relationship.

Ironically, the final piece of advice is that, after brushing up on etiquette, be your natural self. Koreans are more familiar with the West than vice versa. They expect you to be a courteous foreigner, not a mock-Korean. ❏

LEFT: many Korean white-collar workers work six days a week, and long hours.
ABOVE: businessmen's lunch.

TRADITIONAL KOREAN COSTUME

With its flowing lines and distinctive style, traditional dress is still worn on special occasions and holidays by Koreans of all ages

Traditional Korean clothing is usually known as *hanbok*, and consists of a two-part ensemble of short jacket with voluminous skirt for women, and a jacket with loose trousers tied at the ankles for men. As long ago as AD 500, clothing in this style was worn, as we know from wall paintings found in ancient tombs. Tailoring and proportions varied over time, with the Joseon period preferring a short jacket length for women along with very long, trailing skirts.

Since Koreans sat on the paper-covered floors of their houses, rather than on chairs, loose, flowing skirts and trousers were both comfortable and practical. When traveling or visiting outside the home, upper-class men would wear long coats, woven from silk or ramie and lined with fur in the hard winters. This was completed by a distinctive black hat, which hid long hair tied up into a topknot. Commoners had woven straw shoes, or wooden clogs for muddy paths. Indoors, woven shoes of silk, hemp and animal hides were the norm. Children were dressed in bright colors until they reached adulthood, whereas married women wore sober, restrained colors. Clothing marked the wearer's social standing.

Farmers and laborers wore undyed workclothes, although on special occasions they would don bright and festive attire.

▷ **PALACE GUARDS**
Guards at the Deoksugung Palace in Seoul wear long, plain robes and broad-rimmed hats as they beat time with brightly decorated drums.

▷ **MODERN HANBOK**
The bright jacket, *jeogori*, tied with an ornamental bow to the right, contrasts with the darker skirt, *chima*, in this modern version of the *hanbok*.

△ **BIRTHDAY PARTY**
Dressed in a traditional stripe-sleeved silk coat, this child marks his first birthday by choosing an object that foretells his future. Money or rice suggest riches.

▽ **ANCESTOR WORSHIP**
A Confucian ceremony at Jongmyo shrine in honor of royal ancestors. 'Courtiers' wear black silk hats and round-necked robes.

FOLK VILLAGES: A KOREAN SPECIALTY

This actor is playing the role of magistrate at the Folk Village at Suwon, one of many such villages scattered around South Korea. These villages provide a useful introduction to traditional Korean ways of life, as well as to the many types of clothing worn by different people at different times; actors, in appropriate costume, represent the various occupations of traditional Korean society, from laborers and weavers to schoolteachers and officials.

The actor pictured above is wearing the hat and robes of a magistrate, one of the highest officials in the complex government machine of pre-modern Korea. Magistrates were drawn from the ranks of the educated classes and recruited through regular nationwide examinations testing their knowledge of the classic Confucian texts. They were responsible for tax collection and public order in the regions in their control.

◁ **SHAMAN RITES**
The shaman is an enduring feature of Korean society. Here a shaman's assistant wears a hood bearing tri-colored *taegeuk* symbols.

▽ **WORKING CLOTHES**
In contrast to the flowing lines of formal *hanbok*, modern working clothes are designed for ease of movement and comfort.

△ **WEDDING BELLS**
At a traditional wedding, the bride wears red silk embellished with gold leaf; the groom has an embroidered jacket and silk trousers.

▷ **FLOWING LINES**
Hanbok with tapering sleeves and high-waisted skirt makes for a flowing silhouette.

PERFORMING ARTS

Koreans love singing and dancing as forms of entertainment, but these arts are also considered a means of spiritual and political expression

Eolssigu! *Jota!* Such shouts are heard at every party, encouraging people to dance or sing. The clickety-clack of chopsticks beaten against the edge of a table punctuates the hearty, perhaps slightly inebriated, voices. Take a tourist bus and a microphone will be passed around so that everyone can sing, and – though officially illegal – passengers will stand in the aisles and dance. Every street has a *norae bang*, a "song room" at which karaoke is king.

For the average Korean, singing and dancing is an essential part of having fun. The aim is to create something similar to what the Irish would call a "crack", a state of heightened emotion and pleasure known in Korean as *heung* – how you feel when the spirit moves you.

Ancient beats

Korea has a rich and ancient music and dance tradition, dividing into court and folk genres. When Japan made Korea its colony, the court music institute began to struggle for survival. It was resurrected in 1950 as the National Center for Korean Traditional Performing Arts. The Center, now situated next to Seoul Arts Center, employs 350 musicians, dancers, and researchers to preserve traditional court music and dance. Recently, with modernization and urbanization, much of the folk tradition has declined. To counter this, the government passed legislation in 1962 to encourage conservation, appointing specific genres as Intangible Cultural Assets. Today, folk arts contests are held annually, and master musicians and dancers continue to teach and perform. Within just a few decades, traditional music and dance has been reinvented as a symbol of Korean identity.

Court music can seem slow and motionless, a combination of the upright propriety demanded by Confucian etiquette and by the apparent slowing down of many melodies over time. However, it always remains enigmatic. To

LEFT: a *Hwagwanmu* (flower crane) dancer.
RIGHT: performer at the mask dance drama, Hahoe Folk Village.

Western ears it sounds strange since melodic contour is less important than the ornamentation of individual tones, and because pentatonic scales are favored over the Western diatonic system. There is no harmony, and the soft timbres of instruments are tempered by elements of noise – the plucking of a silk string, the sound

of a plectrum hitting wood as well as the string, the rush of air on a wind instrument.

Some of the 65 traditional instruments are restricted to the two surviving court rituals, the twice-yearly Rite to Confucius *(Munmyo jeryeak)* and the annual Rite to Royal Ancestors *(Jongmyo jeryeak).* These rituals date back to two gifts from Song China, received in 1114 and 1116, and revised in the 15th century after the founding of the Joseon dynasty. The first gift was banquet music, the second was ritual music: 428 instruments together with costumes, musicians and dancers. All other Chinese music was soon Koreanized, and today only two pieces are still played, the orchestral *Nagyangchun* and *Boheoja*. A suite based on a poem written by King Sejong (r. 1418–50) to celebrate the creation of the Korean alphabet, *Yomillak*, is more commonly performed in concerts.

Dances – *ilmu* – are prescribed for the two rituals, performed in rigid lines with little spatial movement. The dancers hold symbolic objects, a feathered stick and flute to represent civil paraphernalia, and a military axe and shield. A second dance category, *jongjae*, signifies court entertainments that until the 20th century had never been seen by the public. *Hwagwanmu*, the flower crane dance, is the most commonly performed, followed by the oldest, a mask dance known as *Cheoyongmu*, the *Mugo* drum dance, the *Chunaengmu* nightingale dance, and a solemn ball game, *Pogurak*.

A new musical culture developed from the 17th century onwards beyond the confines of the court. This is normally associated with the emergence of a professional middle class, the *jungin*. The instrumental suite *Yeongsanhoesang* is representative of this music, with a name taken from syllables matched to the melody in the oldest known score: "Mass to the Buddha on Spirit Mountain".

Eight sounds and eight materials

Korean instruments are by tradition divided into "eight sounds" *(pareum)*, according to the material from which they are made: skin, silk, bamboo, metal, earth, stone, gourd and wood. Representative of the skin category is the *janggu*, an hourglass-shaped double-headed drum seen wherever Korean music is performed. Originally from China, *janggu* were present in Korea at least by the 12th century, made with wooden or pottery bodies and skins of ox or horse. Played solo, two sticks are used; played for accompaniment, one stick and the hand punctuate phrases. The *gayageum* is the most popular instrument in the silk category.

This is a 12-stringed zither plucked with the fingers. Legend tells how this was invented in the 6th century by U Reuk in Gaya: King Gasil saw a Chinese zither and commented that, since Korean and Chinese were different languages, Koreans should have their own instruments.

Typifying the bamboo category is the long bamboo flute, the *daegeum*. This features a sympathetic resonator that adds a buzz to pitched tones, and it is prominent in both court and folk music. Again, a legend tells of its invention. A mountain was observed floating in the East Sea late in the 7th century. On it there was a stalk of bamboo that split into two

whenever played in shaman rituals. Bronze bell and stone chime sets, *pyeonjong* and *pyeong-yeong*, long since consigned to history in China, still dominate Korean ritual orchestras. And the *haegeum* fiddle, originally transported via China from Central Asia, is the only instrument considered to be made from all eight materials, with silk strings, a gourd resonator, a bamboo neck, leather on the bow, and so on.

Masks, dance and acrobatics

Scholars believe that the various Korean masked dance dramas *(talchum)* come from a single source. Each offers a similar set of

at night and fused as a single trunk during the day. When it fused, storms abated and the sea was calm. King Sinmun was instructed to make a flute from the bamboo, and it is said that peace reigned throughout the Silla kingdom whenever the instrument was played.

Other Korean instruments derive from Chinese models but, over time, have become closely associated with the peninsula. The oboe, the *piri*, with a large double reed, produces a plaintive sound that is said to attract the spirits

vignettes, portraying the foibles and misadventures of a group of apostate Buddhist monks, a lecherous old man with a concubine, a stupid aristocrat outsmarted by his servant, a charlatan shaman, and dangerous tigers who gobble up unsuspecting children. As actors, participants encourage the audience to laugh at themselves; as dancers, they jump, leap and squat to the rhythmic pounding of a small percussion group. The most famous masked dance is from the village of Hahoe, where unpainted wooden masks are used. The Bongsan and Yangju versions are more frequently performed, using grotesque and brightly painted papier-mâché masks. Masked dances once functioned as a

LEFT: *janggu* (hourglass drum) musician marks time in a Korean classical setting.
ABOVE: a flautist in royal costume.

way for commoners to release their frustrations about landowners and the clergy.

Early visitors to the peninsula often reported their surprise at encountering bands of Koreans playing drums and gongs in the fields or marching from house to house through villages. Percussion bands, known as *pungmul*, may be traced back many centuries. A 3rd-century Chinese source, Chen Suo's *Sanguo zhi*, describes how Koreans in the southwest sang and danced to rhythmic music at times of celebration. Bands were commonly

minyo, from the southwest, are based on a sorrowful tritonic mode; *Gyeonggi minyo*, from the centre, are more joyful and lyrical; *Seodo minyo*, once common in the northwest but now only found around Seoul, feature nasal resonance and much vibrato. From the late 19th century, a second, more popular and professional folksong style began to flourish, giving rise to Korea's most famous folksong, *Arirang*. Eight folksong genres are now preserved with government support as Intangible Cultural Assets. Two folk

used to purify village wells and to protect homes from the unwelcome attention of troublesome goblins. They now play for entertainment, performing at Seoul's *Nori madang*, at festivals, and in inter-village championships. Four styles are distinguished: the coastal *yeongnam* from the southeast, the urban *gyeonggi* near Seoul, and *jwado* and *udo* from the southwest, the former fast and acrobatic, the latter slower but featuring intricate, contrapuntal rhythms.

In rural Korea, egalitarianism and communal activities meant that an abundance of folk songs – *minyo* – accompanied work, entertainment and the rituals surrounding death. Three folk song styles are distinguished. *Namdo*

dances are also Assets – *Seungmu* and *Salpuri*. In the first, the dancer wears a hooded robe with extended sleeves, finding enlightenment as she beats a single drum. *Salpuri* developed from shaman dances in the early 1930s. It is a dance of exorcism in which the dancer, using a long white scarf as her only prop, strives to free her spirit from trouble and anguish.

Very often, Korean folk arts have both amateur/local and professional/urban forms. In contrast to folksongs, the most developed vocal genre is the professional storytelling-through-song tradition, *pansori*. Performed by a lone singer accompanied by a drummer, *pansori* is of epic proportions, for a performance can last five or more hours. The singer, holding just a fan and a handkerchief as props, tells one of five stories through a mixture of singing, narration and basic dramatic action. The stories are well-known: *Chunhyangga* is a Cinderella story in which the daughter of an entertainer falls for an aristocratic Prince Charming; *Simcheongga* is about filial piety, and tells how a blind man's daughter sacrifices herself so his sight can be restored; *Heungboga* critiques the Confucian system in which the oldest son inherits everything, describing an evil older brother and his generous younger brother; *Sugungga* offers a twist on the story of the wily

band playing updated pieces sequencing rhythms from each of the old *pungmul* styles. *Samullori* sit where old percussion bands marched and danced. *Samullori* have proved remarkably popular, and several dozen professional teams now work in Seoul. *Samullori* has revitalized the old, and percussion performances today range from student groups to a massed band of 1,100 that played at the opening ceremony for the 1993 Daejeon Expo. This last, in the words of one drummer, was indeed a "Big bang *Samullori*", and earnt a mention in the *Guinness Book of Records*.

Today, though, the majority of music heard

rabbit and the slow turtle; *Jeokbyeokga* is based on the story of a Chinese battle.

From the 1920s onwards, operatic troupes, *changgeukdan*, toured the countryside performing staged versions of *pansori*. They met an earlier form of itinerant travelling troupe, *namsadang*, who since the early Joseon dynasty had been setting up in market places to perform music, dance and acrobatics.

In 1978, a new urban equivalent appeared. This was *samullori*, a four-man percussion

on Korean radio and TV is Western in orientation. Korea boasts orchestras, opera and ballet companies of international standard, and many Korean musicians are active in Europe and America, including the singer Sumi Jo, the violinist Kyungwha Chung, and the conductor Myunghoon Chung. For *Samullori*, this provides opportunity for fusion, most notably with the jazz group Red Sun.

Ppongjjak and pop

Repeat *"ppongjjak"* a few times, and it becomes onomatopoeia for the foxtrot rhythm that underpins a standard song style, *yuhaengga*. This, often arranged in purely instrumental

LEFT: the farmers' dance celebrates a good harvest.
ABOVE: *pansori* singer.
RIGHT: early 20th-century zither musician.

versions, is the music of preference of many older Koreans. It remains popular fare in cafés, taxis and long-distance buses. The style arrived from Japan in the 1920s, and the best-remembered song is also one of the oldest, "Beautiful Death", a sentimental song by Ivanovich given Korean words and first released in 1923. Speeded up in the 1960s, *ppongjjak* took on elements of rock 'n' roll, with lyrics telling of love and desertion. Lee Mi-ja and Patti Kim are two renowned singers from the time who still remain popular.

By the 1970s, students had taken American acoustic folk guitars and created their own style,

tong guitar. From here, a song movement associated with campaigns for democracy grew, led by Kim Mingi. Kim was duly imprisoned during Chun Doo-hwan's presidency. Through the 1980s, the government continued to censor lyrics, creating a uniformity of style. The style was common to most Asian ballad traditions, and in Korea it was promoted by the likes of Cho Yong Pil and Lee Sun-hee. The lack of copyright control – Korea only became a signatory to international conventions in 1985 – meant that cover versions of songs were common.

Pop music changed dramatically in 1992, when Seo Taiji burst onto Korean TV screens singing rap. Reggae arrived with Kim Gunmo's *Pinggye* ("Excuses"), and by the spring of 1994 the group Roora had fused the two together, trumpeting rap as "The Roots of Reggae". Virtually overnight, musicians scrambled to assimilate foreign styles without taking on board the cultural baggage and identity issues which matter to the musicians of New York or London. By 1996, a single song could mix rap, reggae, rock, house and hip-hop. The rapid innovation helped Korea's recording industry grow; by 1987, Korea was the 13th largest market in the world, with domestic sales of 55 million CDs and 156 million cassettes.

Developing a social conscience

In recent years, democracy has allowed the arts to become a medium for social commentary. The ballad singer Lee Sun-hee in 1992 released an album dedicated to the tragedy of "comfort women" – women forced into sexual slavery by the Japanese military.

Three years later, in 1995, Seo Taiji celebrated the lifting of government censorship with the song *Gyosil idea* ("Education Idea"), criticizing in blunt terms the economic management of the Kim Young-sam administration. Im Chintaek updated *pansori* with settings of Kim Chiha's satirical *Ojeok* ("Five Enemies") and *Ttong bada* ("Sea of Shit").

Film directors have also moved away from recreations of history to social commentary. An early example was the 1981 film *Eodumui Jasikdeul* ("Children of Darkness"). More recently, the director Im Kwontaek returned to *pansori*, but criticized the lifestyles and practices it represented, in *Seopyeonje* (1993). A year later, in *Taebaeksanmaek* ("Taebaek Range of Mountains"), he reassessed the brutal repression of left-wing sympathizers that occurred before the Korean War. The trend has continued, notably with *Kkonnip* ("A Petal"), a 1996 film by Jung Sun Woo that looks through the eyes of a child at the Gwangju massacre of 1980, and the 1999 film by Pak Kwangsu, *Ijaesu ui nan* ("Les Insurges"). Aware of the heritage, but often questioning the past and criticizing the present, contemporary performance arts now reflect both diversity and maturity; Korean yet international, they are surely well worth exploring. ❏

LEFT: Michael Jackson fans in Seoul.
RIGHT: masks and performers of the *Bongsan Talchum* dance, Andong Mask Festival.

ARTS AND CRAFTS

You can trace the development of the country's religious traditions and

its dynastic history by viewing its rich legacy of treasures

From Joseon-dynasty folk paintings and images of Buddhist deities to intricate temple bells and the breathtaking crowns of Silla, from regional pottery to regal riches, diversity and uniqueness are the words that spring readily to mind when exploring the world of Korean arts and crafts. Whether the graceful work of porcelain designers or elaborate jewelry recovered from burial mounds, there is always something surprising to be found in this surprising country.

Ceramics

Throughout Korea, antique shops and museum stores offer visitors original and replica pots. To enjoy the diversity of Korea's ancient and contemporary ceramics, it is important to know a little about the centuries of potters' work and patrons' taste that formed the distinctive ceramic style of Korea.

In the first millennium, when the regions of the Korean peninsula were ruled separately and each had a very distinctive local culture, potters produced vessels of hard, dark stoneware for ceremonies and for burials. Many of these have been excavated in modern times, showing that the kingdoms of Silla, Baekje and Goguryeo all turned out high-fired stonewares in great numbers. Judging from the decorations carved on the sides of some large pots, they were used during ceremonies that connected humans with the heavens or an afterlife. A striking feature of early Korean pots is their shapes, typically a high splayed circular stand, divided into rows or bands of linear perforated patterns, and rising to a bowl or cup shape. Some of these high stands with punched-out holes are of imposing dimensions, reaching 50 or 60 cm (2 ft) in height, but most are smaller, suggesting that their use was widespread, at all social levels.

When the Buddhist faith spread throughout

Korea between the 4th and 6th centuries AD, believers adopted the custom of cremating the dead. This created a need for urns to contain ashes, still greyish in tone, but smaller and more rounded in shape.

Later again, around AD 1000, Korean potters began to produce work in an entirely new style.

Having seen the graceful and attractive pots made in the kilns of coastal south China, potters in Korea began making green-glazed ceramics of their own, establishing large and productive kilns to supply fine vessels for the court. These green-glazed wares of the Goryeo dynasty were produced for aristocratic clients during an era of elegant living and connoisseurship. Ships were loaded with bowls, jugs, wine-cups, vases and even roof-tiles made in the southern kilns, to supply eager clients at the palaces and temples of the capital hundreds of kilometers away in the north of the country.

Today, the ruins of the kilns at Sadangni and Yuchonni can be visited: they are an eloquent

---

LEFT: *Gwanseum-bosal with Willow Branch,* painted with mineral colors on silk by Sogubang, a 14th-century Goryeo artist.
RIGHT: celadon ceramic.

testimony to the sophisticated tastes and impressive organization of the ceramic industry in the Goryeo dynasty. The Korean Ministry of Culture and Tourism has proposed to UNESCO that these early potteries should be preserved as sites of world heritage. Far from the capital, potters in the coastal areas turned out thousands of bowls, wine cups, teapots, incense burners, garden stools, roof tiles, pillows, boxes, bottles and many more. These craftsmen were among the lowest ranks in society; their

GORYEO GREEN CERAMICS

For Koreans, Goryeo period green ceramics are an emblem of national pride. Their lustrous color and marvelous shapes were admired even by the haughty Chinese.

sanggam or inlay decoration, adding sparkling mica and iron-rich clays to the decoration of their pots to produce a unique style. After throwing the vessel on a wheel, the potter let the clay dry for a while before using a bamboo knife to cut designs on the leather-hard surface. The indented pattern was then filled with creamy liquid containing tiny particles of mica. When the excess was wiped off and the piece was covered with glaze and fired in a kiln, sparkling white pictures appeared. By a simi-

profession was handed down from father to son, their payment was poor and their work was anonymous. These days, unblemished Goryeo celadons fetch unimagined prices in antique shops and auction rooms, but their makers gained little benefit from producing them.

Known to Koreans as *cheongja* or green-glazed ceramics, these sought-after pieces take their Western name from a character in a French play. Celadon, a shepherd, wore a cloak of a subtle and unforgettable green color. Somehow, the name of celadon has passed into use among art-lovers, long after the play has been forgotten.

Anonymous potters of the 12th century even introduced a stunning innovation known as

lar process, black patterns could be produced, using an infill rich in iron compounds. The potters in the Goryeo period also took pleasure in making art imitate nature by molding and carving their vessels to resemble fruits, flowers and even human figures. Melons, vines, pumpkins and bamboo shoots were all reproduced in green-glazed stoneware, for the pleasure of a luxury-loving aristocracy. Fine green-glazed ceramics were used to serve food and wine at court and in the residences of the nobility. In Buddhist temples too, delicate green incense burners and water sprinklers played their part in the services and devotions. Ingenious potters carved delicate veins to make leaves and petals even more lifelike. They fashioned spouts and handles in teapots to look like the sections of a stem of bamboo or the tendrils of a vine.

Designs applied to celadons also speak of Korean proximity to nature: cranes flying among clouds over a sea of celadon green, or weeping willow trees with a pair of Mandarin ducks floating in water.

A new type of pottery came into vogue in the early years of the Joseon dynasty. Known to Koreans as *buncheong* or powder-green ware, these ceramics

PORCELAIN DESIGN

Painted Korean porcelains are quite austere in taste, often featuring a single design feature, such as a blossoming spray, a pair of fish, a dragon, or a grapevine, set against the plain white surface of the pot.

The Joseon dynasty (1392–1910) was, like the Goryeo, an important consumer of ceramics at court. The Royal Kitchens ordered tableware and ceremonial vessels to be produced at its kilns. Most prestigious of all were pure white porcelains, imitating the splendid blue-and-white porcelains of Ming-dynasty China. When these were first seen at court in Korea, in the early 15th century, they created a sensation, and no effort was spared in making a Korean version. Blue painted decoration was thought to be

are unpretentious and spontaneous. Painted, brushed, carved, inlaid and stamped patterns were applied to bottles, bowls and vases in plain shapes far removed from the refined and ornate designs of the Goryeo. These plain vessels appealed greatly to the Japanese taste, and since the 16th century have been treasured in Japan as tea-ceremony ceramics. The British potter Bernard Leach also admired Korean *buncheong* wares and introduced them to the West.

particularly beautiful, and designs of trees, birds, flowers, bamboo and coiled dragons are seen on surviving pieces. A cobalt-rich compound was used for the blue designs, and copper and iron pigments to produce red and brown. Lotus flowers, grapevines and spare, finely painted bamboo sprays were popular subjects.

Ceramic revival

Korean ceramics have experienced something of a revival in recent years. University fine art departments train potters who work in different styles, some of them responding to the patterns of Korea's past by creating pots in the celadon, stoneware and *buncheong* styles.

FAR LEFT: Goryeo vase decorated with a stylized pattern of leaves and flowers. **LEFT:** iron bell detail, Bomun-sa Temple, Seongmo-do island.
ABOVE: handicrafts are a great attraction for shoppers.

Working with stone

Koreans excel in granite sculpture, a skill perfected over the centuries in a land where the terrain is 70 percent mountainous granite and limestone. Naturally, Koreans developed a special love for stone and a skill in its use both as building material and for sculptural pieces. Huge dolmens of early times speak of the strength and dexterity of unknown Neolithic inhabitants on the peninsula. By the 4th century AD, the northernmost of the three Kingdoms, Goguryeo, was constructing monumental tombs, half the size of the Egyptian pyramids. They used dressed granite blocks that were so

The Korean peninsula is dotted with Buddhist figures skillfully carved in the granite rocks of the mountains. Images of Buddhist deities were also cast in bronze and iron, the early examples appearing relatively flat and linear, while the later period produced fully three-dimensional work of grace and quiet inspiration. The meditating Maitreya (in Korean, *Mireuk*) figures in the National Museum, and the Seokguram cave-grotto near Gyeongju, date as late as the 8th century, and display a religious tenacity. The cave-grotto has many relief carvings of deities sculpted on rectangular blocks expressing the apogee of the

perfectly engineered that they, as well as the frescoes on their walls, have survived to this day. However, the Goguryeo tombs are difficult to visit, being situated partly in an area of China that was formerly Korean territory and partly in North Korea. One can gain an understanding of ancient beliefs about death from these Korean tombs, with their wall scenes and decorative symbols on the ceilings. Hunters, musicians and dancing girls populate the wall paintings, in scenes that seem to capture the way of life of the tomb's occupant. The ceiling frescoes meanwhile show stars, planets and heavenly creatures, since they portrayed the afterlife – the realm of the spirit of the dead.

Buddhist tradition. In addition, Seokguram contains a giant central free-standing sculpture, representing the quintessence of Buddhism's spiritual momentum in the Far East.

Much of the work of Japan's renowned Asuka period can be attributed to Korea since it was created by Koreans and then exported, or else made in Japan by Korean immigrant artists.

Heavenly bells

It is rarely disputed that the most intricate, melodious and beautiful temple bells in the world were created by Korean artisans. The earliest dated one was cast in AD 725 and now hangs at Sangwon-sa in the Odaesan National

Park area. The most famous is the "divine bell," or the Emille Bell (cast in AD 771), now kept in a special pavilion at the entrance to the Gyeongju National Museum. It is said that the sonorous notes of this 3.6 meter- (12-ft) high bell could be heard 64 km (40 miles) away on a clear day. The sound chamber at the top took the form of a dragon, but the most spectacular decoration consisted of two pairs of Buddhist angels or devas, holding censers of incense and floating on lotus pods amid wisps of vegetation. Gossamer-thin garments swirl heavenward, taking the place of actual wings.

These bells, which played a major role in ritual and worship, are major works of bronze sculpture inspired by Buddhism at its peak.

Silla relics

By the early 6th century, most of the Korean peninsula had adopted Buddhism as a state religion. The kingdom of Silla, however, in the remote and mountainous south-eastern region, was still ruled by shaman kings. The people's belief in spirits was coupled with the custom of cairn-type tomb burial in which shaman royalty went to their graves in full religious regalia. This made the Silla capital, Gyeongju, one of the world's most spectacular archaeological sites. Hundreds of tombs are yet to be explored in this city which has already become a veritable outdoor museum.

Breathtaking crowns fashioned for the king to wear in the afterlife were among the treasures buried in Gyeongju's mounded graves. Their fascination lies not only in the use of precious materials, but also in their intricate design. So far, 10 slightly different "gold crowns of Silla" have been brought to light. Alongside the crowns, other royal possessions have been discovered, such as golden girdles, ornate belts, elaborate earrings, silver and gold goblets, necklaces, bracelets, finger rings and ceramics. One intriguing crown was unearthed in 1973 at the excavation of Tomb No. 155 in the heart of Gyeongju city. When viewing the crown, one first sees its outer circle of beaten gold with jagged wave designs representing the watery nether world. An inner golden cap fits closely to the head. Fifty-eight jade tiger claws

hang from the crown. In the shaman religion, the tiger is associated principally with three things: a strong power to destroy evil forces, human fertility and male virility. These curved pieces carved from jade formed a major part of the symbolism when the gold crowns were worn. They were suspended loosely on thin, twisted gold wires, while several hundred tiny golden spangles, suggesting golden raindrops, were affixed onto the crown with more thin gold wires. When the shaman king, who embodied the power of the sun as well as other forms of nature's energy, moved his head even slightly, he created a dazzling sight and

vibrating sounds. Pendants of thick golden leaf-shaped droplets hung on each side of the crown. The key to understanding the meaning behind all this regal magnificence lies in the three upright pieces attached to the circular headband at the base of the crown. These are in three symbolic forms: deer antlers, stylized trees, and pairs of wings, all carrying shamanistic associations. The antlers symbolized reindeer, whose fleetness the shaman king acquired by wearing their horns. Birds and trees both play important parts in shaman ritual, bearing spirits from one world to the next.

After the excavations in 1973, Tomb No. 155, The Magical Flying Horse Tomb was

---

FAR LEFT: Goryeo artifacts dot the countryside.
LEFT: guardian figure General Kim Yu-sin's tomb.
RIGHT: king's crown from the Silla dynasty.

restored to its original state. Half of it is now supported by a steel framework, and a glass wall has been erected across the mid-section, so that tourists can enter to look at the exact position in which the crown, sword, girdle, pottery and many other objects were buried.

Another fascinating discovery was in a large box at the head of the shaman ruler's tomb. Here, an actual royal horse had been offered in sacrifice, indicating the traditional importance of horseriding to these people, former nomads of northwest Asia. A special horse belonging to this shaman king was believed to be a flying horse. This creature could levitate just as a

powerful shaman could. When the horse was killed, his saddle flaps made of laminated birch bark, sewn together with deer leather trimmings, were buried in the grave along with other horse trappings and treasures. Six of these saddle flaps have been found and they are as amazing as the golden crowns.

Goryeo devotional art

Before an exhibition in Japan in 1978, Koreans knew nothing about the survival of exquisite devotional paintings, made to hang in Buddhist temples. These beautiful Buddhist works of art, painted around 1200–1350, were thought to

FOLK PAINTING SYMBOLS

The major symbols used in Korean folk paintings are:
Four Sacred Animals of Good Luck: Turtle, dragon, unicorn and phoenix.
Ten Symbols of Longevity: deer, crane, turtle, rocks, clouds, sun, water, bamboo, pine, fungus of immortality *(bullocho)*.
Auspicious Ideograms: *bok* (good fortune), *su* (longevity), *nyeong* (peace) and *gang* (health).
Fertility Symbols: pomegranate, jumping carp, 100 babies and "Buddha's hand citron."
Special Guardians: tiger (front gate or front door), dragon (gate or roof), *haetae* (fire or kitchen), rooster (front door) and dog (storage door).

Four Noble Gentlemen: orchid, chrysanthemum, bamboo and plum.
Three Friends of Winter: pine, plum and bamboo.
Individual Symbolic Associations: peach (longevity), pomegranate (wealth), orchid (scholar, cultural refinement), lotus (Buddhist truth, purity), bat (happiness), butterfly (love, romance), bamboo (durability), peony (noble gentleman, wealth) and plum (wisdom, hardiness or independence, beauty, loftiness).

A formal list of symbols was never compiled in writing; it was simply a part of Korean tradition, familiar to everyone from itinerant painter to "drunken master."

have vanished. It remains a painful topic to Koreans today, since almost all these master-works are still in Japanese private and public collections. The paintings depict the Buddha, the goddess of mercy Gwaneum and other divine figures, with shimmering robes of finest silk in a delicate yet precise style that reflects the artists' devout reverence for the Buddhist faith. Buddhist subjects continued to find patrons and artists throughout the following centuries, but the splendour and transcendent beauty of the Goryeo period works have never been equalled.

Joseon genre glimpses

During the Joseon dynasty (1392–1910) an official "Painting Bureau" existed. This was supported by the court, and painters were commissioned to paint portraits of the aristocracy. By the 18th century some artists had begun to paint scenes of common people going about their business. These miniature master-works are treasured both as paintings and as evidence of a way of life that has disappeared.

An entirely different approach to art is revealed in Joseon-dynasty folk paintings. They reflect the actual life, customs and beliefs of the Korean people. Since collectors in Korea and abroad have "discovered" them, the value of such works has escalated.

One example of attractive and now valuable artwork is a kind of screen decorated with letter pictures. Artists rendered the terms for the Confucian virtues into paintings which were mounted on paneled screens in the homes of the well-to-do. Anniversaries were also celebrated by the creation of new folding screens painted with motifs of longevity or good omens.

The animals of the zodiac, yin and yang, and the mushroom of immortality: Based on the belief systems of ancient China, a number of themes appeared in the folk arts of Korea. Among the most important were the correlatives of heaven and earth, yang and yin, male and female, along with five directions (north, south, east, west and center), five colors (black, red, white, blue and yellow), and five material elements (water, fire, metal, wood and earth).

Buddhism too brought a number of emblems and themes into the Korean artistic vocabulary. These include the lotus, the official religious flower, which calls to mind the beauty and purity that emerge out of the mire of human existence. After centuries of religious co-existence, the origins and meanings of the multitudes of symbolic plants, animals and figures found in Korean art can be difficult to determine. For example, the animals of the zodiac are often depicted. They usually relate to time, and astrologers still use them to foretell suitability in marriage. The zodiac was also associated with the Chinese principles of yang and yin (in Korean, *yang* and *eum*). It read, in clockwise order: rat, ox, tiger,

rabbit, dragon, snake, horse, sheep, monkey, chicken, dog and wild boar (or pig). These astrological animals also represented the 12 points of the compass.

Folk painting created for the home was rich in symbolism, and further associations can be seen in furniture, linens, clothes and all accessories, even hairpins. All things, including outside walls, are full of the five elements, the 10 symbols of longevity, the four directional animals, the 12 zodiacal animals and propitious ideographs. Even the educated put some measure of faith in these emblems, partly convinced that such symbols can repel evil and attract good fortune. ❑

LEFT: Joseon-dynasty painting of a *gisaeng* house.
RIGHT: names painted with birds and animals are an old Korean art form.

FOOD AND DRINK

Hot spices and hard drinking are just part of the culinary kaleidoscope in this country that loves to wine and dine

Spicy. Fiery. Earthy. Cool. Korean food is diverse and provocative. Its bold and subtle tastes, textures and aromas are sure to elicit comments, sighs and even tears at every meal from novices and Koreans alike.

Most foreigners associate pungent garlic and hot chili pepper with Korean cuisine. It is true that garlic-eating has been heartily appreciated by Koreans since the earliest days, but few people know – even in Korea – that the chili pepper did not even exist in this country until the 16th century when it was introduced by Portuguese traders.

No matter how these two ingredients may have reached Korean plates and palates, they are now used in many dishes – most liberally and notoriously in *gimchi*. For the newcomer, learning to eat this unique dish is the first step to becoming a Korean food connoisseur.

Gimchi culture

Gimchi is *the* dish that has made Korean food famous. Next to rice *(bap)*, it is the most important component in any Korean meal. It is not known when or how *gimchi* originated, but like curry in India, it's in Korea to stay. So institutionalized is *gimchi* that one of the country's most important annual social events is *gimjang*, or autumn *gimchi*-making. At *gimjang* time, women gather in groups throughout Korea to cut, wash and salt veritable mountains of cabbage and white radish. The prepared *gimchi* is stored in large earthenware crocks, then buried in the backyard to keep it from fermenting during winter months. Throughout the dark and cold winter, when in times past there was little or no fresh produce available to the average citizen, these red-peppered, garlicked and pickled vegetables are a good source of vitamin C.

In warmer seasons, a variety of vegetables such as chives, pumpkin and eggplant are used to make more exotic types of *gimchi*. The summer heat makes it necessary to prepare a fresh batch almost every day, often in a cool, light brine. Raw seafood, such as fish, crab and oysters are "*gimchi*-ed" too, and indeed, in Korea, a woman's culinary prowess is often determined first and foremost by how good her *gimchi* tastes.

Exotic herbs

Not all Korean food ingredients are quite so passionate as the garlic and chili pepper. In fact, the earliest Korean dishes consisted of understated ingredients. To Koreans, almost every plant and animal in their diet has a herbal or medicinal quality and certain dishes are purposely eaten to warm or cool the head and body. Wild aster, royal fern bracken, marsh plant, day lily, aralia shoots and broad bellflowers are just a few of the many wild and exotic plants included in the typical Korean's diet. Others, such as mugwort, shepherd's purse, and sowthistle, are also seasonally picked and eaten.

LEFT: selling seaweed at Seogwipo market, Jeju-do.
RIGHT: *galbi* (beef rib barbecue).

More common table vegetables – such as black sesame leaves, spinach, lettuce and mung and soybeans – are typically grown in the backyard, but others are found only in the wild. All are collectively called *namul* when they are individually parboiled, then lightly seasoned with sesame oil, garlic, soy sauce, and ground and toasted sesame seeds.

Another vital part of the Korean meal is soup *(guk)*, which is said to be one of Korea's earliest culinary techniques. Soup of some kind will always be found at a proper table setting. Especially popular is *doenjangguk*, a fermented soybean paste soup with shortnecked clams

stirred into its broth. Also popular are a light broth boiled from dried anchovies, and vegetable soups rendered from dried spinach, sliced radish or dried seaweed *(miyeokguk)*. A seafood dish of some kind is usually included with various side dishes which are called *banchan*. This may be a dried, salted and charbroiled fish or a hearty and spicy hot seafood soup called *maeuntang*. A delicious *maeuntang* usually includes firm, white fish, vegetables, soybean curd *(dubu)*, red pepper powder, and an optional poached egg for richness.

Probably the most popular Korean entrée ordered or automatically served to Westerners is *bulgogi* (barbecued beef). Most beef-eaters –

whether Texans or Koreans – are unanimous in their appreciation of this dish which is essentially strips of red beef marinated and then grilled over a charcoal brazier. Another popular meat dish is tender and marbled *galbi* short ribs which are marinated and barbecued in the same way as *bulgogi*. *Bibimbap* is a satisfying dish of boiled rice mixed with vegetables, served in an earthenware pot.

Every visitor to Korea should sample the tempting array of snacks at the numerous street food stalls; these are extremely popular throughout the country, and are usually excellent (and very cheap). Try the ubiquitous *tteokbokgi*, spicy rice paste rolls, and *twigim*, a Korean version of Japanese tempura involving seafood and vegetables deep-fried in batter. Other snacks include a variety of pancakes; *pajeon* (green onion) and *bindaetteok* (mung bean) being the most common varieties.

Dining etiquette

When Koreans sit down to a traditional meal, they relax on a clean lacquered paper floor. The meal comes to them on a low table. Usually the food is served in a neatly arranged collection of small metal bowls. The utensils used are a pair of chopsticks and a flat soup spoon.

Westerners may be surprised to find that Koreans will often eat a bowl of rice and maybe have an extra helping even though tastier side dishes remain unfinished. Don't let this preference for rice bother you; to Koreans, rice – not meat – is considered to be the main dish of the meal. In fact, one of the most common street greetings *"Bap meogeosseoyo?"* literally means "Have you eaten rice?". If you run out of a particular item, the lady of the house will bring more. When you've had enough to eat, place your chopsticks and soup spoon to the right of your bowl; do not leave them stuck in the rice or resting on any of the bowls.

A dish of sliced and chilled fruit is usually served as a dessert. Depending on the season, muskmelon, strawberries, apples, pears and watermelon are among the fresh and sweet selections. At major celebrations, special steamed rice cakes *(tteok)* are presented as a tasty ritual treat.

Toasting the spirits

Deep within a cave beneath a hill in northern Seoul, four men sit around a low round table, drinking small bowls of a milky white liquor they pour from a battered aluminum teapot. Step into the *guljip* ("cave-house"), one of Seoul's most unusual drinking spots. A bomb shelter during the Korean War three decades ago, today it is operated as a wine-house by several enterprising aging ladies. The quality of the potent rice *makgeolli* is usually excellent, so *guljip* never lack customers.

There are only a few bomb-shelter winehouses in Seoul, but there are many other places to drink. Within a few minutes' walk of *guljip* are a beer hall with draft and bot-

MOTHER'S BROTH

Seaweed soup made from dried seaweed *(miyeokguk)* is tasty and nutritious. It is eaten mainly by new mothers for iron, to replenish blood lost during delivery.

Floating cups and gisaeng

History doesn't reveal when the Koreans first discovered fermentation, but drinking was an important part of the culture even in the early years. During the Silla dynasty, the king and his court are known to have relaxed at the *Poseokjeong* drinking bower outside Gyeongju. Here a spring bubbled up into an abalone-shaped stone channel. The drinkers set their cups afloat in the channel and competed to compose poems before the cups drifted all the way round.

tled beer, a market wine shop serving alcoholic beverages, and a roadside cart, where passers-by can duck in for a quick drink on the way home.

Drinking is an important part of Korean culture. There are few proscriptions against alcohol here and many social reasons for imbibing. Drinking with Koreans provides an opportunity for a foreigner to penetrate Korean culture. This is partly because of the salience of drinking in the culture and partly because, like anywhere else, alcohol removes inhibitions.

LEFT: red peppers, an important element in Korean cuisine, drying in wicker baskets.
ABOVE: street food stalls in Busan.

Later Korean dynasties continued to enjoy drinking and its associated pleasures. Probably the most popular surroundings were *gisaeng* parties. *Gisaeng* were female entertainers who played musical instruments, sang, danced, composed poetry and practiced calligraphy to amuse the male aristocracy at palace parties. They also poured drinks, served the men food, and flirted. According to tradition, high-class *gisaeng* took lovers but weren't promiscuous. At one point in the Joseon dynasty, there were estimated to be more than 20,000 *gisaeng*.

The most famous heroine in classical Korean history was the *gisaeng* Non-gae, who lived in the late 16th century when the

Japanese invaded Korea. Forced to entertain a victorious Japanese general, the forlorn Nongae beguiled the man into walking with her along the steep cliffs overlooking the Nam River. While locked in embrace, she managed to lure him near the brink and forced him over the edge, sacrificing her own life to kill the hated enemy conqueror.

These days, few *gisaeng* can claim to play classical instruments, compose poetry or write with a brush. Instead, most *gisaeng* parties include a band

GISAENG GIRLS

The main patrons of *gisaeng* parties are Korean businessmen who pay large sums to entertain customers, and Japanese tourists who pay even more in the hope of taking the girls back to their hotels.

wards. According to an old custom, the guests may hang the groom upside down and beat him on the soles of his feet if the alcohol runs out.

At memorial services for ancestors, filial Koreans still customarily set a bowl of wine among offerings on the altar. After the rites are completed, the living consume the wine, toasting the spirits and strengthening the bond between them. Funerals and wakes also involve plenty of drinking – to help the living forget their grief. Friends and relatives will

with drums and electric guitar, with the *gisaeng* and their guests go-go dancing around the table after the meal is finished.

In Confucian cups

Conservative Confucians would be distressed to find what has happened to drinking today. They would be particularly aghast to find college co-eds and other supposedly respectable women drinking freely in public. With closer scrutiny, however, the Confucians would find that not all of the old practices have vanished. There is still the traditional practice where a groom consumes rice wine during his wedding ceremony and at the celebration after-

usually drink, sing and gamble all night at the home of someone who has just died.

Confucians might also be surprised to find that, although bowing while drinking has been largely forgotten, other elements of traditional etiquette still remain. The cardinal rule is that one does not drink alone. Furthermore, a drinker does not pour his own glass, but waits until his companion fills it for him. In this tradition, to serve oneself would be an act of arrogance and greed.

Generally, in a gesture of respect and friendship, a drinker will give his cup to another, conveying it politely with both hands. His companion receives the cup with both hands and holds it thus while it is filled to the brim. He may then drink. After emptying the cup, he again uses both hands to return it to the owner. Then, grasping the wine vessel with both hands, he refills the cup for the owner, returning the favor. In a group, several drinkers in succession may offer their cups to a single person, leaving an array of brimming cups before him. A person who has given up his cup cannot drink until the recipient returns it or someone else gives him his. So whoever has received a cup has an obligation to empty it and pass it on without inordinate delay.

The custom of forcing drinks on each other hardly encourages moderation, which is probably why most drinkers in Korea go home rather tipsy. Drunkenness carries no social stigma. To the contrary, when most Koreans drink, they seem to have a responsibility to do so until they are drunk. The rise in car ownership has reduced this tendency to some extent, but Koreans remain heavy social drinkers.

The working man's brew

A popular Korean brew is *makgeolli*, a milky liquor that most rural households ferment at home from rice. Reputed to be highly nutritious, farmers found that a few cups during a long working day helped stave off hunger. *Makgeollijip*, establishments that serve *makgeolli* vary in style and quality, but are generally comfortable, unpretentious places. The *makgeolli* is dipped out of a hug tub or vat into cheap teapots or bottles, and any old bowl may serve as a cup.

The two most important factors about any *makgeollijip* are the quality of the *makgeolli*, and the kinds of side dishes, *anju*, that it serves, since all drinking in Korea inevitably involves eating. The many types of *anju* that go best with *makgeolli* range from fresh oysters, peppery octopus, dried fish, tasty squid or cuttlefish to tofu, soups, bean pancakes, scallion pancakes and omelettes.

The other beverage with long-standing popularity is *soju*, a cheap liquor distilled from potatoes, of approximately 22 percent alcoholic content, with a quality somewhere between gin and kerosene. Price and the high alcoholic content make it Korea's cheapest

drink. While far from smooth, a bottle of *soju* goes down very well with certain foods, such as pigs' feet, barbecued pork, Korean sausage and other meat dishes.

These days, however, Korean drinking tastes are changing. Beer, popular for years, has now overtaken its rivals to become the top drink, especially with young people. Once a rich man's drink, it is now the ordinary man's choice. Western liquors like scotch and bourbon have always had high import duties in Korea. Since the mid-1970s, Korea has been importing, in bulk, scotch and other spirits and bottling their own brands. The resulting

Korean scotch, gin, vodka, rum and brandy are much cheaper than imported brands.

Where should the foreigner visiting Korea go drinking? To get a feeling for what remains of the traditional, the best place would be a *makgeollijip*. Korea also has plenty of beer halls, known as *hofs*. Try the lively Myeongdong district in downtown Seoul (see page 123) or the Sinchon area in the west of the city, popular with students.

If you are dining at Korean or Chinese restaurants, beer or traditional spirits may complement the meal. Restaurants usually don't serve *makgeolli*, but they will have beer, *soju* or *jeongjong*, a Korean *sake*. ❑

LEFT: picnic at Yongduam (Dragon Head Rock), Jeju-do.
RIGHT: *soju* is the most popular liquor in Korea.

SPORT AND LEISURE

From martial arts and traditional street games to modern Western sports,
Koreans enjoy a wide range of competitive and recreational activities

Sports and pastimes are immensely popular in Korea, and the hosting of the 1988 Olympic Games, and the 2002 soccer World Cup tournament *(see page 99)* have both underlined that enthusiasm. Yet Koreans also keep alive the traditions of the martial arts and sports such as kite-flying and archery.

The Olympic legacy

Korea first participated in the Olympic Games under her own national flag in 1948 in London. These days, athletes train at an indoor 77,000-sq. meter (18-acre) camp at Taenung on the eastern outskirts of Seoul. Sports facilities at Taenung include an indoor pool, shooting range, and gymnasia for wrestling, boxing and weight-lifting.

All kinds of sports events take place at the Olympic Sports Complex in Jamsil which was built for the 1988 Seoul Olympics. The stadium here has a seating capacity of 100,000 and there are world-class facilities for a wide range of sports.

Western sports

Baseball: There has been a professional baseball league in Korea since the early 1980s, with the major teams sponsored by large corporations. Games attract large crowds. As in the US, college and high-school leagues are also popular.

Golf: Increasingly popular in Korea, golf is no longer the exclusive preserve of rich businessmen. Courses are operated on a membership basis, although guests are welcome. Green fees aren't cheap – although they are considerably lower than those in Japan. Most courses are in the environs of Seoul, and all of them are 18-holed. Korea is on the ninth leg of the annual Asian Circuit with a US$30,000 prize.

Horse-racing: There are three race tracks in Korea; the best of these is right next to Seoul Grand Park in Gwacheon (subway line 4, Seoul Racecourse Park Station). This track is run by the Korea Racing Association, which is affiliated to the Ministry of Agriculture and Forestry. Races are held on Saturdays and Sundays. The horses are imported mainly from Japan and the United States and none is privately owned.

Skiing: There are now a number of ski resorts in South Korea, with accommodation, ski lifts, restaurants and coffee shops. Most of the resorts are in Gangwon and Gyeonggi provinces. The best known resort is the Yongpyeong (Dragon Valley) Ski Resort in the Barwangsan. Snow machines have helped extend the ski season from December to March.

Soccer: South Korea has long been established as one of Asia's leading international soccer teams, and has put in an appearance at most of the recent World Cup tournaments. With the co-hosting of the global event (with Japan) in the summer of 2002 in 10 cities around the country, the sport has become more popular than ever.

Outdoor pursuits

Hiking and mountaineering: Walking in the hills is a popular pastime for young and old alike. Hills and mountains cover nearly 70 percent of the peninsula, and the many National

Parks are criss-crossed with an excellent network of hiking trails.

Hunting and Fishing: Hunting on Jeju-do and a few other areas is only for those with a proper license. Hunting equipment, rifles, and dogs are rented. Game animals include the male ring-necked pheasant, quail, turtledove, wild boar, hare, and river and roe deer. The sport attracts thousands of Japanese tourists to South Korea during the season, which lasts from the beginning of November to the end of February.

Fishing is a leisure activity enjoyed along rivers, lakes, reservoirs and the coasts. Fishing gear is sold everywhere.

membership of 80 nations. In Korea, students train at some 1,100 centers. The World Taegwondo Federation has its headquarters at Gukgiwon, the main *taegwondo* practice gym in the southern outskirts of Seoul. Regular exhibitions are staged for tourists.

Yusul ("soft art"), another martial art, was introduced from China to the Korea Royal court in 1150, but declined in popularity by the 17th century. It was a characteristically passive defense which consisted of throwing, choking or blocking an aggressor. *Yusul* was taught to the Japanese, who called it judo, and was later reintroduced to Korea during the Japanese

Martial arts

Taegwondo, literally the way of combat kicking and punching, is a martial art exercise that has been developing in Korea for more than 2,000 years. It focuses the combined strengths of body, mind and spirit in devastating fist and foot blows. This empty hand-fighting technique was originally learned from China during the Tang dynasty and has been developed since the Three Kingdoms Period (post AD 650) into the form in which it is practiced today.

The National Taegwondo Association has a

Occupation when it was restyled and called *yudo*. It is now a compulsory martial art for Korean policemen.

Ssireum – Korean wrestling – was introduced by the Mongol invaders during the Goryeo Period. Once a form of self-defense, *ssireum* today is a simple folk sport for students and villagers. Contestants hold each other around the back and wrap a cloth strip around their opponent's thigh; they then try to throw each other to the ground using leg, hand and body maneuvers. *Ssireum* matches are held during *Dano* and *Chuseok* (spring and autumn festivals, respectively).

Western wrestling is taking a firm hold on

Koreans, since their enthusiasm was fueled by a major victory in the 1976 Montreal Olympics (in the featherweight freestyle event) and by their success at the 1986 Asian Games, which were held in Seoul.

Korean archery

Once a means of hunting, a weapon of war, and a prerequisite for Joseon-dynasty military leaders, Korean archery survives as a recreation. Contests are held at various traditional sites by the Korean Archery Association. One of these ancient sites, Hwanghakjeong (Yellow Crane Pavilion), is located above Sajik Park in Seoul.

SWINGING AND JUMPING-SEESAW

The simple pleasures of swinging *(geune ttwigi)* and jumping-seesaw *(neul ttwigi)* are traditionally celebrated by women during the spring festival of Dano. In the game of *geune ttwigi* young girls stand on swings suspended by 6-meter (20-ft) lengths of rope, and gleefully pump their way skyward. The *neul ttwigi* draws laughter as girls, on either end of a solid length of wood set on large bags stuffed with rice straw, spring each other into the air. These recreations were reputedly designed to allow the aristocratic Korean women of old to see up and over their high compound walls, as they were not allowed out of their premises during the daytime.

Traditional games

Nearly 70 percent of the folk games in Korea are said to have been created and played during the winter months. Traditional games and recreation which are still the delight of Koreans today include:

Chess (janggi): *Janggi* is the Korean version of chess which was introduced from Mesopotamia through China. Men can be seen crouched over engrossing games on sidewalks, in shops, and in parks. Sixteen pieces are given per player: one general, two chariots, two cannons, two horses, two elephants, two palace guards, and five soldiers, which are represented by Chinese characters written on checkers. The object of the game is to checkmate the general.

Game of wits (baduk): *Baduk* (called "Go" in Japan) is a contest of wits between two players to occupy more territory (houses) on a board divided by 19 vertical and horizontal lines. Black and white button-like stones are used as markers. Once exclusively the game of high officials during the Goguryeo and Baekje days, baduk increased in public popularity after 1945. *Baduk* halls have now been established in almost every town.

Cards (hwatu): Korean playing cards are called *hwatu*. A pack consists of 48 matchbook-sized cards, representing the 12 months of the year. January is symbolized by a pine tree; February, a plum tree; March, cherry; April, bush clover; May, orchids; June, peony; July, iris; August, the moon; September, chrysanthemum; October, maple; November, paulownia; and December, rainfall. A bit of gambling spices the game. These flower cards are also used for fortune-telling, and in Japan are called *hanafuda* cards.

Backgammon (yut): *Yut* is a form of backgammon that is often seen being played by old men sitting in the street. Four 10-inch sticks used as dice are tossed in the air, and the player moves his pawns according to the number of backs or faces that turn up on the sticks. The first player who gets all four of his pawns to a goal wins.

Kite-flying (yeon nalligi): Kite-flying has long been a favorite pastime in Korea, both for children and adults *(see page 51)*. ❑

LEFT: a member of the Korean Kite Flyers' Association prepares to fly his fighting kite at the Seoul International Kite Festival.

The 2002 World Cup

The much-quoted saying "Some people think football is a matter of life and death – but it's much more important than that" was really given full meaning in Korea in 2002. For the first time ever, the FIFA World Cup came to South Korea, and as joint host with Japan, the country practically burst with pride and enthusiasm at the idea of so many top-class matches being played out on its home turf.

Even more importantly for South Korea, the arrival of soccer's premier competition marked the nation's return to the world stage. After being battered by the economic woes of the late 1990s, and straitened by the dictates of the International Monetary Fund, Koreans reckoned the World Cup allowed them a chance to show they could walk tall again. Fans who remembered when Seoul hosted the Olympics in 1988 said that 2002 was like a replay, with Koreans determined to demonstrate that whether it was work or play, they ranked with the best. The fact that the team progressed to the semi-finals was a bonus beyond anyone's wildest expectations.

Nothing if not passionate about sports, most Koreans are fanatical about football. Youngsters start playing at school, and competition to get into the team is intense. International as well as local matches are watched intently on television, and it is not unusual for fans to follow the fortunes of perhaps Manchester United or Barcelona as well as their own home team. The game combines all the aggression and sporting prowess that are dear to Koreans hearts, and top players enjoy the same fame as some film stars.

While the honor of hosting the final of the World Cup went to Yokohama in Japan, Seoul was awarded the privilege of kicking off the tournament as the venue for the first match, as well as the opening ceremony, in its stunning new hi-tech, state-of-the-art stadium. Nine other Korean cities were selected to host various matches, with shiny modern stadia appearing in Incheon, Suwon, Daejeon, Daegu, Gwangju, Jeonju, Ulsan, Busan and Seogwipo.

With well over one million spectators attending the matches themselves, and many further millions watching on their TV sets across the world via satellite, staging the World Cup constituted a truly spectacular promotion for South Korea. As was the success of the team.

Football has a long and respectable history in Korea, and while the English might claim to have invented the current game, the concept of football in Korea was first entertained 1,400 years ago with a ball game known as *chukguk*. Modern football took its place on the sporting scene when it was brought to the country in 1882. The forerunner of the Korean Football Association was founded in 1928 and later formalised as the KFA in 1948 when the country participated in the London Olympic Games. In 1954 – incredibly, considering the war had only just drawn to a close and

much of the country was in ruins – the Republic of Korea managed to make it as far as the finals of the World Cup for the very first time. Since 1986, South Korea has qualified for every final tournament, making its five appearances to date a record among Asian countries.

The 2002 tournament was a remarkable success for the Korean team. Shock victories against Poland and Portugal were followed by a dramatic 2–1 win against Italy and a penalty shoot-out defeat of Spain that propelled them into the semi-finals, where only a narrow defeat to Germany put an end to the dream. The entire country was consumed in World Cup fever, with raucous celebrations from Jeju island to the DMZ. ❏

RIGHT: in qualifying for the past five tournaments, South Korea has the best World Cup record of any Asian team.

TRADITIONAL ARCHITECTURE

Buddhist temples, palaces and pagodas provide many
of Korea's imposing architectural treasures

Seoul has five royal palaces. The king's primary residence, Gyeongbok Palace, was a modest facility of about 390 *gan* (a *gan*, the space between two pillars, was an old unit of measurement) finished in 1395. Changdeok Palace, completed by the third Joseon king, Taejong, in 1405, and Changgyeong Palace, restored by King Gwanghaegun as his official residence in 1615, were secondary palaces to the east. To the south lie Gyeongun Palace (renamed to and better known as Deoksugung) and Gyeonghui Palace. Local palaces in Suwon and Onyang accommodated the king's entourage when he traveled, and two refuge palaces were built within Namhansan Fortress to the south and on Ganghwa Island to the west.

The five palaces share a similar plan, with a government area in front of a residential area. Each has an enclosed garden. The government area functioned as the center for activity, and housed the state administration, with the imposing throne hall *(jeongjeon)* positioned in front of state buildings where officials met the king *(pyeongjeon)*. The hidden royal quarters were further back, divided, according to Confucian custom, into separate sections for king and queen. The residential area proper was a set of building clusters for the queen, the crown prince, and other royalty. Gardens were designed to promote harmony, featuring lotus ponds, pavilions, and clusters of trees; the best preserved is the Secret Garden (Biwon), part of Changdeok Palace.

Palace protection

The walls to palaces were originally tapered, with large stones beneath and small stones above. Outside, no building was allowed to be taller than the wall, to ensure privacy for the royal family. Massive gates protected each palace.

In 1927, the Japanese colonial administration moved Gyeongbok Palace's main gate (Gwanghwamun) to behind the east gate and erected a concrete government building directly in front of

the throne hall, spoiling the aspect of the palace as a whole. The new building, in Western style, was used as the Korean government complex after liberation and later as the National Museum. Burned down during the Korean War, Gwanghwamun was rebuilt in 1968 and moved back to its original site. As part of an ongoing 20-year pro-

ject to restore the original palace, the Japanese building was demolished in 1998.

In the 1592 invasion, the king fled his palace. The people were incensed, and burnt it. The palace was reconstructed only in 1867, but on a much larger scale – 350 buildings were erected, symmetrically positioned along an axis running from the North Mountain (Bugaksan) behind to the front gate, on a site 18 times larger than the original. The new throne hall, the *Geunjeongjeon*, was built on two terraces reached by stone staircases. The tall columns are buttressed by smaller wooden beams, and there is a double ornate carved canopy. Outside, ceremonial bronze incense pots are positioned

LEFT: multi-tiered roofs at Gyeongbok Palace in Seoul.
RIGHT: traditionally styled gateway at Gyeongbok.

at the corners, and beneath the terraces are nine pairs of stone markers, each inscribed with ranks: these were where officials lined up. Behind the throne hall, through a gate, is the single-storied and much plainer audience hall, the *Sajeongjeon*. The only surviving residential quarters were for the queen dowager.

Temple treasures

Buddhist temples present some of Korea's greatest architectural treasures. Nine late 4th century sites are known, including Geumgang-

MOUNTAIN TEMPLES

The unified Silla gave Korea its most prized temple, Bulguk-sa; with the rise of esoteric Buddhism, many temples began to be built in secluded highland areas.

thousand granite pagodas, along with some made from brick. The oldest is probably that at Mireuk-sa, a Baekje site; originally built with nine stories, six survive. Two of the most prized are Seokgatap, the Sakyamuni Pagoda, built in three parts to the ratio of 4:3:2, and the sarira shrine Dabotap, "Pagoda of Many Treasures", both in the main courtyard of Bulguk-sa.

Bulguk-sa, built to the east of Gyeongju to protect the capital from Japanese invasion, was begun in 751, along with the nearby Seokguram

sa near Pyongyang, noted for its octagonal pagoda flanked by three rectangular halls. A later flowering of temple construction began in the 10th century. The main halls of temples usually have gabled roofs with single or double eaves supported by brackets, symbolic ornaments flanking the slightly curved main ridges. Often, and typically at a higher elevation to the rear, there are shrines to the mountain god and to the Taoist Big Dipper. Some of the most impressive structures are pagodas, housing relics of Buddha or others who achieved attainment. Early Goguryeo temples copied China's multi-storied wooden pagodas, but none survive intact. There are, however, more than a

grotto. Grotto caves were common in India and China, but this unique Korean example, now with the temple a UNESCO world heritage site, was built by piling stones around a stone cliff face. A rectangular anteroom that was originally tiled leads to a rear rotunda. The rotunda ceiling is of dressed stone slabs with knuckle stones, a central stone shaped as a lotus flower forming a canopy above the seated Buddha. Eight guardian deity sculptures protect the anteroom, clad in armour. Mythical figures, birds and heavenly guardians line the corridor to the rotunda, and surrounding the Buddha within the rotunda are bodhisattvas, gods, and the 10 Disciples. Above the structure, the roof was reinforced with two layers of granite stones covered with earth and clay topped with tiles.

Protecting Gyeongbok palace are fire-eating *haetae*, but access to the throne hall is guarded by four animal deities on the stone banisters to the upper terrace, the symbolism coming from the four directions: the dragon breathing flames, the powerful tiger, the positive phoenix, and the auspicious part-deer *girin*. On the lower banister there are zodiacal animals: time and space were divided into 12. Smaller figures, *japsaeng*, are perched on many palace, temple, and shrine roofs. These offered protection from fire, particularly a phallic man-like figure, a

the swastika. One of the most important symbols is the *taeguek*, the two interlocking commas that represent cosmic creation and the interaction of opposites.

Domestic architecture

Traditional Korean houses recreate the concerns of palace architects in miniature. Walled for protection, gates are offset from the center, to avoid power being lost. Buildings are constructed around a courtyard. To the left, around the drawing room *(sarangbang)* are the men's quarters, where guests were welcomed, and the raised rooms with verandahs – designed to counter

miniature of the *harubang* made from volcanic lava in Jeju Island. Dragons or waterspouts feature on end-tiles. Carvings of lotus, peony and vines are common decorations for roof beams, plaster and wall painting, supplemented by the "eight treasures" taken from Buddhism, the symbol for longevity, and the "four gentlemen". Geometric patterns are everywhere in Korean architecture, symbolizing thunder, fusion and the radiation of divine power – the last being

LEFT: classic Silla-era architecture at Bulguk-sa temple, Gyeongju.
ABOVE: traditional wooden houses at Hahoe Folk Village.

summer heat – were flanked with storage areas. In the center were the woman's quarters *(an bang)*, warmed by *ondol*, the characteristic underfloor heating system – with areas for food preparation and children. Many houses also had ancestral shrines. The lower classes compressed the structure, with a kitchen to the left, an all-purpose living area in the center, and store rooms to the right. Even today, much evidence remains of a time before glass was widely available: doors functioned as windows, constructed with white paper pasted over a wooden lattice frame. Straw thatch marked poor houses; these were replaced by tin during the 1970s, but upper-class houses have always had clay tiles. ❏

PLACES

*A detailed guide to South Korea, with principal sites
clearly cross-referenced by number to the maps*

The various provinces of South Korea defy the logic of their official borders. This land of "10,000 peaks, 10,000 islands and 10,000 waterfalls" is a place of never-ending contrasts. After a few hectic days spent in the bustle of hectic, high-rise Seoul where traditional markets compete for space with burgeoning office blocks, the time soon beckons to venture out into the many unexpected corners of this complex land.

From the beaches and volcanic landscapes of Jeju-do in the south, to the rocky mountains of Seoraksan National Park in the northeast, there is a wealth of diversity to be discovered. Go on the search for the fabled plum blossoms in Gyeonggi Province, the "Realm of the Immortals" north of Seoul, then work your way down into the Chungcheong Provinces of central Korea where the ginseng fields spread out between the ancient capitals full of treasures as yet undiscovered by Western eyes. Delve deep into the history of Korea's southeastern valley region of Gyeongju with its massive burial mounds, keeper of the riches of the long-forgotten dead, or visit some of the 3,000 solitary islands of the southwestern Jeolla Provinces where visitors will be subjected to curiosity, hospitality and friendly warmth.

If the thought of all this activity makes you giddy with exhaustion, head instead for the relaxing beaches of the "Island of the Gods," the southern island of Jeju-do. Still, you may be tempted to reach for those walking boots as you gaze up at the intriguing volcanic landscapes that provide the backdrop.

Korea, this "Land of the Morning Calm," holds 5,000 years of history, art and culture. There are fashionable hotels and shopping precincts, breathtaking scenery and the proud and open people themselves. Discover something of the nature of the ancient kingdoms of Joseon, or take advantage of the daily tours to the Demilitarized Zone (DMZ), now open for the first time since the country's civil war split the country in two half a century ago.

The ice of this "Cold War holiday destination" is slowly beginning to thaw as a result of the Pyongyang summit in the summer of 2000, leading to a growing rapprochment and plans for the reopening of rail links between the two deeply divided parts of the peninsula. Tour groups from the South can now visit by boat a beautiful tract of North Korean territory on the east coast near mystical Mount Geumgang, the Diamond Mountain, an area of exquisite scenery of jagged peaks, ponds and waterfalls.

The time to visit is now, before the tourist hordes descend on this largely unexplored Asian wonderland. ❑

PRECEDING PAGES: looking out over Seoraksan National Park; Dumulli Park at Gyeongju; a stroll through the cherry blossoms in spring.
LEFT: beautiful scenery near Gyeongju.

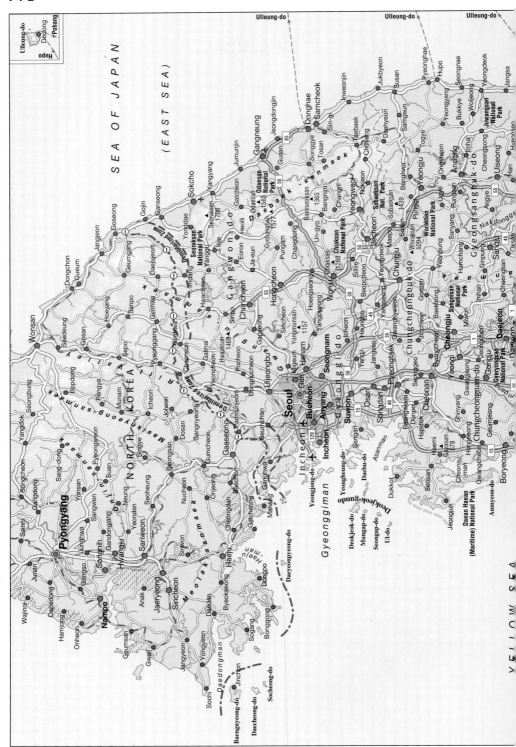

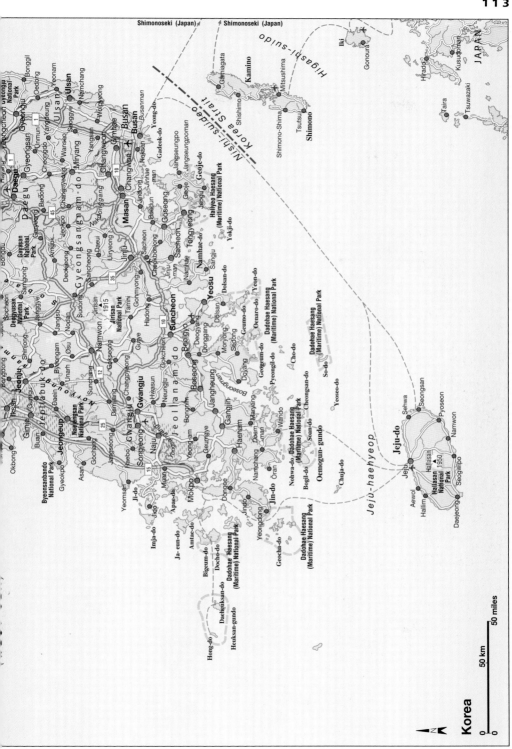

Korea

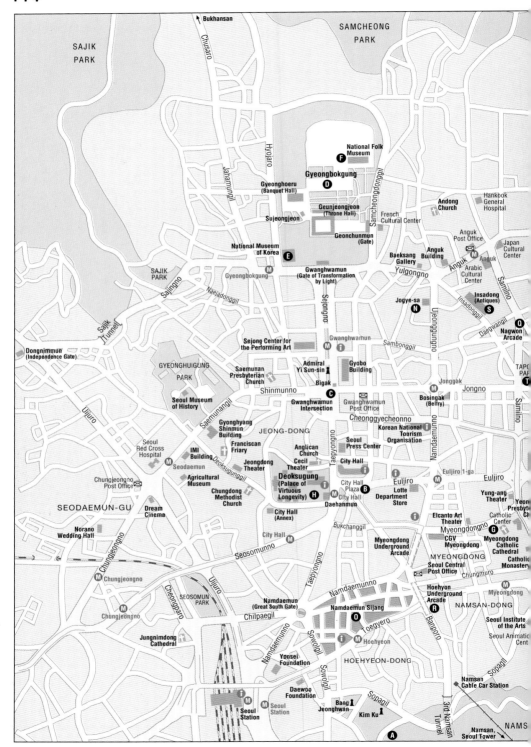

SEOUL

*Seoul is the heart of Korea – a mixture of chic shopping
districts, traditional markets, historic palaces, towering office
buildings, crowded streets and pulsating nightlife*

Map
on pages
114–115

An old Korean saying advises: "If you have a horse, send it to Jeju Island;
if you have a son, send him to Seoul." Jeju Island is the choice for horses
because the grass is green and lush. Seoul is swarming with thousands of
students attending its 18 universities and 15 colleges and the city hosts the head
offices of the country's major enterprises – commercial, financial, and governmental. So sending a son to Seoul gives him the best opportunities.

Seoul – the capital for more than 600 years – is the center of the nation, the
heart of the country to which everything else is drawn (the word Seoul means
capital). It's as if Seoul were a giant magnet attracting to itself filings of trade
and commerce, education, culture and the arts, government, politics – all the
occupations of any nation. So many people, both sons and daughters, have
responded to Seoul's pull that the city is now home to one quarter of the country's population. Its residents now number around 11 million.

Korea's capital has literally risen from the ashes of its wartime desolation
and is now rushing into the mainstream of international activity. Independent
Korea has bred a people determined to improve the homeland and to gain recog-
nition while retaining its values. Seoul's noise and congestion is living proof of
Korea's economic achievements; its calm and grandeur attest to the strength of
Korean culture. As you walk around the city you will
feel the push of the future and the pull of the past.

PRECEDING PAGES:
art for sale in
central Seoul.
LEFT: view of
downtown from
Namsan.
BELOW: looking
towards the Seoul
Tower in winter.

Centers of the vortex

Topographically, the center of the city is wooded
Namsan (South Mountain), a 274-meter (900-ft) hill
topped by the **Seoul Tower** Ⓐ (open daily 9am–
1am; entrance fee), which extends your viewing plat-
form another 240 meters (787 ft). This is a great
place to get your bearings, with spectacular views
across the downtown area to the conically shaped
Bugaksan (North Peak Mountain), and in the opposite direction to the Han River and beyond. Take the
cable car up from the northwestern side of the hill,
and walk back down to the city along peaceful
forest paths.

On the northern slope of Namsan is **Korea House**,
one of Seoul's best Korean restaurants. Several traditional buildings lie in a lovely wooded setting.
There is also a performance theatre, and nearby is
the **Namsangol Hanok Village** showing how life in
Seoul once was.

The old walled city once sprawled between Namsan
and Bugaksan; the 16-km (10-mile) encircling wall
made of earth and dressed stone is gone, but a few
crumbling stretches on Bugaksan and Namsan, and
other restored patches, have survived. Nine gates once
pierced this wall. Five still stand, and the two largest –

Office workers in Seoul's downtown business district, with the Jongno Tower in the background.

BELOW: statue of Yi Sunsin, a 16th-century naval hero.
RIGHT: central Seoul is dominated by giant office blocks.

Namdaemun (Great South Gate) and **Dongdaemun** (Great East Gate) – are regal presences in the midst of the modern city's swirl, and reminders of the capital as it was once laid out.

Some consider the center of Seoul to be **City Hall Plaza B**, the fountain square bounded on the north by City Hall, on the south by the Plaza Hotel, on the east by the entrance to **Euljiro** (one of the main east-west streets), and on the west by Deoksu Palace. Running under the plaza are two subway lines. Traffic flowing in and out of the square from three major arteries swings round the plaza, and pedestrians can walk across it, too. If traffic allows, you can stand in the middle of the north-south street, **Taepyongro**, and look south to Namdaemun and north to **Gwanghwamun** (Gate of Transformation by Light), the reconstructed gate in front of the Gyeongbok Palace. This is City Hall Plaza – a link between the old and new.

Others claim that the **Gwanghwamun intersection C** is Seoul's center. This is the next crossing north of City Hall Plaza, and a looming statue of Yi Sun-sin, Korea's great 16th-century naval hero, dominates it. From that intersection, Taepyongno runs south, **Sejongno** north, **Sinmunno** west and **Jongno** east – the streets change name as they cross. To add to the confusion, the Gwanghwamun intersection is not directly in front of the Gwanghwamun gate for which it is named – that's another long block north of here. People who believe that this intersection is the center of the city probably think so because it is the entrance to Jongno, or Bell Street, the city's original main commercial street. When he established Seoul as the capital in 1394, Joseon dynasty founder Yi Seonggye, whose royal name was Taejo, hung a bell there. The bell was rung at dawn and dusk to signal the opening and closing of the

city gates. The bell, now inside the **Bosingak** belfry at Jongno intersection, was rebuilt in 1984 and is rung only on special holidays.

Palace of Shining Happiness

The governmental heart of the old walled city was **Gyeongbokgung Palace** ❶ (open Wed–Mon 9am–6pm, Nov–Feb closes at 5pm; entrance fee), the Palace of Shining Happiness, which was Taejo's residence and seat of power. He and his successors used it until 1592 when it was burned during warfare with Japan. If you inquire more closely, you will discover that Gyeongbok's throne hall, the **Geunjeongjeon** (Hall of Government by Restraint), rebuilt in 1867, was the very center of Taejo's governmental heart. Here the king sat to receive ministers ranged in orderly ranks before him, made judgements, and issued proclamations. The hall faces south down Sejongno and commands an unob-structed view through Gwanghwamun to Namdaemun.

In 1926, Japanese colonial rulers built a mammoth colonial Capitol Building between the front gate and the throne hall. This was an obvious symbolic severance of the link between the Korean people (the gate) and the royal fam-ily (the throne hall). Finally fed up with this affront, the building was torn down in celebration of Korea's 50th year of independence from Japan. Unfortunately, the old colonial capitol building had served admirably as Korea's National Museum, and the government had to scurry to find a suitable replacement. Currently, many of the museum's most historical items are on view at an interim **National Museum of Korea** ❷ (open Tues–Sun 9am–6pm, Nov–Feb closes at 5pm; entrance fee) in the southwestern corner of the Gyeongbok Palace grounds until a permanent home is ready at the Yongsan Family Park. The museum has

Map on pages 114–115

BELOW: the National Folk Museum, in the grounds of Gyeongbok Palace.

TIP

One of your first stops in Korea should be at the Korean National Tourism Organization's excellent Information Center (open daily 9am–6pm, Nov-Feb closes at 5pm) on Cheonggyecheonno Street. To get here, take subway line 1 to Jonggak Station, or Line 2 to Euljiro 1-ga Station.

BELOW:
Gyeonghoeru, Gyeongbok Palace.

the finest (and largest) collection of Korean antiquities and art in the world. The collection includes over 100,000 items from ancient times through the Joseon Dynasty period. These include Baekje tiles, Silla pottery, gilt Buddhas, Goryeo celadons and Joseon calligraphy and paintings.

Also inside the palace grounds stands the **National Folk Museum of Korea** ❻ (open same days and hours as Gyeongbok Palace; entrance fee), that houses artefacts of everyday use and dioramas showing how they were used. Flanking the palace gate are two stone *haetae*, mythical animals from Korean lore, which have witnessed Seoul's evolution ever since they were carved and placed here in the 15th century to guard the old palace from fire.

When the weather is fine, lines of schoolchildren stream through the gate of the palace. They scatter around the grounds where, with paintbrush and palette in hand, and canvas on easel, they work intently to capture the color of the flowers and leaves, and the charm of interior vistas once seen only by royalty and their attendants. A favorite subject is **Gyeonghoeru** (the Hall of Happy Meetings), a two-story banquet hall that was built in 1412, burned down in 1592, and rebuilt in 1867 when the ruling regent had the entire palace renovated for his son, King Gojong. The hall extends over one end of a spacious square pond. Swans glide over the water and, in winter, skaters glide over the pond's frozen surface. In July, in another pond surrounding the charming **Hyangwon Pavilion** in the northeast corner of the palace grounds, giant pink Indonesian lotus flowers rise on long quivering stems above dinner-plate-sized leaves.

The exact **geographical center of the old city** can be definitely placed, but in the name of progress it's now almost impossible to find. Just off Insadong, an area east of Gwanghwamun known for its art galleries, art supply stores

and antique dealers, there used to be a square granite marker enclosed by short octagonal pillars. That square of granite marked the geographical center of the old walled city. Typically enough, this particular piece of Joseon-dynasty history was ignored: neither the stone itself nor any signboard proclaimed what this spot was. This remnant of history was carted off during construction in the mid-1980s, and a new office block stands in its place. Just by this spot, marked by a plaque, stands the former house of a Joseon-dynasty prince, where leaders of the 1919 independence uprising planned their protest against the Japanese rulers.

Map on pages 114–115

Seoul chic

Many people think Seoul's real center today is modern **Myeongdong**, an area of narrow alleys that starts a 10-minute walk southeast from City Hall Plaza directly across from Lotte Department Store. Myeongdong's main thoroughfare, a one-way street, is lined on both sides with swanky shops that sell chic clothes and accessories, and it ends at the top of a low hill before **Myeongdong Cathedral ⊕** (open daily 9am–9pm). This grand center of Catholicism used to be one of the largest buildings in the city decades ago. Now large hotels and office buildings dwarf it, but it still remains a landmark. In recent years it has become a rallying point for anti-government demonstrators.

Not only has the Catholic faith attracted politically active converts through its human rights stance, but also many protesters ranging from the homeless to radical students have sought refuge within its hallowed grounds. Even in the 1990s, the pungent smell of tear gas from demonstrations often lingered over the area around the cathedral.

Myeongdong Catholic Cathedral. Korea is Asia's second-most Christianized country, after the Philippines.

BELOW: Myeong-dong at night.

NIGHTLIFE

Itaewon is still the main area for foreigners' night-time romping, especially since the government loosened up its regulations, gave this area special tourist status, and allowed the entertainment centers to remain open until the wee small hours – prior to this, a midnight closing time had been strictly enforced since 1990 to combat drink driving and rising crime in the city.

The Sinchon area to the west of the city center is emerging as a new center for nightlife in central Seoul. Myeongdong is lively at any time, and is full of bars. Gangnam – and particularly Apgujeong – south of the river, is also known for its nightlife.

Many first-class hotels have discos but so many similar establishments have opened nearer residential areas that their popularity has declined. Catching the wind of this trend in its sails, the downtown Chosun Hotel turned its disco into a sports bar called O'Kims, the brainchild of the hotel's Irish manager and the most popular downtown lunch and dinner venue for the international business set. Also popular, especially with wealthy young Koreans, is the Grand Hyatt Hotel's JJ Mahoney's bar-and-disco complex that features a dance floor, darts, snooker and an American jazz band.

Myeongdong alleyways come alive in the evening when they are crowded with after-work strollers window-shopping – "eye-shopping" in Korean – past the fancy displays of shoes and handbags, tailor-made suits and custom-made shirts, dresses in the latest fashions, handcrafted modern jewelry, and cosmetics. But these are only the surface attractions of Myeongdong. The district was famous during the Park Chung-hee era for its tiny upstairs and hideaway drinking houses that used to serve cheap liquor up until curfew time. These have been largely replaced by fashionable coffee shops packed with young Koreans.

Namsan, City Hall Plaza, Gwanghwamun, Myeongdong. Perhaps the visitor should think of Seoul as having more than one center: it's certainly a city big enough and old enough for more than one special center of interest.

"Virtuous Longevity"

For a more modern exploratory opener, begin your tour of Seoul at the central and historical **Deoksugung Palace**  (open Tues–Sun 9am–6pm, July–Feb closes at 5.30pm; entrance fee), the Palace of Virtuous Longevity, whose gate faces City Hall Plaza. Deoksu is not the oldest of the surviving palaces – it was built as a villa toward the end of the 15th century – but it is important for its role at the unhappy end of the Joseon dynasty. King Gojong, who was forced to abdicate in favor of his son Sunjong in 1907, lived in retirement and died here in 1919 after having seen his country annexed by the Japanese in 1910 and his family's dynasty snuffed out after 500 years.

Among the most conspicuous structures on the palace grounds, regularly open to the public, is a statue of Sejong, the great 15th-century king who commissioned scholars to develop a distinctive Korean writing system, different

BELOW: the changing of the Palace Gate Guards ceremony at Deoksu Palace.

from the traditional Chinese characters, and officially promulgated it in 1446. There's also a royal audience hall and two startlingly European-style stone buildings, with Ionic and Corinthian columns designed in 1909. These buildings are used to house the **Royal Museum** (open Tues–Sun 9am–5pm, Nov–Feb closes at 4.30pm), exhibiting items once used by the royal court. The palace grounds offer a welcome relief from the modern bustle, especially in the autumn when its aisle of gingko trees is aflame in gold.

Visitors to Deoksu Palace are often surprised to find themselves in the middle of odd-looking, spear-carrying soldiers marching to the beat of huge drums and elongated bugles. This is the ceremony of the **Changing of the Palace Gate Guards** (open Mar–Dec Tues–Sat 10–11.30am & 2–3.30pm), performed much as it was when kings and queens lived and ruled behind palace walls more than a hundred years ago.

Round a secret garden

About a block east of Gyeongbok lies **Changdeokgung Palace ❶** (open Tues–Sun 9.15am–5.15pm, Nov–Feb closes at 4pm; entrance fee), the Palace of Illustrious Virtue, built in 1405 as a detached palace, burned down in 1592, rebuilt in 1609 and used since then as the official residence of various Joseon kings, including the last one, Sunjong, until his death in 1926. The best preserved of Seoul's palaces, Changdeok has a throne room hall surrounded by long drafty corridors leading past reception rooms furnished with heavy upholstered European chairs and sofas. In private living quarters, the furnishings are those of traditional Korea: low, slatted beds, lacquered chests and tables.

Map on pages 114–115

Incongruous architecure at the Royal Museum, Deoksu Palace.

BELOW: Deoksu Palace is very popular for wedding photo sessions.

A quiet spot within the secluded grounds of Biwon, the Secret Garden.

Nakseonjae, a small complex of buildings within Changdeok's grounds, is still the residence of descendants of the royal family: ensconced there are an elderly aunt of Sunjong; the wife of the last crown prince, Sunjong's son (who never ruled); her son; and his wife. In the formal back gardens of Nakseonjae, with a series of stepped granite-faced tiers planted with azaleas, it is possible to feel totally isolated from the sounds of modern Seoul. From within a small raised octagonal pavilion at the top of this garden, you can imagine the royal family sitting here, gazing out over the curved roofs of the palace buildings and the arabesque walls encircling them. Under leafy treetops that stretch towards Namsan in the distance, you can hear court whispers and imagine the turbulence and intrigues of Korea's late Joseon dynasty.

Behind Changdeok lies the extensive acreage of **Biwon** ❿ (entrance through Changdeok Palace, with same opening days and hours; guided tours), the Secret Garden, so-called because it was formerly a private park for the resident royal family. In wooded and hilly terrain, footpaths meander past ponds and pavilions and over small bridges.

The most picturesque of these sites is Bandoji (Peninsula Pond), shaped like the outline of the Korean peninsula. From its shore extending out over the water stands a small, exquisite, fan-shaped pavilion from which Injo, the 16th king, could cast a line for a bit of quiet fishing. Biwon and portions of Changdeok Palace may be visited by joining one of several daily guided tours at the Biwon entrance. The Nakseonjae complex is open to the general public twice a year for royal ceremonies.

One block east from Changdeok lies **Changgyeonggung Palace** ❿ (open Wed–Mon 9am–6pm, Nov–Feb closes at 5.30pm; entrance fee), another palace

BELOW: the walls of Changgyeong Palace.

with its grounds now open to the public (this is the largest public park within Seoul). The complex of buildings dates back to the early 12th century, when it functioned as a summer palace for Goryeo royalty.

Map on pages 114–115

Confucian Seoul

Across the street from Changgyeong Palace lies **Jongmyo** ❶ (open Wed–Mon 9am–6pm, Nov–Feb closes at 5.30pm; entrance fee), the Royal Ancestral Shrine, which, along with Changdeok Palace was designated as a UNESCO World Heritage Site in 1996. This walled complex includes two long pillared buildings housing, according to Confucian requirement, ancestral tablets listing the names and accomplishments of the 27 Joseon kings and their queens. Jongmyo is open to the public and is a favorite strolling ground for young couples. Once a year on the first Sunday in May, a traditional ceremony honoring the spirits of kings and queens is held here. Ancient court music, not otherwise heard, rings eerily over flagstones and beyond cedar pillars. Confucian celebrants pay appropriate respects and offer proper foods and wine to each of the enshrined spirits in a ritual lasting six hours.

The teachings of the great sage Confucius (Gongja), who lived in China about 2,500 years ago, became more deeply rooted in Korea than in their native land, especially during the Joseon dynasty, when they formed the basis of of government and code of behavior in Korean society. Many aspects of Confucianism live on in Korean society, such as the emphasis placed on education, respect for one's elders, and ancestral worship. Twice a year, during the second and eighth lunar months, people gather at the **Munmyo Shrine** located on the grounds of **Sungkyunkwan University** ❶ (open daily

BELOW: Confucian dancers at the Munmyo Shrine, Sungkyunkwan University.

9am–6pm; free) to the northeast of Biwon, to honor his spirit. Sungkyunkwan University is in fact a modern transformation of the old Sungkyunkwan, a national institute sponsored and supported by the Joseon Court. It was here that Korea's best scholars pursued the Confucius Classics and instructed those who aspired to pass government examinations in order to receive official appointments.

The Hangnyeong, the rules which govern students' lives at Sungkyunkwan University, state: "Any student guilty of violating human obligations (prince and minister, father and son, husband and wife, brothers or friends), of faulty deportment, or of damaging his body or his reputation, will be denounced, with drumbeats, by the other students. Extreme cases may be reported to the Ministry of Rites and barred from academic circles for life." After all, the aim of the school was – as its name says – *sung*, "to perfect human nature," and *kyun*, "to build a good society." This is the dual purpose of a good Confucian education.

Buddhism's hub

The Confucian Joseon court tried hard to extinguish the spirit of the Buddha throughout the country, but it failed miserably. Buddhist temples abound. City temples, though, are hardly places of quiet retreat. **Jogye-sa Temple** (open daily, no specific hours) founded in 1910 and the headquarters of the official sect of Buddhism in Korea, is right in the middle of the downtown area, just off Ujeonggungno. As the country's center of Buddhism, it hums with activity, and on the occasion of Buddha's birthday, on the 8th day of the 4th lunar month, it becomes the hub of Buddhist festivities in Korea.

BELOW: lanterns at Jogye-sa, the major temple for Seoul's Buddhists.

On this day, in common with all Buddhist temples in the country, the court-yard in front of Jogye-sa's main hall is strung with parallel strands of wires on support poles. As dusk falls, worshippers come to the temple to buy a paper lantern and candle. The names of all the members of the worshipper's family are written on a tag dangling from the bottom of the lantern. The worshipper fixes the candle into the lantern, lights it, hangs the lantern on one of the wires, then bows and murmurs a prayer when finished. Row after row of flickering candle flames illuminate the courtyard as darkness deepens. If in some stray gust of wind a lantern catches fire and burns, everyone stands aghast and mute at this stroke of ill fortune – an evil omen for the year to come. Meanwhile, within the main hall, devotees light incense on the altar before the Buddha's golden image, bow to the floor three times in reverence and offer prayers. Every part of the temple is thick with people. Anyone may buy and hang a lantern; so many non-Buddhist foreign residents do. Some even march in a long lantern parade that winds through downtown Seoul – an elaborate affair with floats and bands. It's a good way to try to ensure good luck for a year.

Map on pages 114–115

Worshipers in the main hall of Jogye-sa temple.

Seoul's huge traditional markets

Any foreign visitor to Seoul should venture into a proper market; if not one of the neighborhood markets, then certainly into one or both of the great central markets downtown. Take one of the hundreds of neighborhood markets and multiply it by 50, and you have **Namdaemun Sijang ⊙** (Great South Gate Market, located east of the gate itself). The shops and stalls are generally open from 10am until sunset, though it's said that the real bargains are bought after midnight on weekends. Remember to barter for any purchase –

BELOW: lunchtime at Namdaemun market.

MARKET LIFE

By day, the main markets of Seoul are the place to go for a real taste of the city. You can buy almost anything you could think of from herbal medicines to jewelry and furniture. The multi-story hives of shops are connected by alleyways or walkways and cover huge areas of the city. The stores generally open 10am–8pm, while most markets are open from 6am. Sit in one of the many restaurants and you can watch Korean life bustle around you, including the streetside money-changers, purses clutched to their chests, exchanging notes in illegal transactions.

In the evening, another aspect of market life unfolds: the *suljip* or drinking house. A *suljip* is neither bar, cocktail lounge, or beer hall, although these do exist in the city. Rather, it is a mini-restaurant and social hall. Indeed, a stranger could pass through the market unaware that behind a tiny sliding door is a narrow room with four small oil-drum tables, a cluster of tiny stools, and space for 16 customers sitting (and up to three standing at a counter).

Here the men who live and work in the market gather for a few after-work snacks and beer and *soju* liquor, which soon leads to loud singing (accompanied by banging metal chopsticks against the edge of a table) – and so unwinds another working day in a Seoul marketplace.

if you don't, you will end up paying way too much. The stalls selling watches, jewelry, kitchenware and bric-a-brac are everywhere, with clothing outlets occupying most of the shop space. There are also numerous street food stalls, serving a tempting array of seafood snacks.

Triple the size of Namdaemun and you have **Dongdaemun Sijang** ❷ (Great East Gate Market), a large area that stretches south of Jeongno 5-ga and 6-ga.

Feast your eyes on the silk market here (which operates similar hours to Namdaemun) – stall after stall of brilliantly colored silk and synthetic brocades, a truly dazzling display. The history of this market goes back to the 14th century and the roots of the Joseon dynasty. In more recent years, many refugees from North Korea escaping the communist regime rebuilt their lives by taking work at the market. In addition to silks they sell Korean bedding, kitchenware, handicrafts and sports goods.

At either market you can find almost anything you want, and, perhaps, many things you'd rather not find. On weekends the crowds are so intense, you have simply got to move with the flow to survive. Hawkers shout out bargains, and the louder the better, since bargain hunters gravitate to a noisy crowd like a shark to spots of blood. This is also a good place to sit down to a *sundae*, stuffed intestine, or that most pungent of Korean delicacies, *beondegi* (silkworm larvae). Really, you haven't experienced Seoul until you have spent some time at Namdaemun or Dongdaemun markets.

Labyrinthine arcades

BELOW: inside the glitzy Lotte department store.

More convenient and popular than traditional markets these days are the numerous department stores such as Lotte and Shinsegae on Namdaemunno.

South of the river are the Lotte World, New Core, Grace, Galleria, Hyundai and Hanyang department stores. Also south of the river in Apgujeongdong is the informally named "Rodeo Drive," a street of up-market international and local fashion houses.

There are seemingly never-ending streets of shops underground, along Jongno and Euljiro, and smaller and pricier arcades underneath the **Westin Chosun**, **Lotte** and **Plaza hotels**. Above ground there is the **Nagwon Arcade** ❷ (open daily; shop hours generally are 10am–8pm) Jongno 2-ga, and a four-block arcade running north-south from Jongno 3-ga to Toegyero 3-ga.

The Sogong Arcade runs from under the corner of the Plaza Hotel, turns left at the Westin Chosun Hotel and continues alongside Lotte department store to the edge of Myeongdong; the **Hoehyeon Arcade** ❷ (open daily; shop hours generally are 10am–8 or 9pm) starts in front of the Central Post Office and runs up to Toegyero; and other mini-arcades exist where pedestrian underpasses allow room for a few stores. These arcades offer clothes, jewelry, calculators, cosmetics, cameras, and souvenir items, including reproductions of antique porcelain.

Above ground, specialized shops tend to run along together in a row. Barbells, volleyballs and other sporting goods can be found at any one of the half-dozen stores under the shadow of Seoul Stadium (an apt location) at Euljiro 7-ga. Buddhist rosaries hang at the shops near the entrance to Jogye-sa; and puppies and brightly painted dog houses along Toegyero 4-ga and 5-ga. Need hub caps and car seat covers? On a street connecting Cheonggyecheon 5-ga with Euljiro 5-ga. Men's tailored suits? Along Namdaemunno north of Euljiro, in an area called Gwanggyo.

Tea, art and antiques in Insadong

The time-honored location for antique dealers is **Insadong ⑤**, with shops strung along a narrow street leading south from Angukdong. A huge number of small specialist shops sell fine Goryeo celadon, Silla pottery and Joseon furniture are still flourishing here, along with numerous art galleries, art supply stores, teahouses, restaurants and a few bookshops.

Although some of the antique stores face the street, others lurk in back alleys snuggled between tiny restaurants, teahouses, junk dealers and blaring CD and tape stores. Some vendors spread their wares on blankets on the ground. It's a real bargain hunter's challenge.

At weekends, the streets of Insadong take on a festive atmosphere, as Koreans and foreigners (the area is a favorite with the ex-pat community) crowd the streets and shops. A visiting Western urbanologist once wrote, "If you imagine pouring some water onto a pile of large rocks, the pathway found by the water between the rocks, as it flows to the ground, is somewhat similar to the way streets exist in Korean neighborhoods." The urban neighborhood village is typically a maze of small alleyways and side streets and Insadong is one of Seoul's best examples of how the city once was.

The area is a great place for walking. Little alleyways wind and wander past

Map on pages 114–115

TIP

Deluxe taxis are black with a yellow sign on top. They are more expensive than regular taxis (though still relatively cheap), but the drivers are generally more courteous and the vehicles more comfortable.

BELOW: Insadong is the place to go for antiques.

Map
on pages
114–115

*Antique shop in
Insadong, one of
Seoul's most colorful
districts.*

BELOW AND RIGHT:
street food is
exceptionally good
in Korea.

gated doors and tiny stores before ending abruptly. Small shops display snakes embalmed in *soju* (good for a man's stamina, so they say), and behind stone walls where you can hear businessmen singing their hearts out as they entertain each other in expensive salons.

Insadong is also well known for its traditional *(jeontong chatjip)* and not-so-traditional *(dabang)* teahouses, where belljars of dried herbs line the shelves. Although ginseng is the most popular, other homemade brews are also served. These include aromatic ginger tea *(saenggangcha)* made with boiled and strained ginger root and raw sugar; porridges such as *jatjuk*, made of pine nuts, water, rice flour and salt or sugar to taste; and *kkaejuk*, toasted black sesame seeds, water, rice flour and salt or sugar. *Mogwacha* (quince) *daechucha* (jujube), *yujacha* (citron), and *maesilcha* (plum) are a few Korean teas that taste quite sweet but refreshing.

Tapgol Park

At the southern end of Insadong is **Tapgol Park** ❼ (open daily 8am–11pm, Oct–Mar closes at 10pm; entrance fee), also known as Pagoda Park after the Joseon pagoda situated in its center. This became Korea's first Western-style public park when it opened in 1913. Tapgol is famous for its role in the events of March 1919, when the declaration of Korean independence, in defiance of Japanese rule, took place here *(see page 38)*. The wall surrounding the park features scenes depicting the events of the March 1 Movement, and a bronze cast displays the Declaration itself. Every year on March 1 a ceremony takes place to commemorate those who died in the ensuing Japanese crackdown on the nationalist movement. ❑

SEOUL TEAHOUSES

Congestion is a problem in Seoul, both in- and outdoors. Try sitting in a *dabang* (tearoom), for instance. Although there are literally thousands of *dabang* of various sizes in the city, finding a seat in a popular one will be the first hurdle. *Dabang* are popular throughout Korea for their convenience as meeting places. Here friends meet to talk or as a preliminary to going somewhere else, business associates meet to negotiate a deal, prospective bride-and-groom couples meet under the eye of their family and friends. Each *dabang* tends to specialize in a certain clientele – university students gravitate toward some, businessmen to others – largely in response to the kind of music the tearoom offers. A disc jockey in a glass booth, often labeled the "Music Box," will play customers' requests through a powerful stereo system. The mix of loud conversation and loud music, however, can be cacophonous.

A *jeontong chatjip* is a traditional tearoom, with a wide variety of teas and esoteric serving methods *(see page 260)*. Herbs are steeped in earthenware pots (metal is said to deplete herbal potency) over a low-burning *yeontan* (coal briquette) for at least an hour or two until an essence is thus extracted. The Insadong area *(see above)* has a good selection of *jeontong chatjip*.

OUTER SEOUL

*Outside Seoul's historic heart is the modern part of the city,
where you'll find huge department stores and markets, ultra-modern
entertainment complexes and cultural centers*

Map
on page
136

ollowing on the heels of urban expansion, and in tune with a rapidly rising standard of living, many of the outer areas of Seoul have become shopping and entertainment centers that rival those found in the downtown area. With the notable exception of Itaewon, however, they do not attract a lot of foreigners. Part of the reason is that, even though any given point in Seoul seems to be only minutes from a subway station, it can still take an hour or more to travel across town. The subways are quick enough (allow about two minutes between each subway stop); it's just that you can seldom get to your destination without one or two subway transfers, and a taxi ride. Still, there are some interesting places across the Han River that deserve a visit. The thing to do is to make a day of it, and check out several places of interest. And really, there is no better way to get to know modern Korea than by exploring the fringes of Seoul.

LEFT: the Monorail inside the giant Lotte World shopping mall and entertainment complex.
BELOW: Hwanghakdong Flea Market.

Markets for all tastes

Just outside the old city center lies a threesome of interesting specialty markets. Two subway stops east from Dongdaemun (subway lines 2 or 6; Sindang Station) is the sprawling **Hwanghakdong Flea Market ❶** (open daily 8am–6.30pm). If you're looking for a life-size statue of an American Indian, reproduction antique furniture, used ice skates or an old TV, you stand a good chance of finding it here. For the truly bizarre, there is the snake salesman with microphone in hand. He dips his free hand into a bag and brings out a handful of snakes, tossing them into a plastic tub. A few turtles are added for good measure. Somehow he manages to sell this writhing basket of reptiles to one of the middle-aged men crowding around. While the salesman sets up another sale, his assistants boil the basket of turtles and snakes, and quickly bottle them in *soju*. Minutes later, the lucky customer leaves with a big smile, knowing that it will be a long time before he will be suffering from virility problems.

Not far away is the equally unusual **Gyeongdong Oriental Medicine Market ❷** (subway line 1; Jegi-dong Station; open daily 9am–6.30pm except 1st and 3rd Sunday of each month). This is a great place to buy fresh ginseng, or dozens of other odd-looking roots and fungi that are said to be good for a myriad of ailments. There are also a few dealers of dog meat, which is considered a health food in the Orient.

A little more conventional is the **Janghanpyeong Antique Market ❸** (subway line 5; Janghanpyeong Station; closed Sunday). Dozens of small shops are located in several two-story buildings; kind of mini-antique malls. Most of the dealers here do not handle top-of-the line antiques (you need to go to Insadong for these), but since there are regulations concerning

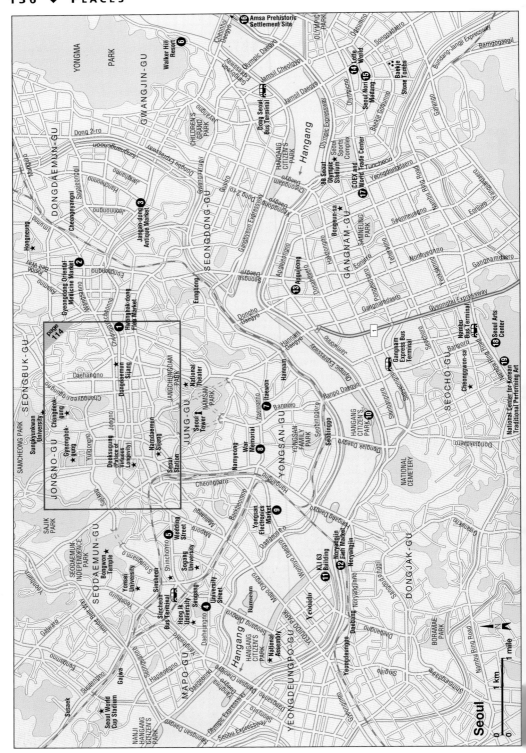

Seoul

the export of valued Korean antiquities anyway, Janghanpyeong is the perfect place to find a funky piece to decorate your living room. How about a large wooden bowl that was once used to clean rice? Or a handmade farmers wood plow? And a Korean ceramic pillow makes a great conversation piece.

Map on page 136

Nightlife and nuptials

Seoul has several entertainment centers that cater to the young, but one of the most popular and interesting is **Daeheungno** ❹, which caters to students from four nearby universities. The streets in this district (Sinchon) have such a profusion of restaurants, bars (some with live entertainment), video arcades, clothing stores and coffee shops that young people from all over Seoul come here on evenings and weekends.

If you are planning on getting married, **Wedding Street** ❺ (shops open daily 10am–8pm) might be the place for you. Rows of shops display fanciful wedding gowns in their windows hoping to entice well-heeled 20-year-olds. Weddings are a serious business in Korea – a wedding gown, make-up, and hairstyle (all these services are offered at the wedding shops), will set Daddy back thousands of dollars. Then there is the wedding hall, the dinner for all the guests, a photographer and wedding gifts (from the parents); a Korean wedding runs into the tens of thousands of dollars.

A lovely spot from which to view Seoul over a proper martini is the **Walker Hill Resort** ❻ complex (subway line 5 to Gwangnaru Station, then take a taxi). This nightlife area of Las Vegas-style revues (dinner shows at 4.30pm and 7.30pm), gambling (in the Sheraton Walker Hill Casino), and resort amenities is located above Seoul's eastern suburbs and overlooks a picturesque bend in the

Coffee shops, a legacy of the American presence, are everywhere in Seoul.

BELOW: shopping in Itaewon.

ALTERNATIVE LIFESTYLES

First-time visitors to Korea are often surprised to see the amount of affection shown by same-sex partners on the streets and dance floors. This is all the more surprising since public displays of affection between a man and woman are strongly frowned upon (and this includes kissing). Physical displays of affection between friends have always been considered acceptable in Korea. Being gay or lesbian, on the other hand, is totally and completely unacceptable. Ask a Korean about homosexuals in Korea, and they're likely to tell you that there aren't any. Of course this isn't true. But in this conservative Confucian society, the alternative lifestyle is a very underground scene. In Seoul, the popular entertainment centers for those with an alternative lifestyle are in Insadong and Itaewon.

Gay bars in Korea are in their infancy, and they are small, basic and limited in their facilities. That there are gay bars in Korea, and that many people know they exist, and the police have not tried to shut them down, is a big step for Korea. Bars in the Itaewon district currently make just enough to keep their doors open, but the crowds, mostly between the ages of 18 and 30, are growing as awareness and acceptance of homosexuality spreads among younger generation of Koreans.

Han River. From Walker Hill's glittering lounges and gardens, you can see Seoul's city lights twinkling in the urban west. Walker Hill was named after General Walton H. Walker, former Commanding General of the US Eighth Army, who was killed in a traffic mishap during the Korean War.

Cruising Itaewon

Itaewon ❼ (accessible via the subway system; alternatively, take a taxi or Bus No. 0014 from Seoul Railway Station) is an urban area that runs down from the southern flank of Namsan and eastward from the fenced edge of Yongsan Garrison, the site of the headquarters of the 8th US Army and the huge War Memorial. The main thoroughfare that bisects the army base into north-south posts similarly bisects Itaewon into an uphill-Namsan side and a downhill side toward the Han River.

For years, that flank of Namsan has been one of the main housing areas for Westerners as the Korea Housing Corporation, a government agency, built and maintained Western-style houses there. That idea is perpetuated, but foreigners, not all of them Western, now occupy multi-story apartment buildings higher up the mountain – a location that gives them a sweeping view of the Han River and mountain ridges south of the city.

Imagine the astonished reactions of the Buddhist monks who, for some 500 years, kept a free hostel for travelers near here. What exists now, albeit breathtaking, may prove to be too developed for their tastes: the Grand Hyatt Hotel's mirrored façade reflecting a setting sun and passing clouds; and the twin minarets of the onion-domed mosque below, from which resounds the muezzin's call to afternoon prayer.

TIP

When bargaining, street vendors and small shops in traditional markets (including Itaewon) usually quote prices 10–30 percent higher than they expect to get. To ask for a discount you can say: *"kkakka juseyo"*.

BELOW: Itaewon is famous for its shopping and nightclubs.

Centuries back, Itaewon was used as a stopover point for visitors to the capital. Then, during the Japanese Occupation, Japanese troops were housed here. These soldiers were replaced after the Korean War with American soldiers stationed at the adjacent Yongsan base, and Korean merchants moved into the thoroughfare to cater to the troops' needs.

Today, Itaewon merchants attract shoppers from civilian ranks as well, and visitors hail from all over the world. By day, bargain-hunters swarm through the hundreds of clothing, leather goods, eelskin, brassware, shoe and antique stores where they stock up on Korean-made goods.

Nightlife in Itaewon

By night, Itaewon attracts hordes of young Koreans as well as foreigners. The Itaewon strip has doubled in length in recent years, with many new discotheques and restaurants catering to a new generation. In former times the hundreds of bars and discos used to rock until the break of day, the alcohol flowed, the crowds got rowdy, and Itaewon earned a rather disreputable name for itself among Koreans. Still, many a cross-cultural marriage had its beginnings in one of the packed clubs. Itaewon has calmed down a little since its heyday, and the lower prices and more varied entertainment options of districts such as Sinchon have diverted a certain amount of the custom. Nevertheless it still attracts the crowds – particularly since it was declared a special tourist zone. The new link to the city subway system should boost numbers further.

A short taxi ride from Itaewon is the impressive **War Memorial** ❽ (open Tues–Sun 9.30am–6pm; Nov–Feb closes at 5pm; entrance fee). Located on the large plaza in front of the Memorial is one of Seoul's better museums, filled with

Map on page 136

The Itaewon district may have calmed down a bit in recent years, but it is still packed with bars and clubs.

BELOW: Seoul youth at Marronnier Park.

South Korean churches come in all shapes and sizes.

Korean War-era airplanes, tanks and artillery pieces. Inside, displays, movies and dioramas tell you everything you ever wanted to know about the Korean War.

You can buy electronics almost everywhere in Seoul, but the largest concentration of discount dealers is in the **Yongsan Electronics Market** ❾ (open daily; 10am–8pm), a short taxi ride to the southwest of the War Memorial. Housed in three multi-story buildings and spreading out to a few smaller arcades, Koreans congregate by the thousands to try out the latest computer games, notebook computers, vacuum cleaners or cameras. Virtually anything electronic can be found here. A lot of expats living in Korea shop here. For visitors, there are a few limitations. For one thing, English software and instructions are rare. Another problem is that Korea runs on 220 volts, so their electronic devices are a bit inconvenient for those 110-volt countries, such as the United States. Unbelievably, Korean companies used to charge outrageously high prices for their goods in Korea (as opposed to their reputation for being inexpensive outside of Korea). With the dramatic devaluation of the won at the end of the 1990s, the prices have became considerably more reasonable. Still, you have to do a lot of shopping to come up with a real bargain.

Tennis, golf, and a picnic in the city

While hiking may be the most popular outdoor recreation, tennis does not lag far behind. Tennis courts can be found all over the city, and Koreans play both in the summer and winter. There are several golf clubs outside the city, but they are expensive. However, the city does offer numerous practice driving nets.

Picnicking elsewhere in the world usually involves just a leisurely meal. In Korea, however, it is a recreation especially popular during the spring and

BELOW: suburban Seoul snowscapes.

Map on page 136

autumn. As part of the beautification program for the 1988 Seoul Olympics, the city cleaned up the once-scruffy and disused banks of the Han River and turned them into the **Hangang Citizen's Park ❿**, a leisure zone for the city's 10 million people. There are facilities for water sports, swimming pools, sports fields, and miles of park area for picnicking and kite flying.

It is quite common to see a group of middle-aged women in long flowing Korean dresses out for an afternoon. At some point, they may relax and form a circle and dance to their *janggu*, waving their arms gracefully and turning slowly and rhythmically.

To the west of the city is the stunning new **Seoul World Cup Stadium** built for the 2002 soccer World Cup and easily reached on subway line 6 – a five-minute walk from World Cup Stadium (Seongsan) Station.

Island in the river

Not too long ago, the island of Yeouido was little more than a large sandbar in the middle of the Han River. During the past 30 years it has been transformed into Korea's version of Wall Street, and an important center for government. The big attraction for visitors is the **DLI 63 Building ⓫** (open daily 10am–8pm), Seoul's tallest building and, along with the Seoul Tower atop Namsan, the city's most visible landmark. The 63-story building (hence its name) may not seem especially tall, but it towers over its surroundings on the banks of the Han River.

There is a terrific observation deck, while the basement houses Seoul's best aquarium, and its grandest IMAX theater. After taking in the view from the top, and perhaps a movie, try one of the many restaurants in the building. Then take

The Seoul Equestrian Park attracts hordes of bet-happy Koreans (mostly men) on weekends from 11am to 6pm. You can watch the races in luxury in a hospitality room on the 6th floor: English-speaking staff make placing a bet or buying a beer a breeze.

BELOW: a bird's-eye view of the Han River.

The Yeouido-Korea Life Insurance Building on Yeouido island. The island is Seoul's financial center.

BELOW: Noryangjin Fish Market.

a walk along Hangang Citizen's Park and watch the members of the Seoul kite club manoeuver their fighting kites – the Hangang Citizen's Park next to the 63 Building is a favored haunt for kite-flying enthusiasts.

If you are really into fish, try the **Noryangjin Fish Market** ⓬ (just across the Han River from Yeouido; subway line 1 to Noryangjin station, then take the walkway back over the tracks), south of the Han River. Fresh fish on ice, crabs waving their claws about, squid trying to slither away, and fat, succulent shrimp all promise gourmet experiences; but you will have to get there in the pre-dawn hours if you want to compete with those who have come here to get supplies for their own fish stalls in neighborhood markets. Perhaps the best feature of the fish market is the raw fish restaurants on the second floor. You can dine in relative luxury while watching all the fish market activity below.

South of the Han River

In contrast to the older residential section of Seoul with its diverging alleyways on the north side of the river, is the southern section of the city. Spreading out from the foot of new Han River bridges, the section is carefully grid-ironed, its streets ruled into right angles. Residents buy everyday necessities in "proper" stores – modern supermarkets where onions come prepackaged in plastic bags. To some, the beige and gray complexes (Jamsil, Yeongdong, Yeouido) lack color and charm; yet to many they offer a kind of beauty of their own, revealed at night by a drive east along the north bank of the Han River from the Hangang Bridge. Across the black water, these façades of tall apartment buildings make a wall of patterned light that shimmers in the reflecting river. The bridges become ribbons of light flung across the water as streamers of automobile headlights mark the passage of traffic between the old center of the city and its new southern sector.

In the high-rent district

Probably the most desirable address south of the river is fashionable **Apgujeong** ⓭, a district of Gangnam. This is a great place to do your people-watching, or to blow that spare cash in your pocket. Apgujeong is where the city's affluent live and shop: on Rodeo Street (as in Los Angeles' Rodeo Drive) are the boutiques of many famous international design houses, as well as a surprisingly large number of Korean designers. The clientele here are worlds apart from the middle-aged *ajumas* found across the river in the traditional markets – the ladies here are carrying Gucci handbags rather than baskets of cabbages.

The area is also known for its nightlife, and for those who feel in need of a kimchi respite, Apgujeong is home to many Western chain restaurants: Outback Steakhouse, Tony Roma's, TGI Friday's and the Seoul Hard Rock Café, to name but a few.

A little east of here (subway line 2; Jamsil Station), but still within Seoul's upscale neighborhoods, is Korea's answer to the American mall – **Lotte World** ⓮ (open daily 9.30am–11pm; entrance fee to amusement park). Actually Lotte World is a mall, entertainment center, amusement park, and sports center all rolled into one. Two Lotte department stores anchor the mall on opposite ends of the complex. There are plenty of independent shops in the basement and adjacent building offering everything from one-of-a-kind dresses to black-market items (purchased on the US military bases and resold at a handsome profit).

One wing of the complex has a sports center complete with an Olympic-size swimming pool. In the center of it all is a huge glass-covered amusement park – Lotte World Adventure – with a bridge leading outdoors to an island ("Magic Island") that looks suspiciously like Disneyland's Fantasyland. There is also a large indoor ice-skating rink, and the equally impressive (in size, at least) Lotte World Folk Museum. Restaurants are on the 11th floor, 3rd floor (the Korean restaurant here gets a lot of good press), and the basement.

By way of variety, a short distance from Lotte World are two areas where you can see tombs that date to the Baekje Kingdom (18 BC–AD 660). The tomb sites (they are large mounds of earth) have been made into attractive parks. It makes an enjoyable trip for hardcore history buffs.

Korean folk performances at the Seoul Nori Madang

Seeming a little incongruous among all the kitsch is the **Seoul Nori Madang** ⓯ (performances on Saturday, Sunday and holidays, Apr–Oct 3–6pm; free), an outdoor amphitheater surrounded by a stone and mud wall – if you ignore the amusement rides twirling around on one side and the hulking Lotte World on the other, it has the feel of a rural Korean village. The surroundings are perfect for the free folk performances held here, and attending one of these provides a rare opportunity to see just how fun-loving Koreans really are (they only look stern!).

Map on page 136

BELOW: ice-skating at Lotte World.

Sculpture at Olympic Park; the park has continued to function as a major venue for sporting events.

BELOW: open-air theater at Seoul Nori Madang.

One of the performances you may see at the Seoul Nori Madang is the Yangju Mask dance. This masked dance-drama was once performed in a small village just north of Uijeongbu. Traditionally, the dances took place during Dano (a spring festival held during the 5th lunar month). This particular folk drama originated in Gyeonggi Province. According to Yangju villagers, about 200 years ago, a troupe from Seoul was invited to perform in Yangju, but broke their engagements several times to perform elsewhere. Instead of enduring more cultural disappointments, the disgruntled villagers took charge and decided to produce their own show and patterned it after the Seoul masked dance-drama. Since then, Yangju's versions have become extremely popular.

Such *Sandae* plays were originally performed only for Joseon-dynasty royalty. Some time around 1634, however, during the reign of Joseon King Injo, this masked dance-drama was discontinued in the court and became entertainment for commoners. To this effect, the entertainment draws heavily from the villagers' perspective of everyday life.

The performance begins with an introductory parade around the amphitheater by the various characters dressed in full costume and dramatic mask (made of paper or gourd). It is a rather colorful and surreal sight to see a monk, a lotus leaf "spirit of heaven," a winking spirit of earth, an acupuncturist, a shaman witch, an aristocrat's concubine, a monkey, a police inspector and 14 other characters (who play some 32 roles using 22 masks) parading around.

A sacrifice to the spirits is conducted shortly after the parade ends at the dance site. Offerings of wine, fruits of three colors, rice cakes (*tteok*), pig's legs, and an ox head are presented and then eaten by the performers – to set them in the right, jolly mood. Then the day's play begins in the open air.

The play satirizes an apostate monk, the *yangban* (aristocrats), corrupt government officials, and other lofty and corrupt people while weaving in contemporary editorial comments. This performance has become a show in which persons and institutions worthy of skewering and grilling are mercilessly roasted with satire that often evokes howls of laughter.

There is also much enthusiastic audience participation. Metal bowls of *makgeolli* rice wine and *tteok* rice cakes are passed around in the audience (who sit in a broad circle around the performers), and when the various characters say something the audience agrees with, the audience calls out, *"Olchi, jalhanda!"* (or "That's right. Well said!").

Ancient and modern

A few subway stops and a short taxi ride from the Lotte World is the **Amsadong Prehistoric Settlement Site** ⓖ (open Tues–Sun 9.30am–6pm, Nov–Feb closes at 5pm), the largest Neolithic site in South Korea. Its former residents lived mainly by hunting and fishing (the site is next to the Han River, though separated by an expressway these days), and some rudimentary farming. Numerous pit-house foundations, pottery chards, and stone tools were found during excavations that began in 1925. This quiet park, on the edge of the city, has an excellent little museum with dioramas, displays of tools, farm implements, and films about Korea's prehistoric past (some displays are in English). On the grounds, nine pithouses have been built to give the visitor an idea of what a village in the Seoul area might have looked like some 8,000 years ago.

Going west from Lotte World is the **Korea World Trade Center** – the center of business for many foreign firms. Several business organizations, including the

Map on page 136

BELOW: the apartment block is home to the majority of Koreans.

Monks at Bongeun-sa; the temple's main hall is known for its murals and is finely crafted both inside and out.

BELOW: the "DDR" ("Dance Dance Revolution") video game is big in Korea.

American, Korean and European Union's Chambers of Commerce are located here. Next door is Seoul's largest convention center, **KOEX** ⑰ (Korea Exhibition Center), which plays host to the annual auto show, travel fair, and other trade shows. Unless you are a businessman, there is probably not much reason to drop by.

If you do find yourself in the area, however, you might want to go to the hill just behind the KOEX, where one of the city's oldest temples is found. **Bongeun-sa** (open daily; 9am–sunset; entrance fee) may not look old (most of the buildings were destroyed during the Korean War, and subsequently rebuilt), but it has been around since AD 794.

Before temples were allowed within the city walls (temples and monks were not allowed within the gates of the city during the Joseon dynasty), this was the largest and most important temple in Seoul. Once the dust settles from all the construction, in and around the temple site, this will be a peaceful retreat for businessmen in need of a short respite from the pressures of making those big deals.

Film and theater

Koreans are avid movie-goers and there are dozens of cinemas (*geukjang*) around the city. Many cinemas show both locally-produced and imported films. Korean films are mostly historical drama or a modern melodrama, although the local film industry is becoming more sophisticated and some films have been lauded at international film festivals). Imports are subtitled American or European films – together with those which originate from Hong Kong's prolific studios.

Seoul also has an active theater scene, with a dozen small theater groups based in the city. The new **Seoul Arts Center** (subway line 3, Nambu Bus Terminal Station, then a ten-minute walk) is a modern building complex south of the Han River. Its location reflects efforts by the city authorities to move many key facilities out of the congested downtown area, and they did it in a big way when they constructed this impressive complex of art and cultural buildings on a picturesque hillside. The Arts Center is now the primary center for Seoul opera (three performance theaters), and hosts big-name international performers and musical companies in the Seoul Concert Hall.

Within the complex are also found an exhibition hall featuring calligraphy (both in Chinese and *Hangeul*), the Seoul Arts library, and the Hangaram Art Gallery that displays exhibitions of Korean and international art works. Outdoor sculptures, a Korean garden and some of Seoul's better restaurants housed in tent structures top it all off.

Adjacent to the Arts Center is **The National Center for Korean Traditional Performing Arts** , where the tradition of Korean court music and dance is kept alive. There are regular performances here on Saturdays (5–6.20pm) that are always popular with tourists.

If you do go to one of the Saturday concerts, get there early and visit the museum next door, which exhibits some odd-looking Korean instruments. On special occasions the courtyard in front of the concert hall is given over to traditional Korean games. Parents join their children in a noisy mêlée of activities including the lively Korean version of the see-saw *(neolttwigi)* which involves jumping onto the plank, a game of tossing arrows into a narrow metal vase *(tuho)*, and large group games such as tug-of-war *(juldarigi)*. ❑

Map on page 136

TIP

Tipping is not expected in Korea. Even taxi drivers give change. You don't need to tip in the luxury hotels, either, though a service charge is often added to your bill in restaurants and bars.

BELOW: traditional dance at the Sejong Center for the Performing Arts.

THE MUSIC LOVERS

Music fans can have their fill in Seoul. Today's typical Korean likes Occidental music the most, whether his tastes are classical or popular. Korean preference in Western classical music tends to the tried and true – Beethoven, Brahms, Tchaikovsky – and opera. Someone once said that the country appears to be made up of thousands of aspiring Italian tenors.

Koreans are very often splendid musicians, as the international successes of such people as concert violinists Chung Kyungwha and Kim Younguk or H.O.T., a pop vocal group, attest. Concert-goers will pay high prices to hear these artists or touring foreign performers but tend to neglect the talent of local performers – except for Korean pop singers who are popular among the young.

Korean traditional folk music is lively, energetic and emotional. The Westerner may consider it to be out of tune and dissonant at first, but the more one listens the more one appreciates its complexity and order.

Musical artists can perform in one of three luxurious concert and theater halls: the National Theater of Korea on the slopes of Namsan, the Sejong Center for the Performing Arts opposite the American Embassy on Sejongno, or the new Seoul Arts Center in Seochu, south of the river.

GYEONGGI PROVINCE SOUTH

Ancient castles, massive mounded tombs, seductive pine glens and moon-watching pavilions pop up like apparitions at improbable bends on southern Gyeonggi's country roads

Map on page 150

Seoul

In contrast to those areas north of Seoul, where development has been hindered by rugged terrain and the close proximity of the DMZ, the area to the immediate south and west of the capital is one of the fastest growing regions in South Korea. Seoul's urban sprawl extends south into the "new cities" of Gwacheon and Bundang, which were nothing more than farmers' fields 20 years ago, but now have row, after row, after row, of apartments housing Seoul's young middle class. Even faraway Suwon and Incheon, by reason of accessibility (both are tied into the Seoul subway system), are like part of the Seoul metropolitan area. You have to venture to the southern and eastern fringes of Gyeonggi Province to escape the tentacles of urbanization.

Despite the inexorable spread of the city, the area has much to offer the visitor. There are royal tombs, mountain fortresses, peaceful temples and one of Korea's best folk villages, and it is still easy to get away from the urban centers and out into the countryside. There are also several amusement parks around the province. All of this is within easy striking distance of the capital. When you finally tire of hectic days in Seoul, take a day off and see what the southern end of the province has to offer.

LEFT: section of wall at Namhansanseong (South Han Mountain Fortress)
BELOW: at a wedding ceremony, Korean Folk Village, Suwon.

Royal tombs and historic battlements

The **Heoninneung Royal Tombs ❶** (open Tues–Sun 9am–6pm, Nov–Feb closes at 5pm; entrance fee), of the 3rd and 24th Joseon kings lie in the southeast outskirts of Seoul in Naegokdong, and are near a green belt area where a variety of crops such as melons, strawberries, eggplant, peppers, corn and rice are cultivated. In late spring, summer and autumn, shady fruit stands are set up in fields so people can sit and enjoy refreshing breezes, sunshine and fresh-from-the-earth fruit before hiking up to the nearby **Heonneung**, the tombs of King Taejong (1367–1422) and Queen Wongyong (1364–1420), and **Inneung**, the tombs of King Sunjo (1790–1834) and Queen Sunwon (1789–1837). All the tombs are guarded by granite statues and by fantastic animal sentries. If you are in Korea on May 8, you may want to attend a *jesa* (ancestor worship) ceremony conducted annually at Heoninneung by Joseon-dynasty descendants.

The grounds at Heoninneung are well manicured, and the area's classical tomb settings make this a popular area for filming historical movies. There are several ways to get to the royal tombs, but perhaps the best is to take bus No 36 from the express bus terminal in Gangnam, in southern Seoul (subway line 3; Express Bus Terminal Station).

You may have noticed that Korea does not have many Western-style parks. Instead, on warm days

families pack a lunch and head for a nearby palace, royal tomb or temple for a day of sunshine and fun. **Namhansanseong** (South Han Mountain Fortress) **❷** (open daily Apr–Oct 7am–8pm, Nov–Mar 9am–6pm; entrance fee), is one such popular weekend picnic and hiking area about 30km (18 miles) southeast of Seoul proper. This grand highland redoubt – with 8km (5 miles) of stone walls – was originally built about 2,000 years ago during Korea's Goguryeo dynasty. Most of the fort's now-visible structures, however, date from the 17th and 18th centuries, when the fortress served Joseon kings of that period as a retreat from invading armies. Like Bukhansan Fortress to the north of Seoul *(see page 162)*, Namhansan is a mountain fortification surrounding a valley.

The fortress once had four main gates (only the west gate survives intact), three command posts, and a few watchtowers. Inside the walls were a palace (retreating royalty had to stay somewhere!), military buildings, warehouses for food and arms, and seven temples (home to warrior monks, dedicated to defending the crown; one temple remains). Unfortunately, this elaborate

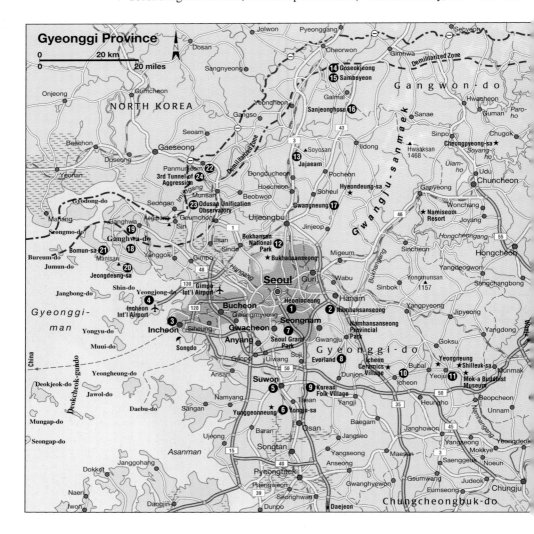

Map
on page
150

fortress was not able to save the king from the onslaught of the Manchus.

In 1636, King Injo, the 16th Joseon monarch, retreated to Namhansanseong on the heels of a Manchurian invasion force. Everything seemed to go wrong for the king. There were inadequate supplies in the fortress, reinforcements did not come on time, and worse, his family was captured. Left with few options, the king surrendered himself, along with some 14,000 of his men, and, in the end, Korea to the Manchurians. After subduing the Koreans, the Manchus then turned to their final objective: the conquest of China.

This spectacular place makes a cool escape on hot summer days, or a pleasant picnic outing on one of Korea's beautiful late autumn days. If you have the energy, you can walk the entire length of the wall, or take a short walk alongside it looking at the remains of the buildings (and a few that have been rebuilt) within the walls. To get to Namhansanseong you can take subway line 8 to Namhansanseong Station, from where it is a short taxi ride to the fortification; alternatively take a direct bus (80 minutes) from Dong Seoul Bus Terminal (subway line 2; Gangbyeon Station).

Incheon – Korea's transportation hub

Around 40 km (25 miles) to the west of Seoul is the city of **Incheon ❸**. Until the 1880s, Incheon was a fishing village called Jemulpo, and for a long time was the only place in Korea foreigners were allowed to visit. Today, it has been transformed into a booming harbor and Korea's fourth largest city. The number of trading ships calling at Incheon has increased with every passing year, and consequently, the stretch between Seoul proper and the Port of Incheon has become the most important sea, road and rail supply route in Korea.

BELOW: enjoying the late autumn sun.

With the opening of the **Incheon International Airport (IIA) ❹** in 2001, the city has become Korea's most important hub for both shipping and air transportation. The new airport sits on reclaimed tidal flats lying between two offshore islands. The construction effort was enormous, beginning back in 1992 and costing more than US$6 billion. The new site replaces the aging Gimpo Airport, which is now used for domestic flights only. The two airports give Korea the best airline transportation facilities in northeast Asia. The new airport currently has two runways (a third is under construction), and handles over 20 million passengers every year. By 2020 there will be four runways dealing with an anticipated 100 million passengers.

Besides the airport facilities, parks have been created (the new airport is quite proud of its environmental record, though this seems a bit misplaced when you consider the massive environmental impact of turning a large area of tidal flats and a few quiet islands into an international transportation hub), and there is an expressway connecting the airport to the Seoul urban area. Adjacent to the airport is an international business center, complete with luxury hotels and high-rise office blocks.

History in Incheon

Incheon is best known as the place where US General Douglas MacArthur directed a brilliant amphibious

The statue of Douglas MacArthur at Freedom Hill, Incheon.

BELOW:
the memorial at Freedom Hill commemorates the turning point of the Korean War.

landing, thus turning the bitter Korean War around for southern Korea and its allies. That landing, code-named Operation Chromite, began at dawn on September 15 1950. Historian David Rees writes in his book *Korea: The Limited War*, that "the successive objectives of the operation called for the neutralization of **Wolmido**, the island controlling Incheon harbor, a landing in the city, seizure of Gimpo Airfield, and the capture of Seoul." Despite fierce objections from his subordinates, MacArthur's strategy proved to have the winning element of surprise.

On D-Day, the 5th Marines poured ashore at Incheon, as Rees writes, "to meet only scattered shots. The flag was raised on **Radio Hill**, dominating Incheon harbor at 0655, and the whole of this 105-meter (114-yd) high feature which had caused the planners so much worry was taken by 0800." US Marines began a bloody advance towards Seoul and, after 12 more days of hellish fighting, took that devastated capital. Today, Radio Hill is known as **Freedom Hill** and looms over an earnest seaport bustling with international trade. Atop the hill, jaunty in sculpted khakis, you will find a 10-meter (32-ft) statue of General MacArthur, gripping a pair of binoculars in his right hand.

The best way to get to Freedom Hill is to take the Seoul Subway train due west through alternating industrial suburbs and rice fields. Once you arrive at **Dongincheon Station**, take a cab or hike up to Freedom Hill above this town of steep streets and endless ocean terminals. The ocean view from up here is overtly industrial, but the sea breezes are crisp, and besides the MacArthur statue you will find a whitewashed replica of America's Statue of Liberty. There is also a pavilion from where you may see a spectacular red fireball sun dropping through container cranes and ships' riggings into an amber ocean.

The walk down from Freedom Hill through old Incheon is a pleasant one,

down cobble- and flag-stoned byways and stairs, past some of Korea's most distinctive verandahs and storefronts. There are several deluxe-priced hotels in Incheon, although if your budget leans towards a more authentic Korean experience, there are numerous *yeogwan* inns to choose from.

Popular nearby diversions include seafood dining on one of the area's land-linked islands, either **Wolmido** (**Moon Tail Island**) or **Sowolmido**. Both sides are famous for their gourmet plates of raw fish and other delicacies from the deep. During the summer, various offshore islands become favored Korean resort destinations. On these islands, you can tan on the white-sand beaches or wallow in lovely manmade lagoons rimmed by colorful cabanas. There are several smaller resort hotels in this area, particularly near big **Songdo Beach** south of the city. For all sorts of sealife, visit the big public seafood market on the southern side of Incheon's tidal basin. Ask for the *Yeonan Budu Eosijang* (fish market) and any *ajumeoni* (housewife) will direct you to this massive covered market next to a sheltered harbor full of fishing trawlers. A local bus service operates from downtown Incheon near the **Olympos Hotel** to the marketplace.

City of strawberries

Suwon ❺, the capital of Gyeonggi Province, is an old fortress-city 51 km (31 miles) south of Seoul. Suwon's name, which means "water-source" or "water-field," derives from its location in an area which was traditionally known for its fine artesian wells.

These days, the city is renowned for its restored castle walls and its *galbi*, or barbecued short ribs. However it's the late spring and summer strawberries (*ttalgi*) that come to most Korean minds when you mention the word Suwon.

Map on page 150

TIP

The best starting point for a visit to Suwon's Hwaseong Fortress is Nammun (Paldalmun), the historic South Gate that sits in the middle of the city's busiest intersection. It's also the best place to find food and lodgings.

BELOW: Incheon still has an important fishing industry.

The 18th-century fortifications at Hwaseong Fortress, Suwon.

BELOW: ubiquitous apartment complexes.

The city can be quickly and easily reached on subway line 1 from Seoul Station to its terminus at Suwon Station. Better yet, take the faster, more comfortable (and more expensive) train from Seoul to Suwon station. Suwon has benefitted greatly from being one of the ten Korean cities chosen as a venue for the 2002 soccer World Cup.

Hwaseong Fortress

The main sight in Suwon is the **Hwaseong Fortress**, with its massive walls, gates, and other historic architectural facilities which meander for 5.5 km (3½ miles) around the old city proper. Construction began during the reign of King Jeongjo (1776–1800), the 22nd Joseon monarch, who established the fortress in memory of his father, Prince Sado *(see page 156)*. The whole complex is an integral part of the city, so there are no opening or closing times or gates to enter.

Historians believe that Jeongjo wanted to move the Korean capital from Seoul to Suwon, but because of various personal and political problems he was never able to realise his ambition. He did, however, create a beautiful fortified city – complete with parapets and embrasures, floodgates, observation platforms and domes, parade grounds, command bunkers, cannon stands and an archery range. Jeongjo's original fortress, known as the "Flower Fortress," was already in a decrepit state when it was heavily damaged by bombing during the Korean War. In 1975 the Korean government undertook a major restoration; the project took four years and cost several million dollars.

The impressive refurbished walls (which average nine metres, or 30 feet, in height) and other structures still look a tad too new, but even so they are an

HIGH-RISE LIVING

You can't miss them – wherever you look you see clusters of high-rise apartments. They appear to be the most impersonal and, yes, even dehumanizing of human dwellings and are a universal turn-off for Westerners. Indeed, the fact that these concrete blocks are taking over the countryside gives even the most avid apologist pause. But there is an obvious reason why construction companies can't build them fast enough – they are popular with Koreans. As Koreans so rightly point out: this is a small (and mostly mountainous) country with over 48 million people. Translated, that means these apartments make good sense. And they really aren't so bad, especially when one considers the drafty, uncomfortable country homes that many of the apartment dwellers grew up in. The high-rise offers relatively spacious living, with hot water, an indoor toilet (which many country homes don't have), a place to park that new Hyundai, and 24-hour security. They are comfortable and modern, offering an improved lifestyle, and though they seem impersonal, the apartments are little villages, with an activity room for seniors, playgrounds and kindergartens for children, and informal clubs where housewives can socialize. So, when you see those slabs of concrete, try to look at them from a Korean's point of view.

irresistible invitation to a city stroll. One particularly lovely spot near the North Gate, Janganmun, is a strikingly landscaped reflecting pond, Yongyeon, which sits below an octagonal moon-watching pavilion called Banghwasuryujeong.

This meditative spot was commissioned by the aesthetically inclined King Jeongjo when he initiated his Suwon fortress-city master plan in 1794. These days it's a gem of a place much favored by neighborhood *harabeoji* (grandfathers), who sit inside its gabled cupola, lighting long-stemmed pipes, drinking sweet rice wine, and bouncing patriarchal thoughts off nearby castle walls. The whole classical effect is officially labeled "The Northern Turret."

The Hwaseong Cultural Festival, held every year in early October in Suwon, features music, theater, dance and exhibitions, as well as memorial services for King Jeongjo and his unfortunate father.

If, after a hike around the "Flower Fortress", you crave fresh strawberries and cool wine, take a bus or taxi to the Agricultural Green Belt area in Suwon's western suburbs near the modern Agricultural College of Seoul National University. There you can eat heaps of sweet grapes and blood-red strawberries at parasol-shaded tables next to the patches and vineyards from where they came, before visiting one of the other Suwon area sites.

Dragon Jewel Temple

Yongju-sa ❻ is a Buddhist temple which, like the Suwon fortress, was built by King Jeongjo in his father's memory. Yongju-sa, "The Dragon Jewel," rests in a rural, piney area about a 20-minute bus ride south of Suwon's mid-town South Gate. Built in 1790 on the site of an earlier Silla-dynasty temple (dating from 856), Yongju-sa's grounds boast a seven-story stone pagoda, a 1,500 kg

Map on page 150

BELOW: Hwaseong Fortress has tremendous views over the surrounding countryside.

(3,300 lb) Goryeo-era brass bell, and in its main hall, a superb Buddhist painting by the Joseon-genre master Danwon Kim Hongdo.

Yongju-sa is a popular place to visit at the time of Buddha's birthday (on the 8th day of the 4th lunar month, usually in late April), when pilgrims from afar arrive here bearing candle-lit paper lanterns and prayers for good fortune.

Tomb of the "Rice Box Prince"

In an appropriately serene setting 20-minutes' walk west of Yongju-sa are the mounded tombs, **Yunggeonneung**, (open Tues–Sun 9am–6.30pm, Nov–Feb closes at 5.30pm; entrance fee) of King Jeongjo and his father, Prince Sado. Jeongjo posthumously awarded his father the title "King Jangjo," and father and son were laid to rest here together.

Jeongjo's grandfather and Sado's father, King Yeongjo (reigned 1724–76), was convinced that his son was attempting to overthrow him, and ordered him to be locked in a rice box until death. He was initially buried in a rather inauspicious location, but when his son became king he had his father reinterred in what was believed to be the best tomb site in the realm.

The location of this tomb, just outside of Suwon, is a fair distance from Seoul, especially when one considers all the hoopla that went on when the king left the safe confines of the palace grounds. Twice a year the king was required to make the journey to pay respects to his unfortunate father's spirit. Each visit took several days and thousands of people to accomplish – it even required a separate palace and the most modern (for the 18th century) of fortifications to protect it all. Thanks to that son's devotion, the fortification at Suwon really is the gem in the crown of Korea's distinguished history of

BELOW: lanterns at Yongju-sa temple.

fortress-building. In 1997, Hwaseong was given the acclaim it deserves when it was designated as a UNESCO World Heritage Site.

Map on page 150

On the lighter side

Nearer Seoul, set in the hills southwest of the city by the satellite city of Gwacheon, is **Seoul Grand Park** ❼ (open daily 9am–6pm, closes Apr and Sept at 7pm, May 8pm, June 9pm, July–Aug 10pm). With a zoo (which features a dolphin show; entrance fee), botanic garden, the **Seoul Land** amusement park (open daily 9.30am–9pm, Sept–Apr closes at 7pm, later on weekends and holidays; entrance fee), the Seoul Horse Race Track (racing weekends 10.30am–5.30pm), and the **National Museum of Contemporary Art** (open Tues–Sun 10am–6pm, Nov–Feb closes at 5pm; free), there is something for everyone. Be prepared for a lot of walking and possible traffic-jams; less so if you go on a weekday. Plan an entire day at the Grand Park; there is a lot to do here, especially if you have children. From the center of Seoul, it takes about a half-hour to get to Seoul Grand Park Station on subway line 4.

The South Korean flag is full of symbolism.

An African safari, American zoo, and Korean amusement park come improbably together at **Everland** ❽ (open daily 9.30am–10pm; entrance fee), a recreation complex on the north side of National Highway 4, 35 km (22 miles) southeast of Seoul. Among its popular attractions are a Korean-style lion safari park, Korea's only pair of pandas (a gift from China after diplomatic relations were established), and a hair-raising 1,000-meter (3,300-ft) jet coaster ride. The **Caribbean Bay** waterpark is a refreshing option on those oppressively humid summer days. Amusement parks are a favorite with Koreans, and if you stay in Korea for any length of time, you're sure to be asked to accompany your Korean friends to one.

BELOW: weaving demonstration at the Korean Folk Village.

Not far from Everland is the **Ho Am Art Museum** (open Tues–Sun 10am–6pm; entrance fee), one of Korea's finest private museums (owned by Samsung, as is Everland). The museum's permanent collection features early devotional art, and, incredibly, 91 of the pieces have been designated as national treasures (the oldest temples can usually claim only a few national treasures). To enter the museum grounds, you pass through a delightful traditional garden, complete with pond and bamboo stand. There are regular shuttle buses operating between Everland and the Ho Am Art Museum.

The Korean Folk Village

The **Korean Folk Village** ❾ (open daily 9am–5.30pm; entrance fee) is best visited as a day trip from Seoul, being located 45 km (28 miles) south of the capital, close to the city of Suwon. Allow several hours to take in the 240 homes, shops and other attractions in authentically reproduced Joseon-dynasty villages from the various regions of Korea. In fact, many of the old buildings here are the real thing, having been transported to the Folk Village from the countryside.

Visit the wide variety of ceramic and bamboo shops, drink rice wines in a wayside tavern, then join the staged wedding procession of a traditionally

Traditional food can be enjoyed al fresco *at the Korean Folk Village.*

BELOW: stylized "spirit-post" guardian, Korean Folk Village.

costumed bride and groom who are transported via palanquin, trailed by a colorful, whirling farmers' dance band.

Skilled silk-weavers, basket-makers, fan-makers, mulberry paper-makers and other skilled craftsmen carry on traditional crafts that have mostly disappeared from the countryside. Even in an entire day, you may not be able to view all the fascinating exhibits in this sprawling museum. The overall effect is memorable, although less so at weekends when things can get crowded. Direct buses leave from the Suwon Railway/Subway Station every hour.

Shopping for pots

The soulful pottery kilns of two of Korea's finest potters are located approximately 70 km (43 miles) southeast of Seoul near **Icheon ⑩** (a short distance north of National Highway 4). With just the right amounts of clay for the post and trees to fire up the kilns, Icheon has been Korea's most important center of ceramic production for over 600 years. Today, the area has 80 kilns firing pots, and dozens of shops and showrooms exhibiting the work of local artists.

At the Icheon Ceramics Village, 4 km (2½ miles) northwest of Icheon at the village of Seokgwangni, it is possible to observe Goryeo celadons being created by ceramics master Yu Geunhyong, and marvel at Ahn Dongo's Joseon-dynasty whiteware as they are pulled hot from his traditional kilns. These gentlemen's fine work can be purchased on the spot or in prominent ceramic art galleries in Seoul. At the other end of the potting spectrum, you will find, here and there in the great Icheon area, row upon row of the ubiquitous shiny, brown, tall and oblong *gimchi* pots. These utilitarian wares are hand-thrown and fired in adobe huts.

Icheon and nearby Yeoju *(see below)* are both good places to shop for ceramics, since prices here are usually lower than in Seoul. You can still pay hundreds or even thousands for pieces from famous artists, though. On the other hand, an attractive Korean tea service can be purchased for less than US$50.

King Sejong's tomb

On the eastern edge of Gyeonggi Province is the modern city of **Yeoju ⓫**, with three or four attractions that might entice one to linger for a few hours before continuing on your way to the natural wonders of Seoraksan National Park *(see page 186)* and the east coast. About 3 km (2 miles) northwest of the city is **Yeongneung** (open Tues–Sun 9am–6pm, Nov–Mar closes at 5pm; entrance fee), the tomb of Korea's renowned and beloved King Sejong (reigned 1418–50). Entering through a forest of twisted trees, you walk past the small shrine and climb the brick walkway to the edge of the tomb. As you get closer, soldiers, scholars and horses – life-size statutes that adorn tomb sites of important officials, and were once thought to have protected and accompanied the spirit on its journey – surround the tomb. The tomb is not a massive mound of earth, like those of ancient royalty in Gyeongju, but still is appropriately sized, on a pleasant forested hillside. From here there is an excellent view of the surrounding countryside.

Far below is a museum filled with displays describing the life of this king that embraced the new ideas entering Korea from east and west. Outside, and scattered around the grounds, are examples of the devices he had a hand in developing – water clocks, sundials, rain gauges and other scientific inventions. Yeongneung is a popular field trip for Korean schoolchildren, and an overlooked but deserving site for foreign visitors. If, after paying your respects to King Sejong, you still have time, you might want to visit **Silleuk-sa Temple** (open daily; Apr–Oct 6am–8pm, Nov–Mar 7am–7pm; entrance fee) beside the Namhangang River. Established in AD 580 by Wonhyo, a celebrated Silla monk, the temple is one of the most important in the province. It is somewhat unique in that it is located by a river rather than in the mountains, as were most temples from this period. On the other hand, its location by the river is rather pleasing, backed by hills and surrounded by a deciduous forest.

The **Mak-a Buddhist Museum** (open daily; Apr–Oct 9am–6pm, Nov–Mar 9.30am–5pm; entrance fee), located on the eastern edge of the city, is one more site which might interest the curious. It is an eclectic display of outdoor sculptures, and devotional art in an indoor museum that will leave you wondering if you have just had a spiritual experience or witnessed one of the tackiest religious displays in Korea. A teahouse on the grounds will give you the time to contemplate your response. As you pass through town, you will notice several pottery shops. While not as important a center for pottery as Icheon, Yeoju has many fine potters and a long tradition of ceramic production. As in Icheon, the prices here are likely to be more favorable than those you'll find in Seoul. ❑

Map on page 150

BELOW: King Sejong's tomb at Yeongneung.

GYEONGGI PROVINCE NORTH

The area north of Seoul is unique: where else has a highly fortified border, seemingly on the verge of full-scale war, been turned into a tourist attraction?

Map on page 150

Beyond Seoul are numerous day outings where one can get away from the hustle and bustle of urban life, all within easy reach of the sprawling city. Do as Koreans do: simply follow your nose until it leads you to a stream filled with plum blossoms, or a meadow bursting with pink cosmos blossoms. The following trips north of Seoul are a sample of the enjoyable and interesting excursions recommended as worth your time.

Plum blossoms in the snow

Visitors and Seoulites alike are often told that they should spend at least one late winter day in the area north of Seoul. This region is dubbed by some as the "Realm of the Immortals." If possible, try to go when plum blossoms – the year's first flowers – begin to bloom in snow-dusted forests and ravines. It is, after all, what the ancients advise: "Do as amused immortals do: whenever the boredom and frustration of a long winter indoors becomes too much for them, they put on their cape and hat, tell the attendant to saddle the donkey, and go out in the snow looking for plum blossoms."

This "immortal" journey will take you on Highway 43 north of Seoul between two popular hiking mountains: **Dobongsan** and **Suraksan**. Dobongsan, the rocky, harsh-looking mountain on the west side of the road, is said to represent the male gender, while the curved and flowing Suraksan on the east side is supposed to personify the female qualities.

Dobongsan, (740 meters/2,428 ft), is one of several pleasant peaks just a few miles north of downtown Seoul. The hike to the summit takes several hours. You may want to linger en route next to a clear stream, or, if you are a camera buff, photograph the many odd rock formations; or you may wish to trek along one of the meandering paths leading to the picturesque Buddhist temples of Mangwol, Cheonchuk, and Hweryong.

Dobongsan lies within one of Korea's 20 national parks – **Bukhansan National Park** ⓬. Further south from Dobongsan there is a triad of granite mountains, Samgaksan (triangle peaks) which is better known as Bukhansan. The tallest of these, at 837 meters (2,746 ft), is Baegundae, from whose ridges you can catch some great views of Seoul. Another peak, Insubong (812 metres/2,664 feet), has a sheer granite face that many have compared to the better known El Capitan in California's Yosemite National Park. Like its California counterpart, Insubong is popular with technical climbers. Bukhansan National Park is a legitimate alpine environment, even if it is surrounded by a sea of concrete apartment buildings, so if you decide to do some hiking, take plenty of water and warm clothes.

LEFT: a walk in the woods. **BELOW:** American sentries at the DMZ.

The rocky peaks of Bukhansan National Park are easily reached from Seoul, and are very popular for weekend hikes.

BELOW: glorious scenery at Bukhansan.

A king's last resort

Besides its natural beauty, Bukhansan National Park also has historic **Bukhansanseong** (North Han Mountain Fortress), one of two major ancient fortresses in the Seoul area – the other being Namhansanseong, to the south of the capital *(see page 150)* – built to defend the royal family against attacking hordes of Manchus and Mongolians when all other defenses had failed. This historical fortress is similar in design and setting to its southern counterpart, and is located above the sprawling northeast suburbs of Seoul along the rocky high ridges of Bukhansan mountain.

Bukhansanseong was originally constructed during the early Baekje period and at various times fell into martial disuse. Following sustained attacks during the 17th century by armies of Qing-dynasty (led by Manchurians) China, the Joseon King Sukjong refurbished its battlements. During that era, the fortification had 13 gates, three command posts, a palace and warehouses within its walls. The walls and buildings were almost completely destroyed during the Korean War, but have since been partially restored to honor their historic importance. Today, you can walk along most of the 8 km (5miles) of wall and see the west gate, and view what remains of the palace and warehouses within the walls. A neat village has grown alongside a stream in the crater-like center of the fortress, and meadows and small forests on its less-populated fringes are favored picnic sites.

Being so close to Seoul, this park is immensely popular for both hikers and picnickers, and the most popular trails and riverside picnicking areas are quite crowded on weekends. Access from Seoul is easy; take line 4 on the subway to Suyu Station, or to Dobongsan Station for the northern part of the park.

A temple, waterfalls, and a feisty carp

Traveling further north, the terrain becomes wilder, with impressive canyons and ravines. Beyond **Dongducheon**, turn at the highway into the **Soyosan Mountains** and make the short hike to **Jajaeam Temple** ⑬ (open daily 9am–sunset; entrance fee), a place famed as the testing ground for a monk's celibacy. Ornately carved dragons snarl out from this quaint temple's eaves. Inside, you will find a pair of tempestuous carved dragons writhing on the ceiling. A spouting waterfall and narrow gorge with a stream complement this little canyon.

An even more dramatic waterfall and river scene is located much further north in the **Sincheorwon** area. Be aware that, because there are several military checkpoints in this area close to the 38th parallel, it is recommended that foreign visitors join a tour if possible (check with the KNTO in Seoul). A massive granite boulder, **Goseokjeong** ⑭, nicknamed "The Lonely Rock", sits in the Hantangang River and invites clambering up to its pine-studded brow. Legend says that this rock rolled in from the east coast and decided to rest at this lovely turn in the fast-flowing river. A pleasure pavilion overlooks the rock and the river's noisy rapids, and local boatmen may be hired for a ride through the narrow river canyons that jut to the north. It is also the most popular rafting spot near Seoul.

Due south of the Lonely Rock – in a deep canyon and off a steep dirt road – is the little-known **Sambuyeon** ⑮ or "Dragon Waterfall". You'll probably see local villagers fishing for carp in pools above the falls. This is an appropriate pastime, because in these parts – and in oriental mythology in general – the carp and the dragon are distant and legendary relatives. A famous story in national lore tells about a carp (regarded by Koreans as a symbol of strength and

Map on page 150

TIP

You can easily access Suraksan from Seoul by taking subway line 4 to its terminus at Danggogae Station, or line 7 to Suraksan Station.

BELOW: hiking in the Soyosan Mountains.

perseverance) that persistently tried to climb up this strong waterfall. On the 100th day of his attempt, this feisty carp succeeded (with the help of the gods) to scale Sambuyeon, and as a reward he was magically turned into a powerful dragon. These falls, however, are rather easy to climb (a well-trodden path runs through a stone tunnel to the right side of the falls); and, of course, there is little worry of being turned into a dragon at the top.

On your return journey to Seoul, you may want to stop off at **Sanjeonghosu Lake** ⑯, an artificial lake built by Japanese engineers during Japan's colonial occupation of Korea. This is a popular skating spot in wintertime, and for most of the year it's a splendid area for hiking (there are numerous hiking trails in the woods around the lake), boating and relaxation. Look out for the large colorful tents which serve as dance halls.

A short detour from the main road leading back to the capital leads to the impressive Confucian-style burial tombs of King Sejo (1456–1468), the 7th Joseon king, and his wife, Queen Yun Jeonghi. Known as **Gwangneung** ⑰ (open Tues–Sun 9.30am–5.30pm, Nov–Mar closes at 4.30pm; entrance fee), these are probably the most idyllically located tombs in the Seoul area, hidden in the midst of a beautiful forest of old trees which shade melodious, trickling streams and wide greens ideal for picnicking. The surrounding woodland is very popular with birdwatchers, being a prime habitat for Tristram's woodpeckers and other rare species.

Close by Sejo's tomb is a small temple, Bongseon-sa, with a 2.6-meter (8½-ft) bell, the third-largest in Korea. Gwangnung is located 28 km (17 miles) northeast of the capital and just past **Uijeongbu**, a satellite city of Seoul, with a military camp made famous in the American movie and television series *M*A*S*H*.

BELOW: Christian kitsch at Uijeongbu.

Ganghwa-do, island of refuge

Ganghwa-do ⑱, an island 50 km (31 miles) northwest of Seoul across the narrow Yeomha Strait, is steeped in history. To get there, catch an express bus at Seoul's Sinchon bus terminal; the journey takes approximately 90 minutes. **Ganghwa town** ⑲ is small and easy-going, ideal for tourists to walk around its marketplaces and handicraft shops. Korea's finest rushcraft weaving is meticulously created on the island, so in local shops you'll find numerous baskets of all kinds. You can also see fine floor mats and doorway hangings that are woven so perfectly they let summer breezes in while filtering out pesky warm-weather mosquitos. Another kind of weaving – silkweaving – is also a specialty of this town – you can hear the sound of machines clacking out reams of silk as you walk along Ganghwa's streets and footpaths.

Take a car ride to the silk factory (off the main street on the road opposite the bridge fronting the marketplace). Since visitors are no longer allowed inside for tours, take a long look instead at a **bronze bell** hanging idly inside a small slatted pavilion next to the factory. Cast during King Sukjong's reign (1674–1720), this bell used to toll at 4am to signal the opening of Ganghwa's city gates. When French troops stormed the city in 1866 to seek revenge for the execution of several French Roman Catholic priests, they attempted to haul this 3,864kg (8,520lb) bell to their ship, but abandoned their efforts because it was too heavy. At the top of this same road is the restored **Goryeo Palace** where King Gojong lived in retreat during his unsuccessful 29-year resistance against invading Mongol hordes in the mid-1200s.

From the Goryeo palace, take a taxi up to the neatly restored North Gate, **Bungmun**, for a view of the distant blue mountains of North Korea. On a clear

Ganghwa-do is one of Korea's main ginseng-growing areas.

BELOW: on board the Ganghwa–Seongmo ferry.

day you can see for several miles across the Imjin estuary and into the forbidden and communist north. The most dramatic view of North Korea, however, is from **Aegibong Peak** (open daily 9am–5pm). Once off-limits, except in December when church groups were able to hold Christmas services at the "Christmas Tree," a pylon decked in colored lights, the peak is now open to civilians. You have to show your ID and fill in a form at a checkpoint before you get there, a reminder that you are at the frontline. It is said that this is the only place in South Korea where you can actually observe villages in the North with the naked eye. Note the brush cleared away from the hillside underneath the North Korean checkpoint (denying cover for southern infiltrators?).

Your next stop should be Korea's oldest and most unusual Episcopal Church, **Gamdeok Gyohoe**. This Christian structure, built in 1900 by Bishop Charles Cort, about 10 years after his arrival in Korea, harmoniously combines Christian, Taoist and Buddhist elements in its overall design.

The front gate of the church is decorated with a large paisleyed Taoist symbol; the church, constructed of wood, is classically Korean in its interior and exterior architecture; a bodhi tree, an old Buddhism-related symbol, was planted in the church's main courtyard at the time of the church's dedication; and atop the roof is a Christian cross trimmed with fluorescent light bulbs which show visitors the way at night.

After seeing this eclectic site, catch a bus at the main terminal and head northwest of Ganghwa town to one of the most mysterious sculptures in Korea, the **Prehistoric Dolmen**. The scenery along this roadway is dominated mostly by fields of ginseng protected by low thatched lean-tos, and typical Ganghwa farmhouses and silos decorated with contemporary folk art. This art is in the form of

BELOW: the Ganghwa Jiseongmyo Dolmen dates back to Neolithic times.

KOREAN DOLMEN

The dolmen on Ganghwa Island are the best known in Korea, but dolmen are found throughout the country. Apparently they protected the burial sites of important people. They would have to have been important, because the size of the rocks would require a significant labor force to put them in place.

There have been both stone tools and a few bronze items discovered in and around the dolmen, though archeologists generally associate the dolmen with the Korean Bronze Age (circa 900–400 BC).

The dolmen found in Korea are of three types. Those on Ganghwa are typical of the Northern Style (sometimes called the Table Style) and have large upright stones in a rough square, covered by a flat capstone.

The Southern Style (found south of the Han River) has a large boulder as a capstone placed atop smaller stones.

The third type of dolmen simply has a large capstone laid over the burial site.

Stone dolmen are not just a Korean phenomenon; they are found throughout central Asia and western Europe. It is rather intriguing to think that Korean dolmen are exactly like those found in Ireland, some 9,600 km (6,000 miles) to the west.

meticulous sheet-metal sculpture attached at the upturns of eaves and along the edge of corrugated metal roofs. Here and there you will see brilliantly painted sheet-metal cranes, lotus blossoms, airplanes and other such symbolic and surrealistic roofcraft.

About 3 km (2 miles) from town, down a dirt path behind a chicken farm, stands a primitive stone structure constructed of three large, flat boulders. Known as the **Ganghwa Jiseongmyo Dolmen**, archaeologists have identified this ancient monument as a Northern-style dolmen (in Korean *goindol* – a sacred tomb or altar) which dates back to Neolithic times. Life goes on around these huge stones, as they stand undisturbed in the midst of peppers, tobacco and ginseng.

Pagodas and panoramas

Further down the bus line, in Hajeommyeon, there is another old but less-visited stone sculpture. It is a five-story pagoda, *seoktap*, that was once a part of a Goryeo temple. The temple is gone but the pagoda stands hidden in the pine forest. If you do seek out the pagoda, which is about a mile's walk from the main road past farmhouses, you might also wish to scale **Bongcheonsan**, the high hill behind it. Hikers are promised a panoramic view of the Imjin Estuary and an opportunity to stomp around the ruins of an old stone beacon tower. This tower supported one of 696 beacon fires lit during the Joseon dynasty to relay national security messages to Seoul. It was rendered obsolete when the telegraph was introduced in 1894.

Now travel back in time to the Three Kingdoms Period. On the southern end of Ganghwado (take a bus to Onsuri from town), about 16 km (10 miles) south of Ganghwa town, is one of the oldest temples in Korea, **Jeondeung-sa ⑳**, the "Temple of the Inherited Lamp". A Goryeo queen named Jeondeung-sa after a jade lamp presented to the temple. Formerly called Jinjong-sa, it was built in AD 381 by a famous monk named Ado. Legend has it that the wall surrounding the temple was constructed by three princes to fortify the monastery. Thus the fortress was named Samnangseong, or the "Castle of Three Flowers of Youth".

The friendly monks here may invite you to share a vegetarian meal with them or guide you to some of the remaining Tripitaka Koreana sculptural wood blocks carved during the 13th century. It took 16 years to carve the Buddhist scriptures on these blocks, a monumental task done in hopes of preventing a consuming Mongol invasion.

On the temple grounds is an iron bell about 1.8 meters (6 ft) tall. It was cast in 1097 during the Northern Sung dynasty in a typical Chinese style. Despite its foreign origin, the bell has been designated a national treasure. Before departing from Jeondeung-sa, examine the unique ornamentation of human images engraved on the eaves of Daeungjeon Hall. This particular design style was popular during the mid-Joseon dynasty and is rarely seen anymore.

About 2 km (1¼ miles) southwest of Jeondeung-sa lies the small town of Sangbangni and the site of

The iron bell at Jeondeung-sa dates from the 11th century.

BELOW: nougat vendor on Ganghwa.

Map on page 150

Traveling north from Seoul there are frequent roadblocks. If you are traveling on a bus, it is likely that soldiers will board the bus and check the IDs of all the young Koreans. They are looking for deserters and possible infiltrators from the North. Foreigners are not usually bothered, but bring your passport just in case.

Dangun's Altar on nearby **Manisan**. It is an arduous climb of almost 500 meters (1,650 ft) up to the summit, where one can get a sweeping view of Ganghwa-do and touch the spot where an important Korean legend was born. Some archaeologists claim Dangun's altar is no more than 400 years old, which would date it considerably younger than Dangun who, according to popular myths, descended to earth from heaven in 2333 BC.

Seongmo-do Island

One last significant full-day excursion is a trip to the "Eyebrow Rock" Buddha at **Bomun-sa ㉑** on the neighboring island of **Seongmo-do**. This pilgrimage starts with a bus ride to **Uipo**, a fishing village on the West Coast. Foreigners may be asked to show their passports before taking the 10-minute ferry ride to the westward island. The bus ride from the landing on the opposite side to Bomun-sa takes about 45 minutes on a bumpy dirt road, but the island destination provides a serene contrast with its endless carpet of rice paddies, punctuated by pointed church steeples.

Bomun-sa is a neatly restored 1,400-year-old temple, behind which, carved into the mountain, is a stone chamber with 22 small stone Buddhas enshrined in individual wall niches behind an altar. The Buddha statues are said to have been caught by a fisherman who dreamt he was instructed by a monk to enshrine them here. Steps lead further above this stone chamber through junipers; at the end of a steep, heart-thumping hike is the massive concave **Ma-ae Seok-buljwasang** ("Eyebrow Rock" Buddha), sculpted into the granite mountainside. He blissfully overlooks the rice fields, the pale blue Yellow Sea, the setting sun and strangely shaped islands that dissolve into the horizon.

BELOW: Bomun-sa's "Eyebrow Rock" Buddha.

Panmunjeom and the Demilitarized Zone (DMZ)

The economic boom of the past two decades and the apparent tranquility of life in suburban Seoul and rural Korea make the possibility of war inconceivable for most visitors. Indeed, it's hard to believe that – after almost 50 years of cease-fire and a Korean War truce agreement – the threat of an all-out war still exists, although tensions have decreased with the recent thaw in North-South relations.

Map on page 150

However, the danger is still there, and to acquaint overly-optimistic tourists about this potentially volatile situation, the Korean government and United Nations representatives have sanctioned one of the world's most unusual tourist outings. This unique visitor attraction is a day trip to **Panmunjeom ㉒**, the site of a small farming village which was obliterated during the Korean War. Panmunjeom (accessible only through an organized tour) is the historic site on Korea's 38th parallel where American and South Korean representatives of a special United Nations Military Armistice Commission have been holding periodic talks with North Korean and Chinese negotiators. Their goal: to mutually supervise a ceasefire truce that was signed here on July 27, 1953. That truce agreement formally divided Korea into North and South political sectors and put an uneasy end to the bloody Korean War.

Geographically, Panmunjeom sits in a wide valley just northwest of the broad Imjin River and about 56 km (35 miles) northwest of Seoul. Cartographically, and therefore politically, Panmunjeom also straddles the stretch of land near the western end of Korea's Demilitarized Zone (DMZ), a demarcation line about 4 km (2½ miles) wide which winds its way for 250 km (150 miles) across the waist of the Korean peninsula. This truce camp is the point of official contact between North Korea and the free world. This is also a heavily mined, barricaded

South Korean guard in the conference room, Joint Security Area, Panmunjeom.

BELOW: American GI at Panmunjeom.

and patrolled "no-man's land" only for well-armed soldiers, a few hundred farmers, and, ironically, several formerly endangered species of birds (such as the spectacular Manchurian crane). These species have flourished within the confines of the DMZ since it was declared off-limits to most of humanity in 1953.

Highway to history

Your Panmunjeom-bound tour bus courses due north of Seoul on national **Highway 1** and follows wartime history through plains and valleys. Not so long ago, these peaceful surroundings were the heavily bunkered scenes of massive military advances and retreats during the Korean War and even during a Mongol invasion a few centuries ago.

This area is green and lush during the summer months, but when the winter chill sets in its beauty turns bleak and brittle. The late author James Wade describes this region best in his book *West Meets East*: "North of Seoul the Korean landscape is austerely beautiful in late winter. A light dusting of snow sets off the dark dots of rice stubble in frozen paddies and the lonely clumps of thatch-roofed farm houses. The steel-gray horizon, rimmed with jagged, ice-streaked mountains, recedes before the jeep as it rumbles past the rail terminal city of Munsanni and approaches the Imjin River, with its symbolically narrow and precarious Freedom Bridge." Suddenly you realize that the bleak new chain of mountains looming up ahead is North Korean territory.

"Freedom Village"

Past the checkpoints and into the DMZ is an enormous South Korean flag. This marks the village of **Daeseongdong** (which means "Attaining Success Town"), a community of ex-refugees allowed to resettle in their native habitat. Called **"Freedom Village"** by the US military, Daeseongdong is about a mile from Panmunjeom. Villagers – and soldiers – have to endure propaganda blasted over from the North Korean side by loudspeakers, but for their pains they enjoy certain benefits; among them exemption from military service and taxation. In fact the residents here are extremely wealthy in comparison with other Korean farmers. Otherwise, life generally goes on here in much the same way it does in other parts of South Korea.

In the distance, across the dividing line in the North Korean half of the demilitarized no-man's-land, is another village. It boasts bigger houses than Daeseongdong and a much bigger flag (so large, in fact, that it flops listlessly against its giant flagpole in anything less than a Force Eight gale). The village is said to be the biggest in the world, but no-one appears to live there. Curiously, even the windows on the buildings appear to be nothing more than black paint. American soldiers are in the habit of calling the North Korean village **"Propaganda Village"**. However, it goes under the official name of **Gwijeongdong**.

View from the top

Once you reach the exact Panmunjeom talks site, you will be escorted around a heavily guarded sector formally known as the Joint Security Area. In the

BELOW: military personnel explain the layout of the DMZ and Joint Security Area to tourists at Panmunjeom.

Conference Room your American military guide will explain another propaganda "war", concerning the question of who had the bigger flag. This "battle" ended in a truce when the flags of the two sides were too large to bring into the meeting room.

From atop ornate Freedom House, you will have a good view of the whole village and from **Checkpoint No 3** you have a panoramic view into North Korea itself, where you can check out billboards plastered with propaganda and listen to loudspeakers blaring out banalities.

Another observatory is the **Odusan Unification Observatory** ❷ (open daily 9am–6pm, Nov–Feb closes at 5pm; entrance fee) a half-hour south of Panmunjeom at the confluence of the Han and Imjin River. There's not a lot to see from here, but it is immensely popular with South Koreans since this is as close as they can get to the DMZ and North Korea without joining the army.

Going underground

If things aren't bizarre enough in the DMZ, some tours take you to the **Third Tunnel of Aggression** ❷ (between Panmunjeom and the Odusan unification observatory; guided tours only). This is one of several tunnels the North Koreans dug under the DMZ in order to sneak troops into the south. This one extends almost a mile into the south and is said to be capable of funneling vehicles and troops to the tune of 30,000 an hour.

Since the discovery of this and other tunnels, in the 1980s, there are round-the-clock tunnel detection teams to make sure the North doesn't do any more "coal mining" underneath the DMZ.

About 150,000 tourists make the DMZ tour from the southern side of the border every year. Since 1987, Western tourists have been able to make the Panmunjeom trip from the northern side. From Seoul this would involve flying to the northern capital, Pyeongyang, via Beijing, and then a morning's drive or a longer, six-hour train journey to Gaeseong, a city near Panmunjeom. In order to avoid unpleasant confrontations, the North and South schedule their tour groups at different times. While south Koreans were banned from travelling to the North for many years, and Panmunjeom is still off limits, restrictions are gradually being lifted (*see box page 172*).

In contrast to the difficulties in reaching the DMZ from the North, getting there from Seoul is extremely easy. The tours are well advertised and run several times a day, six days a week, so it should not be difficult to book one. The most popular tours (and cheapest) are sponsored by the USO (tel: 795-3028), but these tours are often filled a week or two in advance. This must rank as an excursion into the "Twilight Zone", a trip to a spot unlike any other on the planet (*for details of tours, see page 285*).

Private tour companies in Seoul offer tours with English-speaking guides and only require 24-hour advance booking, but they vary quite widely; make sure that they do in fact go all the way to Panmunjeom. Many tours do not include a visit to the Third Tunnel of Aggression. ❏

"The World's Most Dangerous Golf Course", within the Joint Security Area at Panmunjeom.

BELOW: North Korean soldiers taking pictures of tourists.

North and South

While it has been more than 50 years since the end of the Korean War, the hostilities have never ended. North Korea has resorted to subversive acts, trying to disrupt the government and encourage dissident groups in the South. In the 1960s, a special forces unit was sent south in an unsuccessful attempt to assassinate the South Korean president. In the 1980s, agents first set off an explosive that killed 22 South Korean diplomats and journalists on a state visit to Burma. Then they blew up a Korean Airlines passenger jet. In the late 1990s, small North Korean submarines were routinely spotted off South Korean beaches. Then there are the infiltration tunnels dug under the DMZ, the kidnapping of Japanese to help train North Korean agents, the continued threat of nuclear weapon production and test firing missiles over the Japanese mainland. No doubt North Korea has been a major worry to its neighbors, but all this mis-

chief has failed to slow the astounding economic and political progress the South has made over the past thirty years.

The strategy of the South and its primary ally, the United States, has been to isolate the North economically and politically – and this has been surprisingly successful. But the South can't take all the credit. Quirky North Korean leaders had their own policy of isolation, and their disastrous *juche* (self-reliance) economic policies have helped to drive the country to the edge of bankruptcy, making the country an oddity if not a pariah within the global community.

In the mid 1990s, decades of Cold War posturing threatened to turn hot over the nuclear issue, when a visit by former US President Jimmy Carter to Pyeongyang helped to defuse the situation, and the North bartered away their nuclear weapons program in return for nuclear reactors (some called it extortion). However, Kim Il Sung's death less than a month later and the need for his successor (and son), Kim Jong-il, to consolidate power delayed a proposed meeting with his South Korean counterpart.

Since the late 1990s, however, there has been a softening of positions on both sides of the border. For one, the United States and South Korea decided it was time to talk. The South came up with a "Sunshine Policy" that replaced confrontation with dialog, and instead of putting up roadblocks to the North's contacts with other countries, they encouraged them. Consequently, the North has established diplomatic relations with several European and Asian countries. Then the long delayed meeting of the South and North Korean Presidents took place in Pyeongyang in 2000. More recently, the US agreed to end their economic embargo.

South Korean businessmen – spearheaded by the elderly founder of the mammoth Hyundai *jaebeol*, Chung Juyung – made some of the earliest, and most surprising breakthroughs. Concerned that he might die before again seeing the North, Chung arranged to have 500 cows delivered to the village where he grew up. As South Koreans watched on TV, Chung led a caravan of new trucks (included in the deal) packed with cows through the DMZ and on to his old village.

Next, Chung proposed that North Korea

open the scenic Geumgangsan area to South Korean tourists. Surprisingly, the North Koreans not only agreed, but granted Hyundai 30-year exclusivity to operate tours to one of Korea's most scenic mountain regions.

Hyundai quickly leased three former Caribbean cruise ships, constructed their own port facilities on the far side of the harbor (effectively isolating the ships from North Koreans), improved the mountain roads, built an expansive visitors center, performance center and hot springs spa. On the drawing board are plans for a floating hotel, a golf course, a ski area, and cruise ships out of Japanese ports to bolster the 100,000 or so who currently cruise to the North each year.

The South Korean facilities are first-class, and contrast sharply with the poor-quality tourist hotels and restaurants of the North Koreans. At the peak of North Korea's development, back in the 1960s, Geumgangsan was a retreat for the political and military elite. But, if this is any indication, the country has been frozen in time. The two hotels are concrete monstrosities straight from the Stalinist era, with cracked windows and a desperate need for a coat of paint. Even sadder is the fact that the hotels rarely have guests.

Young soldiers decked out in baggy, Soviet-style uniforms stand with blank faces along a roadway lined with chain-link and razor wire topped fencing. The soldiers, and "environmental guides" along the mountain trails are there to ensure that tourists follow the rules: no spitting, no urinating, no littering, no photography (except in designated areas), no smoking, always refer to Kim Jong-il as "Great General", and definitely no political discussions or negative remarks about North Korea. The rules are strictly enforced, as one unfortunate woman discovered when she made an innocuous remark that resulted in several days of detention, and caused a mild political row.

For elderly Koreans with roots in the North, it has been something of a religious experience to again set foot on Northern soil after more than 50 years. But for most, the visit is more about curiosity than sentimentality.

With all the rules, the fencing off of North Korean villages, and extensive propaganda elaborately carved in the canyon walls, the tour *is* a curiosity. As the buses pass villages, South Koreans gaze at farmers plowing with oxen and working the fields with hand tools (there are few tractors). They wave at pedestrians walking on adjacent roadways (no buses or cars, and only a few bicycles), and watch as villagers bathe, fill water jugs and do their laundry along the river.

On the positive side, the homes and villages do look comfortable (even if there is no electricity), and the villagers look healthy and occasionally smile and wave as the buses pass. But it is sobering to think that these villages, because of their exposure to South Koreans, are probably the best in North Korea. And it's pretty obvious that the North is a good thirty years behind the South in economic development. Any reconciliation is going to require South Koreans to dig deep into their pocketbooks. As for the North Koreans, they're in for a little culture shock if they finally get to meet their rich cousins from the South. ❑

LEFT: the Geumgangsan tour gives South Koreans the chance to see the forbidden North.
RIGHT: women from North and South embrace.

GANGWON PROVINCE

If you enjoy mixing sightseeing with skiing, hiking or climbing, then visit Gangwon Province, where you'll find some of the peninsula's most impressive mountain scenery, and a rich cultural past

Map on page 176

W hen a Korean is fraught with wanderlust or feels like hiking into the beauty that has inspired classical paintings, the thing to do is to head northeast to Korea's finest collection of rivers, lakes and mountains to the land "Where Men and Mountains Meet."

This is the great northeast province of Gangwon, where in a day a happy wanderer can bask on a lake or seaside beach, and hike through wispy mountain mists to a 15th-century Buddhist shrine scooped out of a granite cliff.

For centuries Korea has been referred to as "*samcheolli geumsugangsan*," or the land of "3,000 *li* of rivers and mountains embroidered on silk." In Gangwon, for miles in either direction from the North Han River to the Demilitarized Zone (DMZ) and the East Sea this adage rings true. Here you will find a superb scenic tapestry delicately shaded with silken green rice terraces, swaths of amber grain, and pointilist vegetable patches winding hither and thither along cold blue rivers and craggy mountain passes.

You can begin your tour of the East Coast at several points on the East Sea (Sea of Japan), but probably the most central place to use as a pivot point for travel is **Gangneung** *(see page 177)*, the major city in east Gangwon Province. This city of more than 230,000 people is easily reached by train or bus, but the most interesting way to make the 228 km (142-mile) journey from Seoul is by private car.

This route will take you along broad expressways, cutting through quaint little villages with turquoise, tangerine and chartreuse rooftops; glassy rice paddies that reflect neatly marching poplars; pine-green hillsides, and busy logging camps in the bends of timber-clogged rivers.

Land of 10,000 Buddhas

One detour you must make on the way to Gangneung is just beyond little Jinbu village (about 40 km or 25 miles west of Gangneung). This side trip carries you along paved and dirt roads to **Odaesan National Park ❶**, a charming mountain area and the location of two of Korea's best-known temple complexes, Woljeong-sa and Sangwon-sa. The road leading to Odaesan (1,563 meters/5,128 ft) is dotted with tiny secluded hermitages, Zen meditation niches, and other impressive remnants of Buddhism which date from the 7th century and the Silla dynasty.

As cool, dry winds from the Mongolian steppes meet warm, moist air currents off the East Sea in this mountain region, the lush, pine-covered peaks of Odaesan are often wreathed in cool, shifting mists, giving the area a surreal other-worldly aura. It is no wonder that early Buddhist masters chose this place as a prime meditation spot.

LEFT: the summit of Seoraksan.
BELOW: *sarira* (reliquaries) at Odaesan.

Woljeong-sa is one of Korea's most appealing mountain temple complexes.

Woljeong-sa (open daily 8am–sunset; entrance fee), which sits on the southern fringe of Odaesan about 8 km (5 miles) off the expressway, is a sprawling temple complex distinguished by a superb nine-story octagonal pagoda and an unusual kneeling Buddha sculpture. The tiered pagoda, which rises 15 meters (50 ft), is capped with a sculpted lotus blossom and a bronze finial of intricate design; the kneeling Buddha, meanwhile, has well-weathered features, and (because of an unusual cap he's wearing) looks much like a European tin soldier. Both national treasures are located in front of Woljeong-sa's main hall, surrounded by a grass plot and a swastika-motif iron fence.

Along a riverbed road which snakes on up to the higher reaches of Odaesan, you will see occasional shrines and memorials to monks who have lived and died in this region over the centuries. One forest clearing contains tall stone stupas, most of them notably phallic in design, which are said to contain the cremated remains (*sarira*) of famous Buddhist masters.

Even higher up, just east of Odaesan's main peak, and about 200 meters

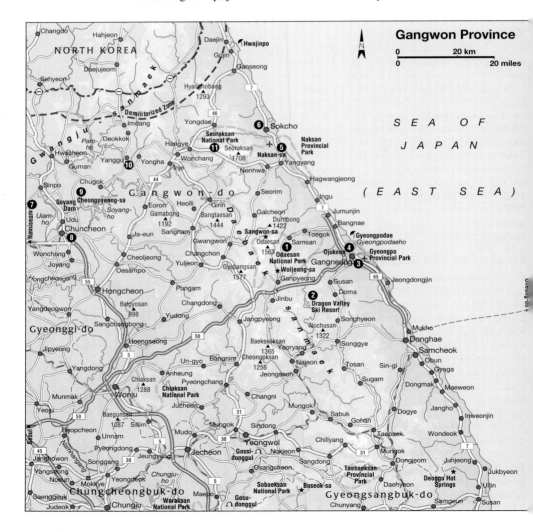

Map on page 176

(650 ft) off the road at the end of a pine-bordered pass, is **Sangwon-sa** (open daily 9am–sunset; entrance fee), another temple established by Jajang. According to an information board there, Jajang built this temple in AD 646 during the reign of the Silla Queen Seondeok. Zodiacal images adorn its walls, and in a wooden pavilion on the grounds is a large bronze bell said to be the second largest in Korea at 1.7-meters (5½-ft) – the largest is the Emille Bell at the Gyeongju National Museum *(see page 231)*. This particular Silla bell is also the oldest known example in Korea. It was reportedly cast in AD 725 during the reign of Silla King Seondeok.

Ski Korea!

Another 12 km (7 miles) south and east of the Yeongdong Expressway is another highland area with a decidedly different aura. This is the Daegwallyeong mountain region where Korea's most modern and best-equipped ski resort is located. In the area are several small resorts centered around a town called Hoenggye, which has produced the best skiiers in Korea. However, insatiable skiers favor the slopes that have been developed in a place called Yongpyeong, or Dragon Valley.

The **Yongpyeong Dragon Valley Ski Resort** ❷ sprawls over 210,000 sq. meters (52 acres) and is equipped with 15 ski lifts covering 31 ski slopes. The resort also has snow-making machines, a ski school, ski rental facilities, and even lighting facilities for night-time skiing. There are long runs down the sides of the area's Gold and Silver slopes on Barwang mountains. The longest run is down Daegwallyeong's 957-meter (3,140-ft) Mt Twin Dragon, which offers a major headwall drop of about 50 meters (164 ft) that quickly tapers off into a series of gentler slopes.

Looming over this snow complex are two first-rate hotels-cum-ski lodges, the Dragon Valley Hotel and the Hotel Ju Won. These lodges offer comfort-seekers both Western and Korean-style accommodation, a "Chalet Grill," billiards lounges, discotheque, heated swimming pool, archery range, tennis courts and rifle range for non-skiers. If these places aren't your style, there are also private villas, *yeogwan* inns and a large dormitory facility in the area, which can be rented at single, double or group rates.

A few more miles to the east of the turnoff to the Dragon Valley and ski country, the Yeongdong Expressway begins to narrow somewhat. Then, after negotiating the Daegwallyeong Ridge, you will begin a final, zigzagging descent to Gangneung town through the famous 99 turns of the Daegwallyeong Pass. On a clear day the view from the top of this granite cliff provides a fine first impression of Gangneung and the deep blue East Sea.

City by the sea

Gangneung ❸ is a sleepy seaside town rich in traditional architecture and hospitable people. It has always been known as the key trading and terminal point in this part of Korea, but has also gained local fame as the site of an annual Dano spring festival, held on the 5th day of the 5th lunar moon, usually in

According to legend, the Buddha appears at Odaesan in the form of a small boy. When King Sejo (reigned 1455–68) came to bathe his diseased body in the mountain's healing waters, a boy came to scrub the king's back. The disease, like the boy, then mysteriously disappeared.

BELOW: learning to ski at Dragon Valley.

May. The festival takes place on the banks of a wide river that divides the town's north and south sectors. This authentic local celebration, rich in shamanistic dancing, rituals and general merrymaking, attracts country folk to its colorful tents, sideshows and carnival atmosphere.

The classical Confucian academy and shrine **Hyanggyo and Daeseongjeon** (call City Hall for appointments, tel: 033-648-3667, 9am–noon) is located in the northwest suburbs of the city on the grounds of the Myeongnyun middle and high schools. This hilltop structure, which was built in 1313, destroyed by fire in 1411, then rebuilt in 1413, has low, brooding rooflines and tapering colonnades typical of Goryeo-dynasty structures. Rooms on either side of this old academy's main hall are filled with boxed spirit tablets that are opened every year when Confucian *jesa* ancestral rites are performed here.

Confucian reflections on rising moons

The resort of **Gyeongpodae Beach**, just a few miles north of Gangneung, has long been a popular Korean recreational spa. Offshore waters here are busy with zig-zagging speedboats and sailing craft, and on shore are numerous tented seafood restaurants where you can choose your lunch live from gurgling saltwater tanks. Korean tourists like to buy bundles of *miyeok* (seaweed for soupmaking), dried cuttlefish, and other exotic delicacies from vendors who ply their trade on this colorful beach.

Just inland of this beach scene, past the clutter of hotels and inns, and rows of kitsch souvenir shops, is mirror-like **Gyeongpodae Lake**. This lake is dotted with islets and once had pavilions set like jewels on her shores. There, local *yangban* aristocrats met with friends to sip wine, compose poems and watch

BELOW: seaside village to the south of Gangneung.

MOUNTAIN SPIRITS

Mountain spirits are a remnant of Korea's shamanistic past when rivers, trees and mountains were believed to have spirits, or spirits residing in them. Since mountains are so dominant on the Korean peninsula, the Mountain Spirit became one of the most important of the shamanistic spirits.

While most young people look upon shamanism as irrelevant superstition, there is a core of rural, older, and traditional Koreans that maintain a deep respect, if not a deep-seated belief in the Mountain Spirit. Shamanistic rituals continue to call on the Mountain Spirit for guidance in many parts of Korea.

At most Buddhist temples in Korea, there is a small shrine to the Mountain Spirit (and Recluse) sitting behind the main temple on a little hill. Look inside and you'll see a brightly colored painting of a bearded, white-haired old man with a mountain tiger, his companion and messenger, at his side.

Gangneung's Dano Festival has its historical precedents in similar ceremonies and festivals that were once held in nearly all villages to pay homage to the Mountain Spirit and request a prosperous future, and to ask for the Mountain Spirit's continued benevolence.

sunsets and moonrises over the nearby Taebaek mountain range. As an old song says, from the old Gyeongpo Pavilion on the lake's northern shore "you can see the rising moon reflected in the lake, in your bowl of wine, and in your sweetheart's eyes".

If such images keep you in a romantic and classical mood, head back across the lake toward Gangneung, then detour to the northwest, and cross a series of rice paddies by footpath until you reach **Seonggyojang** (open daily except major holidays; 9am–6pm, Mar–Oct closes at 5pm; entrance fee). Seonggyojang has an impressive living compound, Confucian academy, lotus pond and pavilion built during the 18th and 19th centuries by members of the prominent Yi Hu family clan. This complex is a perfect example of a *yangban* Joseon-dynasty living compound in Korea. What makes it even better and more authentic is the fact that the Yi family still lives in the main house, just as their ancestors have for the past two centuries.

This compound is picturesque in the wintertime when snow laces its curved roofs, mud and tile walls and cozy thatched servants' quarters; and in the summertime when giant pink Indonesian lotus blossoms rise out of their shallow pond like sleepy dragons.

The Black Bamboo Shrine

Another important Confucian site, just a little way north of Gangneung, is **Ojukheon ❹** (Black Bamboo Shrine; open Wed–Mon except major holidays, 9am–6pm, Nov–Mar closes at 5pm; entrance fee), birthplace of the prominent Confucian scholar-statesman-poet Yi I (1536–1584). Yi I, more popularly known by his pen name Yulgok (Valley of Chestnuts), was one of a select group of

BELOW: portrait of the mountain spirit and his messenger, the tiger.

Traditional fur brushes used in calligraphy.

neo-Confucianists who became quite powerful during the 16th century. Among positions he held were royal appointments as Korea's Minister of Personnel and War, and Rector of the National Academy.

One biographical sketch notes that Yulgok was an infant prodigy who knew Chinese script at the age of three, "and when he was seven he already composed poems in Chinese. At the age of 19, he entered the Geumgangsan Mountains and was initiated in Buddhism, but soon abandoned it for the study of the philosophy of Chu Hsi."

To honor Yulgok's example and memory, the Korean government has in recent years revamped his birthplace site. The memorial, on the west side of the road to Yangyang and Sokcho, is a prim compound in the cheerful yellow favored by the ministry in charge of national parks and memorials.

Ojukheon, which has the aura of a shrine (visitors should be properly dressed, and smoking, gum-chewing and photography are not allowed in the vicinity of Yulgok's memorial tablet house), is a memorial not just to Yulgok but also to his mother, Sin Saimdang, who was revered during her lifetime as a fine calligrapher and artist.

A collection of calligraphic scrolls by Yulgok, his mother, and other members of this Yi family are on display in a small museum at the rear of the Ojukheon compound. Also on display are several original paintings by the talented Lady Saimdang. Her precise and flowing studies of flora and fauna are superbly, artistically executed.

BELOW: a typical east coast fishing village.

Before continuing northwards from this site, marvel for a moment at the fine stand of black bamboo that grows luxuriantly in a garden between the museum and Yulgok's house. Then look west toward the nearby pine forests and consider

these reflective lines from Yulgok's famous poem *Gosangugokga* (The Nine Songs of Mount Ko, translated by Peter H Lee):

Map on page 176

> *Where shall we find the first song?*
> *The sun lances the crown rock, and*
> *Mist clears above the tall grass.*
> *Lo the magic views far and near*
> *Calling my friends I would wait*
> *With a green goblet in the pine grove.*

Coastal road north

Proceeding north on Highway 7, the coastal road, you pass sun-lanced rocks and pine groves against the backdrop of the blue East Sea. Just above **Yangyang**, on the southern outskirts of Sokcho, you will find what is probably the most appealing, and impressive, religious site in this part of Korea. This is **Naksan-sa ❺** (open daily 9am–sunset; entrance fee), a Buddhist temple complex originally established by the Silla high priest Uisang in 671 during the 11th year of King Munmu's reign. The main hall and support structures were rebuilt in 858, burned down during the Korean War, then rebuilt again in 1953 by General Hi Hyongkun and his men.

According to a storyboard, the high priest Uisang prayed here for seven days on a 15 meter (49 ft) high rock by the sea. He wanted to see Avalokitesvara (the God of Mercy), the story notes, but in vain. "In despair he threw himself into the sea and then Avalokitesvara appeared, gave him a rosary made of crystal, and told him where to worship him. Thus Wontongbojeon, the main hall of this

BELOW: squid drying in the sun at Sokcho.

Hangeul, the Korean script

Among Korea's long procession of royalty, King Sejong (reigned 1418–50) is the favorite. In Korea, it is impossible to forget him, since his portrait appears on the 10,000-won note, and everywhere you look you see his most famous invention – Hangeul, the Korean alphabet.

Unusually, the king actually thought a ruler was morally obligated to improve the lot of his subjects. Since the majority of his subjects were farmers, he first concentrated on improving agricultural production. Scholars were sent out to survey farming techniques, bringing back innovative ideas that were then applied to plots within the palace grounds. After years of experimentation, the treatise "Straight Talk on Farming" was published and regional officials disseminated the new farming technologies to the peasants.

In the field of astronomy, King Sejong and his scholars developed a rain gauge, sundial and other devices to measure wind and water.

The king and his scholars then turned their attention to producing a book on Korea's indigenous medicines, resulting in the publication of "The Classified Collection of Medical Prescriptions". A true Renaissance man, Sejong also composed Confucian music with instruments that gave ritual performances at the Korean court a distinctive sound.

His greatest legacy, however, was the development of Hangeul. For centuries, Korea had been using a modified version of Chinese script, made up of thousands of ideograms that required years of study to master. In Korea, only the *yangban* had the time, money (tutors were expensive) or inclination to learn it. Consequently, only Korean males (girls were educated in home duties) from the upper class were literate; this amounted to less than 10 percent of the population. Another problem was that, while Chinese ideograms represented the Chinese language well, the Korean language is quite different from Chinese, making the script awkward to use.

The task King Sejong set his scholars was formidable – create a system of writing that would better represent the Korean language and be simple enough for a peasant to learn. The result was quite remarkable. Discarding ideograms, the scholars developed a phonetic alphabet that used 28 symbols (only 24 are used today). Instead of spending years trying to memorize thousands of symbols, Hangeul could be learned in a matter of weeks, if not days. This made literacy accessible to nearly every Korean.

Unfortunately, it wasn't that simple. Although there were books published in Hangeul, the *yangban* refused to use an alphabet that they felt was suitable for women and farmers, but not true scholars. It was not until the 20th century that Hangeul was widely accepted. Today, Hangeul is a source of considerable pride to all Koreans. It is remarkable when you consider that an alphabet developed over 550 years ago is perfect for the computer age – while the Chinese (and Japanese) struggle to fit ideograms onto a keyboard, the 24 letters of Hangeul fit very nicely. ❑

LEFT: a calligrapher writing "family precepts" in Hangeul at the King Sejong Cultural Festival.

temple, was built on this spot." Another version of this story notes that Uisang "became a Buddha himself when he saw the image of the Maitreya Buddha rising from the sea in front of him following his seven day prayer toward the sea." Regardless of which story holds more truth, this temple stands in Uisang and Buddha's honor.

Several national treasures are housed in Naksan-sa's halls, towers and pavilions. The first item you will notice is a splendid stone gate, Hongyemun, built during the time of King Sejo (reigned 1455–68), who once prayed here. The second impressive structure is a seven-story Goryeo pagoda that stands 6.2 meters (20 ft) high in front of the main hall. Its gleaming finial is composed of finely wrought treasure rings, a fortune bowl and a treasure jewel. Third, but certainly not last, is a large bronze bell, called Beomjong, with four raised bodhisattva images. It was cast in 1496. The bell, 1.6 meters (5 ft) by 1 meter (3 ft) in diameter, is inscribed with poetry and calligraphy by the famous poet Kim Suon, and the calligrapher Jeong Nanjong.

A merciful apparition

On Wontongbojeon's sea side, dominating everything natural and man-made in the area, is a 15-meter (49-ft) white granite statue of Buddhism's Bodhisattva of Mercy, known in Korea as the goddess Gwanseum-bosal, in China as Kwan Yin, and in India as Avalokitesvara (though Avalokitesvara is an earlier male counterpart). This particular Goddess of Mercy faces the southeast atop a 2-meter (6-ft) granite pedestal and open lotus blossom.

The massive statue, the work of Busan sculptor Gwon Jonghwan, was dedicated in 1977. According to Choe Wonchol, then chief priest at Naksan-sa, an old priest appeared to him in a 1972 dream and told him where and how to place this statue. Following this apparition, Choe reported his dream to the religious affairs board of the Jogyejong Order headquarters in Seoul. After considering Choe's vision, the board decided to proceed with the project. Some six months of hard labor and 700 tons of granite stone was required to complete the sculpture. "From the day when the standing granite bodhisattva was solemnly dedicated, Naksan Temple went into a thousand-day prayer for national peace and security," a Dedication Day story stated in *The Korea Times*.

From this statue, standing like an ancient beacon on this quiet and rugged coastline, continue north past Uisangdae and its tiny pink lighthouse to **Sokcho town ❻**. Sokcho is an important coastal fishing port that has long been a stop-off for travelers to seaside resorts to the north. Beyond Sokcho are several quaint fishing villages, exotic inland lagoons brimming with fish and waterfowl, and broad, dune-like beaches as fine as any in California. Private and government enterprise have developed several sandy beach areas north of Sokcho, but the all-time favorite languishing spot is **Hwajinpo Beach** about halfway between Sokcho and the DMZ. Korea's presidents have traditionally maintained summer villas here, as have other comfort- and beauty-seekers.

Map on page 176

Buddhist monk at Naksan-sa.

BELOW: fish restaurant at Sokcho.

The clear waters of Chuncheon lake attract bathers, sailors, water-skiers and fishermen.

BELOW:
rose cabbage,
Chuncheon.

End of the line and as far north as you can go in southern Korea is **Daejin**, a friendly town of tiny streets with people who might still be pleasantly surprised to see a foreigner this far off the beaten path, and boasting one of the most colorful fishmarket docks in Korea.

Glassy lake country

One of the most picturesque routes in Korea is the road from Seoul to Seoraksan and the northeast coast. It takes you north of Seoul on a zigzag course of modern highways, inland waterways and dusty but spectacular mountain roads. This adventure by car or by bus (from Seoul's Cheongnyangni station), heads northeast on Highway 46 through wooded mountains and along and across the snake-like North Han River and its valleys.

Several river and lakeside resorts have sprung up along the highway between Seoul and Chuncheon. Stop and linger a day or two according to whim, but if you would like a suggestion of where to stay, consider **Namiseom ❼**, an island in the middle of the Han River near a quaint highland town called Gapyeong. This is about an hour's drive north of Seoul, followed by a 10-minute ferry ride to Namiseom. There you can rent a small house or cabin and revert to nature, becoming one with the cooing cuckoos, falling chestnuts and pungent pines. Wake up early to see the rising sun slowly but surely burn morning mists out of the little valleys which surround Gapyeong.

About 20 km (12 miles) further north (a journey you can make by leisurely ferry from Namiseom if you have the time), you'll round a hill and descend into **Chuncheon ❽** (pop. 250,000). This is Gangwon's largest city, and a convenient resort for Seoulites who like to get away from it all for a day or week, to enjoy

some of the country's finest lake country. Freshwater fishing, swimming, sailing and water-skiing are readily available at several colorful resort piers which rim spacious **Chuncheon Lake** and other sky-blue waterways in the surrounding area.

In Chuncheon, where violet, yellow and green rose cabbages landscape a series of quaint mini-parks, you can follow your nose in a number of watery and earthy directions. Some people choose to ferry-hop around Chuncheon through river gorges to riverside villages, sandy beaches, waterfalls (the Gugok Falls near Namiseom are a favorite), and jade green pools that have never been reached by car or train. Others continue north to Hwacheon and the peacefully remote **Paroho Lake** north of the Samyeong Mountains.

Probably the most popular local tour is a visit to the nearby Soyang Dam and its attendant **Lake Soyang**. On the north side of this concrete monument of engineering and hydroelectricity, you will find a colorful boat docking area, the **Soyang Pavilion**. Here, a road-weary traveler can leave land and embark on a tour of Korea's most splendid inland waterway. Lake Soyang is hyperbolically, but not unbelievably, called by some Korean travel writers "the largest lake in the Orient made by man." From this pavilion you can proceed for many cool miles on a gliding cruise toward the Seorak Mountains and the northeastern coast.

Temple above the lake

A popular side trip on Lake Soyang involves a brief (15 minutes) cruise by open-air launch to **Cheongpyeong-sa** ❾ (open daily 9am–sunset; entrance fee). There, an ancient Buddhist temple sits about a 20-minute hike and 2.5 km (1½ miles) above a sleepy floating dock and restaurant just north of Soyang Pavilion. This lofty Buddhist retreat provides solace seekers with a simple escape from the asphalt and beeping, fume-spewing buses below. Paths lead from the temple up to the peak of Mt Obongsan.

A well-kept trail to Cheongpyeong-sa rises steeply and steadily along a tinkling, rocky stream to a lovely waterfall and piney crags. All this comes alive at dawn and at sunset with the amazing harmony of sutras being chanted by resident devotees of the Lord Buddha.

There is a small fee to enter this Buddhist center of desirelessness and non-attachment, and on the back of the entrance ticket you'll find this short story, in Hangeul: "This temple originated 1,600 years ago. A Chinese princess of the Tang period visited here to rid herself of a snake. She brought three bars of gold for the expense of rebuilding this temple, in the hope of losing the snake. At this time the gate of the temple was struck by lightning in the midst of a severe storm. The snake vanished, so the gate was renamed 'Transforming Gate' from this incident."

This deliberately perplexing tale only adds to Cheongpyeong-sa's mystique. Art historian Jon Covell theorizes that this story about the princess and a snake indicates shaman influences creeping into Buddhism. Another theory supposes the temple was the refuge-headquarters of a tantric, or erotic, Buddhist cult. Whatever its origins, you will find your visit to Cheongpyeong-sa deeply rewarding, if only to see its fine outer wall murals which include, among other themes, an unusual Gwanseum holding a willow branch, a finely executed Oxherding Series and a well-focused tiger panel.

End of the line

Meanwhile, back on Lake Soyang, you can travel back to Soyang Pavilion near the massive dam, then catch one of many regular commuter specials (these are covered boats with a breezy after-deck) for the hour and 20 minutes glide to a rural docking point just south of isolated **Yanggu** ❿ town. The surrounding mountains, which are ablaze with amber and roseate trees in the crisp autumn months, are reflected by in the calm waters of the lake, and are reminiscent of parts of New Zealand or the American Northwest. At the Yanggu dock you can transfer to a bus or taxi and proceed through the hills to reach the sleepy town itself.

Yanggu, which lies in a pleasant valley a few miles south of the DMZ, has several *yeogwan*, restaurants and all the other amenities normally available in small-town Korea. From this point, regular buses race the short distance through the corn and cabbage country to Inje, which is the gateway town to the spectacular mountains of **Seoraksan National Park** ⓫ (*see page 186*). ❏

Map
on page
176

The Seorakdong resort complex in the Seoraksan National Park is one of the finest places in Korea for leisurely hiking and al fresco meals. Nature trails here accommodate everyone – from the languid wanderer to the rock-climbing fanatic.

BELOW: dragon guardian at Cheongpyeong-sa.

Map on page 187

● Seoul

SEORAKSAN NATIONAL PARK

At Seoraksan you can find beautiful mountain temples, remote hermitages, hot springs, world-class mountain trails, and a mountain resort with deluxe accommodations and gourmet dining

BELOW: Seoraksan's more remote temples are only accessible by foot.

Seoraksan, the "Snow Peak Mountain," is now more formally known as **Seoraksan National Park** (open daily, entrance fee). It is not just a lone mountaintop, but actually a series of peaks in the mid-section of the spectacular Baekdudaegan or "Great White Range," Korea's most prominent geographical region. This panoramic backbone of South Korea's northeast province of **Gangwon** is a tourist destination which lives up to its public relations hype. The Seoraksan area is a true mountain wonderland, and after a visit you'll understand why early Zen (or Seon) Buddhist monks chose this region to sit and strive to become one with the universe. Despite the crowds this park attracts, it is possible to enjoy some solitude within this jewel in the crown of Korea's extensive National Park system – just try to avoid visiting at weekends and during school holidays.

The most popular section of the park is **Outer Seorak** (Oeseorak). This region is east of the mountain divide, closest to the East Sea and furthest from the interior of the peninsula (hence "Outer Seorak"). Visitors to the park usually end up staying in the heart of Outer Seorak, at the resort village of Seorakdong. According to park literature, up to 26,000 people can be housed within the park (it seems like more on holidays), and 90 percent are in Seorakdong. **Inner Seorak** (Naeseorak), the western section of the park, has the advantage of fewer visitors, and the disadvantage of having fewer attractions.

There are several ways to get to the area from Seoul. The quickest is on a domestic flight to **Sokcho** (40 minutes), then by bus or taxi to **Seorakdong** (another 20 minutes). You can also take a train or bus to the terminal fishing town of Sokcho. Korean old-timers, in less of a hurry to get to this place, prefer to enter Seoraksan slowly, from the country's scenic interior (as outlined in the preceding section on the Lake Country), and drift into the area's magic on paved, winding roads that meander through the wilds of Inner Seorak.

Mountain roads

Inje, the renowned "Gateway to Inner Seorak," is a good place to begin a tour of the area. Even in Inje town you'll first have to decide which of two scenic ways you want to take to the Seorak range.

The more straightforward Southern Route winds its way through Inner Seorak, before climbing the **Hangyeryeong Pass** and passing through the southern fringes of Outer Seorak to emerge at lovely **Yangyang** town by the East Sea. The route is gently meandering, enabling you to take in the gorgeous sights in comfort. The Northern Route twists through **Misiryeong Pass**, before descending into Sokcho on the East Sea. Most people prefer the Southern Route, both for the comfort and scenery. If, on the other hand, you're up for a bit of "roughing it," head north.

En route you will encounter, at Jangsudae, numerous nature trails (abloom in the spring and ablaze in the autumn), veil-like waterfalls, red-bellied frogs, quiet creeks, and at Osaek Yaksu, mineral springs famed for their therapeutic properties *(see below)*. Some travelers like to pause at **Jangsudae ❶** and hike up to the **Daeseung** waterfalls (it takes just over an hour), then upward to **Baekdam-sa** (plan on taking the better part of the day for this excursion), a charming Buddhist temple smack in the interior of Inner Seorak. Ex-President Chun and his wife spent a year here over 1989–90 "repenting" for the sins of his 1980–87 dictatorship. Both hikes are spiritually healing after bustling Seoul, but be prepared with warm clothes, good walking gear, food and drink, especially if camping overnight.

Further east at the top of the **Hangyeryeong Pass ❷**, you can begin yet another trek: this one climbs all the way to the top of Mt Seorak (also known as Daecheongbong), the highest peak in the area and the third highest mountain in Korea at 1,708 meters (5,604 ft). You can navigate onward and enter the Seorakdong resort complex by its back door. However, be warned that the steep zigzagging path can be slippery and dangerous during the winter months.

A recuperative soak in the **Osaek Yaksu (mineral springs) ❸** at the far east end of the Hangyeryeong Pass road are well worth stopping for (there are several hot spring baths in the hotels, as well as a few public baths). If you're feeling fit, though, you may want to rush on down to sea level to a grand seafood meal at Yangyang, Naksan or Sokcho. Appetite thus satisfied, and braced by cool breezes off the East Sea, you are now ready to tackle mountainous Outer Seorak.

Seoraksan is famous for its fiery autumn colors.

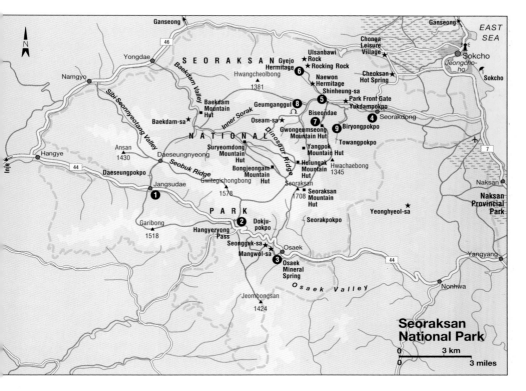

Seoraksan National Park

Mountain resort

The 15-minute bus ride from the sandy East Coast into the **Seorakdong resort complex** ❹ is a grand transition from beach cabana chic to mountain resort cool. One moment you're tasting raw fish under a beachside umbrella, the next, you're in a pine lodge choosing between hot buttered rums and pinenut soup.

The resort complex has become one of the finest places in Korea for leisurely hiking and *al fresco* dining. Nature strolls here can accommodate everyone from the most languid non-hiker to rock-climbing fanatics. There's even a modern cable car that will carry the less active to a properly catered promontory where they can meditate on the famous rock structure of *Biseondae*. When you have settled into one of Seorakdong's deluxe hotels or simple *yeogwan* inns, your next decision will be which of the many mountaineering-excursion themes to pursue.

Temple with a view

A large, detailed sign on the roadside offers a few suggestions as you take an easy stroll up the main fir-lined path to **Sinheung-sa** ❺ (open daily 9am–sunset). This ancient Zen (Seon) temple, originally built near its present location in AD 652, when it was called Hyangseong-sa, or the "Temple of Zen Buddhism," and was destroyed by a forest fire in 707. It was rebuilt in 710, burned again in 1645, and rebuilt a third time at its present location in 1648.

"If the signboard date at Sinheung-sa is correct," writes Zen and oriental art authority Dr Jon Carter Covell, "then Sinheung-sa is the oldest Zen temple in the world. Nothing in China or in Japan is of this age, not by many centuries."

Just before you reach the actual temple compound, you'll pass (on the right side of the cobble path) a neatly kept and fenced-in cemetery full of unusual bell-

Seoraksan is wall-to-wall with people during holiday periods, from late July to early August, and during October when the leaves take on beautiful colors. During these busy times, people often wait in line just to begin their hikes on the most popular paved trails. Avoid these periods, or go to the less popular areas on the fringes of the park.

BELOW: hiking is a national obsession in Korea.

HIKING KOREAN-STYLE

Considering they live in a country covered by mountains, it is not surprising that Koreans love to hike. Actually, they call it mountain climbing, and the dyed-in-the-wool "climbers" are to be found in the mountains every weekend. For thousands of years, mountains in Korea have sheltered temples, hermits and some of the world's finest ginseng. They also provide a welcome respite to thousands of pilgrims weary of urban life who, on the weekend, hike the trails in droves. Since Koreans tend to be social, they often hike with their friends, and many belong to climbing clubs. It's a great way to keep in touch with old buddies from primary or high school.

Whether a hardcore climber taking on the big mountains or a lightweight that goes for the gentler trails, you have got to look the part. In Korea, that means donning huge hiking boots and pulling big heavy wool socks over the pants. With the boots, socks, vest and hats, well-outfitted Korean hikers look like they're ready to take on the Matterhorn. Thanks to the Koreans' almost religious dedication to proper hiking, camping and enjoyment of the great outdoors, the government has made new far-sighted investment in wilderness areas such as Outer Seorak, where they have created a superb mountain resort.

Map
on page
187

shaped tombstones, erected to honor former illustrious Zen monks who spent much time meditating in this area.

In the temple itself, which sits on a bluff with a superb view of the surrounding mountains, you'll pass through lattice doors carved and painted with a floral motif. You'll then come eye-to-eye with a standard Amit's Buddha flanked by Gwanseum and Daiseiji bodhisattvas. On a more light-hearted note, you'll also be confronted by "the two crazy idiots of the 7th century", Hansan and Seupdeuk (known in China as Han Shan and Shih Te), who grace the temple's north wall. These absurd, grimacing, "crazy" fellows are often found in such spiritual surroundings, where they temper our overly-serious lives by laughing at the absurdity of existence.

Sinheung-sa offers more such fantasy, drawing on combinations of shaman, Taoist and Buddhist imagery. Consider the creatures which are half-tiger, half-leopard, and the writhing dragons, cranes and bats all brilliantly painted on the ceiling. Or the drawing on the main hall's rear wall that shows a Zen patriarch offering his severed arm to a higher-ranking Zen master.

On the spiritual path

Next, proceed up this spiritual path to the **Gyejoam Hermitage** ❻ (open daily 9am–sunset), about 3 km (2 miles) up, along a singing streambed. Gyejo Hermitage, a subsidiary of the mother Sinheung Temple, is partially built into a granite cave at the base of Ulsan-bawi, a spectacular granite formation that dominates this part of the Seorak area. Some say that the rock, which the hermitage is located in, resembles a *moktak*, a hollow wood block that monks rhythmically beat while chanting. Legend says that because of this, it takes a monk only five years to complete his studies rather than the ordinary 10 years.

Temple guardians provide protection from evil spirits.

BELOW: the hills of Inner Seorak.

Map on page 187

The cable car to the top of Biseondae (Flying Fairy Peak).

BELOW: on top of Biseondae.
RIGHT: swaying footbridge to Biryong waterfall.

Like much of Seorak, and like the famous Geumgangsan Mountains across the DMZ in North Korea, Ulsan-bawi's face is rich with anthropomorphic images. Indeed, about halfway up the Gyejo Hermitage, an enterprising fellow with a high-powered telescope sells lingering peeks at one particularly erotic formation at Ulsan-bawi's mid-section.

The hermitage is identified by a bright red Buddhist swastika carved and painted over an entrance arch. A narrow corridor leads to the cave interior where candles on an altar burn before a small but exquisite golden Buddha. When monks are inside this ancient niche chanting sutras, and clacking wooden bells sound in the flickering candlelight, the effect is Zen Buddhism at its most atmospheric and mystical.

Fronting the Gyejo Hermitage and Ulsan-bawi is another geological curiosity that has become a major tourist attraction over the years. This is the famed **Rocking Rock**, a massive boulder that rocks back and forth in its secure place when given a solid nudge. Being photographed in front of this tipsy ball of granite is a tourist's must. If you enjoyed your ramble to the Rocking Rock, then you're ready for a more challenging trek, this time on the southern trail, to Geumganggul (cave) above the aforementioned Biseondae.

Flying fairies and dragons

The hike to **Biseondae** (Flying Fairy Peak) **❼**, a vertical rock that juts heavenward at the entrance to a breathtaking gorge, is easy enough. At every turn you'll find yourself gawking at the beauty of chill pools and waterfalls. In the autumn, fire-red maples and golden gingkos are the seasonal attraction. "In Canada you'd have to do a lot of bushwhacking to see country like this," commented a visitor from Vancouver. Vendors sell cooling bowls of *makgeolli* rice wine and *meorujeup*, a beverage made from the berries of a local plant related to the grape. It is best to avoid weekends if possible when the trails become very crowded.

From this restful camp at the base of Biseondae, devoted Buddhist pilgrims head up a smaller path to **Geumganggul Cave ❽**, which is located near the top of Biseondae and requires serious genuflection to attain. After negotiating 649 stairs to reach this charming cave-shrine, your heart will be pounding, but the extraordinary view from the top (as well as a halfway point promontory) will be your earthly reward. Inside the cave is a small Buddha surrounded by burning candles, incense and food offerings. Artifacts found in the cave indicate monks have been seeking meditative isolation in this cave for centuries.

Meanwhile, back at the Seorakdong base camp, other hikers opt to take the waterfall trail, and visit Yukdam and Biryong, and Towangseong waterfalls. **Biryong** (Flying Dragon Waterfall) **❾** is located halfway between the two, at the top of a lovely gorge beneath the 1,345-meter (4,412-ft) Hwachaebong. A suspension bridge across the narrow gorge and stream leads to the Flying Dragon. Legend says that a dragon once lived beneath the waterfall. The bothersome dragon was sent flying to the heavens after villagers sacrificed a maiden. ❏

KOREA'S BEAUTIFUL MOUNTAIN TEMPLES

While the urban centers have their attractions, a visit to Korea would be incomplete without experiencing the peace of these rustic hideaways

Korea's largest and most historic Buddhist temples are found in mountain valleys far removed from the hectic urban centers. Many of Korea's artistic treasures are to be found within the temple grounds, although the greatest treasure may be the beauty of the temples and their pristine natural setting. These mountain shrines and their grounds have become the centerpieces of Korea's well-developed system of Provincial and National Parks, from Jirisan in the south to Seoraksan in the north.

It is not happenstance that the temples are located in beautiful mountain locations. For most of the staunchly Confucian Joseon dynasty (1392–1910) Buddhist temples, and even monks, were banned from entering the cities; the mountains were their refuge. Today, these temples in the hills provide visitors with a quiet opportunity to calm, refresh and renew their spiritual side.

VISITING THE TEMPLES

The temples, along with their surrounding mountain trails, are popular weekend destinations for both Korean and foreign tourists. If you choose to visit one of the temples, make a day of it. Take time to explore the main temple complex and to appreciate the charm and delicate details of the many buildings. On the doors of the Main Hall, colorful demons repel evil, and lotus flowers promise the hope of nirvana. Inside, look up and you're likely to see dragons and cranes softly suspended from the rafters. And finally, visit the small shrine on a hillside behind the main buildings and pay homage to the Mountain Spirit and Recluse.

▷ **A MONK'S LIFE**
Korea's monks and nuns spend a good deal of the summer and winter months in meditative retreat. Autumn and spring are for travel and personal reflection.

▷ **STONE PAGODAS**
Maisan Temple is famous for its delicate, sometimes outrageous, stone pagodas built over several decades by a local hermit.

△ **KEEPING GUARD**
The temple guardian repels evil and reminds the faithful they are entering a world of peaceful solitude.

THE FOUR TEMPLE GUARDIANS

The Four Heavenly Guardians stand watch at the entryway of almost every Buddhist temple in Korea. In the larger temples, the Guardians are gigantic wooden or concrete statues housed in the temple's second gate. At smaller temples, Guardians are painted on the wooden doors of the temple gate.

The Guardian of the North stands with a pagoda, a reliquary for the ashes of monks, as this is the direction of death. The Guardian of the South controls the weather with his lute, and the Guardian of the West carries a sword that is able to multiply whenever needed. Finally, the Guardian of the East holds a dragon to ensure good fortune.

First-time visitors are often taken aback by the ferocity of the Guardians. They stand with sword, dragon or lute in hand; wide-eyed and with ferocious grins. Underfoot a bizarre little gremlin winces in anguish. But don't worry, their ferocity isn't directed at visitors with a pure heart; they're there to protect the temple against evil from the four directions of the compass, standing ever vigilant against devils and demons trying to enter the temple grounds.

◁ GIANT BUDDHA
Size matters, at least when it comes to Buddhas. The larger and more ornate statues are a symbol of the devotion of their creators.

▽ TEMPLE WORSHIP
Several times a day, monks can be heard chanting while striking a wooden gong. Layman worship involves a series of bows to the main Buddha statue.

△ TIME OUT
Whether nestled in a remote mountain valley or just off a busy street, temples offer a peaceful escape from today's stresses and worries.

▽ MOUNTAIN SPIRIT
To the rear of almost every mountain temple are shrines to the Mountain Spirit and The Hermit, both remnants of a shamanistic past.

CHUNGCHEONG PROVINCES

Country roads, vineyards, ginseng fields draped in black; hot springs, beaches and shrines; National Parks and ancient capitals – central Korea is full of surprises waiting to be discovered

Map on page 198

Tourists often get only a fleeting look at the Chungcheong Provinces as they speed through on buses and trains heading for Gyeongju or Busan. Yet these two central provinces have a lot to offer anyone willing to take the time to explore their highways and byways. Chungcheongnam Province boasts dozens of historical sights, temples and an attractive coastline. Landlocked Chungcheongbuk, to the east, is an area of forested hills and small villages, a quiet, rarely visited rural backwater.

Chungcheongnam-do

To reach Chungcheongnam from the capital, head south on Highway 1, the Seoul-Busan Expressway (also called the Gyeongbu Expressway), then veer west and southwest on Highway 21 into the lush, terraced valleys and rolling hills of the province. First, you might consider stopping off at the **Independence Hall of Korea ❶** (open Tues–Sun 9.30am–6pm, Nov–Feb closes at 5pm; entrance fee) near to the town of Cheonan. This is much more than a "Hall" – it's a full-scale museum (the largest in the country, in fact), with several gargantuan sculptures, a half-dozen museum buildings, and a plaza that could hold a hundred thousand people. It takes half a day to fully appreciate this monument to Korea's determined, and ultimately successful, resistance to foreign aggression throughout its long and turbulent history. Unfortunately captions in English are few and far between.

The complex was completed in 1987, and no expense has been spared in developing displays containing historical artifacts, life-size recreations of Korea resistance fighters, and even reproductions of torture scenes that are sure to give nightmares to the squeamish. After a visit here, you'll understand the nearly universal bad feelings Koreans have for Japan (you may even wonder if this museum doesn't actually contribute to those feelings).

Travelers en route from Seoul to the west coast may find **Onyang ❷**, 18 km (11 miles) west of Cheonan on Highway 21, to be a refreshing stop along the way. Well established attractions here include the **Hyeonchung-sa Shrine** (open Wed–Mon 9am–6pm, Nov–Feb closes at 5pm; entrance fee), dedicated to Korea's great 16th-century naval hero, Admiral Yi Sun-sin. The **Onyang Folk Museum** (open daily 8.30am–6pm, Nov–Mar closes at 5pm; entrance fee) in **Gwongokdong** is touted as having the best all-around collection of Korean folk art in the world. The privately owned museum boasts over 7,000 traditional Korean folk articles, although this represents only a portion of the vast collection Kim Wondae has accumulated

PRECEDING PAGES: verdant fields near Daejeon. **LEFT:** Chungcheong is Korea's major ginseng-growing area. **BELOW:** the Independence Hall of Korea.

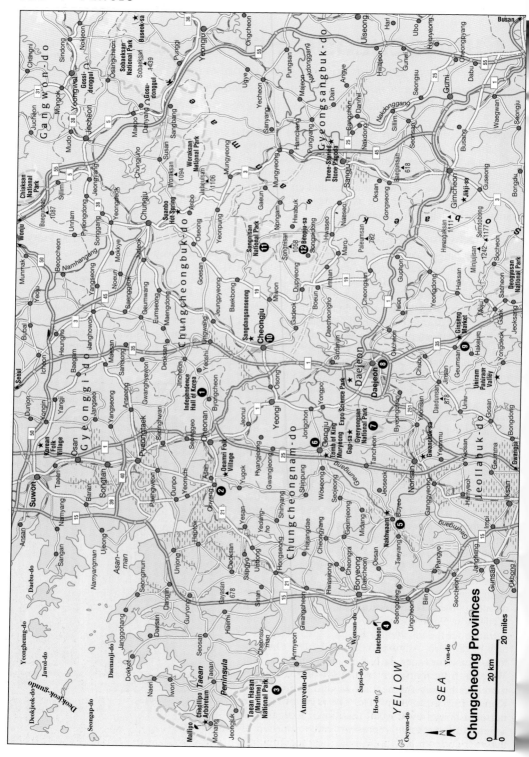

Chungcheong Provinces

Map
on page
198

over the past two decades. Three diorama display halls depict the life and traditions of Koreans with authentic household articles, work utensils, and religious, recreational and scholastic items.

Onyang's **hot spring** feeds soothing mineral waters to several hotels and public baths in the area. If you have not experienced a Korean public bath, take your time to immerse yourself into the almost unbearably hot tub, then hop into the invigorating cold tub. Do this a few times, and you'll be ready for anything. Primed after a stimulating hot bath, a pilgrimage to Admiral Yi's shrine, and insights into Korean culture, head westward to the coast, Mallipo Beach and Korea's largest arboretum.

West coast attractions

Korea's convoluted west coast, cut by the shallow waters of Yellow Sea, is dotted with myriad peninsulas and small islands, and bordered by sandy beaches overlooking quiet pine glens. Along this coast, village fishermen and seasonal beachgoers regulate their activities according to tidal changes, because the tide differential is so extreme. In certain areas at low tide, the Yellow Sea exposes vast mud flats a long distance offshore, owing to the huge tidal range on this coast, second only to the Bay of Fundy in Nova Scotia.

Taean Haean Maritime National Park ❸ extends north-south for some 70 km (45 miles) along the Chungcheongnam coast, its protected waters punctuated by a string of popular beaches such as Mallipo and Cheollipo. There is a rich variety of marine life here, although controlled fishing is permitted, and the area is well known for its seafood. The 200-acre sanctuary at Cheollipo protects more than 7,000 varieties of plants.

The **Cheollipo Arboretum** (not open to the public for conservation reasons; some admissions allowed if reserved two weeks in advance; tel: 041-672-6310) was founded by Ferris Miller, a naturalized Korean originally from Pennsylvania, who lived in Korea for over five decades. Some of the plants in Miller's arboretum are indigenous, while others were imported from around the world. There are, for example, two varieties of magnolia indigenous to Korea at Cheol-lipo, and 180 varieties from elsewhere (the entire magnolia family accounts for 800 members). Hollies have been hybridized at the arboretum, and there are presently 450 hollies there. Among the many botanical wonders flourishing in Miller's arboretum are rare species such as the *glyptostrobus lineatus,* a conifer from southern China, and *magnolia biondii* from north-central China. The arboretum was donated to the country when Mr Miller died in August 2002, and it is now being managed by a group of specialists.

Daecheon

Veteran Westerners in Korea have long favored **Daecheon Beach** ❹, as a summer seaside resort. This attractive stretch of sand, about 14 km (9 miles) from Daecheon town (also known as Boryong), can be reached by bus, train or car from Seoul. As you near Daecheon town, fields of yellow barley, the staple added to rice or boiled into a drink, cut bright

BELOW:
Daecheon Beach, a
well-established
seaside resort.

yellow swaths across the summer rice terraces. Daecheon is in the middle of a lush agricultural area, but it is also well known in Korea for its coal mines in the surrounding hills, contributing the base fuel from which *yeontan*, or charcoal heating briquettes, are made.

Daecheon Beach is unofficially divided into two sectors: a northern stretch called "KB," or the "Korean Beach," and a southern stretch called the "Foreigners' Beach." This was originally a Christian missionaries' resort, and many Daecheon homes are still occupied by missionaries or their descendants, by members of Seoul's diplomatic and banking corps, and more recently by wealthy Korean business and government leaders.

The Korean Beach, where discos and wine houses co-exist with sleepy fishermen's huts, is a non-stop party scene during the peak summer season, while the well-manicured Foreigners' Beach maintains a residential dignity.

Baekje capitals

About a half-hour's drive from the coast is the town of **Buyeo** ❺, famous throughout Korea for its relics from the Baekje kingdom (18 BC to AD 660). For openers, at Jeongnim-sa, a Baekje temple site in the center of town, is a seated stone Buddha and a five-story stone pagoda, one of three remaining from the Three Kingdoms Period (57 BC to AD 918). Other precious relics are displayed in the **Buyeo National Museum** (open Tues–Sun 9am–6pm, Nov–Feb closes at 5pm; entrance fee). Prehistoric stoneware vessels, shamanistic instruments, gilt-bronze and stone Buddhist statues, gold and jade ornaments and other treasures attest to the development and excellence of Baekje artists and craftsmen. The Buyeo museum building is something of a curios-

BELOW:
Baekje incense
burner, Buyeo.
BELOW RIGHT:
stone Buddhist
statue at Buyeo.

ity in that it was designed by a Korean architect along traditional Baekje lines, which were then adapted by the Japanese.

The Baekje legacy extends itself beyond the museum. Along the serene Geumgang River at **Baengmagang** (White Horse River), remnants of the grandeur and the fateful fall of the Baekje kingdom of some 1,300 years ago are preserved. Picnic on the flat rock (Nanseok, Warm Rock) on the riverbank at Saja, just as the Baekje kings used to. On the opposite side of the river is the picturesque **Nakhwaam** (Rock of the Falling Flowers) bluff with a pavilion on its brow. Tradition says that the Tang dynasty general Su Tingfang lured a protective dragon out of the river with a white horse's head, and thus was able to cross the river and conquer Buyeo.

Out of loyalty to their king and to preserve their dignity, court women jumped to their deaths from Nakhwaam into the river. As recorded in some Korean epics, they looked like falling blossoms as their colorful *chimajeogori* dresses billowed in their deadly flight.

Travel another half-hour to the northeast to reach **Gongju ❻**. The city was established in 475 AD, and was once the capital of the Baekje Kingdom until it was moved south to Buyeo. In Gongju, a **National Museum** (open Tues–Sun 9am–6pm, Nov–Feb closes at 5pm; entrance fee) was dedicated in 1972 to house relics found around town. Almost half of the 6,800 display items were excavated from the King Muryeong (r. 501–523) tomb. As you browse past Muryeong's gold crown ornaments, his exquisitely engraved bronze mirror, and other Baekje articles, remember that it was this same craftsmanship which was taught to the Japanese by emigrant Baekje artisans.

After visiting the museum, you may want to see where many of the items

Map on page 198

The five-tiered granite pagoda at Jeongnim-sa, in the center of Buyeo.

BELOW:
Gongsangang Fortress, Gongju.

Carved from granite, the Eunjin Mireuk statue is thought to have taken almost 40 years to complete.

BELOW: the Eunjin Mireuk at Gwanchok-sa is the largest standing stone Buddha in Korea.

originally came from – the **Tomb of King Muryeong** (open daily 9am–6pm, Nov–Feb closes at 5pm; free). The tomb was accidentally discovered in 1971 during a construction project, before which it had been undisturbed for 14 centuries. The 3,000 items pulled from the tomb have offered valuable insights into 6th-century Korean life. A model at the site illustrates the technique used in the construction. The tomb is a five-minute taxi or bus ride (Gongju Intercity bus Terminal) west of the city. Close by is another set of tombs, the **Songsanni Burial Mounds** (open daily 9am–6pm, Nov–Feb closes at 5pm; free).

Not far from downtown Gongju is an earthen (from the Baekje Period) and stone (from a 17th-century reconstruction) fortification, **Gongsanseong** (open daily 9am–6pm; entrance fee), lying beside the Geumgang River and surrounded by woods. To get there, you can catch a city bus at the Gongju Intercity bus terminal.

From Gongju, head southeast to **Gyeryongsan National Park** ❼, a beautiful area popular with hikers as well as with those taking time-out for deeper reflection. Long considered a propitious site, Gyeryongsan is home to several minor religious sects. In the 14th century a spot here was selected for the capital city and construction began before it was decided that Seoul would make a better site. Further west you can visit the Expo Science Park at Daedok, featuring a funfair and some permanent exhibitions from the Daejeon Expo which was held here in 1993.

These two sites are worth at least a day on their own if you have the time. Then you could return to Gongju and head 50 km (31 miles) southwest, traveling deeper into Baekje history to Buyeo on the curving Highway 23. Along the way, pause at the **Gap-sa temple** (open daily 8am–6pm; entrance fee), one of Korea's oldest temples, on the edge of Gyeryongsan National Park.

The Eunjin Mireuk

Head southeast from Buyeo, or south from Gongju, to the town of Nonsan; a short distance south of here is **Gwanchok-sa**, Temple of the Candlelights (open daily 7am–6pm; entrance fee), with one of the most impressive Buddhas in Korea. As you scale up the stone steps on the Banya hillside to the temple all the superlative descriptions you've ever heard regarding the the 1,000-year-old **Eunjin Mireuk** – the largest standing stone Buddha in Korea – stir you with anticipation. Your curiosity is piqued when, at the top of a flight of stairs, your first glance at the Eunjin Mireuk is through the clear, horizontal window of the temple (if the temple doors are open). All you can see of the "Buddha of the Future" is its face, its eyes peering back at you through the holy sanctum.

The "Standing Stone Gwanseum Maitreya" is awesome in its totality. Its disproportionate massiveness, crown, large hands and extended earlobes all suggest a higher evolved spiritual being. Its face, however, which is occasionally scrubbed clean, has flat features and almond-shaped eyes (not unlike the Koreans) and sculpted toes all of which lend tangible human qualities. Situated in the rear of the temple courtyard, the Eunjin Mireuk stands sedately at the foot of a stand of dwarf maple and scrub pine. Also included at Gwanchok-sa are a five-story stone pagoda, lantern, and altar which were constructed while the Eunjin Mireuk was being sculpted.

Map on page 198

Science City – Daejeon

With a population of 1.4 million, **Daejeon ❽** (240 km/150 miles south of Seoul) is Korea's sixth largest city and the largest in the Chungcheong Provinces. The city sits (more or less) in the middle of the country, and if you're traveling south from Seoul, you're sure to be going through Daejeon at some point. As Korean cities go, it's pleasant enough, but there really isn't much here to entice visitors to linger – although it is surrounded by beautiful mountains and lakes. The major city attraction is the **Expo Science Park** (open daily 9.30am–6pm, Nov–Feb closes at 5pm; entrance fee) on the northern edge of town. In 1993 this was the site of the Daejeon Expo. Since then, it has been reinvented as a science theme park with the 13 major pavilions housing a variety of themed attractions (space exploration, recycling, automobiles, to name a few) with displays emphasizing technology and the future.

In keeping with the futuristic theme, pavilions come in imaginative shapes, sizes and colors. A monorail, cable cars and tram shuttle people between the pavilions, performance centers, the Expo Theatre, and restaurants. The park complements a couple of top-notch science and technology universities, and a nearby science research center that has made Daejeon Korea's principal city for science and technology. The city's profile was further boosted when it was selected as one of the venues for the 2002 soccer World Cup.

On the KTX, the new high-speed bullet train, you can travel from Seoul to Busan in 2hr 40min, at an average speed of 300 kmh (190 mph). There are two lines: Gyeongbu-seon (Seoul–Daejeon–Daegu– Busan) and Honam-seon (Seoul–Gwangju–Mokpo).

BELOW: the ginseng harvest near Geumsan.

Ginseng

Among the herbs in Korea, the "cure-all wonder," panax ginseng, referred to as *insam* in Korean, is by far the most popular. As far back as the 3rd millennium BC in China, herbal potions and poultices were used to maintain and restore the internal eum-yang (i.e. the negative-positive, base-acid, female-male) forces to proper balance by stimulating or repressing either aspect. Ginseng, which originally grew wild in ravines and the forests of Korea and Manchuria, was found to be bursting with yang energy. It became a vital ingredient used in a vast range of medications prescribed in the first Chinese pharmacopoeia.

If consumed regularly in small doses, scientists claim the root will help stimulate the central nervous system. Larger doses, however, depress the nervous system by buffering out physical and chemical stress, and by promoting cell production that counteracts anemia and hypertension. Ginseng thus reportedly increases physical and mental effi-ciency, and enhances gastrointestinal functions. It is widely believed in Korea that the regular use of ginseng will extend one's life.

Ideal climatic conditions in Korea, especially between northern 36° to 38° latitudes, where an optimum mountain-forest simulated environment is maintained, have allowed the production of a cultivated root that is considered to be the international standard. Korea's main ginseng-growing area is in the central region, south of Daejeon around the small city of Geumsan where the air is filled with the aroma of the root being processed, and there is a very active market attracting buyers from throughout Asia.

The growth and maturation cycle of Korean ginseng takes one to six years depending on the intended use of the root. In mid-May, the plant flowers. Seeds of the strongest, most mature, five-year-old plants are selected in mid-July and planted in late October. After harvest, the roots are washed, peeled, steamed, and dried. They are then produced in two grades white *(baek)* and red *(hong)*. Around 60 percent of the best ginseng is selected for the red variety which is further processed to preserve the potency of its chemical components. The root takes so many minerals from the soil, that once the fields have been harvested the land will not be planted with ginseng again for at least 10 to 15 years.

Valued more highly than gold in ancient times, Korean ginseng today is still a costly commodity. While some Koreans eat ginseng raw, most will try this bitter experience only once. Better to have some fresh ginseng in the very popular *samgyetang* (ginseng chicken soup). Perhaps to placate Western consumers, ginseng comes conveniently packaged in modern products. For internal rejuvenation there are pills, capsules, extracts, jellies, teas, soft drinks, jams, candies, chewing gums, and, ironically, even cigarettes. For cosmetic needs, there are ginseng body creams and shampoos.

At the Geumsan Ginseng Festival (mid-September) you can dig up your own ginseng, have a bowl of *samgyetang*, and even have an oriental medicine doctor carry out an analysis of your health and stick a few pins in you. ❏

LEFT: ginseng root on sale at Geumsan Market, the center of the ginseng trade.

Ginseng country

The hills and valleys south of Daejeon are ginseng country. Ginseng fields are easy to spot – they're usually on a hillside or rocky slope and covered by black sheets of plastic to protect the shade-loving plants. The little city of **Geumsan** ❾ is smack in the middle of ginseng country, and is home to the largest and most active ginseng market in Korea (which would probably make it the largest in the world). It is possible to buy ginseng along with a bewildering assortment of herbs, roots, fungi, dried lizards and toads, scorpions and god-knows-what else at the many oriental medicine shops along the main thoroughfare and the side streets leading off it. But if you want to go when the place is really hopping, go on the 2nd, 7th, 12th, 17th, 22nd and 27th day of each month. That's market day in Geumsan, and farmers from throughout the province bring in fresh ginseng, and a variety of vegetables and fruit to sell to busloads of elderly tourists who come for the best selection and prices in the country.

Gateway to Chungcheongbuk Province

Cheongju ❿ is the gateway to the natural attractions of Chungcheongbuk Province. First you may want to stop and rummage around a few museums to get some historical background for your visit. The **Cheongju National Museum** (open Tues–Sun 9am–6pm, Nov–Feb closes at 5pm; entrance fee) has three rooms which display the museum's permanent collection on the prehistoric period, the Three Kingdoms Period, and historical art. Cheongju prides itself on being the first place where movable metal printing type was used (in 1377, well before Gutenberg printed his famous Bible), even if the technology did not take hold within Korea. The **Cheongju Early Printing Museum** (open Tues–Sun except major holidays; 9am–6pm, Nov–Feb closes at 5pm; entrance fee) displays artifacts and histories of Korea's early dabbling with printing presses.

A 30-minute drive into the mountains northeast of Cheongju will take you to **Sangdang sanseong**, a mountain fortress that has a long, if muddied, history. It was first built during the Baekje Period, then renovated during the Silla and Joseon eras. Four gates and most of the wall still stand, and it has been made into a mountain park that is popular with locals. It is also a pleasant place to relax before heading off to a trio of national parks strung out along the southeastern borders of the province.

Songnisan National Park

Of these three parks, **Songnisan National Park** ⓫, a mountain retreat an hour and half from Cheongju, is the most popular. A visit here is superb any time of the year, but is most favored by discriminating Korean weekenders in the autumn when its trees are aflame with color. Oaks, maples and gingkos try to outdo each other in their autumnal radiance. As one romantic Korean travel writer once wrote of Songnisan: "The tender green for spring, abundance of forests for summer, yellow leaves for autumn, and snow for winter all deserve appreciation."

Indeed, since ancient times, Songnisan has been a preferred resort area, and appropriately, the word

Map on page 198

Ginseng farming can be a very profitable exercise.

BELOW: golden hues at Songnisan National Park.

songni means "escape from the vulgar." To achieve this Songni escape, travel from Seoul to Daejeon by train, then transfer by bus or car through Okcheon to the Songni area. Alternatively, you can also travel directly by car or bus from Seoul via **Cheongju City**. It is about a three-hour car journey one way. After passing through Cheongju City and beginning an ascent to idyllic Songni, you will enter the steep Malttijae Pass which serves as an unwinding transition from harsh urbanity to comforting nature at its freshest.

The ministerial pine

Just beyond a glassy reservoir, on your final approach to the **Songni highlands** and **Songni village**, your local guide will no doubt point out the most distinguished tree in Korea. This is an old pine on the left side of the road called the Jeongipum Pine, so named because the Joseon-dynasty King Sejo (r. 1455–68) granted this hoary fellow the official bureaucratic title of Jeongipum, a rank equivalent to that of a cabinet minister. Legend and even history note that this humble tree was granted that distinction because it lifted its boughs in respect one day as King Sejo and a royal entourage passed by. The pine's loyalty and politeness was duly rewarded by the flattered king.

Just beyond this ministerial pine is the final approach to **Songnidong**, a mountain village famous for the semi-wild tree mushrooms cultivated in this area and sold at roadside stands. Seoulites try to arrive in Songni village at lunchtime, when they can enjoy a fabled Songni mushroom lunch featuring as many as six different mushroom dishes served with a dizzying array of side dishes, gimchi and rice. Be sure to buy a bag of these tender air-dried morsels for later munching at home.

BELOW: Beopju-sa.

The Biggest Buddha

After this mushroom-fest, proceed uphill to Songnisan's biggest attraction, **Beopju-sa** ⓜ (open daily 8am–sunset; entrance fee), a large temple complex dominated by a massive Mireuk Buddha of the Future, appropriately fashioned from modern poured cement. This 27-meter (88-ft) image, completed in 1964, is often identified by tour guides as "the biggest Buddha in Korea."

Map on page 198

This sprawling temple complex was first built at the base of Mount Songni in the 6th century, shortly after Buddhism had been carried into Korea from China. Records note that work began in 553, during the 14th year in the reign of the Silla king Jinheung. The original founder and spiritual master was the high priest Uisin, who had returned home from studies in India. Uisin contributed several Buddhist scriptural books to Beopju-sa's first library.

Author-historian Han Gihyung, a former assistant editor of the *Korea Journal*, writes that this temple, "one of Korea's oldest," was reportedly "renovated during the reigns of Kings Seongdeok and Hyegong (702–780)." This fact can be confirmed by observing the ancient stone buildings of the temple surviving to date.

According to Han, the monarchs of not only the Silla dynasty but also the Goryeo and Joseon dynasties protected the temple. In the 6th year (1101) of King Sukjong's reign (in the Goryeo era), the king gathered 30,000 priests from all over the country to pray for the health of ailing Royal Priest Uicheon. In the Joseon era, King Sejo (1455–68) presented the temple with large tracts of paddy fields, grains and slaves. Kings Injo (1623–49), Cheoljong (1849–63), and Gojong (1864–1906) all had the temple renovated. Remnants of this favored temple's days of spiritual grandeur can be found in every section of the compound. Consider the famed Cheolhwak, a massive iron rice pot which was cast in 720, during the reign of Silla King Seongdeok, when some 3,000 priests were living and eating here. This grand mass facility is 1.2 meters (4 ft) high, 2.7-meters (9 ft) in diameter, and 10.8 meters (35 ft) in circumference. These days you'll find perhaps only 2 percent of that previous number of gray-robed, sutra-chanting monks, so the pot no longer has its utilitarian purpose.

Perhaps the most celebrated historical treasure at Beopju-sa is the **Palsangjeon**, or **Eight Image Hall**, which rises in symmetrical splendor above the complex's roomy main courtyard. As Han notes: "This five-story building, presumably reconstructed during the second year of King Injo's reign (1624) in the Joseon era, is a rare architectural work for Buddhism not only in Korea but also in China, and can be compared with a similar five-story pagoda at Nara, Japan."

Other Beopju-sa curiosities include a large deva lantern surrounded with relief bodhisattvas, a second stone lantern supported by two carved lions, and, outside the temple, a large "ablution trough" carved in the shape of a lotus. To the left side of the main entrance you'll also find a huge boulder that has come to life with a serene Buddha sculpted into a wide and flat façade. If such art boggles your mind, head for natural beauty in the surrounding hills that are laced with excellent hiking trails. A view of the Beopju-sa complex from one of Songnisan's upper ridges is just reward for the huffing and puffing it takes to get up there. ❑

BELOW: monk farmers at Beopju-sa.

GYEONGSANGBUK PROVINCE

Map on page 212

Gyeongsangbuk Province has the most varied cultural landscape in Korea, with traditional folk villages, white-sand beach resorts and thoroughly modern cities

The logical starting point for a dip through Korea's southern crescent area is the large city of **Daegu ❶**, capital of Gyeongsangbuk Province. Daegu serves as a clearing house for a variety of produce harvested in this agriculturally rich region, and is also an industrial center. The city was hit by tragedy in February 2003 when a suicidal man set fire to a subway train, killing 125 people.

At first glance Daegu may appear to be either a half-hearted attempt at a city or an overgrown village, but a closer inspection reveals it to be a uniquely Korean compromise between urban and rural extremes: it is big enough to offer good hotels, restaurants and 21st-century entertainment, yet small enough to retain a relaxed ambience that is lost in Seoul or Busan. Few of Daegu's buildings are so imposing as to obstruct the view of the surrounding mountains. Pedestrians rather than cars dominate the streets. Traditional clothing is still very evident, especially (for no apparent reason) in the environs of Dalseong, an earthwork fortress from the prehistoric Samhan era. And the city is famous for its apples – the Daegu apple is renowned throughout Asia.

Dalseong was originally constructed of several artificial hills in the middle of the broad plain that is now largely filled by Daegu. Presumably these hills supported a Korean variant of the motte-and-bailey forts once common in Europe. Late in the 14th century, at the end of the Mongol occupation and the beginning of the Joseon dynasty, the fort was enlarged and stones were added to its existing earthworks. In 1596, during the Imjin War, the fort was again enlarged to its present circumference of 1,300 meters (4,265 ft) and height of 4 meters (13 ft). The fort is now a popular park, called **Dalseong** (open daily 5am–10pm, Nov–Feb closes at 7pm; free), complete with a small zoo that includes several claustrophobic lions donated by the local Lions Club. The entrance to Dalseong is a favorite meeting place for the city's senior citizens, who lounge amicably along its cobblestone walkway, traditionally sartorial in pastel silks and cotton voile.

West Gate Market *(seomun sijang)*, one of the largest and oldest in the country, is just a short walk away, across Dongsan Hospital. The narrow alleys of the market are lined with cauldrons of noodle soup billowing steam, mobile vendors with carts devoted exclusively to such specialized merchandise as sewing needles and arcane mousetraps. Clustered networks of permanent stalls deal in even more mundane necessities.

Redolent pharmacopeia

Yakjeon Golmok, "**Medicine Alley**", is the site of one of Daegu's most notable sensory delights. The street is a center for wholesale purveyors of traditional medicines. A stimulating barrage of scents oozes out of

PRECEDING PAGES: the Silla tombs at Gyeongju. **LEFT:** mask-dance drama at Hahoe Folk Village. **BELOW:** healing herbs at Daegu's "Medicine Alley".

Gyeongsang Provinces

0   20 km

0   20 miles

buckets and boxes of prepared pharmacopoeia and wafts up from magical herbs drying on woven mats under the sun. The blend of aromas shifts gradually as one wanders down this pungent street. Indeed, mere inhalations will probably relieve you of any afflictions of the nasal passages or even the soul. Should this prove ineffective, there are several licenced herbalists who will willingly prescribe healing brews.

Daegu has its own brand of nightlife that, if lacking the polish of posher establishments in Seoul, is well endowed with enthusiasm. Most after-hours partying in Daegu is centralized in several blocks near the "old station" at the center of town. Standing with your back to the station, expensive "businessmen's entertainments" are to your right; on your left are rock 'n' roll clubs and wine stalls. Adjacent to the latter is one of the city's larger markets. At night the two merge in a spirited confusion of side alley vendors, eclectic shopfronts, blasting nightclub bands, and throngs intent on entertaining themselves.

Start your Daegu evening with a sidewalk snack of steamed crab, or, if you dare, raw sea cucumbers. Continue with dinner in a smoke-billowing bulgogi house or in an inexpensive but elegant Western-styled restaurant, then move out to explore the many raucous bars.

Time travel by bus

In addition to the train station and the highway bus terminal adjacent to it, Daegu has four depots for back-road buses, one for each of the cardinal directions. These buses serve remote villages and mountain hamlets out of range of highway express buses or trains, and in many of these places foreign visitors are still a considerable surprise. Goats, chickens, and pigs on their way to market are often among the bus passengers. Disembark with them and their owners and you'll be rewarded with a rare glimpse of a genuine village market. Transistor radios and plastic serving trays may now be bartered for livestock and vegetables, but the rural setting has yet to lose its timeless appeal.

The annual cycle of village life fluctuates between intense periods of field labor and long stretches of off-season leisure. Rise at dawn and follow the *makgeolli* merchant on his delivery rounds to village taverns. Clusters of children in their school uniforms hurry through the morning fog to schoolyard chores. Farmers sometimes still lash wooden plows on the backs of bullocks and lead them out to rice fields. The resounding toll of a brass gong announces a funeral. Join the stragglers in the procession led by a bier laden with paper flowers, and you will witness a remarkable blend of solemn ritual and carefree frivolity as the deceased is escorted to the netherworld. On festive days, such as Chuseok and Lunar New Year's Day, everyone gathers to dance to the pulsing rhythms of hourglass drums and clanging gongs. There are no strangers on a country festival day: exhibit the slightest touch of whimsy and you will be accosted, festooned with ribbons, plied with liquor, and dragged into a frenzied dance.

Back-road buses are cheap, crowded and not especially comfortable; but, except for a possible stiff

Map on page 212

Daegu has developed rapidly and is now South Korea's third-largest city.

BELOW: rural tranquility near Hahoe.

TIP

There is a new subway in Daegu. The first line opened in 1997, with more lines to follow. For most visitors, however, the major city sites are near the railway station, or a short taxi ride away.

back, they offer a low-risk gamble for anyone keen on exploration. Pick a destination at random (place names ending in "sa" are safest, as they promise a temple at the very least), stock up on emergency provisions and try your luck.

Temple-hopping around Daegu

The bus to **Unmun-sa ❷** (open daily 8am–sunset; entrance fee) from Nambu Terminal (South Depot) is a challenging, but rewarding, test of stamina. After enduring several hours of some of Korea's most jarring dirt roads, you will be left at a dead-end town consisting of a gas station, a few inns and restaurants, along with a few dozen farmhouses, including some handsome examples of traditional folk architecture. The path to the temple follows a rambling stream through a spacious pine forest. The surrounding mountains harbor several small hermitages. Set in an open field, Unmun-sa is a sanctuary for a community of Buddhist nuns, who go about their work and worship unperturbed by occasional visitors who drift through for the many fine paintings adorning the temple walls.

The favorite destination for Daeguites with a free afternoon is **Palgongsan Provincial Park ❸**, only a few minutes drive north of the city. The attractions here are the gentle mountains, clear mountain streams, as well as the numerous restaurants along the roads. In season, apples, grapes and fresh vegetables are sold from roadside stands.

During the Silla Dynasty, Palgon Mountain was one of five sacred mountains, and numerous temples were built and pilgrimages were made to make offerings to Buddha and the Mountain Spirit. There are still several temples in the mountains and valleys of this park. The largest is **Donghwa-sa** (open daily; 7am–sunset; entrance fee), a center for practicing Zen (called Seon in Korean),

BELOW: traditional wooden houses at Hahoe Folk Village.

with several hermitages located in the mountains. The temple has recently expanded, and a giant granite Buddha was added in the hope that it would speed up the reunification of North and South Korea. Koreans come to make an offering and pray for peace at the foot of the Buddha.

High above Donghwa-sa, and reached by trail from the temple, is **Gatbawi**, a 1,000-year-old Buddha carved from mountain stone and serenely looking out over the mountains and valleys from his lofty viewpoint. Being a curing Buddha, Gatbawi is thought to have special medicinal powers, and believers come to pray for the health of their family and friends. It is commonly believed that Gatbawi will answer at least one of your prayers. Just below Gatbawi are shrines to the Mountain Spirit (Palgonsan is also an important mountain in shamanism) and Dragon. Directly across from the shrine is a cafeteria serving free vegetarian meals. Gatbawi is open 24 hours, and you will find people praying at almost any hour, but if you go late bring a flashlight. There are stone stairs leading up the mountain (a short, but steep climb), but no lights.

Needles and noodles

Jikji-sa ❹ (open daily 7am–7.30pm; entrance fee), easily reached from Daegu via Gimcheon (about an hour and half to the north), is a gem of a temple, recently repainted in an entrancing blend of blue, magenta and gold. Exquisite figures and landscapes embellish virtually every external wall space, and Jikji-sa's shrines are populated with a bewildering array of finely carved statues. A quick stroll through the temple grounds might induce a giddy overload of visual stimulation, but taken slowly, Jikji-sa is a rare pleasure. Its beauty has not gone unnoticed: it is one of several temples associated with Samyeong Daesa, who was both a Buddhist saint

Map on page 212

Gatbawi, the 1,000-year old stone Buddha on Palgonsan Mountain.

BELOW: Jikji-sa has a superb mountain setting.

Outside of Andong is a seven-story brick pagoda, Chilcheung Jeontap, with Unified Silla era (AD 668–918) relief engravings of god-generals and divas. This pagoda is thought to be the oldest, biggest pagoda in the country. You'll find it in Sinsedong along the railroad tracks.

and a military hero. Samyeong was born in the town of Milyang in 1544. His family was of the *yangban* class (aristocrats) and he was educated in the Confucian Classics. After losing both his parents, Samyeong left his home to wander in the mountains. He eventually made his way to Jikji-sa where his study of Zen led to his attainment of enlightenment. He became chief priest of Jikji-sa in 1574.

Soon after, he set out wandering again and met Seosan, the most prominent Korean Buddhist master of the period. According to legend, they engaged in a contest of magic. Samyeong began by arduously transforming a bowl of needles into noodles. Seosan received the bowl of noodles, promptly turned it upside down, and needles crashed to the floor. Samyeong's next feat was to stack eggs end-to-end vertically, several feet into the air. Seosan followed suit, but started from the top. Samyeong responded by turning a clear blue sky to a thunderstorm and challenged Seosan to return the torrential rain to the sky. Seosan calmly met the challenge and added his own flourish by transforming the ascending droplets into a flock of birds. Duly humbled, Samyeong asked to become a disciple of the greater master.

Several years later, the Japanese invasion began and Seosan emerged as leader of a voluntary militia of monks, which eventually grew to a force of 5,000. Seosan was too old for battle, so he appointed Samyeong as field commander. Under Samyeong's command, Korea's warrior monks earned a reputation for their fierce courage and played a major role in repulsing the Japanese.

Stately Harabeoji

BELOW: *haraboji* (grandfather) at Andong.

Andong ❺ is one city where Joseon dynasty *yangban* still walk down the streets. Andong has become synonymous with *yangban* since the Andong Kwon clan served in high government positions during Korea's last dynasty.

From Daegu, Andong can be reached via expressway in just over an hour, or alternatively via a 6-hour-long, roundabout train ride from Seoul which only begins to get interesting as the train enters the outskirts of Andong town. The monotony of hills and grain fields and modern Saemaul cement villages is broken by sturdy, wooden houses with white rubber *gomusin* (Korean shoes with upturned toes) lined up outside lattice doors on the *maru* (wooden porch).

Andong is full of surprises and ironies. Expect to see stately *harabeoji* (grandfathers) dressed in *hanbok* (traditional Korean clothes), and sporting horn-rimmed glasses and wispy beards, strolling around town. Although modern times have encroached on this provincial town with a multi-purpose dam and concrete architecture, a few *yangban* manors have managed to survive through the ages with a traditional graciousness and charm. These houses are easily recognized by their roofs of charcoal-colored tile which curve upward over thick wooden beams; beneath are white and cement-covered mud walls, windows and doors of paper and wood, a hard wooden *maru*, and weathered wood railings that surround the house. Above the front entrance, a signboard in an ancestor's finest calligraphic script proclaims the dignity of the dwelling. These old houses preserved to this day are not without modern trappings. You can easily spot electrical wiring and the ubiquitous TV antennae.

About 3 km (2 miles) east of the city center is the **Andong Folk Museum** (open Tues–Sun except major holidays; Mar–Oct 9am–6pm, Nov–Feb 9.30am–5pm; entrance fee), surrounded by traditional-style homes and outdoor displays. This little folk village is pleasantly situated, and many of the homes have been turned into restaurants that serve a local clientele (always a good sign), as well as welcoming visitors.

Map on page 212

Dosan Seowon – the 1,000-won academy

An epitome of Confucianism that should not be missed while in the Andong area is **Dosan Seowon Confucian Academy** ❻ (open daily 9am–6pm, Dec–Feb closes at 5pm; entrance fee). The academy is a 28-km (17-mile) inter-city bus ride north of Andong, and a 2-km (1¼-mile) walk down a winding paved road that overlooks a peaceful blue lake and green rice paddies.

Dosan Seowon was initiated by Yi Hwang (also known as Toegye, Dosu and Toedo; 1501–70), one of the foremost Confucian scholars of Korea and once Chief of Confucian Studies and Affairs. The name Dosan Seowon was given to the academy in 1575 by King Seonjo. The government also later acknowledged Yi Hwang and his academy by depicting both of them on the commonly circulated 1,000-won note.

Confucianism is no longer instructed at Dosan Seowon, but one can stroll through the hallowed Dosan Seodang lecture hall at the main entranceway, see the wooden plates that were used for printing lessons in the Janggyeonggak archive, and study some of Yi Hwang's relics, such as his gnarled walking cane and books of his teachings rendered in his personal calligraphy. The wooden, tiled Joseon dynasty house behind the academy and over the ridge has been the abode of Yi Hwang's descendants for the past 16 generations.

An older institution, and one which is still very much alive with followers, is the **Bongjeong-sa** ❼ Buddhist temple, 16 km (10 miles) northwest of Andong city. Perhaps a more awesome sight is the 12.4-meter (40-ft) **Amitaba Buddha** carved on a mammoth boulder on the mountain at Jebiwon, 5 km (3 miles) from Andong en route to Yongju on Highway 5. This Buddha, which dates back to the Goryeo dynasty (AD 918–1392), stands on single lotus petals. Its robe and hands are carved into a massive granite boulder, and its head and hair are carved from two separate pieces of rock set into holy place. A stone pagoda sits higher on the slope among gnarled pines.

Charming Hahoe

A purer essence of Joseon dynasty architecture and rural life has been maintained for the past 500 years in a hamlet called **Hahoe** ❽ (open daily 9am–7pm, Nov–Feb closes at 6pm; entrance fee). This village is a half-hour ride southwest of Andong. During the Joseon dynasty Hahoe was celebrated for its literati and military leaders, and for a form of mask dance drama that evolved there. Today, it is appreciated for its rustic, traditional aesthetics.

Child wearing Hanbok at the Andong Folk Museum.

BELOW: the Amitaba Buddha.

Ornamental mask in the mask museum at Hahoe Folk Village.

BELOW: Hahoe is perhaps the most authentic "Folk Village" in Korea.

Hahoe is certainly off the beaten track, which has helped to keep it traditional. The Andong inter-city bus makes infrequent round-trips as far as Jungni (about 4 km or 2½ miles north of Hahoe). You can take a taxi or wait at a bus stop at the western fringe of town for a privately run bus to Pungsan, which is 16 km (10 miles) west of Andong. Pungsan is your last glimpse of paved Korea; the zigzagging 8 km (5-mile) dirt road to Hahoe passes Jungni, cutting through grain and vegetable fields, and, finally, the bus deposits you in 16th-century Korea. Earthen thatched huts, larger *yangban* manors of wood and tile, the surrounding Sobaek Mountains, and the serpentine Nakdonggang River bending around Hahoe; this is the Korea that is warm, hearty and strongly rooted in tradition.

The dirt path that wends around the hamlet is inlaid with chips of ceramic and tile. Cows are tethered in the front yard, chewing on hay. Under the tiled and thatched cave of each home is a row of fermented soybean (*doenjang*) patties drying in the sun. *Jige*, or A-frames, used for carrying heavy loads, lean against mud walls. In all its natural, raw beauty, Hahoe is perhaps the most picturesque village in Korea. Admittedly, there are a few modernities; even the oldest house – said to be around 550 years old by the local museum curator – is equipped with a refrigerator on its hard wooden *maru* and a TV antenna on its lichen-covered roof.

Across the path from the *yangban* manor is a museum that imitates Joseon architectural lines and is painted in bold Saemaul colors. This museum honors an educated 16th-century aristocrat from Hahoe, Yu Seongryong. Yu competed with Admiral Yi Sun-sin for court favors during the Japanese Hideyoshi invasions of the 1590s, and eventually became the king's prime minister. Yu's voluminous books of genealogy, personal articles and government documents

FOLK VILLAGES

There are two types of "folk villages" in Korea. One is a commercial endeavor where the buildings have either been built or moved and a village constructed on the spot. People working in the village are experienced in traditional ways, but they are being paid (though not a lot), and this is not their home.

The other, more authentic, type of folk village is that which has chosen to maintain its traditional ways, limiting the construction of modern buildings, and hanging on to customs long-since forgotten in Korea's cities. It is here that you will experience Korean rural life more or less as it has been lived for centuries. There are only a handful of these villages that have been officially recognized (such as Hahoe), but driving through the Korean countryside you are bound to notice a considerable number of villages that appear "traditional".

The fact is that life in the countryside, for many, is not a whole lot different than how it was 50 years ago. People generally live in the same homes their grandparents did, farm the same plot of land, live the same hard-working, yet quiet, life. Yet, as elsewhere in the world, this way of life is under threat, as more and more young people leave for the hustle and bustle of the modern city.

are displayed in the museum. The Yu clan remains the most influential in Hahoe.

Probably the most glaring visual obstruction in Hahoe is an off-white school building. It stands out most noticeably when seen from the hilltop across the river. The school was a Saemaul Undong (New Community Movement) project. The Hahoe villagers vetoed future Saemaul developments, and with the blessing of government officials, managed to keep their home town in thatch.

The village is quite popular with Koreans and foreigners alike, even if it is a little out of the way. When Britain's Queen Elizabeth II paid a visit to Korea in 1999, Hahoe was the one place outside of Seoul she chose to visit. Naturally, this is quite a feather in the cap for the little village and a museum has been set up to house the photos and other mementos from the visit. More interesting is the new **Hahoe Mask Museum** (open daily 9.30am–6pm; entrance fee), displaying Korean masks on the first floor and international masks on the second floor. Hahoe is famous for its *Byeolsingut Tallori*, a mask dance drama that is part shamanistic ritual and part slapstick comedy. At weekends (May–Oct Sat and Sun 3–4pm; Mar, Apr, Nov: Sun 3–4pm; entrance fee), villagers perform the dance drama in the amphitheater located near the village entryway (across from the parking lot). If you are going to Hahoe, the dance drama will make the long trip worthwhile.

The "floating rock"

Another place that is rather inaccessible but really should be seen while in the Andong area is **Buseok-sa ❾** (Floating Rock Temple; open daily 6am–sunset; entrance fee), 60 km (37 miles) due north of Andong along Highway 5 and a long, bumpy road. For the serious student of ancient culture, this is one of the country's most rewarding detours. The temple was established in 676 by High Priest Uisang, who returned to Korea from China with teachings of Hwaeom Buddhism. The legend relates how Uisang's former lover reunited with him in the form of a huge granite "floating rock." She later transformed herself under the main hall, her head beneath the gilded-clay Buddha and her tail 18 meters (60 ft) away under a stone lantern so she could help protect Uisang's temple. That same "floating rock" still hangs protectively and precariously outside Buseok-sa's main hall.

Despite the floating rock protectors, the temple was burned down by invaders in early 14th century, and then reconstructed in 1376. Fortunately, it was just beyond Hideyoshi's destructive reach in the 1590s, so the famed Muryangsujeon (Eternal Life Hall) main hall has been preserved to this day. This hall is considered to be the oldest and most classical wooden structure in Korea. Its Goryeo style is said to have been influenced by Greek artisans through India, and this structural theory is evidenced by the hall's main support pillars that gradually taper off at the ends.

Predating the temple by at least 50 years and complementing its Goryeo architecture is a 2.7-meter (9-ft) gilded-clay sitting Buddha, the only one of its kind in Korea. Also, Buseok-sa's Goryeo interior of Buddha and the Four Kings are considered to be the oldest wall paintings in Korea outside ancient tomb art.

Map on page 212

BELOW: *Byeolsingut Tallori*, the mask dance drama at Hahoe.

Sun, sea and sand at Pohang beach.

BELOW: the East Sea (known to non-Koreans as the Sea of Japan) is a source of wonderful seafood.

Crabs and beaches

The east coast of Gyeongsangbuk-do is known for two things: beaches and crabs. Beaches are scattered along the coast from Pohang north to the border. Most of them can boast fine white sands which, except for weekends, remain surprisingly free of crowds. Granted, these beaches don't qualify as undiscovered tropical paradises, but they do offer a chance for sunbathing, some beachcombing (glass floats from Japanese fishing boats sometimes wash ashore), and an occasional dip in the chilly waters of the East Sea. You're likely to see a busload of older Koreans, who are out for a day of sightseeing, stop to have lunch. After that, they'll crank up the radio for some impromptu dancing and singing, while a few of them will head off for a walk along the beach in their Sunday best.

You really must combine a visit to the beach with some fresh seafood. Raw seafood restaurants (usually referred to as *hoetjip*) are very popular with Koreans, and Korea's best seafood is found on the east coast. Just south of the city of Yeongdeok is the fishing village of **Ganggu** ❿, which becomes jammed with visitors on weekends. You can buy fresh crab, have it steamed and then sit at a sidewalk table, perhaps with a beer or soju accompaniment, and enjoy a Neptunian feast while watching all the action around you. Koreans eat everything but the crab "lungs"; they swear that the most delicious parts of the crab are wasted by Westerners. In late summer the streets are lined with squid hung out to dry, another specialty of the coast.

Steel city

At the southern end of Gyeongsangbuk-do's coastline is **Pohang** ⓫, a seaport and resort area that since 1968 has been the jewel in Korea's industrial crown.

This is because Pohang is the location of the model Pohang Iron and Steel Company Ltd (POSCO), Korea's successful producer of industrial steel and its profitable by-products.

Map on page 212

Situated on the rim of **Yeongil Bay** and the East Sea, POSCO is one of the world's biggest steel producers. Pohang itself is not just dominated by POSCO. It *is* POSCO. Just as **Ulsan** is "Hyundai Town" where every major firm is part of the Hyundai group, so Pohang appears a one-company town. Schools, gymnasia and housing complexes are all part of POSCO.

Were it not for the fact that this is capitalist South Korea, one might say the firm has achieved the socialist ideal in which everything is run for and provided by the state, or in this case, the company. POSCO is also an environment-conscious company and the town is remarkably clean considering it is based on steel production.

Bogyeong-sa

In the foothills of Naeyeonsan, just about 15 km (9 miles) north of Pohang, is **Bogyeong-sa** ⑫ (open daily 5am–7pm; entrance fee), a temple that offers a long history and a hike to a nearby pool and waterfall.

A Western-style *yeogwan* down the road to the right is a good spot to stay overnight. It offers a picturesque view of the mountains and is within drum-beat range of the Buddhist temple. If you can sleep with one ear alert for the early morning drum-call to prayer, wait outside for the sight of a sunrise and birds leaving their nocturnal perches. The only human sounds you'll hear will be your own stirring and distant sutras being chanted by monks celebrating all life on earth.

BELOW:
sorting the day's catch at Pohang.

Chinese mirrors of Madeung and Beomnan

Once sleep is washed from your eyes, stroll over to Bogyeong Temple. Just before reaching the temple proper, you will see a walled-in hermitage. Next to it is Bogyeong-sa where monks hold retreats for lay Buddhists. According to the sign posted at Bogyeong-sa, this temple was built during the Silla dynasty when Buddhism was first introduced to Korea. At that time, priests Madeung and Beomnan returned from China with the new religion and two mirrors. One mirror had 12 facets and the other had eight. The eight-faceted mirror was given to Priest Iljo, one of their disciples, who was told that if he went eastward he would find a deep pond in **Jongnamsan** on the east coast of the Silla kingdom. If he threw the mirror into the water and filled the pond with earth and built a temple there, Buddhism would flourish.

The eight-faceted mirror is said to be buried under Bogyeong-sa's **Jeong-wangjeon Hall**. Fine Buddhist paintings are hung in Jeongwangjeon and Dae-ungjeon, but what distinguishes this temple from most others is its backdrop of waterfalls streaking the mountains that form this lush valley. An easy hiking trail beside the temple leads to a clear pool, and further to 11 other waterfalls where you can enjoy a cool summer splash.

Ulleung-do

Few foreigners venture out to this remote island 268 km (166 miles) northeast of Pohang, about halfway between Korea and Japan. Indeed, because of its location **Ulleung-do** ⓭ is one of Korea's best-kept secrets, although this is changing as it is being promoted as a tourist destination by the government. It is an easy place to promote: a stunningly beautiful, verdant Eden, a perfect

BELOW: remote Ulleung-do is one of the most beautiful places in Korea.

place to get away from it all. The island, which is the remains of an extinct volcano, rises precipitously out of the East Sea to the summit of Seongin-bong at 984 meters (3,228 ft), with wild forests and dramatic sea cliffs towering over rocky beaches with superb snorkelling and scuba diving (but dangerous currents) in the clear waters.

Ulleung-do was settled during the Silla dynasty, before becoming depopulated around 1400. After centuries of obscurity when the island was the haunt of pirates, settlers returned in the 1880s. These days the population of 9,600 makes its living from fishing and, increasingly, from tourism. Until the late 1970s there were no roads on the island. Now the round-island road is almost complete (still very rough in spots) and, of course, there are cars and trucks. However, the air is still sea-fresh and the stars still shine brightly in the clear night skies.

Dodong and the mineral springs

Embark on a speedboat ferry in Pohang, and three hours later you'll be strolling into Dodong town on Ulleung-do's southeast coast (you can also take a ferry from Mukho, in Gangwon Province). There are many *yeogwan* in town, almost all of them without locks on the doors – attesting to Ulleung-do's reputation for being theft-free. Clapboard walls without windowpanes flimsily divide the outside from the indoors during the warm season. A few of the *yeogwan* fronting Dodong Harbor have rooftop decks where one can sip a beer at sunset and watch fishermen dock their boats.

Behind the town and up a path towards the rugged mountains is **Dodong Yaksu** mineral spring park (open 24 hours; free), with a mineral water fountain

Maps on pages 212 & 223

Ferns thrive in the warm, wet island summers.

BELOW: traditional Ulleung-do dwelling.

Ulleung-do

0   2 km
0   2 miles

N

SEA OF JAPAN
(EAST SEA)

Gongam (Elephant Rock)
Samseonam
Cheonburi
Gwaneum-do
Seommok-do
Natural growth of Chinese Junipers
Hyeonpori
Juk-do
605
Nari Basin
Taeha-ri
Mireuksan 901
Yonggul
Bongnae-pokpo
Manmulsang
Seonginbong
Jotaeam (Sea Stack)
Primeval Forest 984
Jeodong
Guam
Daewon-sa
Dodong
Namyang
Sadong
Nonggumi

Mukho   Pohang

Map on page 223

Ferries can be delayed or cancelled without notice as sea conditions change quickly. You are advised to check ferry shedules prior to your trip. Pohang, tel: (054) 242-5111; Mukho, tel: (033) 531-5891.

BELOW: spectacular scenery on the north coast of Ulleung-do. **RIGHT:** the rocky coast and blue waters of the East Sea (Sea of Japan).

that spews from a stone-carved turtle's mouth set in the mountainside. Visitors often like to splash a bit of Johnnie Walker "on the rocks" and mix it with the fresh mineral water. This water is very soft (as you'll find out when you bathe), and is also pure enough to drink straight from water pumps. Close to the spring is the **Dokdo Museum**, showcasing the history and culture of the island. A cable car leads to the summit of Manghyangbong (315 meters/1,033 ft), while further up the valley is the attractively located temple of Daewon-sa.

Sights around the island

Just up the coast from Dodong, **Jeodong** is the island's main fishing port. From here you can take a boat across to **Juk-do**, a flat-topped islet jutting out across the water to the northeast. Approach this island from the south side, then scale its steep hillside. The hike up the steps to the top may seem arduous, but the men on this island actually carry calves on their backs all the way up to this island's highland farm. The fattened, corn-fed cattle are then lifted off the island by rope onto barges and sent to Ulleung-do for beef. This Juk-do beef is renowned as the tastiest and tenderest in Korea. Four families who live on this small island mountaintop also grow watermelon (which some say is the sweetest in Korea). The young, thin bamboo growing here is used for stretching out and drying squid. Large mulberry leaves are grown here, too, for silkworm production on the mainland. Indeed, though the island is small, there is even room for a camellia forest which blooms in early to late February. Next to the camellia forest are paulownia trees – the only tree, according to mythology, on which a phoenix will land.

About 3 km (2 miles) inland from Jeodong is Ulleung-do's most famous waterfall. The 25-meter (80-ft) **Bongnae** falls are impressive, and a pleasantly cool spot in the humid summer months, although the clumsy concrete viewing tower tends to spoil the effect.

All along Ulleung-do's coast, steep mountainsides drop straight down to a sea which is a most unusual, clear shade of blue – like liquid blue laundry bleach. Off the northeast coast is a sea grotto of unique, craggy candlestick rock formations with nesting sea birds. The northernmost rock, Gongam, has a hole through which you can boat.

The road from Dodong to the small settlement of **Namyangri** on the southern coast makes for a spectacular drive. Keep going to reach **Taehari**, the west coast landing site of the first Koreans to migrate to the island over 1,000 years ago. Nearby is **Sataegam Beach**, a cove with warm, calm waters that are ideal for safe swimming. On the headland to the north is a fine stand of Chinese juniper trees.

To get a memorable 360 degree view of Ulleung-do, hike up Seonginbong, the island's highest peak. Set off from Dodong at daybreak (take the path past the Mineral Park) and you'll be resting high among the clouds by mid-morning and back down just when the sun's heat turns oppressive. To circle the island, you can either hike 40 km (25 miles) across valleys and along the coast (which takes three days), or take a boat trip (two hours). Either way, you'll find coves with bat caves (in Korean, *bakjwigul*) and sun-toasted beaches with cool, clear water. ❑

Maps:
area 212
site 228–9

GYEONGJU

*Rich in artifacts from Korea's Silla Dynasty, the
southeastern valley region of Gyeongju is the place to visit
if you want to delve deeply into the peninsula's history*

It's the massive burial mounds, brown and dusted by frost in the winter, and carpeted with a dark-green nap in the summer, which punctuate any visit to **Gyeongju** ⓮. Rising here and there in populated and rural areas, they dominate all other physical realities in this riverine valley between Daegu and Busan. The mounds, memorial tombs or *neung* in Korean, represent the glory that was Silla, and the wonders contained within are now waiting to be unearthed. The area around the city is also full of interest – secluded temples, including famous Bulguk-sa, abound in the wooded hills of Namsan and Tohamsan.

Opulent shaman kings

Gyeongju was well known to Asia's ancients as Geumseong, the home of powerful and opulent shaman kings. Today, it's an easy-going resort town where rice cultivation and tourism are more important than wars of conquest. Its distinction as a one-time seat of power, however, cannot ever be forgotten. This 214-sq. km (83-sq. mile) valley is dotted with burial tombs – most from the 1st to 8th centuries but some more recent – tired pagodas, fortress ruins, granite sculptures, palace grounds and other remnants of the rich Three Kingdoms Period.

Gyeongju is one of the three most popular destinations in Korea (the other two being Seoul and Jeju Island), and Koreans have an immense pride in Gyeongju and the Silla Kingdom that was able to unite the peninsula for the first time. Like the corresponding Tang Dynasty in neighboring China, the Silla period is considered the epitome of Korean art and culture. In early Silla, the dominant belief system was based on shamanism, that magical world inhabited by benevolent mountain spirits, and malevolent demons. The huge tombs of Gyeongju and other areas on the Korean peninsula date from this period, as do wondrous golden crowns decorated with amulets. Eventually Buddhism was accepted by the royal families and spread rapidly throughout the kingdom. The religious fervor sparked by this new religion resulted in a flowering of the arts that remains unsurpassed. Much of the art was religious in nature, pagodas, statues and magnificent temple compounds, all in praise of the Buddha.

Artifacts remaining from Silla are only a fraction of what was produced. When rebels overran Gyeongju, a wagon train several kilometers long hauled out the city's treasures. Later, in 1592, the Japanese invaded and completed the looting of Korea. What remains are those items too large to haul off, or those that were buried in tombs, lakes and such. Nevertheless, they are impressive and prove that Gyeongju was the cradle of Korea's Golden Age.

BELOW:
granite Buddha
statue at Gyeongju.

The Silla tombs

There are several routes you can take to see Gyeongju's sites, but since **Dumulli Park ⓐ** (open daily 8.30am–6pm, Nov–Mar closes at 5pm; entrance fee) sits near the middle of the historic part of the city, it's a good place to start. This is a unique 15-hectare (37-acre) "tomb park" on the southeast side of Gyeongju with some 20 tombs of varying sizes that were originally heaped into place as early as the mid-1st century. Until 30 years ago, this restored, beautifully landscaped and lamplit complex of mounded graves was just another ordinary neighborhood in Gyeongju. When private individuals and government archaeological teams began to find literally thousands of important items here, however, the area was quickly cleared of homesites and was designated as a national museum and site of major historical significance. The restoration of Dumulli Park began in 1973, and the complex was officially dedicated and opened to the public in 1975.

The entrance to Chonmacheong, the "Heavenly" or "Flying Horse" tomb.

The largest of the tombs, that of King Michu (r. 262–285), has been identified in ancient chronicles as the "Great Tomb." However, a secondary tomb (No. 155), the so-called Cheonmachong, or "Heavenly Tomb" or "Flying Horse Tomb", is probably the best-known gravesite in Dumulli Park. This tomb, about 50 meters (164 ft) in diameter and 12.7 meters (42 ft) high, was excavated in 1973, and in its collapsed wood and stone burial chambers were found numerous important treasures including sets of gold and jade tiger claw earrings, a solid gold, 125-cm (40-in) long belt-girdle with dangling gold and jade ornaments, a 32-cm (12-in) high gold foil crown embellished with 58 carved jade tiger claws, and an unglazed stoneware pot ornamented with a dragon's head and turtle's body.

BELOW: the Dumulli Park moundscape.

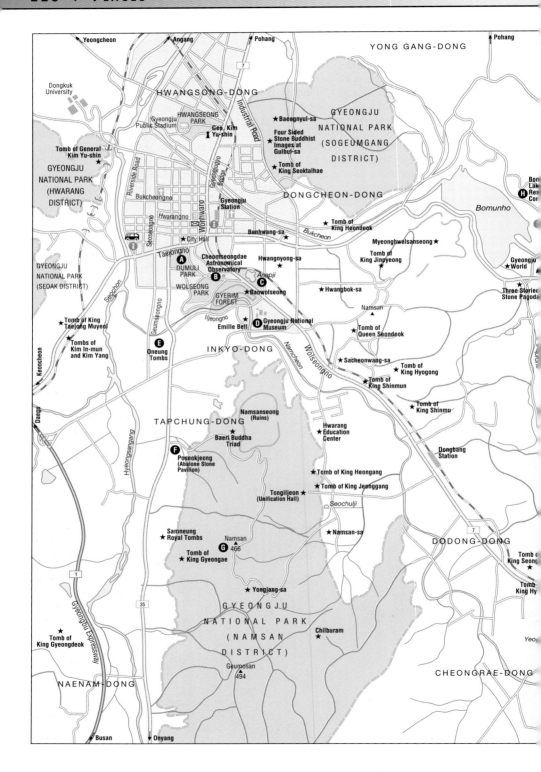

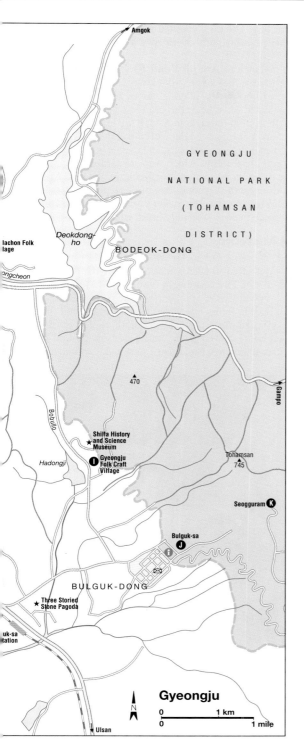

More than 10,000 objects were discovered in this unknown king's tomb, but the most celebrated find was a painting of a galloping, winged horse. This flying horse study, the first early Silla painting ever discovered, was painted onto a birchbark saddle flap in white and vermilion and bordered by a rococo frame. Visitors to this tombsite can now literally walk into the tomb, which has been scooped out and converted into a contrastingly modern domed glass, metal and concrete gallery. On display here are a detailed diorama-model of the tomb's burial chamber, photographs of the actual excavation in progress, and more than 100 excavated Silla pieces. Many of the most important treasures are safely displayed in larger national museum structures at Seoul and at the nearby Gyeongju National Museum (see page 230).

An ancient observatory

Directly across from Dumulli Park is **Cheomseongdae** Ⓑ (open daily 9am–9pm; entrance fee). This astronomical observatory tower, one of the oldest structures in Korea, was built during the reign of Queen Seondeok (reigned 632–647), Silla's 27th ruler. Astronomers question just how the tower was used, but they point with intrigue at the following coincidences: 365 stones, the number of days in a calendar year, were used in its construction; and there are 12 rectangular basestones, plus 12 separate levels of stones above and below a central window. Could this constructional recurrence of the number 12 imply the zodiac, or the number of months in a year? This telescope-shaped tower probably served several generations of Silla geomancers who attempted to foretell astrological fates in this historic region.

Across the road is an old hardwood forest known as the **Gyerim (Chicken) Forest** . This is the legendary birthplace of the first Kim (the most popular of the Korean family names). Legend says that a white cock was heard crowing under a golden box hanging from a tree branch within the forest. The king was summoned, and when he opened the box

The 7th-century astronomical observatory tower of Cheomseongdae is one of the oldest structures in Korea.

he found a beautiful infant boy. The king adopted the child and gave the child the surname of Kim. This popular picnicking spot has been known as the chicken forest ever since.

Head north for a short distance to **Anapji Pond** Ⓒ (open daily 9am–6pm, Nov–Feb closes at 5pm; entrance fee) where Silla kings and queens spent their leisure moments relaxing, writing poetry, playing games and entertaining visiting dignitaries. This was said to have been the grandest garden in the orient, with trees and plants brought in from throughout Asia. It lay in ruins for centuries, until 1975, when a team of archaeologists began working at the site. To their surprise, hundreds of dishes, tiles, religious artefacts, and even a boat were found at the bottom of the silted pond. These items, which were discarded or accidentally dropped by royal revelers, can now be seen at the Gyeongju National Museum. Today, the pond is back, along with reproductions of three pavilions that once stood at the water's edge. While Anapji may never regain the glory of its Silla days, it remains a pleasant place to take a leisurely break while touring Gyeongju.

Gyeongju National Museum

Gyeongju is often called "Korea's Open-Air Museum". The phrase is apt, because so many of Gyeongju's treasures are outdoors where they can be seen, touched, and experienced. Yet in **The Gyeongju National Museum** Ⓓ (open Tues–Sun 9am–6pm, Nov–Feb closes at 5pm; entrance fee), you can see some of the finest of more than 80,000 items unearthed during recent and old-time digs in this area: metal work, paintings, earthenware, calligraphic scrolls, folk art objects, weapons, porcelains, carved jades, and gold, granite and bronze sculptures wrought in various shamanist, Buddhist, Taoist and Confucian motifs.

Only about 10 minutes by bicycle from Anapji Pond, a visit to this world-class museum will put your tour of Gyeongju's other historic sites into perspective.

Among the museum's important pieces is the huge bronze Emille (pronounced "Em-ee-leh") Bell, The Divine Bell for the Great King Seongdeok, which is one of the world's oldest, having been cast in AD 771. It is also one of the largest, weighing 20 tons and measuring 3 meters (10 ft) in height and 2.3 meters (7½ ft) in diameter. This Buddhist bell, which originally hung in a pavilion at nearby Bongdeok-sa Temple, is embellished with four relief devas who kneel facing each other on lotus blossom cushions. It is said that the bell's sonorous tones can be heard 64 km (40 miles) away on a clear day. The bell's name, it has been written, comes from an ancient Silla term that literally means "mommy". The bell was given this name because its sound resembles the voice of a lost child crying for its mother.

West of Namsan

The **Oreung Tombs** ❺ (Five Royal Tombs; open daily 9am–6pm, Nov–Feb closes at 5pm; entrance fee) are in a beautiful, tree-covered park setting. It is believed that these are the tombs of the first Silla king and queen, as well as the second, third and fifth kings of Silla. While not as dramatic as Dumulli Park, this shady little corner of Gyeongju provides a welcome retreat on hot summer days.

A little further out of town on the western edge of Namsan is **Poseokjeong** ❻ (The Abalone Stone Pavilion; open daily 9am–6pm, Nov–Feb closes at 5pm; entrance fee). This site received its name from the shape of a curving, stone-rimmed ditch cut in the ground next to a pleasure pavilion used by Hyeongang, the 49th Silla king. This winding ditch was a large board game of sorts that

Map on pages 228–229

TIP

Many of the ancient sites are near the city, and the best way to reach them is by bicycle which can be rented from sidewalk traders. Regular bus services can get you to outlying areas.

BELOW: Buddhist monks, tutors to the elite Hwarang youth.

HWARANG EDUCATION CENTER

On the rolling, forested eastern slope of Namsan is a cluster of traditional Korean buildings housing the Hwarang Education Center. These buildings were built in 1973, but during the Silla Dynasty the best and brightest young men of the kingdom underwent mental and physical training among these same hills. The early Hwarang (Flower Youth) have a mystique surrounding them that is analogous to knighthood in medieval Europe. The Hwarang were teenage sons from the aristocracy who were trained by Buddhist monks in the art of warfare, philosophy, history, and even dance. Many of Silla's prominent rulers, scholars and monks received training with the Hwarang. The five tenets that these "Flower Youth" lived by are a blend of Buddhist and Confucian thought: (1) to serve the king with loyalty, (2) to serve one's parents with filiality, (3) to practice fidelity in friendship, (4) to never retreat in battle, and (5) to refrain from wanton killing. The thought of young teenagers undergoing rigorous training and performing heroics in battle has considerable appeal for modern-day Korean youths. Stories of the Hwarang are frequently featured in TV sitcoms and novels. Perhaps the Hwarang Education Center will again produce leaders like those that once roamed the foothills of Namsan.

With a comprehensive network of trails linking its numerous temples and pagodas, Namsan is a wonderful place for hiking.

BELOW: the view from Seokguram of the forested hills around Gyeongju.

involved the drinking of wine and the impromptu composition of poetry. Nearby stream water was channeled in, on which cups of wine were set afloat. A guest was challenged to compose a proper poem before his cup made a floating round of the channel. If he didn't compose a satisfactory poem, he had to drink his entire bowlful of wine and try again. According to ancient chronicles, it was great royal parlor fun. It is said that the last Silla king was indulging his pleasures at Poseokjong when the city was overrun by rebels.

Namsan ❻ (South Mountain) is a veritable cornucopia of history. During the Silla Dynasty, this was a sacred mountain. The sites of over 100 temples have been found on and around the mountain, and there are still a few active ones. In addition, there are some 60 religious images carved from the mountain's granite, and 40 pagodas lying alongside the mountain trails, as well as a fair share of royal tombs along its base. It would take several days to explore all the trails and sites of this unusual mountain, but if you have only a few hours you might try hiking the trail that begins at Namsan Village and goes to the top. There, perhaps after an hour of huffing and puffing, you'll find amazing Buddhas and attendant bodhisattvas etched into sheer granite boulders and cliffs. All look east, like the Seokguram Buddha, towards the rising sun.

East of Namsan

On the east side of Namsan is **Bomun Tourist Town** ❽ (20 minutes from Gyeongju by bus, taxi or hotel shuttle). Alongside this attractive lake are Gyeongju's deluxe and mid-range hotels (inexpensive *yeogwan* are found in the city). The setting is pleasant enough, with a brick path alongside the lake, an 18-hole golf course (expensive), marina and clubhouse, and a lakeside amusement park

(tacky), but the attractions are geared more to Koreans on holiday. You'll proba-bly want to spend most of your daylight hours visiting the historic sites or hiking the trails of Namsan. The town plays host to two annual festivals. At the end of March there is the Korean Traditional Drink and Cake Festival. Then, in every third year (the next is in 2006) in early autumn, there is the Gyeongju World Cul-ture Expo, featuring performing groups from Korea and other countries.

Map on pages 228–229

Down the road from Bomun Tourist Town is the **Gyeongju Folk Craft Village ❶** (open daily 9am–5pm; free). There is a large building selling crafts made by local potters, wood carvers, and other local artisans, who live and work in the small village directly behind. Those who take the time to walk through the village can often observe artisans at work. Much of their work reproduces designs and pieces from the Silla period, an indication of the influ-ence this culture still has on Korea a millennium after its demise.

Temple of the Buddha-land

Still furthur down the road (30 minutes by bus from Gyeongju Station) lies **Bulguk-sa ❷** (open daily 6.30am–6pm, Nov–Mar closes at 5pm; entrance fee). This sprawling temple complex about 16 km (10 miles) due south of Gyeongju on the western slopes of Tohamsan is one of the oldest surviving Buddhist monasteries in Korea. First built during the reign of Silla King Beopheung (r. 514–540), Bulguk-sa, "Temple of the Buddha-land," is also Korea's most famous temple. Its renown comes not from its age or size but probably because it stands, flawlessly restored, as a splendid example of Silla-era architecture in a spectacular hillside setting lush with manicured stands of pine, plum, peach, pear, cherry and cryptomeria trees. It also enshrines some of the country's and

BELOW: a school outing to Bulguk-sa.

Colorful guardian deity at Bulguk-sa; the temple complex is famous for the quality of its paintwork.

BELOW: Dabotap pagoda is decorated with lanterns on Buddha's birthday.

Korean Buddhism's most important national treasures. The historical significance of Bulguk-sa and the nearby Seokguram were recognized when they were listed as UNESCO World Heritage Sites in 1975.

Wonderfully stone-crafted steps and bridges carry the visitor on an uphill stroll to the broad granite block terraces on which this pristine temple compound stands. Almost all of the hand-painted wood structures on these terraces are of recent Joseon-dynasty construction, but most of the stone structures – large granite blocks fitted together without mortar – are original. The architect credited for this stone masterwork, Kim Daeseong, also supervised the construction of the nearby Seokguram Grotto, an annex to Bulguk-sa and one of Buddhism's most-celebrated shrines. Architect Kim honed his design and structural skills during the reign of King Gyeongdeok, the 35th Silla king (reigned 742–765), when Bulguk-sa underwent several major modifications and restorations.

Blue and white clouds

Two double-tiered stone staircases – the Seokgyemun – used to lead pilgrims and tourists up to Bulguk-sa proper. The larger, 33-stepped staircase to the right has been given two names, one for its lower flight (called Cheongungyo, the Blue Cloud Bridge), and the other for its upper flight (Baegungyo, the White Cloud Bridge). The smaller, left staircase, meanwhile, was similarly named. Its lower flight is called Yeonhwagyo (Lotus Flower Bridge), and the upper flight is Chilbogyo (the Seven-Treasure Bridge). The Blue Cloud and White Cloud bridges terminate at an entrance gate called Jahamun, while the Lotus Flower and Seven-Treasure bridges climb up to a secondary entrance gate known as Anyangmum. Both are grand entry-ways, but these days tourists and devotees alike have to enter the temple via new stairways and gates on the left and right sides of the temple.

Pass through the small Jongnu entry pavilion to arrive at Bulguk-sa's main worship hall, Daeungjeon. This is an expansive courtyard dominated by two unusual and impressive multi-tiered Silla pagodas.

The smaller of the two pagodas, called Seokgatap, is 8.2 meters (27 ft) high and the larger Dabotap is 10.4 meters (34 ft) high. While Dabotap was built by Kim Daesong for his parents, legend has it that Seokgatap was built by Asadal, an esteemed artisan who came to Silla from Baekje.

Both stone pagodas (which have been restored in recent years) are considered premier examples of such Silla pagoda construction. Inside a niche on the left side of the Dabotap you'll spot a small growling lion sitting on a neat lotus pedestal. He's Dabotap's (the Many-Treasured Buddha's) guardian.

The smaller pagoda, Seokgatap, is not quite as quaint, but many relics of great historical and artistic value were found inside this pagoda in 1966. According to a government survey: "The relics included a sarira box containing gold images of Buddha and a scroll of Dharari sutras, the oldest Buddhist literature of its kind remaining in the world today. The inscriptions engraved on the cover of the relic box say that in AD 706 King Seongdeok placed within the pagoda four *sarira* (remains of Buddha or high priests), a gold

Amita figure, and a volume of sutras in memory of three deceased royal family members: King Sinmun, Queen Mother Simok and King Hyoso".

Other Bulguk-sa sights deserving meditative attention are the nine-pillared Museoljeon hall, the compound's oldest, largest structure; the Birojeon, which houses a Birojana Buddha found clutching his right forefinger in an overtly sexual Diamond First mudra position; and Gwaneumjeon, a hall which is home to a 10th-century wooden image of Gwanseum-bosal, the popular Bodhisattva of Mercy known to Chinese Buddhists as Kwan Yin. Most of the halls are painted in the flamboyant colors typical of Joseon dynasty buildings.

Temple in a grotto

Seokguram Ⓚ (open daily 9am–6pm, Nov–Mar closes at 5pm; entrance fee), the Stone Cave Hermitage, is located several winding miles northeast of Bulguk-sa proper, and has become a major pilgrimage site for practitioners and students of Buddhism and Buddhist art. Seokguram is a grotto temple, set among pines and maples, which enshrines a white granite Sakyamuni Buddha image considered by some to be the most perfect of its kind anywhere.

Unlike grotto temples in other parts of Asia, Seokguram was not carved out of a granite hillside or built inside an existing cave. Rather it is an artificial chapel built of large granite blocks placed on a summit. After a pleasant hike through a lower woods and up a flight of stairs, you will enter as classical a Buddhist shrine as you would ever expect to see in the Far East.

The base of the Seokguram structure consists of a square antechamber and a round interior chamber with a graceful dome-shaped ceiling. As you enter the chapel you will first pass stone images of the Eight Generals, each representative of one of the Eight Classes of Beings. Next are the Four Deva Kings, Guardians of the Four Quarters. A pair of these directional deities cavorts on either side of the main passageway. Framed in the radiant aura of haloes, they are also depicted stomping on little demons.

Inside the main chamber is Sakyamuni, sitting in repose on a lotus dais. At his forehead is a typical protuberance, and atop his head are neatly cropped spirals of curly hair. Facing the grotto's entrance and the East Sea, the Buddha Sakyamuni sits with his right palm downward over his right leg. This is the mudra position referred to as "Calling of the Earth to Witness." The left palm faces up in a meditation pose. While the individual sculptures may be matched by some of those in the cave temples of China, the chapel as a whole is unequalled in the art of the Far East.

Also high on the Gyeongju must-see list is the impressive tomb of General Kim Yu-sin, which is rimmed by carved stone zodiac figures, and the Bunhwang-sa Temple with the oldest datable pagoda in Korea.

Still craving Silla-era Buddha images? Then head for the *Tap* Valley on the eastern slopes of Namsan, the Buddha Valley just north of *Tap* Valley, the *Guksa* Valley east of Namsan, or the more remote *Seonbang* Valley. This litany of treasures grows longer and more awesome with every passing lunar year and every new discovery in Gyeongju. ❑

Map on pages 228–229

TIP

For such a small city, Gyeongju has an active nightlife. Wait until dark, then head downtown to streets full of young people, fast-food joints, *norabongs* (singing rooms), games rooms, coffee houses and bars.

BELOW: the Sakyamuni Buddha at Seokguram grotto.

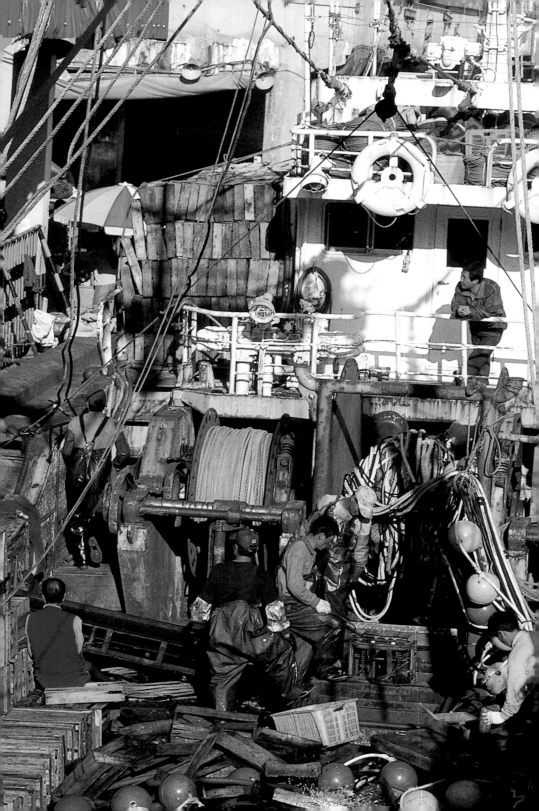

GYEONGSANGNAM PROVINCE

*Visitors are drawn to Gyeongsangnam's beaches, seascapes
and historical sites, which chronicle the often volatile relationship
with its neighbor across the East Sea – Japan*

Maps:
area 212
city 239

I n 1592, the Japanese warlord Hideyoshi dispatched 150,000 troops in an
ambitious assault on the Chinese Empire. Korea had the misfortune of being
in the way and of being loyal to China. When the Korean government refused
to grant Japan free access across its frontiers, the Japanese dispensed with
courtly etiquette and proceeded to fight their way through. After six years of war,
they finally retreated, failing to conquer China, but thoroughly devastating
Korea. Thousands of Koreans were either killed or taken to Japan as slaves.
Vast tracts of crucial farmland had been razed, the country's social order was in
shambles, and much of Korea's great cultural legacy was destroyed or stolen.
Nearly four centuries have passed since this tragedy, yet all along Korea's
southern coast monuments and memorials remain to keep alive the Imjin War.
The dominant theme in this region, despite more recent wars and wrenching
transitions, is still the Japanese invasions.

LEFT: trawler at
Jagalchi Fish
Market, Busan.
BELOW: annual
memorial service
at Chungyeol-sa
Shrine.

Busan

The first south coast city to fall during the Hideyoshi invasion of 1592 was
Busan Ⓖ, wedged between a range of mountains and the sea. It was then, as it
is now, Korea's most important port city, and these days has a population of
around 4 million. The city is a raucous mélânge of
masts, loading cranes and buildings; honking cabs,
train whistles and the throbbing air horns of passing
ferries are heard; suited businessmen, deck hands,
navy cadets and fishmongers mingle. Tiny punts propelled by a single sculling oar slip through the shad-
ows of huffing tankers. Urban gentlemen in angler
outfits toy with their delicate bamboo poles, waiting
patiently for nibbling minnows, while scruffy trawler
crews unload the day's catch of squid and dog sharks.
Dockside fish market matrons hawk abalone, brilliant
orange sea apples, deep-sea clams and fish of all sizes,
shapes and colors.

Near the main nightlife district is **Yongdusan** Ⓐ, a
small park made conspicuous by the imposing Busan
Tower dominating the city's skyline. The park has
two statues; one is a kitsch representation of a dragon,
the legendary king of the sea; the other is of the patron
hero of the south coast: Admiral Yi Sun-sin.

Right on the Busan waterfront is the highly
animated **Jagalchi Fish Market** Ⓑ (open daily
except the first Sunday of the month, major holidays
and the following day; 6am–8 or 9pm), a great place
to wander around, with rows of fish sellers hawking
their oceanic fare. Do as the Korean tourists do – buy
some fresh fish (or octopus, squid, or sea cucumber)
and take it to one of the nearby seafood restaurants
where they'll prepare it for you (most Koreans prefer

Beomeo-sa is known for its three gates. Walking through the second gate, you will pass by the four temple guardians, which are the ferocious protectors of the temple. The third gate, the gate of Non-Duality, symbolically suggests that, even though you are passing from the secular world into the spiritual, the two are the same.

BELOW:
looking towards Yeong-do island from Busan Tower.

to eat their fresh fish as sashimi – i.e. raw) and add some side dishes and drinks.

A few blocks north of the fish market, and opposite Busan railway station is **Texas Street** , sometimes called Russian Street or, in Korean, Choryang. This shopping district has clothing and accessory stores, as well as restaurants and nightspots that cater to the tastes of foreigners. As its alternative name implies, a lot of Russian sailors call in at Busan's port and this section of town. But it's not just Russians who make this the one of Busan's liveliest entertainment centers; like Itaewon in Seoul, Texas Street has an international following. A large underground shopping arcade runs parallel with the main drag for those who want to burrow deeper for a bargain.

Around Geumjeongsan

Admiral Yi's staunch patriotism and military skills prevented the Imjin War from becoming a total disaster for Korea. But for the Busan and Gyeongsang-nam Province, it was a bona fide disaster. Korea simply was not prepared for the battle-hardened samurai who took less than a month to burn and pillage their way to Seoul. At **Dongnae Fortress** (where you can still see a small portion of the old wall), defenders were faced with an overwhelming invasion force, but managed to put up a valiant resistance. When the Japanese asked the Korean Governor to surrender, he responded by saying; "It is difficult to make way for your forces, but easy to fight and die." While the Japanese overran the fortress, the commander calmly composed a last poem for his father. **Chungyeol-sa Shrine** (open daily 9am–6pm, Nov–Feb closes at 5pm; entrance fee), sits on the battle site, and is dedicated to the memory of those brave soldiers who found it easier to die than allow a foreign force to occupy their land. The shrine is near

a busy intersection, and offers a quiet retreat from the hassles of the city. Locals sit with friends under trees in the Korean garden while children feed goldfish in the pond. The shrine's exhibition hall displays graphic paintings of the battle, along with period uniforms on display.

A short taxi ride to the west of Chungyeol-sa Shrine will take you to the base of Geumjeong Mountain, and **Dongnae Hot Spring E**, whose waters fill the baths of several dozen hotels and *yeogwan* (making this is a good place to get rooms at a reasonable rates). A few of the larger hotels have public baths open to the general public. On **Geumjeongsan F** are the remains of a mountain fortress, **Geumjeongsanseong** (open daily, all hours; entrance fee) built during the Joseon Dynasty. Four kilometers (2½ miles) of the original 18-km (11-mile) wall remain, as do two of its four original gates, surrounded by thick forests and unusual rock formations. A cable car (open daily 9am–7pm) runs between **Geumgang Park** (near Dongnae) and the ridge at the top of the park. The mountain is a favorite with weekenders hiking its numerous trails.

At the north end of the mountain, not far from the north gate of the fortress, is the city's most important temple, **Beomeo-sa G**, (open daily 8am–sunset; entrance fee) headquarters of the Dyana sect. Legend says that there is a golden well nearby in which a golden fish from Nirvana lives; in its early years (it was built in AD 678) it was known as the temple where fish from Nirvana play. It was, of course, burned to the ground during the Japanese invasion of 1592, but the main hall that was rebuilt in 1613 still stands. The courtyards of the temple are well landscaped in traditional Korean style with trees, stone lanterns, relics and a pagoda dating back to the Silla dynasty. There are almost a dozen hermitages spread out in the mountains around the temple.

> Maps
> on pages
> 239 & 240

Texas Street (aka Russian Street), a magnet for Russian sailors.

BELOW: Jagalchi Fish Market.

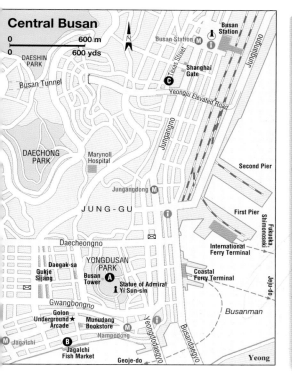

*Spectacular cliffs at
Taejongdae, at the
southern tip of
Yeong-do island.*

BELOW:
Busan harbor is
congested with all
kinds of boats.

Local beaches

Ask any Korean what Busan is famous for, and they will probably tell you the beaches. There are several to choose from. For those willing to dare the murky water of Busan harbor, **Songdo Beach** ⓗ is just a stone's throw southwest of the downtown area. Even if you prudently abstain from swimming, it offers an interesting alternative to staying in town, as there are several inns and hotels with a uniquely Busan flavor. Considerably cleaner waters are available at three sandy beaches to the east of the city. The most popular is **Haeundae** ❶, which has good hotels and a bustling resort town. At the southern end of the beach are cliffs overlooking a rocky beach below, with the white sand beach beyond. On one of the rocks below the cliff, the Little Mermaid (*à la* Copenhagen's famous sculpture) gazes longingly out to sea. Koreans are almost comically conservative when it comes to beach attire, creating some interesting contrasts when a Western tourist wearing only his thong walks alongside an old grandfather in coat and tie – but no one seems to mind.

Immediately to the south of downtown Busan is the island of Yeong-do, built up to the north, but covered in thick forest towards the south. **Taejong-dae Park** ❶, at the southern tip, features impressive cliffs and a lighthouse dating from the late 19th century. The view over the ocean is tremendous, and on a clear day it is just possible to make out the Japanese island of Tsushima. On the coast to the west of Busan are Masan and Jinhae, the two urban ports of the area north of Geoje-do island. **Masan** is a gritty industrial city, struggling to catch up with its status as a Free Port. **Jinhae**, smaller and more spacious, is a naval station famous for the cherry trees that swathe the city with blossoms each spring.

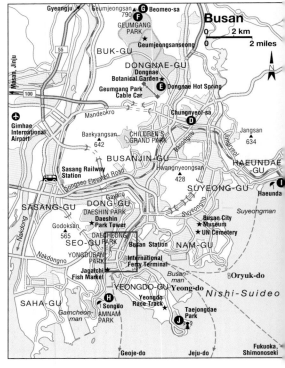

Along the south coast

Geoje-do ⓰ is Korea's second-largest island (after Jeju) and one of the most beautiful areas of the country. Regular jetfoils run from Busan's Coastal Ferry Terminal to Jangseungpo on the northeastern side of the island. This is a good place to get the feel of a tiny Korean coastal town.

The southern coast of Geoje-do is particularly attractive, and is easily explored by driving along the coastal highway. One of the best known beauty spots is **Haegeumgang**, a striking camellia-covered rock outcropping undercut with anemone-infested caves. An alternative way to see this beautiful coastline is to take a tourist excursion boat from Jangseungpo or Tongyeong. Much of the area lies within the Hallyeo Haesang National Park.

It is also possible to access Geoje-do by road, via the bridge from **Tongyeong ⓱** (also known as Chungmu), a pleasant town on the Goseong peninsula. Tongyeong's small dock is always busy with ferries returning from neighboring islands, small private fishing trawlers, tourist boats, and all manner of hired craft that take people out for an afternoon of fishing or skin-diving. The marketplace begins on the dock, where catches are sold directly from piers, and continues a considerable distance into town, where local specialties such as traditional horse-hair hats, reed baskets and, of course, all kinds of fish are available. The restaurants in town serve the usual variety of seafood. Clams, oysters, soft-shelled crabs and unidentifiable mollusks are thrown into everything, to the delight of those who have an appetite for submarine curiosities and to the horror of those who don't. Tongyeong has plenty of inexpensive *yeogwan* and makes a good base from which to explore Geoje-do and the other islands in the vicinity.

Maps:
area 212
city 240

Tongyeong is noted for its craftsmen who make lacquerware furniture and jewelry with mother-of-pearl inlay. The most expensive piece of furniture in a Korean home is usually an elaborate wooden and lacquerware closet.

BELOW:
Geoje-do fishtraps.

*Namhae suspension
bridge crosses the
Noryangjin Strait.*

Across the narrow channel from Tongyeong is the island of **Mireuk-do**, linked to the town by an unusual pedestrian tunnel built by the Japanese in 1932 and originally designed for vehicles. On the north slope of a mountain that dominates the island is **Yonghwa-sa**, a tiny temple with an unusual set of appropriately diminutive altar paintings. **Gwaneum Hermitage**, a short walk away, has a lawn instead of a courtyard, and a handsome stone gate; careful landscaping manages to convey a sense of serenity, despite the incongruity of stone lanterns wired with electric lightbulbs.

To the west of Geoje-do, between Tongyeong and Yeosu and forming the western part of the Hallyeo Haesang (Maritime) National Park, is the **Hallyeosudo waterway**, sheltered from the open sea by hundreds of islands that are the ancient peaks of an inundated mountain range. Submerged valleys have become countless secluded harbors, many of them now crowded with the vibrantly painted boats of fishermen and divers.

The attractively situated town of **Yeosu** can be reached by train, bus and ferry from Busan, and shuttles run from here to the nearby islands of Namhae and Odong-do, both of historic and scenic interest. (Yeosu and Odong are in fact within Jeollanam Province, but for convenience are included in this chapter). **Odong-do** is covered with camellia and bamboo and was where bamboo arrows were made for Admiral Yi's fighting men. **Namhae-do** is connected to the mainland by a suspension bridge that crosses the strait of Noryangjin, where Yi was killed.

Jinju and the patriotic Ju Nongae

BELOW: coastal
scenery at Namhae.

Buses connect Namhae, Yeosu and Sacheon to **Jinju** ⓲, one of Korea's most enchanting and least-visited small cities. The Nam River runs through the center of the city. In early morning mists, ghostly anglers squat along the shore with the patience of statues, and elderly gentlemen in traditional dress stroll along the winding walls of **Jinju Fortress** (Jinjusanseong; open daily 9am–10pm; entrance fee), bringing the distant past breathtakingly close. Even the perfectly mundane concrete traffic bridge that crosses the river takes on an air of timelessness.

Jinju Fortress was attacked in one of the first battles of the Imjin War. After a heroic defense by the Korean army assisted by a civilian militia, the attack was repulsed, and a planned drive into Jeolla Province was thwarted. Less than a year later, the fortress was the site of an equally heroic defeat after 10 days of fierce fighting. The Japanese celebrated their victory with a banquet in **Chokseongnu** (open daily 9am–6pm, Nov–Jan closes at 5pm), a spacious pavilion within the fortress. One of the Korean women brought in to provide entertainment was Ju Nongae, a *gisaeng* hostess whose patron, a Korean military official, had lost his life in the battle for Jinju. During the banquet, Nongae lured one of the Japanese generals to the edge of the cliff between the pavilion and the Nam River. There she threw her arms around his neck and dived into the river, dragging him down with her to a patriotic and much-celebrated suicide-assassination (*see page 93*).

Nongae's selfless courage is commemorated now, four centuries later, in a special ritual held in July or

August (according to the lunar calendar) at a small shrine built in her honor, **Nongae Shrine** (open daily 8am–10pm), above the rock from which she jumped.

The walls of Jinju Fortress and Chokseongnu have been tastefully reconstructed and several shrines, temples and pavilions are preserved within the fortress grounds. The most imposing structure is Chokseongnu, which is raised on stone pillars to provide a view of the Nam River below. A small gate leads to the cliff where Nongae lured the general to his (and her) death. Evidently the river was considerably deeper then or the general was a remarkably poor swimmer; or else they were killed by hitting the rocks along the shore and not by drowning. A peculiarly Korean form of graffiti embellishes the cliff, with names (presumably of Nongae's posthumous admirers) carved into the rock. Off to one side of Chokseongnu is the shrine in Nongae's honor, which contains her portrait.

Jinju is one of few Korean cities that has developed into small urban centers without losing their individual identity or rural ambience. Wander through the narrow streets, browse in the tiny shops, visit one of the several small temples, or spend the day rowing a rented boat around **Jinyang Lake**.

Korea's largest temple

Directly north of Busan is a mountainous region known as the **Yeongnam Alps**. These gentle mountains (the name is something of a misnomer) harbour several well-known temples in peaceful highland settings. The best known of these is **Tongdo-sa** ⓭ (open daily 9am–6pm, Nov–Feb closes at 5pm; entrance fee) about a half an hour to the north of Busan along the expressway to Gyeongju. The road leading to the temple is a long, slow incline, sheltered by a forest whose name means "pine trees dancing in the winter wind."

Map on page 212

TIP

If you are driving, the Yeongnam Alps region is a great place for a spot of temple-hopping. Besides Tongdo-sa, there are many other temples and hermitages in the area.

BELOW: statue of Admiral Yi at Busan.

ADMIRAL YI

In 1591, Korean Admiral Yi Sun-sin was appointed fleet commander for the eastern coast of Jeolla Province. A year later the Japanese invaded. In less than a month they had overrun the country, routed the untrained and ill-equipped Korean army, and occupied the capital.

Admiral Yi quickly became the bane of the Japanese navy, which gradually disintegrated during a series of Korean victories, climaxing in a naval rout at Hansan-do, near the port of Tongyeong (Chungmu).

Later in the war, Yi suffered his second demotion, and the Korean navy was turned over to a rival, Won Gyun. Under Won's command the navy was promptly decimated. Yi was hastily pardoned and asked to resume command of the admiralty, but his once-powerful navy now consisted of only 12 ships. Exhibiting a remarkable blend of strategic genius and gall, he led his paltry fleet in an assault of 133 Japanese ships and won.

This astonishing victory revived the dwindling Korean resistance, marking the turning point of the entire war. Tragically, less than a year later, as the Japanese were attempting to retreat from their debacle without further loss, Yi was mortally wounded by a stray bullet in the last battle of the war.

Memorial service for Jajang, the 7th-century founder of Tongdo-sa temple.

BELOW: ceremony to commemorate those who died in the Imjin Wars against Japan.

With a total of 65 buildings, Tongdo-sa is Korea's largest temple. Many of the buildings are dispersed throughout the surrounding mountainside, so the temple does not appear especially big at first sight. However, virtually every major Buddhist deity is honored in a separate shrine in the central cluster of buildings, unusually liberal even for so large a temple compound. The buildings themselves comprise a variety of exceptional architecture, some left pleasantly unpainted or faded to the muted brown of weathered pine. Clustered around several courtyards, Tongdo-sa is guarded by a massive quartet of wooden divas, each rendered in vivid and intimidating detail. Inside, one fine mural depicts a boat escorting the deceased to paradise. In addition to the many fine statues housed in the shrines, an excellent collection of artwork is on display in the temple museum. Woodblock prints are available for purchase.

According to legend, Tongdo-sa was founded in 646 by a Korean religious leader named Jajang who traveled to China in search of a truth to save his nation. There he experienced a miraculous visitation by a holy being who presented him with relics of the Buddha, including his yellow robe. Jajang returned to Korea to create his temple, naming it "Tongdo," which means "salvation of the world through mastery of truth." The gifts received in his vision are preserved in a stone monument in the temple.

Haein-sa's ancient library

On Gyeongsangnamdo's northern border, and just over an hour's drive west of Daegu, is one of Korea's most famous temples. Ritual drums thunder down from the mist-wreathed **Gayasan Mountain** (open daily, sunrise–sunset; entrance fee), temporarily silencing the clack of prayer knockers and ethereal

JAPAN AND KOREA

Acrimony has long characterized the relationship between the two neighboring countries of Japan and Korea. From the Korean point of view, the Japanese have made a habit of invading and terrorizing their peninsula. In the early days, it began with pirates periodically ravaging coastal villages. Then came the brutal invasion at the end of the 16th century, followed by centuries of Japanese attempts to force trade and political concessions onto the Koreans, finally culminating in colonization from 1910 to 1945.

The list of injustices heaped on the Koreans during this last occupation are, by now, familiar to most people: repression of any form of independence (including language and culture), forced laborers for Japanese Empire expansion (the beginnings of the Korean Diaspora), and sex slaves at the frontlines.

Perhaps worst of all has been the reluctance of the Japanese government to acknowledge and apologize (at least to the satisfaction of the Koreans) for its misdeeds. There have been some overtures from both sides to end the feud, and some young Koreans who will tell you openly that they do not despise the Japanese. The joint hosting of the World Cup in 2002 was seen by many as a positive step towards reconciliation of the two nations.

Map
on page
212

chanting. The smoke of cooking fires mingles with the aroma of incense as the monks of **Haein-sa Temple** ❷⓪ (open daily sunrise–sunset; entrance fee) prepare a meal of unpolished rice, mushrooms and mountain herbs.

Undoubtedly the most rewarding of Korea's more accessible temples, Haein-sa is still isolated enough to be a meditative haven; yet it is only an hour from **Daegu** by bus, and accommodations are available within easy walking distance of the temple grounds. As with many of Korea's mountain temples *(see page192)*, Haein-sa is set in wonderful forested surroundings; the scenery of **Gayasan National Park**, beautiful in any season, is stunning in the autumn, with craggy peaks and languid streams surrounded by fiery maples and oak.

Haein-sa houses the **Tripitaka Koreana**, a collection of more than 80,000 woodblocks engraved with Buddhist scriptures. This vast library was completed in 1252, during the Goryeo dynasty, after nearly two decades of labor. It was a mammoth task undertaken twice. A first set, carved as a plea to the Buddha for aid against invading Khitan tribes, was destroyed by Mongols when they took their turn at invasion. Retreating to virtually impotent exile on Ganghwa Island, King Gojong ordered the creation of a second set in hopes of inducing an avataristic intervention against the Mongols. It is difficult to assess whether the king's hopes were justified or not: the Mongols finally departed in 1382 due to the collapse of their dynasty in China.

The Tripitaka library was moved early in the Joseon dynasty, from Ganghwa Island, which was too near the capital for safety, to Haein-sa. The building that now protects the woodblocks was constructed in 1488. It was designed with an adjustable ventilation system to prevent deterioration of the blocks. A recent concrete structure utilizing an array of modern devices to ensure a controlled environment was intended as a new and improved replacement; but it now sits neglected within smirking distance of the more effective old library. The temple, its repository and the Tripitaka have been designated a UNESCO World Heritage Site.

One of the first statues you are likely to encounter in the temple complex is not a gilt deity but a curious self-portrait of a monk carved in wood and painted true to life. The figure sits in apparent *rigor mortis* in a glass case in Haein-sa's small museum, surrounded by displays of elaborate embroidery and remnants of the temple's past. More typical statues are to be found in the compound's numerous shrines, including an imposing 18th-century trinity (with Virochana at the altar's center) in the main hall. Outstanding among the paintings inside this hall is a mural depicting scenes from the Buddha's life. In common with most of Korea's major temples, Haein-sa has several hermitages scattered through the surrounding mountains. All are a lure to meditative exploration.

Sacks of dried wild mushrooms spill out into the streets of the local "resort" town and in several restaurants you may indulge in a fungus-eating spree in a semi-private *ondol* (floor) 0heated room. While most of the town's inns are adequate, there is a virtual palace located on a low hill at the western edge of town, traditionally styled with pinewood. ❑

BELOW: the Tripitaka Koreana library at Haein-sa.

JEOLLA PROVINCES

These two southwestern provinces contain some of Korea's finest rural landscapes, along with 3,000 seldom-visited islands, and the best food in the country

Map on page 248

onsidered the "rice bowl of Korea," the two Jeolla Provinces are a veritable cornucopia of food. In the late spring, ample rains water the fields, and the farmers can be seen bent over, planting even rows of rice. As might be expected with such an agricultural region, the women from this area are considered the best of Korea's cooks.

Many of the residents of the Jeolla Provinces feel that the area has become an economic backwater. No doubt there is a lot of truth to this. The provinces have experienced an intense rivalry with the neighboring Gyeongsang provinces to the east, and unfortunately for Jeolla, politicians from Gyeongsang have tended to dominate federal politics. Much of the failure to develop this region was probably intentional. Jeolla was finally able to celebrate when their favorite son, Kim Dae-jung, became the first opposition candidate to be elected to the Korean presidency in December 1997.

The conspicuous lack of heavy industry in the Jeolla Provinces does have certain advantages, however, as the region has perhaps the cleanest air and best-preserved natural environment in Korea. A ride through the countryside reveals scenes that are only a memory in the more developed provinces. The Korean curve motif is everywhere in this pastoral scene – in the subtle curves of terraced rice paddies, the rolling curves of mountains, hills and burial mounds, and the upcurved roofs of traditional farmhouses.

LEFT: tea plantation near Boseong.
BELOW: Jeonju is famous for its *bibimbap*.

Jeollabuk-do (North Jeolla Province)

Jeonju ❶, located approximately 240 km (150 miles) south of Seoul, is the provincial capital of Jeollabuk-do. It is the ancestral home of the descendants of Yi Seonggye (Taejo), founder of the Joseon dynasty, and is famous throughout Korea for its paper and paper products (such as fans and umbrellas), delicious *bibimbap*, and food in general.

The Chinese introduced papermaking to Korea about 1,000 years ago. The Koreans, however, became so adept at this fine craft that both Chinese and Japanese calligraphers came to favor Korean papers over their own. Technology has encroached on the handmade papermaking industry to the extent that very little can be found now, a sad state of affairs when you consider that just 15 years ago villagers near Jeonju perpetuated the tradition in their homes and in makeshift factories. You could hear the sound of new paper pulp swishing in water, and white sheets hanging out in backyards like drying laundry were a common sight. All may not be lost, however. Ask in town where the papermakers are still operating.

Despite modernization, papermaking is still best done by hand. Fibers of the *dak* (paper mulberry tree),

Jeolla Provinces

0 — 30 km

0 — 30 miles

mulberry stems, bamboo (all brought from other areas in Korea), and other flora are stripped and cooked into a soft pulp and then bleached in a soda solution. They are then transferred to a large wooden and cement vat. Rectangular bamboo mat screens suspended from resilient bamboo poles are dipped in and out of these pulp-filled vats, and with a rhythmic finesse that has made this process a fascinating sight, a sheet of sopping-wet paper is eventually sieved onto the bamboo screens. The various types of paper stocks include: *unhyangji* of coarse mulberry, a basic wrapping paper; *whaseonji* for brush painting; *jangji* ("paper of 1,000 years") from the *dak* tree for calligraphy; *jangpanji* for *ondol* floors; *ttae juji*, algae paper; *jukji*, bamboo paper; *biji*, bark chip paper; and recycled paper made from various secondary papers.

But if you ask any Korean what Jeonju is really famous for and the answer will be *"Bibimbap."* Don't leave Jeonju without tasting this dish of rice and vegetables. At the long-established **Hanilgwan Restaurant** (open Mon–Sat 6.30am–9.30pm), the *bibimbap* comes with the rice deliciously mixed with soy sprouts and topped with broiled and sliced meat, fern bracken, strips of boiled squid, bluebell roots, toasted sesame seeds, pine nuts and a sunny-side-up egg. This savory dish is further accompanied by a bowl of beef broth and side dishes of cool seaweed and onion soup, then spiced further by at least five kinds of *gimchi*. Indeed, even at the simplest Jeonju restaurant expect to see amazing foods piled up at your table, in some cases at least as many as 20 different side dishes. When in Jeonju, don't be shy, eat!

A Jeonju city bus or taxi will get you out to **Songgwang-sa** (open daily 7am–7pm, Nov–Feb closes at 6pm; entrance fee), a fine Buddhist temple to the northeast of the city. Located in a corner of a quaint village that produces *jangpanji* paper for *ondol* floors, Songgwang-sa offers the jaded temple seeker some of the finest mineral color murals in Korea. Flying fairies and *mudang* (sorceresses) are painted directly on the walls and ceiling of this temple. These 150- to 200-year-old artworks were rendered in earthy and warm greens, orange, blues and yellow. The characters posture and prance as if they were part of a modern animated film. Carved wooden fairies, wispy as clouds, are suspended from the ceiling above three enormous gilded Maitreya Buddhas. Even the main altar is splendidly wood-carved.

Horse Ears and frozen fairies

The winding road on to **Maisan ❷**, Horse Ears Mountain, is a joyful cruise in its recently paved condition. There are charming and classical sights at nearly every highway turn. Just five minutes outside of Jeonju, for example, you will see on your left a series of hills covered with hundreds of traditional Korean grave mounds. This is an unusually crowded pre-Christian-style cemetery.

A few miles further, a splendid Buddha can be seen enshrined in a large granite bluff. All along this 34-km (21-mile) haul eastward and over the Jinan Plateau to Jinan, farmers are out planting rice in the late spring, and, at other times, tending their plots of hay, tobacco, onions and ginseng.

The famous Maisan "Horse Ears" are not visible

Map on page 248

Looking down the aisle at Jeonju Catholic Cathedral.

BELOW: papering a screen at Jeonju.

until you get quite close to Jinan town. There, off to the right, they spring up from behind a large knoll above a meandering riverbed. From Jinan, lovely Maisan is but a 3-km (2-mile) hike southward through an oak forest where mushrooms are cultivated under short logs leaning against trees.

As everything in Korea has its divine or mythical reason for existence, the two Maisan peaks are no exception. Legend notes that, before Maisan was created, two fairies – one male, the other female – lived there. They were enjoying their respite on earth when one day their heavenly creator called for them to make their ascent back home. He warned them to let no mortal eye witness their flight, so they carefully planned their departure for the next full moon night. This was so the moon could light their path to heaven.

The chosen night was overcast, so they decided to wait until dawn, an escape deadline decreed by their creator. As the two fairies were ascending to heaven, however, an early-rising housewife spotted them. They looked back at this eagle-eyed mortal, and were transformed into stones and fell back to earth as the two curious peaks of Maisan (moral: don't procrastinate). If you are curious as to which frozen-in-place fairy is which, the peak to the left is called *Sut Mai* (Male Horse Ear) and the one to the right is *Am Mai* (Female Horse Ear).

A hermit's stone vision

Once you reach **Maisan Provincial Park** (open daily 9am–sunset; entrance fee), your expedition will have just begun. The hike through narrow Jonghwang Pass between the two horse ears is a heart-thumping,132-step climb. Up there, near **Hwaeom Cave**, you can rest a while and enjoy a panoramic view of Jinan and environs. Continue into a small valley on the south side of the ears,

veer to your right (while negotiating another 181 steps in segments) and you will come to one of the most bizarre Buddhist temples in Korea. Built by the hermit monk Yi Gapyong, this **Tap-sa** (Pagoda Temple) religious site is a collection of stone pagodas, some of them 9 meters (30 ft) high. All were built without mortar and have stood in surrealistic splendor in this narrow valley since the early part of this century. The Spanish architect Gaudí would be thrilled if he could return to life and study hermit Yi's architectural fantasy. Past these "Shaking Pagodas," the path continues through the steep mountains to temples such as Eunsu-sa, Geumdang-sa and Isanmyo Shrine, all about a half-mile walk away.

A white statue of the Hermit monk Yi sits comfortably at the foot of his Maisan temple complex. Yi holds on to a wooden walking staff and stares west toward the rising sun that bathes him, his narrow valley home and his zany pagodas with an amber morning light. Several *yeogwan* on Jinan's road to Maisan offer accommodations to the weary body and soul who is not so keen to rush back to civilization.

Moaksan Provincial Park

Geumsan-sa (Gold Mountain Temple) on the western slope of **Moaksan Provincial Park ❸** (open daily 6am–7pm, Nov–Feb 7am–6pm; entrance fee), is reputedly the most beautiful temple in Jeollabukdo. It is about 34 km (21 miles) southwest of Jeonju. To visit it, take the old Highway 1 heading southwest from Jeonju toward Gwangju, and some 26 km (16 miles) later, just north of Wonpyeongni, veer eastward along a side road that will lead up to Geumsan-sa.

The pathway to the temple entrance is adorned with a line of cherry trees and Himalayan pine and a pool off to the right side of the path. This short walkway induces a meditative calm that prepares the traveler for Geumsan-sa itself.

First built in 599, Geumsan-sa was rebuilt in 766 by High Priest Jinpyo Yulsa during the Silla dynasty, and enlarged in 1079 (during the Goryeo period) by High Priest Hyedeok Wangsa. The complex was burned during the 1592 Hideyoshi invasion, then finally rebuilt in 1626. Today, its main hall, *Mireukjeon*, stands three stories high, making Geumsan-sa the tallest temple in Korea. This spaciousness is devoted to housing 10 cultural assets from the Silla, Baekje and Goryeo periods. *Mireukjeon*, a worship hall for the god Avalokitesvara, is one of these 10 great treasures.

Inside *Mireukjeon*, a huge golden Maitreya (Buddha of the Future) stands 12 meters (39 ft) tall, holding a red lotus blossom in its left palm. It is flanked by two crowned bodhisattvas, Daemyosang and Bophwarim. Below the statues, behind the wooden grill, there is a stairway. One may walk down the steps to kiss the candlelit Maitreya's feet as a sign of respect and make an offering.

Next to *Mireukjeon*, above the left slope of the hill, is a stupa made of stone and a five-story granite pagoda where a monk's body minerals are enshrined after cremation. The pagoda's roofs are flat and subtly curved at the corners, in traditional Baekje style. The roofs to all of the temple structures, in fact, were never measured with anything but the naked human eye.

Map on page 248

At Eunsu-sa Temple, just above Tap-sa, there is an unusual building dedicated to ginseng. Ginseng is grown on the farms around Maisan. Look for freshly planted fields that have been covered with straw.

BELOW: the golden *Mireukjeon* Buddha at Geumsan-sa, Moaksan.

The *Daejangjeon* worship hall looms behind wood-carved doors that survived the 1592 Hideyoshi invasion. In the hall sits a gold-gilt Sakyamuni Buddha with a symbolic mandala around it – a rarely seen embellishment.

In the second largest hall, the *Nahanjeon* Buddha sits with 500 sculptured disciples, each amazingly exhibiting different facial expressions. On the way back down the path, there is a Zelkova elm tree. Large and branching, it is renowned as a fertility tree. If someone throws a stone up the tree trunk and the stone does not drop, legend says that person will soon have a child.

"Inner Sanctum" mountain

From Geumsan-sa, traverse tobacco fields along the main tributary road and rejoin the world's mainstream traffic on the Honam Expressway bound southwest for **Naejangsan National Park** ❹ (open daily sunrise–sunset; entrance fee), where an entry tunnel of red maple trees reflects fiery autumn colors on the faces of incoming visitors.

The journey up to Naejang (Inner Sanctum) Mountain National Park near Jeongeup is a peaceful prelude to a pilgrimage to Baegyang Temple. Up here, in maples and mist and steep mountain passes, you will find a pleasure pavilion placed aesthetically onto a massive, real-life scroll painting.

Upon reaching the **Baegyang (White Sheep) Temple** you will already be properly inspired and in the mood to consider this place and its Seon, or Zen, Buddhist origins. Originally built in AD 632, Baegyang-sa was then called Baegam-sa after Mt Baegam. Son master Hwangyang Seonsa renamed it Baegyang-sa in 1574. Despite its reclusiveness, this temple befell malevolent forces, being destroyed four times by invaders. It was rebuilt a fifth time by Son master Songmanam Daejongsa in 1917. In its present form it sits like a jewel in the midst of lush mountain foliage that seems to be aflame during the late autumn. An aged bodhi tree broods all on its own in the temple's main courtyard.

Jeollanamdo (South Jeolla Province)

Gwangju ❺, the ancient provincial capital of Jeollanamdo, is a low-key city where at night, in many areas of the center, vehicular traffic ceases and streets become pedestrian malls busy with strolling townfolk.

Gwangju competes with Jeonju for honors such as "best food in Korea" and "the most food served in Korea." This is because in the past wealthy landlords established gracious food standards, and because the lush Honam Plain in Jeollanamdo has provided food for the city's gourmets. Also, the country's best *jeongjong* (barley and rice wine) and *makgeolli* (a simpler form of rice wine) are served here with an array of *anju* (drinking snacks) which make a veritable dinner out of a drink.

The best time to visit Gwangju is during one of its two popular festivals. If you have developed a taste for the pride of Korean cuisine, visit during Gwangju's Gimchi Festival. The festival is held over an extended weekend in late September or early October. Here you can get a taste of every gimchi imaginable, and some (such as gimchi pizza) that you never imagined. As with other Korean festivals, there are plenty of regional games and local talent performing to keep the crowds happy.

The other major festival is the Gwangju Biennale, which runs Sept–Nov every even-numbered year. This is Korea's premier exhibition for the arts, displaying works from Korea's best artists, as well as contributions from artists from more than 50 other countries.

The two-story **Gwangju National Museum** (open Tues–Sun 9am–6pm, Nov–Feb closes at 5pm; entrance fee) was built to house Yuan dynasty booty that was discovered in a sunken 600-year-old Chinese ship in the Yellow Sea in 1976. This archaeological find is exhibited on the ground-floor gallery. A map there illustrates the spread of Yuan-dynasty kilns throughout Eastern China down to Hong Kong, across to Korea's west coast, and on to Japan, Denega Island and Okinawa. Among the finds are early 14th-century Luang Juan wares, including celadon vases with two rings and a peony design in relief, cups shaped like flowers, and a celadon druggist's mortar and pestle.

Upstairs on the second floor is a gallery of Jeolla Province treasures which includes Neolithic Korean relics from Daeheuksan-do, 11th- to 14th-century bronze Buddha bells, Joseon-dynasty scroll paintings and white porcelain.

Mudeungsan (Peerless) Mountain hovers like a guardian over Gwangju City. A resort area has been created at its base among acacia trees and beside a whispering stream. Along Mudeung's right flank are two factory buildings that are used for tea production during the spring and autumn tea-harvesting seasons. A tea plantation previously owned by the famous early 20th-century Joseon-dynasty artist Ho Baeknyon is now cared for by Buddhist monks and sprawls next to **Mudeung's Jeungsim-sa (Pure Mind) Temple** (open daily). Perhaps

Map on page 248

Foreigners attempt to make gimchi at the Gwangju Gimchi Festival.

BELOW: Gwangju is known for its food and drink, and has a lively nightlife.

it is true that tea has helped purify the minds of local monks. A monk at Jeungsim-sa explained that in Korea green leaf tea was traditionally the preferred brew of only monks and scholars. They believed this tea purified their blood and stimulated them so that they could resist sleep and study until dawn. It must work, because even today Mudeung-sa monks cultivate *chunseol* "Spring Snow" tea on slopes adjacent to their temple.

The small, tender *chunseol* leaves must be cut at a very early stage of growth and steamed and dried nine times in the early morning dew and mist (intense heat or cold spoils the delicate leaves). This is a very tedious tea-cultivation process that apparently only Buddhist monks have the patience for. The resulting tea, which smells of aromatic persimmons, is said to aid digestion and whet the appetite.

Damyang bamboo

One of the most revered plants in Korea is bamboo, called *daenamu* in Korean. It is splintered into chopsticks, carved into spoons, harvested for its delicious tender shoots, and immortalized in paintings and poetry.

The center of bamboo cultivation and craftsmanship in Korea is **Damyang** ❻, north of Gwangju on the main highway. The best time to visit Damyang is on market day, which falls on days that end with the number 2 or 7. The market is held along the Gwanbangcheon stream, opposite a bright chartreuse bamboo forest. Usually, the bamboo is not cultivated longer than three years, as its purpose is not for sturdy construction but specifically for gentle basket-weaving. Villagers bring these utilitarian objects down from their nearby village homes on market day, which starts at around 6am and peters out by 3pm. Straw and bamboo mats are sold near the market above the riverbank.

BELOW: traditional farmers band performance at Gwangju Gimchi Festival.

In the center of town stands what locals claim to be the only museum devoted to bamboo. Check out the many uses made of this most utilitarian of plants in **Damyang's Bamboo Crafts Museum** (open daily 9am–6pm, Nov–Feb closes at 5pm; entrance fee).

Map on page 248

Namwon's legendary pavilion

Along the Olympic '88 expressway east of Damyang is the ancient city of **Namwon ❼**, which is the birthplace of Chunhyang, the favorite heroine of Korean literature. It is not known whether her birth was more than a literary event, as no proof of Chunhyang's actuality exists. However, the story of her life is set in Namwon, and she has had sufficient effect on Korean life and thought for quibbles to be immaterial.

"Chunhyangjeon" ("The Story of Chunhyang") is a simple, romantic tale of forbidden love and sacrifice. Mongnyong, the son of an aristocrat, falls in love with Chunhyang, the daughter of a *gisaeng* (female entertainer). The two secretly marry, and soon after, Mongnyong's father is transferred to a government post in the capital, separating the two lovers. A lecherous governor is appointed in Namwon who is determined to add Chunhyang to his roster of lovers. Remaining faithful to Mongnyong, she flatly refuses to comply with the governor's wishes. She is promptly imprisoned and beaten under the personal supervision of the enraged governor. Meanwhile, Mongnyong is appointed Royal Inspector of Jeolla Province. He soon hears of Chunhyang's maltreatment and comes to rescue her and punish the governor. The two lovers return to Seoul where they of course live happily and prosperously to a grand old age.

Chunhyang's staunch fidelity is still revered today, and her story is an essential

Damyang is the center of Korea's bamboo production.

BELOW: the cherry blossom comes early in the southern provinces.

part of Korea's literary legacy. She is honored in Namwon with a shrine as well as an annual festival held for a week or so in early May.

On the edge of Namwon is Gwanghallu Garden (open daily 8am–10pm; entrance fee), a wonderful Korean-style park complete with ponds and streams. Gwanghallu Pavilion, where it is said the two lovers in the Namwon legend spent their evenings, is the major attraction. The huge Gwanghallu Pavilion was rebuilt in 1638 (after a fire), and is one of Korea's four famous pavilions.

Jirisan National Park

Ask a Korean which is the most beautiful mountain, and they are likely to tell you Jirisan. The highest point of the Sobaek Range (indeed the highest point of mainland South Korea) and sitting in the northeast of **Jirisan National Park ❽** (open daily; unlimited hours for most roads; fees for major temples), Jirisan is a stark jumble of snow-covered peaks in winter, cool and lush in summer, and brilliant with turning foliage in the autumn. There are many small temples in the valleys of the mountain and two major ones Hwaeom-sa and Ssanggye-sa are both easily reached from Gurye.

Hwaeom-sa (open daily 7am–7pm; entrance fee) was founded in the Silla dynasty. A 4.5-meter (15-ft) stone lantern, the largest in Korea, is preserved on the temple grounds. The dominant structure of the temple is the imposing, two-story Gakhwajeon ("Awakening Emperor Hall"), built in the 18th century and named in honor of the Chinese Emperor credited with funding its construction.

According to legend, **Ssanggye-sa** was founded by Priest Sambeop in 723 during the Silla dynasty. Sambeop dreamed of becoming a disciple of the great Buddhist master of the time, Hyeneung, a patriarch of the Tsaochi sect of

BELOW: village on the slopes of Jirisan.

CONFUCIAN CHEONGHAKDONG

Hidden in a high valley on the eastern face of the sacred Mount Jiri, above Hadong, is Cheonghakdong, one of a few traditional villages that have been granted permission to abstain from Saemaeul Undong, the "New Community Campaign."

The colorful concrete rooftiles, ersatz chalets, paved roads, electricity and modern plumbing that have redefined most Korean villages have not affected Cheonghakdong. "Monoleum", though, a soft, flexible linoleum in vogue in Korea, has infiltrated onto some porches and living-room floors.

The formal courtesy of Confucianism is meticulously observed in Cheonghakdong. Unmarried men still wear their hair in single long braids, and education is still conducted in the old Joseon-dynasty style: the teacher wears his horse-hair hat while lecturing on the Confucian Classics to his students (who sit cross-legged on the *ondol* floor dressed in traditional white *hanbok*).

Visitors are obliged to impose themselves on the hospitality of village residents, as no inns, hotels or restaurants are available.

Cheonghakdong is not easily accessible to visitors, and the isolation protects this timeless place from change.

Chinese Zen Buddhism. Hyeneung, however, died before this dream could be realized. Sambeop found some consolation in studying transcriptions of Hyeneung's discourses that were brought to Korea. This motivated him to visit Gaiyum Temple in China, where Hyeneung's skull had been preserved. While there, Sambeop bribed a priest at the temple into giving him the revered skull. Having returned to Korea, Sambeop made his way to Jirisan where he built a shrine for his pilfered relic. This shrine gradually developed into Ssanggye Temple.

Map on page 248

Pagoda and lanterns at Hwaeom-sa.

Songgwang – a Zen temple

To the south of Gurye lies the city of Suncheon, with a regular bus service to **Songgwang-sa** ❾ (open daily 7am–7pm, Nov–Feb closes at 6pm; entrance fee). This is one of three "treasure temples" in Korea, representing Buddha's followers: monks, nuns and laity. It has become a center of Seon (Zen) Buddhism, and houses the International Zen Center where non-Koreans can study Buddhism in a peaceful mountain setting.

Originally a small hermitage built during the Silla dynasty, Songgwang-sa was expanded in the 13th century after Bojo, a Seon Master, settled there with his followers. Destroyed during the Japanese invasion of 1592, the temple has slowly been rebuilt. Today it is a sprawling complex of buildings and courtyards nestling in a pleasant mountain valley.

A tiny, intricately carved, wooden statue of Buddha, believed to have been carried by Bojo in his travels, is preserved in the temple. The temple includes a number of architectural treasures. The oldest is the 400-year-old *Guksajeon*, or National Priests' Hall, that contains the portraits of prominent monks that

BELOW: the entrance bridge to Songgwang-sa.

have called Songgwang-sa home. One unique feature of Songgwang-sa is the pair of arched, covered bridges spanning a shallow stream that meanders quietly in front of the temple entrance. To the southeast of Suncheon is the town of **Yeosu**, at the western end of the picturesque Hallyeosudo Waterway *(see page 242)*.

About 30 km (18 miles) south of Songgwang-sa is **Boseong ⑩**, and Korea's major tea-growing center is just south of this small city. From atop the mountain pass, you can look down upon neatly groomed tea bushes lining the steep hillsides. Women can be seen harvesting year-round, though spring is the best time to pick the new leaves. The tea plantations welcome visitors, and are a wonderful place to take a casual stroll among tree-lined lanes, or perhaps peek into a shed to watch workers drying and sorting the day's pickings. Afterwards, tea can be sampled in the plantation teahouses.

Mokpo and the southwestern islands

At the southwestern extreme of the Korean peninsula is the port city of **Mokpo ⑪**, a rather drab shipping town with one or two indulgences for the visitor. Mokpo's docks abound in coarse vignettes: 2-meter (6-ft) sharks for sale in a fishmonger's shop, a trawler festooned with gaudy banners, sulking ponies hitched to heavy cartloads of produce, and blubbery hogs screeching in protest as they are hauled ashore.

The major distraction of this city is the interesting view from Yudalsan, a craggy twin-peaked mountain that cuts into the city center. Several miles of winding pathways allow visitors to earn a vista proportionate to their degrees of health or ambition.

BELOW: picking
tea on a plantation
near Boseong.

Probably Mokpo's most interesting attraction is the National Maritime Museum (open Tues–Sun 9am–6pm, Nov–Feb closes at 5pm; entrance fee). The museum displays a wooden ship that had been mired in the mud of nearby tidal flats for several hundred years. Its cargo included over 30,000 pieces of Goryeo celadon, along with thousands of other trade goods. Other goods on display, many of Chinese origin, suggest that Mokpo was once a very important link in pan-Asian trade.

Mokpo is the chief point of departure for some 3,000 islands, many of which make up the **Dadohae Haesang Maritime National Park**. Most of the islands are no more than clumps of rock covered with evergreen trees, surrounded by cliffs, with an occasional beach littered with millions of small stones. Life on the islands is centered around the ocean: harvesting fish, seaweed, kelp, clams, and anything else even remotely edible.

The two best-known islands in the national park are Heuksan-gundo and Hongdo. **Heuksan-gundo** ⓬ is actually a group of 100 islands, the largest of which is Daeheuksan-do. Daeheuksan-do has several small hotels, though rooms can be difficult to find during the peak travel season of late July and August. A few of the islands of Heuksan-gundo are large enough and flat enough to support agriculture. Stone walls, rustic homesteads and pastoral scenes set against an ocean backdrop make these islands exquisite beauties.

Hong-do (a nature preserve with a small entrance fee) is a rugged piece of rock to the west of Daeheuksan-do. Hong-do, the "Red Island," is named for the pink hues of its rock and is famous for the imposing, contorted rock formations and precipitous cliffs that line its coast. The best way to see this small island is by boat. There are rooms to let at the larger of the two villages. The fast ferries from Mokpo can get you there in just over two hours.

Canines and miracles on Jindo

Less demanding is a trip south to **Jin-do (Jin Island)** ⓭, a large island that is only two hours by ferry from Mokpo. For those traveling by car, the island is also connected to the mainland via Korea's longest suspension bridge.

Jindo is famous for two things: a rare breed of dog and an unusual natural event. The pedigree *Jindot-gae* (literally translated as Jin Island dog) has a short, nearly white coat of fur with a touch of ochre along the inner curve of its characteristic arched tail. An annual Jindo dog show is held in autumn and billed in the English-language press as a "beauty contest."

Jin-do's other claim to fame is its impressive low tides. Twice a year (end of February and mid-June), the tides are so low that a small island nearly 3 km (2 miles) offshore becomes accessible by foot. In the 1970s, a Frenchman likened it to Moses's parting of the Red Sea, and the "Moses Miracle" moniker stuck. In recent years it has become an impressive event, with thousands of people walking between the two islands.

The event has reached festival proportions, and become a showcase for the island's cultural traditions and enthusiastic local talent. ❏

Map on page 248

The Saemaul express train covers the Seoul–Busan and Seoul–Mokpo routes quickly and comfortably.

BELOW: sardines and seaweed.

THE WAY OF TEA – KOREAN STYLE

Green tea is increasingly popular worldwide, and Korean green tea is the best there is. Yet almost no-one seems to have heard of it

The drinking of tea *(cha)* was introduced to Korea and Japan around the 7th centuries AD by Buddhist monks from China. Over the following centuries, tea drinking remained closely linked with Buddhism; when a new dynasty, the Joseon, took control of the Korean peninsula in the 14th century and decided to break the power of Buddhism, the tradition was almost completely lost. In the 19th century the Buddhist monk Cho Ui, followed by Hyodang in the 20th century, led revivals that are only now beginning to bear fruit.

KOREAN TEA TODAY

Today, tea ceremonies are a popular activity among housewives, while Buddhist monks and many ordinary people enjoy drinking green tea in an informal manner. To enjoy the full experience, look for a *jeontong chatjip* (traditional tea house). In Seoul, the alleyways of the Insadong district offer a fine selection of these. Staff will gladly show you how to prepare your tea, if you are unsure. The most important thing to remember is that the water must not be too hot or the delicate taste will be spoiled. Tea is reckoned to contain five or six tastes: salt, sweet, bitter, tart, peppery, in varying proportions. Ordinary tea will have lost most of its flavor after three servings, but very good tea may be used to make four or five rounds. Koreans will tell you that Chinese tea has perfume, Japanese tea has color, but Korean green tea has a deeper, richer taste than either. And it is better for you, too!

▷ **WHISKED TEA**
Finely powdered tea is whisked to a froth in warm water, in one version of the tea ceremony; more usually, green tea is brewed in a teapot and poured into small cups.

▷ **DRYING THE LEAVES**
The very finest green tea is slowly dried over a fire in an iron cauldron, the leaves stirred and rubbed between the tea-makers' hands.

▽ **TRADITIONAL TEA HOUSE**
Young couples, as well as monks, frequent Korean tea houses, drinking green tea slowly in a relaxed atmosphere.

GREEN TEA?

When the freshly sprouting leaves are plucked from the tea bushes in late April or May, they are a vivid green color. To make green tea, they have to be dried before they wither; this means within a few hours of being picked. Tea bushes only grow in the far south of the Korean penisula, on the southern slopes of Jirisan, around Boseong, and on the hills of Jeju Island off the south coast. On the slopes of Jirisan, individual tea-makers spend hours crouched over heated cauldrons, turning and rubbing the tea by hand until it is perfectly dry. This is the finest and most expensive variety of Korean tea, although tea made industrially by such large companies as Taepyong-yang can also be very good. The first, small sprouts gathered in April give the most delicate tea, known as "Ujeon". The leaves gathered in early May yield "Sejak" and in the last weeks of May, when the taste of the leaves is beginning to grow weaker, the tea is known as "Jungjak". Menus in tea houses will often list green tea by these categories.

◁ **POINT OF ORIGIN**
Green tea, Chinese tea, and the black tea from India or Sri Lanka are all made with leaves from the same bush, *Camellia sinensis*.

△ **FORMAL CEREMONY**
Holding their cups in both hands, first admire the color, then inhale the fragrance, then drink and savor the aftertaste.

△ **HARVEST TIME**
The Taepyongyang company's tea plantations at Boseong employ dozens of women during the brief tea-picking season between April and June.

▷ **TOOLS OF THE TRADE**
Korean potters copy some of the country's finest ancient pottery to create a Korean style of tea service.

JEJU-DO

Balmy temperatures, volcanic landscapes, great beaches, first-class hotels and a rich (and distinctive) cultural history have made the island of Jeju-do Korea's top holiday destination

Map on page 266

PRECEDING PAGES: the rocky coastline of eastern Jeju. **LEFT:** traditional and modern housing at Daepyongri village. **BELOW:** enjoying shellfish at Yongduam (Dragon's Head) Rock.

eju-do is Korea's top holiday destination – and it is not difficult to see why. The island has a benign climate, beautiful beaches, wonderful seafood, spectacular volcanic peaks and craters, and superb tourist facilities including international-class hotels, golf courses, challenging hiking trails and sports-fishing grounds. Similarities to idyllic islands further south have also played their part; *The Asian Wall Street Journal* called Jeju the "Bali of North Asia", while the Korean government has dubbed the island "Korea's Hawaii" and "The Hawaii of the Orient." More recently, the island has been referred to, appropriately, as the "Honeymoon Island."

Whichever sobriquet you choose for Korea's biggest and most famous island, such descriptions completely debunk stereotypical visions of this northern country as a land of frozen mountain passes and howling Siberian winds. There are indeed several geographical similarities between Jeju-do and the Hawaiian archipelago. On this egg-shaped island, which lies about 160 km (100 miles) south of the mainland, offshore waters are of the same aquamarine hue as those of Hawaii. These colors lap against the similar black lava shelves, jagged outcroppings and steep cliffs that rim the islands of Oahu, Maui, Kauai and the Big Island of Hawaii. The most famous of these is curious Yongduam, the Dragon's Head Rock *(see page 269)*.

Like its Hawaiian counterpart, Jeju has some superb beaches. Favorite crescents of sand are located at Hyeopjae, Gwakji and Hamdeok along Jeju's upper half, and at Hwasun, Jungmun, Pyoseon and Sinyang in the south sector. Most of these resorts feature superb seafood restaurants, gaily painted tent cafés, and rentable recreational facilities. Other highlights include the breathtakingly massive Hallasan, and, if you visit in the springtime, brilliant rape fields that paint broad yellow splotches across Jejudo's fertile pastureland.

However, due to the realities of Jeju's temperate locale and the subsequent absence of coconut palms (though there are pineapple fields), romantic comparisons to Hawaii and Bali must end once winter sets in; chill winds knife across Jeju-do and shatter all Polynesian allusions from mid-November through March.

To get your bearings, a simple tour around the island, or a cruise along one of the two crosscut highways which skirt Hallasan's west or east slopes, are both worthwhile. Whichever course you choose, you'll soon find yourself driving past a variety of pine forests, tangerine orchards, pineapple fields, mushroom caves, dancing waterfalls, odd rock formations and rural charms that will draw you yet deeper into Jeju-do's calm and complex beauty.

If you like stone gardens (as a lot of Koreans do), don't miss the Mokseok-won, a garden with unusual displays of Jeju stones and dried tree roots. Mokseokwon is south of Jeju City, on the road to Hallasan.

The island can be easily reached either by ferry from Busan, Mokpo or the island of Wan-do (*see pages 282–3*); or by regular Korean Air and Asiana Air-lines flights from the major mainland airports, and from Tokyo, Osaka, Nagoya and Fukuoka in Japan.

Mountains, waterfalls and lava caves

Volcanic, cloud-wreathed **Hallasan** (Mt Halla) ❶ (open daily; admission times for climbers: Mar–Apr & Sept–Oct 5.30am–2pm, Jan–Feb & Nov–Dec 6am–1.30pm, May–Aug 5am–2.30pm; check with the control office in bad weather, tel: 064-742-0384; entrance fee) at 1,950 meters (6,400 ft), is the highest peak in South Korea, and a walk up to the summit is one of the highlights of a visit to the island. It dominates Jeju-do and, indeed, if there were no volcano there would be no island. The slopes of Hallasan are included within **Hallasan National Park**, and have fauna and flora unique in Korea. If you want to climb to the top, plan on a good half-day. There are four park entrances, each with a path up the volcano. The north and south slopes are the most strenuous hikes, while the eastern slope is the easiest.

Rivers and waterfall come tumbling off of Hallasan. The best known are a series of waterfalls on both the east and west sides of lovely **Seogwipo Town**. The stunning **Jeongbang Falls** ❷ (open daily 7.30am–6.30pm; entrance fee) right in Seogwipo town is often referred to as "the only waterfall in Asia that plunges directly into the sea."

Unlike Hawaii, however, Jeju-do cannot advertise that its deep fissures and frozen lava swirls are the products of still active volcanoes. On the other hand, it can claim the world's longest known lava tubes, the Gimnyeongsa and Man-

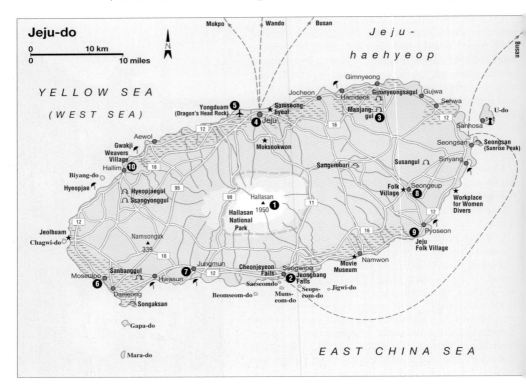

jang Caverns located at Gimnyeong between Jeju City and Seongsan. The **Man-jang cavern ❸** (open daily 9am–7pm, Nov–Feb closes at 5pm; entrance fee), the longer of the two tubes, is a mind-boggling 13.4 km (8½ miles) in length (although only 1km/⅔ mile is open to the public) with a diameter that ranges from 3 to 20 meters (10–66 ft). In the summer, tourists can join lamplight tours of these caverns filled with bats, spiders, centipedes and unusual lava formations. You are advised to dress warmly as temperatures inside the caverns stay between 10–20°C (50–68°F) throughout the year.

Probably Jeju-do's most distinctly Hawaiian-like phenomena are man-made structures. Particularly similar are low walls of lava-rock construction that lace the Jeju countryside. Many are almost exact replicas of lava-rock walls that wind hither and thither in rural Hawaiian areas.

Map on page 266

Legendary guardians and petrified dragons

One of the more fascinating remnants of pre-historic Jeju (and a prominent symbol of the island) are the *dolharubang*, or **grandfather stones**. These carved lava-rock statues, 52 in all, are seen in every part of Jeju-do. Anthropologists say they probably represent legendary guardians who once flanked the entrances to Jeju's largest townships. Other scholars compare them to mysterious statuary found in various locales such as some parts of the southern Korean peninsula, Tahiti, Okinawa, Fiji and even Easter Island. Suitable places to study these images up close are at the entrance to the **Jeju-do Folklore and Natural History Museum** (open daily except major holidays; 8.30am–6pm, Nov–Feb closes at 5pm; entrance fee) in Jeju City or in front of **Gwandeokjeong** (a 15th-century pavilion), the oldest standing building on Jeju-do, which faces Jeju City's main

Dolharubang *(grandfather stones) are a symbol of Jeju-do.*

BELOW: Seongsanpo crater, the easternmost point of the island.

Hard times for shopkeepers

For as long as anyone in Korea can remember, the way to break the cycle of poverty or escape the drudgery of farm life was to own your own business. Even the smallest of towns has a row of little shops selling groceries, shoes, clothing, toys and furniture, along with karaoke rooms, restaurants and coffee shops.

Some of the older shops in the villages, which are no bigger than a modest bedroom, have a quaint lean to them, the windows plastered over with ads for cigarettes and soju, and a single, bare bulb providing light to the dingy room. Many families were raised in the backroom of these tiny stores. Now these old shops are being rapidly replaced by three- and four-story concrete and brick buildings filled top to bottom with small shops. The buildings can be built in a few weeks, and before you know it, a half-dozen businesses have already

come and gone. These multi-story shophouses so dominate the Korean city that it seems as if the streets are identical.

Over the past decade, however, there have been some major changes in the way Koreans shop, and it doesn't look good for some small traders. It started 20 years ago when the first department stores were built. They stocked a lot of imports and high-end items, and worse, each had a supermarket in the basement. Still, the prices and quality of products were usually higher than the smaller stores, and the department stores were only located in the larger cities.

Next came the supermarkets, with their big inventories and low prices. Since they have begun sprouting up in the smaller towns, the small grocers and butchers have been pushed to the edge. Real problems for shopkeepers began when huge discount stores moved in – Carrefour from France, Walmart and Costco from the States, and several homegrown versions such as Kim's Club and HomePlus. Koreans have taken to them like a fish to water. The combination of better selection, lower prices, and one-stop shopping have given these discount stores over half the retail market in barely a decade.

While it is true that these new shopping centers have made life difficult for many shopkeepers, this has not deterred the small businessman in Korea. It seems there is always room for another restaurant, coffee shop or tavern. With Internet games enjoying phenomenal popularity among high school and university students, thousands of "PC rooms" have recently opened. Middle school students are flocking to crowded and noisy video game rooms, where the DDR (dance machine) has taken the country by storm. Then there are all those shops selling cell phones, and instant photo shops that emboss friendship on a button.

So "Mom and Pop" shopkeepers face difficult times ahead, as computer technologies and the increased spending power of the young are creating a new generation of small business entrepreneurs. It looks like there is still room for the small shop owner in Korea; it just requires a little creativity. ❑

LEFT: modern department stores are a threat to traditional Korean shops.

square. If you find the *dolharubang* charming, miniature lava-rock reproductions are for sale at souvenir shops scattered throughout the island.

Jeju City ❹ is comfortably the largest urban area on the island, yet is noticeably laid back in comparison to similar-sized cities on the mainland. About 300 meters (330 yards) from the KAL Hotel are the **Samseonghyeol** (open daily 8am–6.30pm, Dec–Feb closes at 5.30pm; entrance fee), three holes in the ground, from whence emerged three male demigods, Yang, Go and Bu. According to Jeju myths, these were the original inhabitants of the island. These male progenitors were hunters and fishermen who had the good fortune to later meet three princesses who brought with them grains, livestock and other forms of agriculture. Yang, Go and Bu married these princesses and thus Jeju society was born. The births and meetings of these original Jeju ancestors are celebrated on special feast days every April, October and December by locals.

Yongduam, the **Dragon's Head Rock** ❺ is a rocky formation by the sea in Jeju City's western suburbs near Jeju's main airport. According to local legends, this dragon descended from Hallasan and, upon reaching the sea, petrified in place. These odd-shaped rocks are a hit with Koreans, and no Jeju honeymoon is complete unless the happy couple has their photo taken with Yongduam as a backdrop.

Map on page 266

Tangerines thrive in the southerly climes of Jeju-do.

Tammora, Doi, Tangna

Until about AD 1000, Jeju, like many other remote island spots in Asia, developed in relative isolation and it wasn't until around the end of Korea's Goryeo Dynasty (918–1392) that it was influenced by off-island events. It was during the reign of Goryeo King Gojong (r. 1213–59) that Jeju received its present name. *Je* means simply "across" or "over there." *Ju* in earlier times referred to an administrative district. Therefore, Jeju is the *do*, island, in the district over there. Previously, the island was variously known as *Tammora*, *Doi*, *Tangna* and *Tamna*, the last being the most common version in historical references.

BELOW: an elderly Jeju resident.

In the 13th century, after the Goryeo kingdom had been subjugated by Mongol invaders, Jeju-do became a Mongol possession for about 100 years (from 1273–1374). Professor Sang Yongick of the Jeju National University reports that during this time the armies of Kublai and Genghis Khan "used Jeju-do as a bridge to invade Japan." One invasion of Japan led by Kublai Khan involved 33,000 men and 900 vessels. Many of the ships were in fact constructed of wood milled from trees on Hallasan.

These Mongol conquerors permanently altered Jeju ways. The present-day dialect (unlike the language spoken on the Korean mainland) is a direct result of influence by the Mongols. Not so long ago, it was still possible to find Mongol-styled leather hats, fur clothing and fur stockings in use in the mountain areas of Jeju-do. Through the Mongols, Jeju became a stock-raising area, a famous breeding area for horses. Also, the Mongols, along with temples and statues, brought Buddhism to Jeju.

The first Westerners to visit and tell the outside world about Jeju-do (as well as the Korean mainland)

Old-style water jar at Seongeup village, one place on Jeju-do that has escaped major development.

were Dutch sailors who were shipwrecked at **Moseulpo** ❻ on Jeju's south shore on August 16, 1653. These men of the Dutch ship *Sparrow Hawk* en route from Batavia to Taiwan and then Nagasaki had ventured into fierce typhoon winds, which, according to survivor and author Henrik Hamel, "blew so boisterously, that we could not hear one another speak, nor durst we let fly an inch of sail…"

It wasn't until 1958 that the first group of tourists descended on Jeju-do. Frederic Dustin was a member of that initial exploratory tour, which was led by the late Ferris Miller *(see page 199)*. Dustin quotes Miller as saying: "Over 100 people went, by boat of course since there were no commercial planes then, and the occasion was considered so important that the governor and the mayor of Jeju City met the ship. There were no hotels, so we rented all of the seven or eight inns in town, staying three nights. We also took over two bath houses, one for men and one for women, with runners to guide visitors to them through the unpaved, unlit streets."

That idyllic portrayal of Jeju City has changed considerably. Most of the island is now criss-crossed with paved streets and highways and dotted by hotels and *yeogwan*. Hotels on the island even have casinos, a rarity in Korea.

A US$700 million development project at **Jungmun** ❼, on the south side of the island, includes major international hotels and other facilities including a golf course and botanical gardens. If you are traveling on a budget, you had better look for a hotel in Jeju City or Seogwipo, or near one of the beaches.

Looking for old Jeju

On the eastern end of the island are two "folk villages" which are a good mirror to Jeju's past. **Seongeup** ❽ is an old inland village that not so long ago was the

BELOW: Jeju-do is Korea's number one honeymoon destination.

HONEYMOON ISLAND

For more than 20 years, the idyllic island of Jeju-do has been *the* place for Koreans to spend their honeymoon. Its beaches, expensive hotels and image as a tropical, exotic destination made it a perfect romantic escape. Isolated for centuries, this place of myth and magic also benefited from its warm southern climate, subtropical greenery and volcanic scenery. It didn't hurt, either, that it was nearly impossible for Koreans to travel outside their own country (due to inflexible passport restrictions and financial considerations). By 1990, however, the government had loosened up and Korean tourists were finally allowed to travel overseas.

On the wave of a seemingly non-stop economic boom, Koreans took full advantage of their new-found freedoms, and Jeju's allure was soon eclipsed by Guam and Saipan (only a few hours from Seoul), and even Hawaii and Thailand. With the economic downturn of the late 1990s, though, Korea's honeymooners again returned to the island, which lies just 160 km (100 miles) off the southernmost tip of the peninsula. Who knows – with an increasing number of Japanese (and Chinese) visiting the island, it may become the honeymoon destination of choice for East Asia.

administrative center of the island. There are several old government buildings and a shrine, indicators of the village's past position. Even more interesting are the quaint homes, rock walls and narrow alleyways which visitors are free to wander about (but don't go *in* the houses, someone lives there!). Thankfully, the construction of concrete tower blocks has been limited in Seongeup.

Not far from Seongeup is a folk village with a more commercial bent, the **Jeju Folk Village** ❾ (open daily 8.30am–6pm, Oct–Mar closes at 5pm; entrance fee). Like its more authentic counterpart, the Jeju Folk Village leaves you with a good sense of what the island was like before it was discovered by Japanese jet-setters. Different areas of the Folk Village replicate village life, as it would have been a hundred years ago in the mountain, plains and fishing villages of Jeju. Many of the buildings are authentic, and have been moved here. There is a performance area where you can watch local traditions of song and dance – most of which have links to the island's shamanistic past.

You might also try dropping in on the **Hallim weavers village** ❿ on the northwest shore. This village once had an unusual cottage industry that was begun in the early 1960s by Father Patrick J. McGlinchey, who imported 500 sheep and the proper grass to grow for grazing. Trained by Columbian Roman Catholic priests and nuns, this quiet little village once created some of the finest Irish woollens outside Ireland.

You may still be able to buy superb woollen sweaters, ponchos, caps, mittens, skirts, scarves, blankets and berets, produced at the old Hallim Handweavers Factory, though it's unlikely you will see any village weavers these days – they have moved on to higher paying jobs in the tourism industry.

Diving women

Jeju's famous diving women, the *haenyeo*, have long been a symbol of the island and its purported matri-archal culture, famed for centuries by the people of Jeju-do and Korean mainlanders alike. They are immortalized in folk songs, contemporary promo-tional brochures, as plaster-of-Paris sculptures, and on postcards, souvenir pennants, cups and plates. When conditions are favorable, scores of the *haenyeo*, who range from teenagers to wrinkled grandmothers, can be seen bobbing offshore between free dives for seaweed, shellfish and sea urchins. Fewer dives take place in winter, when the water temperature falls to around 10°C (50°F). There are still several thousand women on the island still practising the tradition, and drawing in the tourists.

In times past, when the *haenyeo* would plunge into the waters clad only in loose white cotton, it was illegal for any man to set eyes upon them. Things have changed, and these days, in their slick black head-to-toe wetsuits, face masks and snorkels, the sexy sirens of the past look more like members of a navy demo-lition team. Nevertheless, they are still the favorite target of every camera-toting tourist who visits Jeju. Do remember, though, to ask for permission before photographing the *haenyeo*, since they are often camera-shy, and some might want to be paid for hav-ing their picture taken. ❏

Map on page 266

TIP

There are a lot of tour buses operating on the island, but this is one place (it's rural and small) in Korea where renting a car for a day is a good idea.

BELOW: *haenyeo* (diving women) souvenir.
FOLLOWING PAGE: early morning walk.

Travel Tips

INSIGHT GUIDES Phonecard

One global card to keep
travellers in touch.
Easy. Convenient. Saves
you time and money.

It's a global phonecard

Save up to 70%* on international calls
from over 55 countries

Free 24 hour global customer service

Recharge your card at any time via customer
service or online

It's a message service

Family and friends can send you voice
messages for free.

Listen to these messages using the phone*
or online

Free email service - you can even listen
to your email over the phone*

It's a travel assistance service

24 hour emergency travel assistance –
if and when you need it.

Store important travel documents online
in your own secure vault

For more information, call rates, and all
Access Numbers in over 55 countries,
(check your destination is covered) go to
www.insightguides.ekit.com or call
Customer Service.

JOIN now and receive
US$ 5 bonus when you
join for US$ 20 or more.

Join today at

www.insightguides.ekit.com

When requested use ref code: **INSAD0103**

OR SIMPLY FREE CALL
24 HOUR CUSTOMER SERVICE

UK	0800 376 1705
USA	1800 706 1333
Canada	1800 808 5773
Australia	1800 11 44 78
South Africa	0800 997 285

THEN PRESS 0

For all other countries please go to "Access Numbers" at
www.insightguides.ekit.com

* Retrieval rates apply for listening to messages. Savings based
on using a hotel or payphone and calling to a landline. Correc
at time of printing 01.03

(INS001)

powered by ekit

"The easiest way to make calls and receive messages around the world"

CONTENTS

Getting Acquainted

The Place

Area: South Korea covers an area of 98,500 sq. km (38,000 sq. miles). The country is bordered on the north by North Korea, on the west by the Yellow Sea (Bo Hai), known to Koreans as the West Sea, and to the east and south by the East Sea, which Japanese refer to as the Japan Sea.

Population: 48 million.

Major Cities: Seoul (10.3 million); Busan (4 million); Daegu (2.5 million); Incheon (2.3 million).

Time Zone: Korean time is GMT +9 hours. There is no daylight saving time. When it is noon in Seoul it is 3am in London (4am during British Summer Time), and 10pm the previous day in New York (11pm from April to October).

Religion: There is no official state religion. Many Koreans practice a mix of Buddhism and Confucianism, with folk influences and shamanism. Approximately one quarter of the population would define themselves as Christian.

Language: Korean.

Currency: won (W). In August 2004, the exchange rate was W1,110 to 1 US Dollar, and W2,050 to 1 Pound Sterling.

Electricity: 220 volt outlets are standard throughout Korea. Super deluxe and deluxe hotels also have a few 110 volt outlets.

Weights and Measures: Metric.

International Dialing Code: 82.

Economy

An "Asian Tiger" *par excellence*, the Korean economy has achieved astounding growth in the past forty years. Since the 1960s, an enviable annual growth rate has fostered prosperity, and a burgeoning white-collar middle class has developed. More recently, the Korean auto industry has established itself in overseas markets. Today the country's traditionally protected markets are being opened to outside competition – Korea has been a member of the Organization for Economic Cooperation and Development (OECD) since 1996. In the past few years, the easing of political tension on the peninsula has resulted in an increased interest in investment opportunities and trade.

The economy is based on the Japanese model of state involvement and regulation. However, recognizing that its interference has deterred potential importers, the government has tried to adopt more liberal trading policies as set by the international General Agreement on Tariffs & Trade (GATT). Following the Asian slump of 1997 and 1998, the economy has recovered strongly. Although there are still some problems, from the preponderance of monopolies to the level of military spending, South Korea can look forward to the future with justifiable optimism.

Government

South Korea is a democratic republic with authoritarian overtones. Although government is constitutionally divided into executive, legislative and judicial spheres, power is centered in the office of a powerful executive president. The legislature is represented by the single-chamber National Assembly, which is currently composed of five parties. Out of 299 members who serve

Climate and When to Go

Korea's location on the eastern edge of the Eurasian landmass results in a continental climate, with cold winters (rather milder along the south coast and in Jeju-do) and hot, humid summers. Seoul's rather unpredictable weather is often compared to that of New York City.

From December to early March the weather is generally cold and sunny, with occasional snowfalls. Afternoon temperatures in Seoul are usually around freezing; Busan is a few degrees warmer. The cold is enhanced by the Siberian winds that whip down the peninsula, often in a cycle of three consecutive cold days followed by four milder days.

A spring thaw comes in mid-April and lasts little more than two months. In early spring north-westerly gusts bring swirls of dust from the Gobi Desert and a light rain. As summer approaches, humid southerlies vie for control and the spring drizzle becomes an occasional downpour, culminating in three or four weeks of heavy rains during the late July and early August monsoon season.

July and August are the hottest, most humid months, and are particularly enervating in the inland basin around Daegu, where afternoon temperatures climb into the lower 30°s centigrade (around 90°F). Temperatures in Seoul are more often around 28°C (82°F).

Between mid-July and the end of September occasional typhoons move north from the East China Sea to bring torrential rain and strong winds to the Korean peninsula, although these are rarely damaging as they are further to the south (Jeju-do is more at risk).

Autumn arrives in early October when the air currents shift back to the crisp northerlies. The weather is normally dry and sunny.

The best months for visiting are mid-April to mid-June, and September to October just before and after the summer rains. Autumn has the advantage of the wonderful displays of foliage in the Korean forests, while spring is famous for the cherry blossom.

four-year terms, 243 are elected on a constituency basis, while the other 56 are awarded proportionately to parties that win not less than three percent in the polls. The president appoints leading officials such as the prime minister, his right-hand man. A State Council with nominally executive powers includes ministry and department heads, but has only an advisory role to the president.

Korean democracy is evolving but remains delicate. In 1987 the country experienced its first peaceful transfer of presidential power after years in which elections were little more than fig leaves covering coercive governments that were obsessed with secrecy and dependent on military support. In today's atmosphere of rapprochement with the North and greater popular awareness of the outside world, students, liberals and intellectuals are making some headway in opening Korean government to greater scrutiny.

Culture and Customs

Etiquette

To many Westerners, Koreans can seem rather formal, with rigid codes of behavior. Heavily influenced by Confucian ethics, the Koreans place great emphasis on respect for one's elders. Greetings, and saying thank you, are considered important. Direct physical contact, unless between close friends, is limited to a courteous handshake.

Remember to always remove your shoes before entering a Korean home, although bare feet are considered insulting.

When out for a drink or a meal with a group, be prepared to take on the role of guest, or host: Koreans will seldom pay separately. Talking a lot during a meal is impolite, as is blowing your nose at table and resting your chopsticks in the rice. Oddly enough, public drunkenness is quite acceptable, as long as the inebriated individual is not being aggressive or offensive.

The National Flag

The Korean flag, *Taegeukgi*, was adopted as the national flag in August, 1883, not long after the "Hermit Kingdom" opened its front and back doors to foreign aggressive powers. The flag symbolizes the oriental yin-yang (in Korean, *eum-yang*) philosophy of the balance and harmony in nature of opposite forces and elements which are in perpetual motion.

The colors of the flag are red, black, and blue against white. The red and blue circle in the center of the flag symbolizes the dualism of the universe. The upper red paisley represents *yang* nature: positive, masculine, active, constructive, light, heat, and dignity; complemented by the lower blue paisley, *eum* nature: negative, feminine, passive, destructive, dark, cold, and hope.

The black trigrams in each corner are also of Chinese origin (from the *Tao Te Ching*). They basically symbolize the four seasons and cardinal directions. Going clockwise from the upper left corner, the three solid bars *(Geon)* represent heaven, spring, east and benevolence; the upper right bars *(Gam)* signify the moon, winter, north, and wisdom; the lower right bars *(Gon)* symbolize earth, summer, west, and righteousness; and the lower left bars *(Ri)* represent the sun, autumn, south, and etiquette.

Korean Names

As with Chinese names, Korean surnames appear at the start of a person's name. Most surnames consist of a single syllable, and are as easy to learn as they are to forget. The problem is that many Koreans share the same romanized surname (although some of the Chinese characters may be written differently). Thus referring to someone by his surname can only become confusing and futile after meeting many Koreans. To add to the confusion, Korean wives retain their maiden names. Thus, it is best to learn the entire Korean name.

Korean surnames were derived

Public Holidays

- **1 January** New Year's Holiday.
- **Feb** Lunar New Year *(Seollal)*. Businesses closed for 3–5 working days.
- **1 March** Independence Movement Day *(Samiljeol)*.
- **5 April** Arbor Day *(Singmogil)*.
- **5 May** Children's Day *(Eorininal)*.
- **mid-May** Buddha's Birthday *(Seokga Tansinil)*.
- **6 June** Memorial Day *(Hyeonchungil)*.
- **17 July** Constitution Day *(Jeheonjeol)*.
- **15 August** Liberation Day *(Gwangbokjeol)*.
- **Sept** Chuseok, harvest festival; the Korean equivalent of the American Thanksgiving festival. Takes place on the 15th day of the 8th lunar month.
- **3 October** National Foundation Day *(Gaecheonjeol)*.
- **25 December** Christmas Day

from the Chinese during the early Three Kingdoms period (57 BC–AD 918). The most common surnames are Kim, Yi (Lee, Rhee), and Pak (Park), followed by Choi, Chung, and Cho. Throughout the ages, surnames have dictated one's social position, a tradition still honored only in isolated villages. Whether *yangban* (aristocrat) or *pyeongmin* (commoner), however, one's name was recorded in a family-tree book, *jokbo*, which traced an individual's lineage back to the origin of the clan.

Dojang (House Seals)

Seals, engraved by professional artisans, are used in lieu of personal signatures, especially on legal documents. The use of seals was originally a borrowed custom from China, initially a status symbol used by royalty. During the Three Kingdoms period, a dethroned king had to symbolically transfer power by handing over his imperial seals.

Seals today are as popular as ever, and are commonly used by government offices, companies, and organizations, and for personal flourishes on stationery. The seals are carved of ivory, stone, marble, plastic, wood, smoky topaz, jade, and other materials. The ink is made of sticky scarlet vegetable dye that is permanent.

Business Hours

Banks
Weekdays 9.30am–4.30pm; Saturday, Sunday and Public Holidays closed.

Department Stores
All week and some public holidays 10.30am–7.30pm.

Embassies
Weekdays 9am–5pm, usually closed one hour for lunch; Saturday, Sunday and Public Holidays closed.

Government Offices
Weekdays Mar–Oct 9am–6pm (5pm Nov–Feb); every other Saturday 9am–1pm; Sunday and Public Holidays closed.

Post Offices
Weekdays 9am–6pm; every other Saturday 9am–1pm; Sunday and Public Holidays closed.

Private Companies
Weekdays 9am–6pm; Saturday 9am–1pm; Sunday and Public Holidays closed. More and more companies are adopting a five-day working week.

Planning the Trip

Entry Regulations

Visas & Passports
Visitors from most countries may stay for up to 90 days without a visa if they have confirmed outbound tickets. Most European, and many Asian and South American countries have agreements that permit citizens to stay for longer without a visa. Canadian citizens can stay for 6 months. Note that any traveler holding a US, Canadian or Japanese visa is granted a 15-day, visa-free stopover.

Customs
You may bring in 200 cigarettes, (50 cigars or 250 grams of tobacco), one liter of liquor and two fluid ounces of perfume. Items for personal use (except goods such as vehicles, guns and musical instruments) may be brought in duty free, but visitors must leave with these items.

Korean antiques pre-dating 1910 should be checked and appraised by the Arts and Antiques Assessment Office and a permit should be secured. For five or fewer antiques, checking may be done at Seoul City Hall (tel: 02 3707-9443). A limit of three kilograms of red ginseng with a sales receipt is acceptable.

Korean Embassies Overseas

Australia, 113 Empire Circuit, Yarralumla, ACT 2600.
Tel: (02) 6270-4110.
Canada, 150 Boteler Street, Ottawa, Ontario K1N 5A6.
Tel: (613) 244-5010.
China, 3, Fourth Avenue East, Sanlitun, Chaoyang, Beijing 100600.
Tel: (10) 6532-6778.

France, 125 rue de Grenelle, 75007, Paris. Tel: (01) 4753-0101.
Germany, Schoenberger Ufer 89–91, 10785 Berlin.
Tel: (030) 26065-0.
Hong Kong (consulate general), 5/6 Floor, Far East Finance Centre, 16 Harcourt Road, Hong Kong.
Tel: 2529-4141.
Japan, 1-2-5 Minami-Azabu, Minatoku, Tokyo.
Tel: (03) 3452-7611/9.
New Zealand, 11th Floor, ASB Bank Tower, 2 Hunter Street, Wellington. Tel: (04) 473-9073/4.
Singapore, 47 Scotts Road, #08-00 Goldbell Towers, Singapore 228233. Tel: 6256-1188.
United Kingdom, 60 Buckingham Gate, London SW1E 6AJ.
Tel: (020) 7227-5500/2.
United States, 2450 Massachusetts Avenue, N.W. Washington D.C. 20008.
Tel: (202) 939-5600/4.

Health Precautions

South Korea is a healthy place, although it is recommended that you take out comprehensive travel insurance before traveling. In the UK, detailed health advice for visits anywhere in the world is available from MASTA (Medical Advice for Travellers Abroad), tel: 09068 224-100 (premium rate). They have a website at www.masta.org.

Recommended vaccinations for South Korea include hepatitis A and polio, as well as tetanus and diphtheria boosters. Except for those whose itineraries include cholera-infected areas, no certificate of vaccination is required. Japanese encephalitis inoculations are recommended for those staying in rural areas in the summer months. *For more on health, see page 280.*

Money Matters

Currency
Korean *won* comes in 1,000, 5,000 and 10,000 denomination notes and 10, 50, 100, and 500 *won* coins. Bank drafts for large amounts (normally W100,000) are available.

Changing Money

Procuring *won* outside Korea may be difficult. Once you have arrived, however, there are foreign exchange counters at the airport, large tourist hotels (usually less favorable rates), and major banks (some with branches in large hotels), and a few department stores (such as Lotte) in Seoul. The most viable currencies to carry in Korea are Japanese yen and US dollars, although other major foreign currencies can also be exchanged. Remember to retain all exchange receipts for reconversion on departure.

Credit Cards and ATMs

Credit cards are commonly used by Koreans, but may not be accepted by small shops and businesses. American Express, Visa, JCB, MasterCard, and Diners Club cards are readily accepted in major hotels, department stores and restaurants as well as many tourist-oriented shops.

There are numerous ATMS dispensing cash advances on credit cards. They are found at hotels, department stores, subway stations and tourist attractions across the country, with instructions in English.

Banking in Seoul

Banks are open Mon–Fri 9.30am–4.30pm.

Korean Banks in Seoul

Bank of Korea, tel: 759-4114.
Choheung Bank, tel: 2010-2114.
Export-Import Bank of Korea, tel: 3779-6114.
Hana Bank, tel: 2002-1111.
Kookmin Bank, tel: 7073-7114.
KORAM Bank, tel: 3455-2114.
Korea Development Bank, tel: 787-4000.
Korea Exchange Bank, tel: 729-8000 ext. 9.
Korea First Bank, tel: 3702-3114.
Shinnhan Bank, tel: 756-0505.
Woori Bank, tel: 2002-3000 ext. 0.

Foreign Banks in Seoul

American Express, tel: 1588-8100.
American Express Bank, tel: 399-2929.

Tourist Offices Overseas

Websites of KNTO overseas offices can be accessed through www.knto.or.kr/eng/overseas.html

North America

Los Angeles
4801 Wilshire Blvd, Suite 103, Los Angeles, CA 90010, USA
Tel: (323) 643-0280
Fax: (323) 643-0281
e-mail: la@kntoamerica.com

New York
One Executive Drive, Suite 100, Fort Lee, NJ 07024, USA
Tel: (201) 585-0909
Fax: (201) 585-9041
e-mail: ny@kntoamerica.com

Chicago
737 North Michigan Ave, Suite 910, Chicago, IL 60611, USA
Tel: (312) 981-1717/9
Fax: (312) 981-1721
e-mail: Chicago@kntoamerica.com

Toronto
Suite 1903, 700 Bay Street, Toronto, Ontario M5G IZ6, Canada
Tel: (416) 348-9056
Fax: (416) 348-9058
e-mail: Toronto@knto.ca

Asia-Pacific

Hong Kong
Suite 4203, 42/F, Tower 1, Lippo Center, 89 Queensway, Admiralty, Hong Kong
Tel: 2523-8065; Fax: 2845-0765
e-mail: general@knto.com.hk

Singapore
20-01, 24 Raffles Place, Clifford Centre, Singapore 048621
Tel: 6533-0441; Fax: 6534-3427
e-mail: kntosp@pacific.net.sg

Bangkok
15/F, Silom Complex Building, 191 Silom Road, Bangkok 10500, Thailand

Bank of Tokyo-Mitsubishi, tel: 399-6439.
Banque Nationale de Paris, tel: 317-1700.
Chase Manhattan Bank, N.A., tel: 758-5114.
Citibank, tel: 2004-1760.
First National Bank of Chicago, tel: 316-9700.

Tel: (2) 231-3895
Fax: (2) 231-3897
e-mail: kntobkk@knto-th.org

Beijing
Rm 508, Hyundai Millennium Tower, 38 Xiaoyun Rd, Chaoyang District, Beijing 100027, China
Tel: (10) 8453-8213
Fax: (10) 8453-8147
e-mail: bjknto@a-1.net.cn

Tokyo
Rm 124, Sanshin Bldg 1-4-1, Yuraku Cho, Chiyoda-ku, Tokyo, Japan 100
Tel: (3) 3580-3941
Fax: (3) 3591-4601
e-mail: Tokyo@tour2korea.com

Sydney
Level 40, Australia Square Tower, 264 George St, Sydney, NSW 2000, Australia
Tel: (2) 9252-4147
Fax: (2) 9251-2104
e-mail: visitkorea@knto.or.au

Europe

Frankfurt
Basseler Str, 48, D–60329, Frankfurt am-Main, Germany
Tel: (69) 233226
Fax: (69) 253519
e-mail: kntoff@euko.de

Paris
Tour Maine Montparnasse 33, Avenue du Maine, BP 169, 75755 Paris Cedex 15, France
Tel: (1) 4538-7123
Fax: (1) 4538-7471
e-mail: knto@club-internet.fr

London
3rd Floor, New Zealand House, Haymarket, London SW1Y 4TE, United Kingdom
Tel: (20) 7321-2535
Fax: (20) 7321-0876
e-mail: koreatb@dircon.co.uk

HSBC, tel: 1588-1770.
Standard Chartered Bank, tel: 750-6114.

Photography

Due to high import taxes, cameras are expensive in Korea. This has encouraged a demand for second-

Emergencies

Police: 112
Fire and Emergency Ambulance:
119
Medical Emergency: 1339
International SOS Korea provides
a **24-hour emergency service for
foreigners**, acting as a link
between patients and Korean
hospitals for a fee.
Tel: (02) 790-7561.

To recover lost possessions,
including those left in taxis,
contact the nearest police box
(these are on every major street)
or ask the hotel front desk clerk
to help you do so. The Seoul
Metropolitan Police Lost and
Found Center is at 102,
Hongikdong, Seongdonggu.
Tel: 2299-1282; Fax: 2298-1282.

hand equipment, although this is
still quite pricey.

Prices for print and slide film
vary widely from one place to
another, so shop around. Hotel
stores are the most expensive.
Chungmuro is the area to shop
(subway lines 3 and 4) where
professional labs and specialist
shops selling a wide range of new
and second-hand cameras are lined
up, and where you can also buy
black and white films. Also, you
must specify the kind of processing
you desire for all film – if you don't
say Kodak, they'll use a local
processing company, which may be
of poorer quality.

Opportunities for photography
in Korea abound but it is
important that visitors respect the
privacy of their hosts. Koreans do
not like ceremonies to be
photographed and older Koreans
don't like photos at all. Ask before
you shoot.

Getting There

BY AIR

With the opening of **Incheon
International Airport** (IIA) in 2001,
Korea greatly increased its air
traffic handling capacity and is now
one of East Asia's major transport
hubs. The new airport is 52 km
(31 miles) west of Seoul, and 15 km
(9 miles) west of Incheon *(see page
282 for more details on travel to
and from the airport)*. For airport
information, tel: (032) 741-0114.

Korea is connected with the
United States by Korean Air, Japan
Airlines, United Airlines, and
Northwest Airlines among others.
Carriers routed through Seoul
include Cathay Pacific, China
Airlines, Malaysian Airlines and
Singapore Airlines. It is less than
13 hours from the US West Coast,
11 hours from London, 2½ hours
from Tokyo, 3½ hours from Hong
Kong, and 1½ hours from Beijing.
Gimpo Airport, 19 km (12 miles)
west of Seoul now operates
domestic flights. For airport
information, tel: (02) 2660-2475.

Korea's other international
airports are at Busan (Kimhae
Airport) and on Jeju Island;
these operate flights to major
cities in the region, mostly to/from
Japan.

Following is a list of airline
offices in Seoul; add the 02 prefix if
dialing from outside Seoul:
Aeroflot, tel: 551-0321.
Air Canada, tel: 3788-0100 ext. 1.
Air China, tel: 774-6886.
Air France, tel: 318-3788.
All Nippon Airways, tel: 752-5500.
Asiana Airlines, tel: 669-4000.
Cathay Pacific, tel: 311-2800.
China Eastern Airlines,
tel: 518-0330.
China Southern Airlines,
tel: 3455-1600.
Garuda Indonesia Airline, tel: 773-
2092.
Japan Airlines, tel: 757-1711.
KLM Royal Dutch Airlines,
tel: 2011-5500.
Korean Air, tel: 1588-2001 ext. 5.
Lufthansa German Airlines,
tel: 3420-0400.
Malaysia Airlines, tel: 777-7761.
Northwest Airlines, tel: 732-1700.
Philippine Airlines, tel: 774-3581.
Qantas Airways, tel: 777-6871.
Singapore Airlines, tel: 755-1226.
Thai Airways International,
tel: 3707-0011.
United Airlines, tel: 757-1691.

All passengers are subject to a
W27,000 airport tax (normally
included in air ticket prices).

BY SEA

To/From Japan

Overnight ferry services operate
between Busan and the Japanese
port of Shimonoseki on the western
tip of Honshu (Bukwan Ferry, tel: 02
738-0055). Busan and Hakata, the
port of Fukuoka, are connected by
daily jetfoils (Korea Marine Express,
tel: 02 753-6661) and ferries
(Korea Ferry, tel: 02 775-2323).
There are also ferries to other
Japanese ports like Kokura,
Hatakatu, Izuhara, Osaka, and
Hirosima. It is best to check the
latest schedule and fare with KNTO
(tel: 02 729-9496) and then to
contact individual ferry operators or
a travel agency.

It is possible to purchase all-in-
one train-ferry combination tickets
for travel between South Korea and
Japan, for instance from Seoul to
Osaka via Busan.

To/From China

There are extensive ferry services
from Incheon to several Chinese
ports such as Dandong, Weihai,
Qingdao, Tianjin, Dalian, and Yantai.
They are overnight ferries and
operate three times per week
except for Tianjin (twice a week).
Travel time is 11 hours to Dalian for
the shortest (Daein Ferry, tel: 02
3218-6550) and one full day to
Tianjin for the longest (Daeah
Travel, tel: 02 515-6317). It is
advisable to check the latest
schedule and fare with KNTO first
(tel: 02 729-9496).

Korea–China through-tickets
which combine train and ferry
services are also available.

Call the following companies for
information on ferries traveling
between Korea and China and
Japan:
Beetle II (Busan)
Tel: (051) 465-6111
Camellia Line (Busan)
Tel: (051) 466-7799

Camellia Line (Seoul)
Tel: (02) 775-2323
Korea Marine Express (Busan)
Tel: (051) 465-6111
Korea Marine Express (Seoul)
Tel: (02) 730-8666
Bukwan Ferry (Busan)
Tel: (051) 464-2700
Weidong Ferry (Seoul)
Tel: (02) 3271-6753

Embassies in Seoul

*Note: if calling from outside of
Seoul add the 02 telephone prefix.*
Australia, 11th Floor, Gyobo
Building, 1 Jongno 1-ga, Jongnogu.
Tel: 2003-0100.
Canada, 9/10th Floor, Kolon
Building, 45 Mugyodong, Junggu.
Tel: 3455-6000.
China, 54 Hyojadong, Jongnogu.
Tel: 738-1038.
France, 30 Hapdong, Sodaemungu.
Tel: 3149-4300.
Germany, 308-5, Dongbinggodong,
Yongsangu. Tel: 748-4114.
Ireland, 15th floor, Daehan Fire &
Marine Insurance Building, 51-1
Namchangdong, Junggu.
Tel: 774-6455.
Japan, 18-11, Junghakdong,
Jongnogu. Tel: 2170-5200.
New Zealand, 18th Floor, Gyobo
Building, 1 Jongno 1-ga, Jongnogu.
Tel: 730-7794.
Singapore, 19th Floor, Samsung
Daepyongno Bldg, Daepyongno
2-ga, Junggu.
Tel: 774-2464.
United Kingdom, 40 Taepyeongno,
4 Jeongdong, Junggu.
Tel: 3210-5500.
United States, 32 Sejongno,
Jongnogu. Tel: 397-4114.

Practical Tips

Media

South Korea has 10 national daily
newspapers, five economic dailies
and three sports dailies, plus three
English newspapers – *The Korea
Herald*, *The Korea Times* and
Joongang Daily, which carry
international news. The *Asian Wall
Street Journal*, *International Herald
Tribune* and *Far Eastern Economic
Review* are also circulated locally.

Weeklies, bi-weeklies, monthlies
and bi-monthlies flood the
bookstores. The most popular
English-language periodicals are the
Korea Economic Weekly and the
monthly *Korea Economic Report*.
Time and *Newsweek* are prominently
displayed in bookstores.

Major hotels carry satellite news
services like BBC and CNN, as well
as other channels like MTV and Star.
American Forces Korean Network
(AFKN) broadcasts in English in
Seoul on 1530 AM, 88.5 and
102.7 FM. AFKN TV programing is
carried on local TV when US military
installations are located nearby;
check TV channel 2, or UHF
channel 30.

Postal Services

Seoul's Central Post Office is
currently located just off the busy
Myeongdong area, by the old
Yeongnak church. The Gwanghwamun post office branch is located
near the corner of Taepyeongno and
Jongno. General post office hours
are 9am–6pm Monday to Friday and
9am–1pm on Saturday. Aerograms
cost W400 and postcards W350. A
10-gram airmail letter to Europe,
North America or the Middle East is
W580, and to southeast Asia,
W520. Letters to the US and
Europe take 6–8 days. You may
make further enquiries at the
Central Post Office (tel: 2278-
5152), Gwanghwamun Post Office
(tel: 3703-9011) or International
Post Office (tel: 2645-0004).
Ministry of Information and
Communications: www.mic.go.kr

For a faster service, there are
international courier services such
as DHL (tel: 716-0001), UPS (tel:
3665-3651) and Hanjin (operated
by KAL, tel: 738-1212).

Telephones

Using a public telephone can be
something of an endurance test in
Korea. There are three different
types: coin phones, card phones and
credit card phones. Of course it is
also possible to make local, long-
distance and international calls
direct from your hotel room, although
you will pay more for the privilege.

Phone cards come in
denominations of W3,000, W5,000
and W10,000 and are sold at
banks and convenience stores such
as LG25 and 7-Eleven.

To make an international call,
first dial the access code 001
(002 or 008 are also used),
followed by country code, area code
and the number. International calls

Telephone Area Codes

Seoul 02	Gangwon-do 033
Busan 051	Gyeonggi-do 031
Chungcheongbuk-do 043	Gyeongsangbuk-do (Gyeongju) 054
Chungcheongnam-do 041	Incheon 032
Daegu 053	Jeju-do 064
Daejeon 042	Jeollabuk-do 063
Gyeongsangnam-do 055	Jeollanam-do 061
Gwangju 062	Ulsan 052

and collect calls can be made through the operator by dialing 00799. Dial 00794 for information on international calls.

Cellular phones can be hired at Incheon Airport.

Useful Numbers
Directory Assistance (multiple enquiries at one time) Tel: (080) 211-0114.
Directory Assistance (local call) Tel: 114.
Directory Assistance (long distance) Tel: (area code) + 114.
Tourist Information Tel: 1330.
Tourist Complaint Centre Tel: (02) 735-0101; Fax: (02) 777-0102. e-mail: tourcom@mail.knto.or.kr

Internet

Most hotel business centers can provide internet access, although it can be pricey. However the internet (especially internet gaming) has caught on in a big way, and there are dozens of "PC Rooms" wherever there are young people. All you have to do is walk in to one, mention "internet", and they'll set you up. Charges are generally in the range of W1,000–2,000 for the first 30 minutes, and W1,000 for each additional half hour. Free internet access is available in KNTO, banks, airports, major train stations and some tourist information centers in busy districts.

Useful Websites
www.knto.or.kr/english
Comprehensive, informative website of the Korea National Tourism Corporation.
www.english.tour2korea.com
Up-to-date and comprehensive tourist information provided by KNTO.
www.visitseoul.net
Well-organized and detailed information on Seoul provided by Seoul city.
www.kimsoft.com
Independent Korea Web Weekly site covering history, politics, culture and the economy, with a great array of links.

www.koreaherald.co.kr
Colorful and well-organized site of *The Korea Herald*, featuring latest exchange rates and breaking news stories.
www.han.com/gateway.html
Well-organized, easily accessible list of links to all things pertaining to the country and its people.
www.lifeinkorea.com
Well-presented and researched site designed for foreigners living in Korea, with a wide variety of features and links.
www.kimsoft.com/dprk.htm
Everything you ever wanted to know about North Korea, including surprisingly candid news features.
www.koreatimes.co.kr/times.htm
The *Korea Times* homepage, featuring a great archive, and language tutorials.
http://iml.jou.ufl.edu/projects/ STUDENTS/Hwang/home.htm
An excellent guide to Korean food in all its pungent forms.

Medical Services

Many kinds of medicines and healthcare goods – from bottled sweetened vitamin tonics to contraceptives – are available at local pharmacies.

Immunizations are administered at the International Clinic at Severance

Drinking Water

Potable water is available in hotels. In establishments for locals, *boricha* (roasted barley boiled in water), distinguished by its light brown colour, is served instead. In traditional Korean restaurants, you may be served another water substitute, *sungnyung*, tea boiled from browned rice gathered from the bottom of a rice pot. It is also quite safe to drink water which springs from certain mountain sites at temples in the countryside. Unboiled tap water is never advised for drinking. Bottled water can be purchased from supermarkets or convenience stores.

Hospital, which uses disposable needles, and at the Seoul Quarantine Office, located to the right of the USO compound in Galwoldong, Yongsangu.

Dentists and optometrists are generally reliable and their work is reasonably priced. Major hotels have house doctors.

The following is a list of major hospitals for foreigners in Seoul:
Asan Medical Center, tel: (02) 3010-5001.
Cha General Hospital Foreign Clinic, tel: (02) 3468-3113.
Gangbuk Samsung Hospital, tel: (02) 2001-2911.
International Clinic (Itaewon), tel: (02) 790-0857.
Samsung Jeil Hospital, tel: (02) 2273-0151.
Samsung Medical Center, tel: (02) 3410-0200.
Seoul Foreign Clinic (Itaewon), tel: (02) 790-0075.
Seoul National University Hospital, tel: (02) 760-2890.
Severance Hospital (International Clinic), tel: (02) 361-6540.
Soonchunhyang, tel: (02) 709-9158.

Tourist Information

A wide range of tourist information and related services are readily available at the KNTO head office in Seoul, which has an information counter, reservation and ticketing desk, tourism exhibition hall, book and souvenir shop and a small theatre. It also has a comprehensive library. KNTO's TIC (Tourist Information Center), 10 Dadong, Junggu, Seoul, is open daily 9am–8pm.

There are also information centers at Gimpo, Gimhae, and Jeju airports. They provide you with city maps, brochures and useful information on tours, shopping, dining and accommodation.

Tourist Information by Phone
Dial 1330 for detailed tourist information in English, Japanese and Chinese. Local call rates apply. If you require information for another region to the one you are dialing from, dial the appropriate area code followed by 1330 (for

Local Tourist Offices

Seoul
KNTO Head Office, 10 Dadong, Junggu, Seoul 100-180. Tel: (02) 729-9600; Fax: (02) 757-5997; www.knto.or.kr
Gimpo Airport
Tel: (02) 3707-9465
Incheon Airport
Tel: (032) 743-0011
Incheon Ferry Terminal,
Tel: (032) 891-2030
Itaewon, tel: (02) 794-2490
Myeongdong, tel: (02) 757-0088
Namdaemum Market, tel: (02) 752-1913
Sinchon, tel: (02) 363-2883
Dongdaemun, tel: (02) 2236-9135
Gyeongbu Line, tel: (02) 535-4151
Honam Line, tel: (02) 6282-0808
Deoksugung, tel: (02) 756-0045

regional telephone codes in Korea see yellow panel on page 279). Lines are open 24 hours.

Tipping

Tipping is not the norm in Korea, and is expected only in businesses that cater primarily to Westerners. A 10 percent service charge is automatically added to major hotel room and restaurant bills (read the bill to make sure before tipping). Airport baggage porters are tipped at the exit door according to a set standard. Taxi drivers do not expect a tip unless they perform an extra service, although they may not return your change if it is only a small amount. Bellhops usually receive around W1,000 tip per bag.

Religious Services

There are numerous places of worship in Seoul catering to many different faiths. Details of service times are published in the Saturday edition of English-language newspapers, and your hotel concierge will also be able to provide information. Or you can call one of the churches with English-speaking services (unless noted) below:

Busan
Gimhae Airport
Tel: (051) 973-4607
Busan Railway Station
Tel: (051) 441-6565
Busan Ferry Terminal
Tel: (051) 465-3471

Jeju
Jeju International Airport
tel: (064) 742-8866
Jungmun Tourist Information
tel: (064) 738-8550

Gyeongju
Gyeongju Railway Station
Tel: (054) 772-3843
Bulguksa Temple
Tel: (054) 746-4747

Seoul Union Church,
Sunday worship 11am.
Tel: (02) 333-7393.
Seoul Church of Christ, non-denominational. Sunday Bible class 4pm, worship 5pm.
Tel: (02) 2605-2309.
Seoul International Baptist Church,
Sunday worship 11am, Bible classes Sunday 9.45am and 5pm.
Tel: (02) 333-0662.
International Lutheran Church,
Sunday worship 9am followed by brunch. Tel: (02) 794-6274.
Anglican Church, Sunday worship at 9am. Tel: (02) 730-6611. Anglican Holy Communion Sundays at 7am, 9am and 11am offered at the Missions To Seamen, Marine Center, in Busan. Tel: (051) 644-7787.
Myeongdong Cathedral, for information on daily masses and for appointments for confession in English, call (02) 774-3890 ext. 0.
The Seoul Central Masjid, prayers in Korean, Arabic and English. For daily schedule call (02) 794-7307.
Lotus Lantern International Buddhist Center, ceremony Sundays 6pm. Exploring Buddhism on Thursdays 1.30 to 3pm.
Tel: (02) 735-5347. For meditation programs, call (02) 735-5347.
Seoul International Zen Center,
Meditation and Dharma talk,
Sunday 1pm. Hwagye-sa Temple.
Tel: (02) 900-4326.

Women Travelers

Women take second place to men in Korean society, and generally can expect to get served last whether at a restaurant or standing in a queue. This can be galling to observe and to experience, but a pithy two-minute lecture delivered at top volume is not going to alter the attitudes of millennia. Foreign women, whether on holiday or business, can look forward to rather more courteous treatment. Sexual harassment is rare, but alcohol inflames Korean men like nothing else. Take care.

Traveling with Kids

As in many Asian countries, children enjoy a special place in society, and are cosseted and fussed over, especially by older Koreans. Arriving with a family in tow is like having an "extra passport" – you can expect special service in restaurants, hotels and many other public places. Note that larger babies may not fit Korean-size diapers/nappies, while Korean food may not be to toddlers' tastes, so plan accordingly. If your children can be persuaded to learn a few word of Hangeul expect some bonus points!

What to Wear

Korean businessmen wear suits and ties, even in the summer. Otherwise, dress is casual. Mini-skirts and shorts are acceptable, although foreigners are advised to avoid being too skimpily clad. An umbrella, sunglasses, and rainy day footwear are practical accessories to pack. In the summer it is worth bringing a light sweater for mountain regions and to combat fierce air-conditioning in hotels and restaurants. Bring extra-warm clothing for the chilly winters, made even colder by the considerable wind-chill factor.

Business Travelers

As well as heeding the advice given in Business Etiquette (see page 71) business travelers should beware of some of the pitfalls of getting around Seoul, where most major companies are located. Rush-hour traffic jams can throw well-laid schedules awry, and occasional lack of clear addresses can make finding office buildings tricky. And few taxi drivers speak anything apart from Hangeul. A well briefed chauffeur, hired from your hotel, can save a lot of time.

Gay Travelers

Thanks in part to the liberating influence of the Internet, Gay Korea is gradually coming out of its shell. Buddy, a gay magazine, is being sold freely and a gay film fest, previously banned by police, takes place every year. A number of bars, saunas and night spots are thriving in Busan and Seoul, and while Korea remains a highly conservative country, the theory that Gay = Aids or that homosexuality is itself a disease is gradually losing credibility.

Disabled Travelers

Disabled travelers will find that Korea is not the easiest country to get around. Few concessions are made, for example, for wheelchair users, in the way of lifts or ramps. However, on the plus side, Koreans are extremely hospitable and courteous and will go out of their way to help foreigners in obvious difficulties. Depending on your level of mobility, plan ahead on what you want to do, and if possible bring along someone who can assist you.

Getting Around

From The Airport

INCHEON

By bus
Until the airport express railway is completed in 2005, the best way out of Incheon International is by bus, with routes to Gimpo (now the main airport for domestic flights), numerous points in downtown Seoul, Incheon City and Gyeonggi Province. Departures coincide with the first and last flights and run regularly all the time in between. Buses normally take about 50 minutes to travel between the airport and downtown Seoul.

The Limousine Bus service covers Gimpo and Seoul, with tickets priced at W6,000 and W12,000 respectively.

The "Seat Style Bus" (SSB or jwajeok in Korean) covers 14 destinations in Seoul, and is much cheaper, with fares ranging from W4,500–W7,000.

Travel Agents

The following agencies have English- and Japanese-speaking guides and operate tours of various lengths all over Korea.
Freedom Travel, tel: (02) 777-7114
Global Tour, tel: (02) 776-3153
Joy Travel, tel: (02) 776-9871
Korea Travel Bureau, tel: (02) 778-0150
Marco Polo, tel: (02) 757-2300
Minyoung Travel Services Co., tel: (02) 752-1626
Star Travel Service, tel: (02) 569-8114
Zenith Travel, tel: (02) 508-5781

Both SSBs and Limousine run to various destinations in Incheon city at costs between W3,000 and W6,500.

There are long-distance limousine services to Gyeonggi Province and as far as to Dajeon, Gwangju and Mokpo with tickets costing W7,000–W33,000.

By taxi
Taxis are the most expensive method of airport transfer, and they are by no means immune to city traffic jams. From Incheon to downtown Seoul costs approximately W64,000 by deluxe taxi, or W45,000 in a regular cab.

More information is available at www.airport.or.kr/eng

GIMPO

By bus
The **KAL Limousine Bus** stops right outside 17 of Seoul's major hotels and has plenty of room for luggage, plus free water and a phone on board. There are four routes to choose from and tickets (W6,000) are available from KAL counters inside the terminal. The stops are prominently signposted, and buses leave every 15–20 minutes. Call (02) 2667-0386 for information.

Airport Direct Buses (jikhaeng bus) travel on four different routes to Seoul, operating from

The **Korean Tourism Association** can be reached on tel: (02) 757-7485. **The Korean Association of General Travel Agents (KATA)** are on tel: (02) 752-8692.

Two organizations in Seoul who plan tours for resident foreigners but also welcome outsiders are:
The Royal Asiatic Society (RAS), Christian Building, 6/F, Room 611, Jongno 5-ga, tel: (02) 763-9483.
The USO (United States Service Organization), 104 Galwoldong, Yongsangu, tel: (02) 792-3028.

5.20am–11.40pm, and costing W1,300–W3,300. Note that these do not have space for large suitcases. Call (02) 2665-1094 for information.

Airport Limousine Buses go direct to the Korea City Air Terminal (KCAT) leaving every 10 to 20 minutes between 7.30am and 10.20pm. Tickets (W6,000) are available from the counters on the first floor of the airport. Call (02) 551-0751 for information.

By subway
Subway Line 5 is cheap (W900) and leaves directly from the airport, but flights of stairs in the stations make this method impractical for anyone with heavy suitcases.

By taxi
Expect to pay about W19,000 from Gimpo to downtown Seoul for a deluxe taxi; and W13,000 if you take a regular cab. The exact fare will depend on traffic conditions and your final destination.

Domestic Travel

BY AIR
Two airlines, Korean Air and Asiana, conduct all air travel within Korea. Daily flights from Gimpo Airport to Jeju-do, Busan, Gwangju, Daegu, Yeosu, Pohang, Jinju and Ulsan are available on both domestic carriers with flight times of 40–65 minutes. Flights from Seoul to Yangyang in Gangwon Province are available only on Korean Air. Visit www.airport.co.kr/eng for daily schedules. Tickets are available at major hotels and tourist and travel agencies. Security at the airport is tight; passengers and baggage are checked, and cameras, knives, and certain other articles are withheld during the flight.

BY SEA
Numerous ferries and jetfoils make regular connections between the mainland and the outlying islands. There are daily sailings between Busan and Jeju City (11½ hours); Busan and Sogwipo (15 hours); and Mokpo and Jeju City (5½ hours). Daily ferries operate between Pohang and Ullungdo (7½ hours).

Several routes on the south coast in the Hallyeosudo Waterway may be traveled by jetfoil from Geoje-do.

Ferry schedules change frequently and operators will cancel trips at short notice if the weather gets bad. Travel arrangements should be made with travel agents and time should be allowed for last-minute changes if you travel during the monsoon season. The Korean National Tourism Organization (KNTO) provides information on schedules, itineraries and fares, call (02) 729-9498.

BY RAIL
The introduction of the locomotive to Korea was not without political motives. Several foreign powers, including Russia, Japan, France, and the United States, bid hard for the contract, which was eventually awarded to an American, James R. Morse. Soon after initiating construction, Morse, beset with financial difficulties, was forced to pass the project to the Japanese. The Korean government directed Japan to complete the line in the standard gauge system Morse used rather than import narrow-gauge rails in from Japan. The first railroad, which linked Seoul to Incheon, was opened in September 1899. Other major lines were laid by the Japanese, including lines originating in Mokpo and Busan to Seoul and to Sinuiju in North Korea, which linked with the Trans-Siberian Railway. At one time it was possible to take the train from Busan to Paris. The railway suffered considerable damage during various wars, but since 1953 the network has been steadily modernized to accommodate tourists comfortably.

Today three kinds of service are available in Korea's efficient and fast inter-city train system: KTX is the high-speed bullet train with the

Sightseeing Tours

Panmunjeom and the DMZ: The Korea Travel Bureau offers tours to the Panmunjeom area, the Folk Village, Gyeongju, Busan, and around Seoul by day and night. Reservation counters can be found at several main hotels. Their offices can be found in the Lotte Hotel in downtown Seoul, tel: (02) 778-0150. You must book at least one day in advance. Cost is around US$50. Similar guided tours are organized by USO (tel: 792-3028), Global Tour (tel: 776-3153) and Panmunjeom Travel Center (tel: 771-5593).

The trip, including lunch and a briefing by the US military, takes eight hours; children under ten years of age are not admitted. Visitors must be smartly dressed and well groomed, and must carry their passport during the tour.

Mt Geumgang Tour: The chance to visit North Korea, and a beautiful mountain area, means this tour is very popular. You need to book at least 15 days prior to departure. There are ½ day and ⅔ day programs costing between W200 and W900 depending on the season and the type of accommodation. For details, tel: (02) 739-1090. Note that due to the political situation, these tours are not guaranteed year-round.

best facilities; the super-express *Saemaulho* is fast, comfortable and air-conditioned and usually has a dining car; the express *Mugunghwaho* may also have a dining car and sleeper facilities. All three types of train have comfortable seats with plenty of leg room and may also have private compartments for families. If you are planning to travel on a weekend or public holiday, it's advisable to book at least two weeks in advance. For information, call 1544-7788 ext. 1. The KNTO also provides detailed information, tel: (02) 729-9496–9.

For more information browse www.korail.go.kr.

BY ROAD

Inter-city Buses:
There are four kinds of inter-city buses: the *Udeung Gosok*, which is the most comfortable and includes a public phone and a video; the *Gosok* express bus (cheaper long-distance); the *Jikhaeng* (first class local and direct route); and the *Wanhaeng* (round-about with frequent stops). It is advisable to buy bus tickets in advance for a reserved seat. Listed below are eight main bus stations in Seoul and their major destinations (check Seoul map for locations; add 02 telephone prefix for the following numbers):

Gangnam Express Bus Terminal/Central City Terminal: The main bus terminal, located across the Han River in Banpodong, provides only the express bus service to cities out of Seoul. Has its own subway station, "Express Bus Terminal", on lines 3 and 7. Tel: 782-5551 for Gyeongbu Line (to Gyeongsang-do Province); tel: 6282-0600 for Jeolla Line (to Jeolla-do Province).

Dong Seoul Bus Terminal: Located near the river and Gangbyeon subway station (line 2); buses run to destinations south and east of Seoul including Chuncheon, Seoraksan, Sokcho, Yangyang, Gangneung, Gwangju and Andong. Tel: 446-8000.

Nambu Bus Terminal: South of the river with its own subway stop (line 3); services to Buyeo, Cheongju, Gongju, Jonju, Songnisan, Jeongju, Daejeon. Tel: 521-8550 ext. 0.

Sinchon Bus Terminal: Five minutes walk from Sinchon subway station (line 2); non-stop buses to Ganghwa-do: 6am–10pm; trip takes 1 hour 15 minutes. Tel: 324-0611.

Sangbong Bus Terminal: Close to Sangbong subway station (line 7). Most buses are for destinations to the east of Seoul. Tel: 435-2129.

Seoul Seobu Bus Terminal: In Pulangdong (northern Sodaemungu); service to Haengjusanseong, Uijeongbu. Tel: 382-5103.

Car Rental

Foreigners are advised to avoid driving in Korea. The accident rate is one of the highest in the world and, in a legal dispute, foreigners tend to come off worse unless accompanied or supported by a local. Many road signs are only in Korean hangeul script. It's best to take on a chauffeur with your rental car, which costs around W150,000 inclusive for a ten-hour day. Hertz and Avis are represented by local companies **Kumho** (tel: 02 797-8000) and **VIP** (tel: 02 838-0015 ext. 9).

Taxis

Taxis are cheap and plentiful (except late at night, when they can be hard to find), fill in the gaps left by the bus and subway networks, and provide a handy alternative when you don't feel like braving the crowds. Cabs cluster outside hotels and in ranks in busy city areas, and in Seoul may also be requested by phone (02-3431-5100). Most drivers do not speak English, however, and some have a rather hazy knowledge of the geography of their home town; unless your destination is a major hotel, transport facility or landmark, it's best to have clear instructions written in hangeul – and, if possible, a map too.

There are two types of taxi – regular and deluxe. Cabs may be hailed to the curbside and can be shared with other passengers bound in the same direction. Each passenger pays only for the distance he travels (two or more traveling together pay as one passenger). This taxi-sharing system is called *hapseung*.

Fares for regular cabs begin at W1,600 for the first 2 km (1¼ miles) with W100 for each additional 168 meters. The meter also runs on time when movement is slower than 15 kilometers per hour and W100 is charged for every 41 seconds in addition to the basic fare. Between midnight and 4am fares are automatically increased by 20 percent.

The deluxe *mobeom* taxis – with the black and yellow livery – cost W4,000 for the first 3 km (2 miles) and W200 for each additional 205 meters or each 50 seconds if the speed drops below 15 km per hour. Receipts and in-car phones are available and there is no late-night surcharge.

Also available are taxi vans (*daehyeong taxi*); their fare system is the same as *mobeom* taxis. They can accommodate up to eight passengers and have plenty of space for luggage. They can be requested on tel: (02) 888-2000.

US military ID holders may also use Army–Air Force Exchange taxis, which charge slightly higher rates in dollars.

City Transport

The majority of people living in Seoul depend on public transport. The subway is efficient and foreign-user-friendly, the bus system less adapted to non-Korean speakers but still workable, while taxis seem to swarm everywhere.

City Buses

During less hectic commuting hours, getting around on the local city bus can be interesting, quick and cheap. The driver usually turns up his radio so everybody can listen to the local baseball game, a soap opera, or to the latest hits. Confucian ethics generally prevail on board the bus: students offer their seats to mothers toting babies and to the elderly, and out of mutual consideration, those seated relieve those standing of their schoolbooks and shopping bags. Smoking is prohibited.

Buses run frequently from 5am to around 11.45pm daily. The fare is W900 and can be paid in cash or by prepaid bus card.

In addition to the regular city buses, there are "Seat Style Buses" (*jwajeok*, see page 282),

Sample Name Changes

OLD	NEW		
Cheju-do	Jeju-do	Kyŏngju	Gyeongju
Chikji-sa	Jikji-sa	Kyŏngsang	Gyeongsang
Chiri-san	Jirisan	Paekche (dynasty)	Baekje
Chŏlla	Jeolla	P'anmunjŏm	Panmunjeom
Ch'ŏngju	Cheongju	Pulguk-sa	Bulguk-sa
Chŏnju	Jeonju	Pusan	Busan
Chosŏn (dynasty)	Joseon	Puyŏ	Buyeo
Ch'ungch'ŏng	Chungcheong	Shilla (dynasty)	Silla
Inch'ŏn	Incheon	Sŏgwip'o	Seogwipo
Kŏje-do	Geoje-do	Sŏrak-san	Seoraksan
Kongju	Gongju	Taegu	Daegu
Kwangju	Gwangju	Taejŏn	Daejeon
Kyŏngbok (Palace)	Gyeongbok	Tŏksu (Palace)	Deoksu
		Ullŭng-do	Ulleung-do

Where to Stay

Choosing Accommodation

which follow similar routes but with fewer stops and for a somewhat higher fare. These are designed for commuter use and generally make few stops downtown.

A word of caution: beware of pickpockets on the bus and at crowded bus stops.

Destinations are written on the side of the bus in hangeul and on street signs at the bus stops. Route maps for the entire system are virtually non-existent and change so frequently that it is impossible to keep track. The routes are mapped out on a panel inside the bus, but destinations are again written only in hangeul. The best way to get around the matter is with directions from a hotel concierge or a business partner. Two rules of thumb: when the bus comes, run to where it stops and leap on; at the other end, get to the exit before the bus stops and jump off just as fast.

Subway

Roomy, inexpensive, color-coded, prominently signed in English and Hangeul, Seoul's subway system – first opened in August 1974 – is the most convenient form of public transport for visitors. There are eight lines, and the subway also hooks up with the Korean National Railway. From Seoul Railway Station, it goes to six major destinations: Cheongnyangni Railway Station and Songbuk district to the north, and, to Incheon (39 km/24 miles west),

Suwon (41 km/25 miles south), Jamsil and Guro. One-way tickets cost a basic W900, although you can buy stored value tickets for up to W10,000. The computer chip fare cards you will see locals using are only available to Korean bank account holders. Trains run from 5am to midnight at three minute intervals during rush hours, and six minute intervals at other times. Smoking is prohibited on platforms as well as in the cars. The following are points of interest within walking distance of each subway stop within the city walls:

City Hall (Taepyeongno): City Hall, Deoksu Place, British Embassy, major hotels, banks, department stores, Seoul Tourist Information Center.

Jonggak (Jongno): Bosingak (city bell tower), bookstores (with foreign language sections), Korean National Tourism Organisation, Jogye-sa (Buddhist Temple), Communications Memorial Center, Seoul Immigration Office, Gyeongbok Palace, National Museum, Folk Museum, Embassies of USA, Japan, and Canada, Sejong Center for the Performing Arts, Yi Sun-sin statue at Gwanghwamun intersection.

Jongno 3-ga: Pagoda (Tapgol) Park and shopping arcade, Jongmyo (Royal Confucian Shrine), Insadong (antique shops, art galleries, etc.).

Jongno 5-ga: Dongdaemun market, herb shops.

Dongdaemun: Dongdaemun (East Gate), Seoul Baseball Stadium.

Many international hotel chains have properties in Korea, vying for business with accommodation that ranges from five-star to the most basic homestays. Suffice to say that there is something for all budgets and tastes in the accommodation stakes.

The accommodations and services at Korea's **international class hotels** are superb. And since a lot of wheeling and dealing takes places in the coffee shops, lounges and restaurants of these hotels, they are amongst the finest in the world. As might be expected, a stay at an international hotel is going to be expensive. At these hotels you can expect health clubs, swimming pools and extensive conference and business facilities. In the resort areas of Jeju-do and Gyeongju some even have indoor driving ranges, bowling alleys, tennis courts, casinos and hot spring baths.

While not as luxurious as international class hotels, you can still expect **superior class hotels** to provide excellent accommodations and services. Superior hotels tend to be smaller (between 200–300 rooms) and older than their international class counterparts. There will also be fewer restaurants and recreation facilities, along with smaller facilities for conferences and business meetings.

Standard class hotels are generally older hotels that cater primarily to Korean businessmen and travelers. These hotels usually have around 100 rooms, with a restaurant, lounge, and perhaps an exercise room. Some have public baths, saunas and nightclubs.

Budget hotels cater to the casual Korean traveler and their families. They are usually clean, and a good place to sleep if you're looking at cost rather than amenities. The rooms are likely to be small, and very basic. In the cities, some of the staff are likely to speak some English.

Thousands of **yeogwan** (Korean inns) have popped up all over the countryside where they are often the only option for the weary traveler. In the city, yeogwan seem to cluster together, especially near transportation centers. Most are very pleasant but some can be rather dirty – the exterior and lobby are a good indicator of how clean the rooms are. For the budget traveler they provide an inexpensive place to sleep. You may find yourself on the upper floors, since many yeogwan also double as "love hotels", where the lower-level rooms are let by the hour. Yeogwan are a favorite of Western English teachers in Korea, and other extended travelers. Most are family-owned and operated, and unlikely to have English-speaking staff.

Another type of Korean inn is the **yeoinsuk**, which offers lodging in a private compound and isn't as consistently convenient, nor as appealing as the yeogwan. Room rates are even lower, though, and accommodation is native all the way.

The **hasukjip** (boarding house) has its place among students, working bachelors, and itinerants. Rooms are rented by the month. Rent includes very simple home-cooked meals.

For the working foreigner, the **setbang** – a rented room in a local home – is yet another option. Except for the fact that he happens to share the same roof with others, the tenant is generally on his own.

A chain of **youth hostels** has been established in many of the provinces, and hostels are open to international members. The charge for one night ranges from W9,000–W20,000. Reservations or further information can be obtained from the Korea Youth Hostel Association, tel: (02) 725-3031; www.kyha.or.kr.

The Korea Labo Corp arranges **home-stays** (minbak) for foreigners with Korean families who may speak English, Japanese, Chinese, Spanish, French or German. If you want to take part in this program, you should contact Labo by e-mail: labo@labo.or.kr at least two weeks in advance with details of where you want to stay, when and for how long. Rates start at US$30 per person per night, which includes breakfast. However, a four-week stay costs only US$500. Labo will then find a family and send you some information about them and arrange a rendezvous. For more information tel: (02) 736-0521, fax: (02) 359-0527.

For those who would like to experience the old Korean lifestyle, **hanok**-stay is recommended. Bukchon is the area where traditional Korean houses are extremely well preserved and there you can find inexpensive hanok guesthouses: Bukchon Guesthouse, tel: 743-8530; Seoul Guesthouse, tel: 745-0057; Urijip Guesthouse, tel: 744-0536. Easy access from Anguk station on subway line 3. Room rates are generally between W30,000–70,000.

Hotel Listings

SEOUL

INTERNATIONAL CLASS
Grand Hilton
201-1 Hongeundong, Seodaemungu
Tel: (02) 3216-5656
Fax: (02) 3216-7799
www.hilton.co.kr
A very swish hideaway at the foot of Mount Baengnyonsan in the northwest of the city.
Grand Hyatt
747-7 Hannamdong, Yongsangu
Tel: (02) 797-1234
Fax: (02) 798-6953
www.seoul.hyatt.com
Apart from all the joys of the "Hyatt touch" (the swimming pool becomes an ice rink in winter!) the reputation of JJ's nightclub here has assumed legendary proportions. Located in the Itaewon district in the south of the city.

Grand Inter-Continental
159-8 Samseongdong, Gangnamgu
Tel: (02) 555-5656
Fax: (02) 559-7990
www.seoul-grand.intercontinental.com
A business-oriented hotel on Seoul's "Wall Street" in the Gangnam district south of the river.
Lotte Hotel Seoul
1 Sogongdong, Junggu
Tel: (02) 771-1000
Fax: (02) 752-3758
www.lottehotel.co.kr
Located next to the lively Myeongdong district in the heart of the city center, and ideal for those with retail therapy on their mind.
Lotte Hotel Seoul-Jasil
40-1 Jamsildong, Songpagu
Tel: (02) 419-7000
Fax: (02) 417-3655
www.lottehotel.co.kr
Situated south of the river, right next to Korea's answer to Disneyland, this is a family fun hotel rather than an executive's boutique haven.
Millennium Seoul Hilton
395 Namdaemun 5-ga, Junggu
Tel: (02) 753-7788
Fax: (02) 754-2510
www.hilton.co.kr
A mainstream conference hotel, but one that still retains an intimate and friendly atmosphere.
Radisson Seoul Plaza
23 Daepyeongno 2-ga, Junggu
Tel: (02) 771-2200
Fax: (02) 755-8897
www.seoulplaza.co.kr
Smart, fashionable and excellently located for exploring the center of the city.
Renaissance Seoul
676 Yeoksamdong, Gangnamgu
Tel: (02) 555-0501
Fax: (02) 553-8118

Korean-style Rooms

Just about every hotel in South Korea has a number of Korean-style rooms. These come with traditional ondol underfloor heating and a Korean mattress (yo) on the floor. Room rates are normally the same as a standard double room, but some hotels charge up to 50 percent extra.

www.renaissance.co.kr
A smart hotel south of the river, with the airy, spacious top-floor Club Horizon, which serves one of the best breakfasts in Seoul.
Ritz-Carlton
602 Yeoksamdong, Gangnamgu
Tel: (02) 3451-8000
Fax: (02) 3451-8188
www.ritz.co.kr
Discreet, tasteful and head and shoulders above many of its competitors south of the river when it comes to service and facilities.
Sheraton Walker Hill
Gwangjangdong, Gwangjingu
Tel: (02) 455-5000
Fax: (02) 452-6867
www.walkerhill.co.kr
Dame Fortune rules at this Mecca for gamblers, which infuses the entire hotel with an aura of excitement. Located on the eastern edge of the city.
Shilla
202 Jangchungdong 2-ga, Junggu
Tel: (02) 2230-3131
Fax: (02) 2233-5073
http://seoul.shilla.net/eng
On the northeast edge of Mount Namsan, this is the grande dame of Seoul hotels, with an especially picturesque sculpture garden.
Westin Chosun
87-1 Sogongdong, Junggu
Tel: (02) 771-0500
Fax: (02) 756-8848
www.westinchosun.co.kr
Patrons return time and again to sample the charm of this downtown five-star anchored by the rumbustious Irish bar O'Kims.

SUPERIOR CLASS
Holiday Inn Seoul
169-1 Dohwadong, Mapogu
Tel: (02) 717-9441
Fax: (02) 715-9441
www.holiday-inn.co.kr
Located in the Mapodong district to the west of Itaewon. Has 367 rooms (four Korean-style). Health club, sauna and nightclub.
Novotel Ambassador Doksan
1030-1 Doksan 4-dong, Geumcheongu
Tel: (02) 838-1100
Fax: (02) 854-4799
www.ambatel.com/doksan

Price Guide

Prices are per night for two people sharing a standard double room.
International: over US$150
Superior: US$100–150
Standard: US$70–100
Budget: below US$70

Health club, sauna and bar, and 239 rooms (five Korean-style).
Novotel Ambassador Gangnam
603 Yeoksamdong, Gangnamgu
Tel: (02) 567-1101
Fax: (02) 564-4573
www.ambatel.com/gangnam
Indoor pool, bar, health club, sauna, and 336 (six Korean-style) rooms.
Olympia
108-2 Pyeonchangdong, Jongnogu
Tel: (02) 2287-6000
Fax: (02) 396-6633
www.olympia.co.kr
Has 270 rooms (four Korean-style), indoor and outdoor pools, health club, sauna, theatre, restaurant and cocktail lounge.
Sofitel Ambassador
186-54 Jangchungdong 2-ga, Junggu
Tel: (02) 2275-1101
Fax: (02) 2272-0773
www.ambatel.com/sofitel
Large hotel with 432 rooms (six Korean-style), health club, indoor pool and sauna.

STANDARD CLASS
Airport
11-21 Gonghangdong, Gangseogu
Tel: (02) 2662-1113
Fax: (02) 2663-3355
www.hotelairport.co.kr
Has 55 rooms (ten Korean-style).
Crown
34-69 Itaewondong, Yongsangu
Tel: (02) 797-4111
Fax: (02) 796-1010
www.hotelcrown.com
Nightclub, sauna and 170 rooms (13 Korean-style).
Hamilton
119-25 Itaewondong, Yongsangu
Tel: (02) 794-0171
Fax: (02) 795-0457
www.hamilton.co.kr
Has 139 rooms (one Korean-style), a nightclub and outdoor pool.

BUDGET CLASS
Central
227-1 Jangsadong, Jongnogu
Tel: (02) 2265-4121
Fax: (02) 2265-6139
Facilities include nightclub, sauna. The hotel has 72 rooms (eight Korean-style).
Seoul
Cheongjindong, Jongnogu
Tel: (02) 735-9001
Fax: (02) 733-0101
Moderately priced hotel with 102 rooms (15 Korean-style). Facilities include a sauna.
YMCA
9 Jongno 2-ga, Jongnogu
Tel: (02) 734-6884
Fax: (02) 734-8003
Not so great, but in a good location with 79 rooms.

GYEONGGI-DO

Suwon
SUPERIOR CLASS
Castle
Umandong, Paldalgu, Suwon
Tel: (031) 211-6666
Fax: (031) 212-8811
Business center, sauna, nightclub, and 81 rooms (two Korean-style).

STANDARD CLASS
Regency
47 Gucheondong, Baldalgu, Suwon
Tel: (031) 246-4141
Fax: (031) 243-9296
Good location near the south gate, with 53 rooms (four Korean-style).

Incheon
SUPERIOR CLASS
Paradise Hotel Incheon
Hangdong 1-ga, Junggu
Tel: (032) 762-5181
Fax: (032) 763-5281
www.paradiseincheon.co.kr
Central location by the inner harbor. Casino (for foreign guests only), sauna, nightclub, and Korean, Japanese and Western restaurants. Has 195 rooms (20 Korean-style).
Songdo Beach
812 Dongchundong, Yeonsugu
Tel: (032) 832-1311
Fax: (032) 832-1325
www.songdobeach.co.kr

Located next to Songdo Amusement Park. Health club, sauna and cocktail lounge. Has 195 rooms (20 Korean-style).

STANDARD CLASS
Pupyung
181 Galsandong, Bupyeonggu
Tel: (032) 504-8181
Fax: (032) 504-8182
Has 31 rooms (four Korean-style), a sauna and cocktail lounge.

BUDGET CLASS
Soobong
618-2 Dohwadong, Namgu
Tel: (032) 868-6611
Fax: (032) 868-4333
Has 30 rooms (six Korean-style), a cocktail lounge and sauna.

GANGWON-DO

Yongpeong Dragon Valley Ski Resort
SUPERIOR CLASS
Dragon Valley Tourist Hotel
Yongsanri, Doam-myeon, Pyeongchang
Tel: (033) 335-5757
Fax: (033) 335-0160
www.yongpyong.co.kr
Well-equipped with health club, sauna, driving range, indoor golf course, ski slope, nightclub and 191 rooms (150 Korean-style).

Gangneung
STANDARD CLASS
Gangneung
Ponamdong, Gangneung
Tel: (033) 641-7701
Fax: (033) 641-7712
With 74 rooms (38 Korean-style), this hotel is located between the railway station and the police station.
Gyeongpo Beach
303-4 Gangmungdong, Gangneung
Tel: (033) 644-2277
Fax: (033) 644-2397
Situated right on the beach to the northeast of the city, with 60 rooms (31 Korean-style). Facilities include a nightclub and Western and Korean restaurants.

BUDGET CLASS
Sun Castle
Jumunjinri, Jumunjineup, Gangneung
Tel: (033) 661-1950
Fax: (033) 661-1958
Facilities include a tennis court. Has 52 rooms (18 Korean-style).

Sokcho
BUDGET CLASS
Sokcho Beach
478-19 Jungangdong, Sokcho
Tel: (033) 631-8700
Fax: (033) 631-6758
Located right on the beach, about 1km (½ mile) north of the inter-city bus terminal, with 70 rooms (40 Korean-style), and a nightclub.

Seoraksan National Park
SUPERIOR CLASS
Sorak Park
74-3 Seorakdong, Sokcho
Tel: (033) 636-7711
Fax: (033) 636-7732
Located about 1.5 km (1 mile) from the park entrance, this is the region's top hotel, with 139 rooms (18 Korean-style). Excellent facilities include casino, cocktail lounge, nightclub, sauna and health club.

STANDARD CLASS
Soraksan
61-1 Seorakdong
Tel: (033) 636-7101
Fax: (033) 636-7106
Close to the park entrance, with an ice-skating rink and swimming pool. Has 124 rooms (36 Korean-style).

CHUNGCHEONGBUK-DO

Songnisan National Park
SUPERIOR CLASS
Lake Hills Songnisan
Sanaeri, Naesongnimyeon, Boeun
Tel: (043) 542-5281
Fax: (043) 542-5198
Has 132 rooms (88 Korean-style), cocktail lounge and outdoor pool.

Cheongju
STANDARD CLASS
Cheongju Tourist Hotel
844 Bokdaedong, Cheongju

Tel: (043) 264-2181
Fax: (043) 266-8215
www.cheongjuhotel.com
Bar, nightclub and 70 rooms (19 Korean-style).

BUDGET CLASS
Jinyang
1831 Bongmyeongdong, Heungdeokgu, Cheongju
Tel: (043) 267-1121
Fax: (043) 263-9532
Has 36 rooms (five Korean-style) and cocktail lounge.

CHUNGCHEONGNAM-DO

Onyang
SUPERIOR CLASS
Onyang Grand Park
300-28 Oncheondong, Asan
Tel: (041) 543-9711
Fax: (041) 543-9729
Sauna, swimming pool, nightclub and Western and Korean restaurants. Has 151 rooms (53 Korean-style).

STANDARD CLASS
Onyang Plaza
228-6 Oncheondong, Asan
Tel: (041) 544-6111
Fax: (041) 542-6100
Sauna, hot spring baths, cocktail bar and 143 rooms (73 Korean-style).

BUDGET CLASS
Kongju
139-1 Sansongdong, Gongju
Tel: (041) 855-4023
Fax: (041) 855-4028
32 rooms (17 Korean-style). Sauna.

Daejeon
SUPERIOR CLASS
Riviera Yuseong
445-5 Bongmyeongdong,

Price Guide

Prices are per night for two people sharing a standard double room.
International: over US$150
Superior: US$100–150
Standard: US$70–100
Budget: below US$70

Yuoseonggu
Tel: (042) 823-2111
Fax: (042) 822-0041
www.hotelriviera.co.kr
Health club, sauna, hot spring
baths, indoor and outdoor pools,
nightclub, and 216 rooms (43
Korean-style).

STANDARD CLASS
Chateau Grace
72-5 Yongjeondong, Donggu
Tel: (042) 639-0111
Fax: (042) 639-0077
Has 102 rooms (37 Korean-style), a
sauna and nightclub.

GYEONGSANGBUK-DO

Daegu
SUPERIOR CLASS
Grand
563–1 Beomeodong, Suseonggu
Tel: (053) 742-0001
Fax: (053) 742-0002
www.taegugrand.co.kr
Luxury hotel with 86 rooms (11
Korean-style), located about 3 km
(2 miles) southeast of the city
center. Health club, sauna and
nightclub.
Prince
Daemyeong 2-dong, Namgu
Tel: (053) 628-1001
Fax: (053) 650-5600
www.princehotel.co.kr
Located near Daegu University.
Health club, sauna and nightclub,
and 117 rooms (12 Korean-style).
Daegu Park
San 98-1 Manchondong, Suseonggu
Tel: (053) 952-0088
Fax: (053) 953-2008
www.ibhotel.com
Out on the eastern edge of the city
by the river and Mangu Park. Has
133 rooms (36 Korean-style),
swimming pool, indoor golf range,
sauna and nightclub.

STANDARD CLASS
Kumho
28 Haseodong, Junggu
Tel: (053) 252-6001
Fax: (053) 253-4121
Downtown location with 56 rooms
(14 Korean-style), bar, nightclub
and sauna.

Crown
330-6 Sincheon 4-dong, Donggu
Tel: (053) 755-3001
Fax: (053) 755-3367
Has 56 rooms (14 Korean-style), a
bar and sauna. Handy for the
railway station.

BUDGET CLASS
Empire
63 Bisan 2-dong, Seogu,
Tel: (053) 555-3381
Fax: (053) 559-9056
Near Dalsong Park in the west of
the city; 47 rooms (23 Korean-style)
and nightclub.
New Hilltop
3408-35 Daemyeongdong, Namgu
Tel: (053) 651-2001
Fax: (053) 651-2006
A short distance south of the
Daegu Tower, a reasonably priced
hotel with 52 rooms (16 Korean-
style).

Andong
BUDGET CLASS
Andong Park
Unheungdong, Andong
Tel: (054) 275-2000
Fax: (054) 275-2218
Has 41 rooms (15 Korean-style)
and a bar.

Pohang
SUPERIOR CLASS
Cignus
145-21 Yongheungdong, Pohang
Tel: (054) 275-2000
Fax: (054) 283-4075
Well-equipped hotel with 112 rooms
(16 Korean-style), sauna, hot spring
baths, health club and nightclub.

GYEONGJU

INTERNATIONAL CLASS
Concorde
410 Sinpyeongdong, Gyeongju
Tel: (054) 745-7000
Fax: (054) 745-7010
www.concorde.co.kr
On the shores of Bomun Lake, this
luxury hotel has 319 rooms (12
Korean-style), swimming pool,
sauna and disco.
Gyeongju Hilton
370 Sinpyeongdong, Gyeongju

Tel: (054) 745-7788
Fax: (054) 745-7799
www.hilton.com
324 rooms (13 Korean-style). Close
to the convention center on the
shores of Bomun Lake, the Hilton
has full facilities including health
club, tennis courts, indoor and
outdoor swimming pools and a
casino.
Hyundai
477-2 Sinpyeongdong, Gyeongju
Tel: (054) 748-2233
Fax: (054) 748-8112
www.hyundaihotel.com
On Bomun Lake, with 482 rooms
(33 Korean-style). Fully equipped
luxury, with indoor and outdoor
pools, health club, tennis court and
hot spring baths.
Kolon
111-1 Madong, Gyeongju
Tel: (054) 746-9001
Fax: (054) 746-6331
Situated close to Bulguksa, a luxury
hotel with 354 rooms (34 Korean-
style), swimming pool, tennis court,
indoor driving range, casino, sauna,
hot spring baths, golf course and
nightclub.
Wellich Chosun
San 410, Sinpyeongdong,
Gyeongju
Tel: (054) 745-7701
Fax: (054) 740-8349
Another luxury hotel right on
Bomun Lake, with tennis courts,
swimming pool, hotspring, sauna,
nightclub. Has 337 rooms (37
Korean-style).

SUPERIOR CLASS
Gyeongju Spa
145-1 Gujeongdong, Gyeongju
Tel: (054) 746-6661
Fax: (054) 746-6665
Close to Bulguk-sa station, with
104 rooms (80 Korean-style),
sauna and nightclub.

BUDGET CLASS
Bulguksa
648-1 Jinhyondong, Gyeongju
Tel: (054) 746-1911
Fax: (054) 746-6604
80 rooms (58 Korean-style). As
its name implies, this hotel is
located close to the Bulguk-sa
temple.

Gyeongju Park Hotel
170-1 Noseodong, Gyeongju
Tel: (054) 742-8804
Fax: (054) 742-8808
Good location near the bus terminal
and Dumulli Park in downtown
Gyeongju.

GYEONGSANGNAM-DO

Busan
INTERNATIONAL CLASS
Haeundae Grand
651-2 Udong, Haeundaegu
Tel: (051) 740-0114
Fax: (051) 7400-141/3
www.grandhotel.co.kr/eng
Located west of the city at
Haeundae beach resort, with 325
rooms (38 Korean-style), fitness
center, bowling alley, indoor golf
range, movie center, disco.
Lotte
503-15 Bujeongdong Busanjingu
Tel: (051) 810-1000
Fax: (051) 810-5110
www.lottehotel.co.kr
Super-luxury hotel with 806 rooms
(15 Korean-style) and a spectacular
lobby. Located in the Somyon
district of the city close to a lively
market area, the hotel has a full
range of amenities, several
restaurants and fabulous views
from the top-floor bar.
Marriott
1405-16 Jungdong, Haeundaegu
Tel: (051) 743-1234
Fax: (051) 743-1250
www.marriott.com
363 rooms (27 Korean-style). Full
facilities include health club, sauna,
indoor pool, tennis court, hot spring
baths and nightclub.
Westin Chosun Beach
737 U1-dong, Haeundaegu
Tel: (051) 742-7411
Fax: (051) 742-1313
www.chosunbeach.co.kr
Resort hotel with 305 rooms (10
Korean-style), health club, sauna,
indoor pool and hot spring baths.

SUPERIOR CLASS
Commodore
743-80 Yeongjudong, Junggu
Tel: (051) 466-9101
Fax: (051) 462-9101

www.commodore.co.kr
Has 326 rooms (10 Korean-style),
health club, sauna, indoor pool and
nightclub. Between the railway
station and downtown.

STANDARD CLASS
Paragon
564-25 Goebeopdong, Sasanggu
Tel: (051) 328-2001
Fax: (051) 328-2009
West of the city, near the airport,
with 132 rooms (eight Korean-
style), golf shop, sauna and
nightclub.

BUDGET CLASS
Dong Bang
210-82 Oncheon 1-dong,
Dongaegu
Tel: (051) 552-9511
Fax: (051) 552-9274
44 rooms (16 Korean-style). Sauna
and hot spring bath.
Hillside
743-33 Yeongju 1-dong, Junggu
Tel: (051) 464-0567
Fax: (051) 464-1214
40 rooms (15 Korean-style). Sauna.

JEOLLABUK-DO

SUPERIOR CLASS
Jeonju Core
627-3 Seonosongdong,
Deokchingu, Jeonju
Tel: (063) 285-1100
Fax: (063) 285-5707
110 rooms (27 Korean-style).
Sauna, bar and nightclub.

STANDARD CLASS
Naejangsan
71-14 Naejangdong, Jeonju
Tel: (063) 538-4131
Fax: (063) 538-4138
104 rooms (54 Korean-style).
Sauna, bar and nightclub.

JEOLLANAM-DO

Gwangju
SUPERIOR CLASS
Grand
212 Bullodong, Donggu
Tel: (062) 224-6111
Fax: (062) 224-8933

65 rooms (23 Korean-style). Sauna,
cocktail lounge and nightclub.
Mudeung Park
9-2 Jisandong, Donggu
Tel: (062) 226-0011
Fax: (062) 226-0020
110 rooms (35 Korean-style). Well
equipped hotel with a health club,
sauna, tennis court, hot spring
baths and nightclub.

STANDARD CLASS
Riverside
72-1 Honamdong, Donggu
Tel: (062) 223-9111
Fax: (062) 223-9112
35 rooms (11 Korean-style). Bar
and nightclub.

JEJU-DO

INTERNATIONAL CLASS
Cheju Grand
263-15 Yeondong
Tel: (064) 747-5000
Fax: (064) 742-3150
www.grand.co.kr
Large resort hotel with 517 rooms
(30 Korean-style), casino, cocktail
lounge, health club, outdoor pool,
nightclub, sauna.
Cheju Oriental
1197 Samdo 2-dong
Tel: (064) 752-8222
Fax: (064) 752-9777
www.oriental.co.kr
330 rooms. Casino, bowling alley.
Cheju Shilla
3039-3 Saekdaldong, Seogwipo
Tel: (064) 738-4466
Fax: (064) 735-5415
www.chejushilla.com
422 rooms (ten Korean-style).
Casino, cocktail lounge, health
club, indoor and outdoor
pools, tennis court, nightclub,
sauna.
Hyatt Regency Cheju
3039-1 Saekdaldong,
Seogwipo
Tel: (064) 733-1234
Fax: (064) 732-2039
www.hyattcheju.com
Complete with casino, cocktail
lounge, health club, indoor and
outdoor pools, tennis court,
nightclub, sauna and 224 rooms
(25 Korean-style).

Price Guide

Prices are per night for two people sharing a standard double room.
International: over US$150
Superior: US$100–150
Standard: US$70–100
Budget: below US$70

Jeju Lotte
Sackdaodong, Seogwipo
Tel: (064) 731-1000
Fax: (064) 738-7305
www.lottehotel.co.kr
500 rooms (45 Korean-style).
Spectacular resort hotel with every conceivable luxury and all amenities.

SUPERIOR CLASS
Cheju KAL
169-9 Ido 1-dong
Tel: (064) 724-2001
Fax: (064) 720-6515
282 rooms (ten Korean-style).
Casino, cocktail lounge, health club, indoor pool, nightclub, sauna.
Crowne Plaza
291-30 Yeondong
Tel: (064) 741-8000
Fax: (064) 746-4111
www.crowneplaza.co.kr
224 rooms. Health club, sauna, swimming pool, casino.

STANDARD CLASS
Cheju Pearl
277-2 Yeondong
Tel: (064) 742-8871
Fax: (064) 742-1221
88 rooms (28 Korean-style).
Cocktail lounge.

Youth Hostels

There are 63 youth hostels in Korea which are members of the Korea Youth Hostel Association. For information and booking, call the association on (02) 725-3031; www.kyha.or.kr
Seoul
Olympic Parktel
88, Bangidong, Songpagu
Tel: (02) 410-2114
Fax: (02) 410-2100

Gyeonggi-do
Ganghwa
Oepori, Naegamyeon, Ganghwa
Tel: (032) 933-8891
Fax: (032) 933-9335
Gangwon-do
Naksan
Jeongjinri, Ganghyeon-myeon, Yangyanggun
Tel: (033) 672-3416
Fax: (033) 671-4620
Seoraksan
Seorakdong, Sokcho
Tel: (033) 636-7115
Fax.(033) 636-7107
Chungcheongbuk-do
Sajo Maeul
Oncheonri, Sangmo-myeon, Chungju
Tel: (043) 846-0750
Fax: (043) 846-1789
Chungcheongnam-do
Samjung Buyeo
Gugyori, Buyeoeup, Buyeo
Tel: (041) 835-3102
Fax: (041) 835-3791
Gyeongsangbuk-do
Bulguksa
Jinhyeondong, Gyeongju
Tel: (054) 746-0826
Fax: (054) 746-7805
Gyeongsangnam-do
Namhae
Geumsongri, Samdongmyeon, Namhae
Tel: (055) 867-4848
Fax: (055) 867-4850
Jeollanam-do
Mokpo
Sanjeongdong, Mokpo
Tel: (061) 243-0475
Fax: (061) 243-0476
Jeju-do
Seogwipo
Beophwandong, Seogwipo
Tel: (064) 739-0114
Fax: (064) 739-7552

Eating Out

What to Eat

Below is a list of the types of restaurants you are likely to encounter in Korea.
Barbecue meat restaurants (Bulgogijip). Beef (sogogi) and pork (doejigogi) and short rib (galbi) are marinated in soy sauce, sesame oil, garlic, green onions, and toasted sesame seeds, then char-broiled.
Raw fish restaurants (Saengson Hoejip). Fresh raw fish is served sliced with a soy sauce (ganjang) or red pepper sauce (chojang). Other kinds of fish dishes such as maeun tang (hot pepper soup of fish, soybean curd, egg, and vegetables) are served.
Ginseng Chicken Soup restaurants (Samgyetangjip). Chicken stuffed with rice, white ginseng, and dried oriental dates are steamed and served hot. Deep-fried chicken and other chicken dishes are also served.
Dumpling restaurants (Mandujip). Meat, vegetables, and sometimes soybean curd are stuffed into a dumpling and steamed, fried or boiled in a broth. Chinese-style cookie pastries baked in the restaurant fill the display window.
Noodle restaurants (Bunsikjip). Noodle dishes are the specialty but so are easily prepared rice dishes. Some of the popular dishes are Momil guksu – buckwheat noodles served with a sweet radish sauce; naengmyeon – cold potato flour or buckwheat flour noodles topped with sliced meat, vegetables, a boiled egg, and a pepper relish sauce and rice; kongguksu – wheat noodles in fresh soya milk; odeng guksu – wheat noodles topped with oriental fishcake in a broth; Ramyeon – instant noodles in

instant broth; *udong* – long, wide wheat noodles with onions, fried soybean curd, red pepper powder, and egg; *bibimbap* – rice topped with parboiled fern bracken, bluebell root, soysprouts, spinach, and a sunny-side-up egg, accompanied by a bowl of broth; and *japchae* – rice vermicelli stir-fried with vegetables and meat slices.

Steamed rice restaurants
(Baekbanjip). A bowl of rice is served with a variety of *gimchi*, *namul* (parboiled vegetables), fish, and soup (usually made of soybean paste) – the basic Korean meal. Other simple dishes, such as *naengmyeon* and *bibimbap* are often on the menu.

Dog Meat Soup restaurants
(Bosintangjip). *Bosinhada* means to build up one's strength. Thus, to the people, dog meat soup, *bosintang*, is considered to be a delicacy. Other popular Korean dishes include: *sinseollo* – chopped vegetables, meat, quail egg, fish balls, and gingko nuts in a brazier; *seolleongtang* – rice in a beef and bone stew; and *bindaetteok* – the Korean bean flour and egg pancake filled with different combinations of vegetables and meat.

Chinese Shantung restaurants are as popular as Korean restaurants. They are designated by a red or green door plaque draped with a red strip of cloth. Homemade wheat noodles with various sauces make for a slurpy meal. *Jjajangmyeon* is a popular order consisting of pork, seafood, and vegetable tidbits stir-fried in a sweet-sour black bean sauce. Larger Chinese restaurants have a more varied menu that includes delicacies such as sweet-sour fried fish and meat.

Japanese restaurants complete with *sushi*, *sashimi* and *tempura* (deep-fried battered fish and vegetables) are all over Seoul, and are even more common in the southern port of Busan.

Where to Eat

Koreans have great pride in and an enduring love affair with their own cuisine. It's not uncommon to hear a middle-aged businessman boast that he only likes Korean food. And the difference between most Korean dishes and those favored by Westerners is as different as the Korean language and English. But there is some hope for those who simply cannot get used to the pungent smell of *gimchi*. There are many Western chain restaurants in Seoul (and a few in Busan and Daegu, but good luck finding one elsewhere), and there are a few independently owned Western restaurants. These restaurants cater to a younger Korean clientele, upper-class Korean families, and foreigners.

The best hotels have fine Western restaurants and good Japanese and Korean restaurants; though they are expensive by Korean standards. But visitors to Korea really should try to breach the language barrier and experience Korean food. There is little doubt that Korean restaurants offer the best value and (according to most expats) the tastiest meals in Asia.

SEOUL RESTAURANTS

Korean – Traditional
Gayarang
239-4 Itaewon 2-dong, Yongsangu
Tel: (02) 797-4000
Daily 11.30am–3pm,
5.30pm–midnight.
Specializes in royal cuisine; the staff are fluent in English, Japanese and Chinese.

Jihwaja
National Theater
14-67 Jangchungdong 2-ga, Jeunggu
Tel: (02) 2269-5834
Daily noon–3pm, 5.30–9pm. Closed first and third Sunday every month. Famous for its original royal cuisine recipes from the Joseon dynasty.

Korea House
80-2, Pildong 2-ga, Jungu
Tel: (02) 2266-9101
Daily: lunch: noon–2pm; dinner: 5.30–8.40pm; one-hour traditional music and dance performances at 7 and 8.40pm (except Sunday).
Exceptional surroundings on a hillside with traditional Korean buildings, serving food formally reserved for royal families, and with entertainment. Expensive.

Lotte World
40-1, Jamsildong, Songpagu
Tel: (02) 411-2000
Daily 11am–11pm.
There are many restaurants in this maze of stores and entertainment centers, but try one of the four traditional Korean restaurants on the third floor. Reasonably priced.

Samcheonggak
Seongbuk 2-dong, Seongbukgu
Tel: (02) 3676-2345
In a quiet, wooded environment behind the Blue House is a large complex with traditional Korean buildings and gardens that are used as a restaurant, teahouse, function rooms, exhibition venues and performance theaters. Asadal, the restaurant, serves fine Korean delicacies.

Sawon
84-11 Gwanhundong, Jeongnogu
Tel: (02) 732-3002
Mon–Sat noon–2pm, 6–10pm.
Modern Korean cuisine, set at the back of a striking art gallery.

Seokparang
125 Hongjidong, Jeongnogu
Tel: (02) 395-2500
Daily noon–10pm.
Located in a 19th-century mansion, surrounded by beautiful gardens, Seokparang serves authentic Korean food.

Sokran
50-5 Daeshindong, Sodaemungu
Tel: (02) 393-4690
Daily 11.30am–10pm.
A 300-seater restaurant with fast service and helpful staff.

Yongsusan
118-3 Samchongdong, Jeongnogu
Tel: (02) 732-3019
Daily noon–3pm, 6–10pm.
Features a battery of specialist chefs, who each only ever make their own signature dishes.

Youngbin Garden
50 Gwanhundong, Jongnogu
Tel: (02) 732-3863
Daily 11am–10pm.
Pleasant setting in the heart of Insadong; terrific *galbi* at a moderate price.

Korean – Vegetarian
Pulhyanggi
726-54 Hannamdong, Yongsangu
Tel: (02) 794-8007
Daily 11.30am–10pm.
The best of three branches of
Pulhyanggi – the others are in
Jungno and Kangnam.
Sanchae
411-7 Dogokdong Gangnamgu
Tel: (02) 579-2923
Sun–Fri 11.30am–10pm.
The owner is a health-food
specialist. Most popular is the
Sanchae set menu with dishes
made of fresh vegetables and
natural condiments.
Sanchon
14 Gwanhundong, Jongrogu
Tel: (02) 735-0312
Daily noon–10pm; entertainment
from 8.15–9pm.
On a little side street in Insadong,
Sancheon is owned by an
ex-monk and serves superb
traditional Buddhist monk
vegetarian dishes. Entertainment
with dinner in the evening.
Moderately priced.
Shigolsaenghwal
16-1 Nonhyeondong, Gangnamgu
Tel: (02) 511-2402
Sun–Fri 11.30am–9pm.
This restaurant's all-you-can-eat
buffet is one of the best deals in
town at just W7,000.

Chinese
Dongbosung
50-7 Namsamdong 2-ga, Jeunggu
Tel: (02) 754-8002
Daily noon–9pm.
Full range of Chinese dishes,
with flavours adjusted for Korean
tastes.
Ho Lee Chow
119-25 Itaewondong, Yongsangu
Tel: (02) 793-0802
Daily noon–10.30pm.
On the second floor of the Hamilton
Hotel in Itaewon, the favorite
Chinese restaurant of expats in
Seoul. Reasonably priced.
Lotus Garden
689-12 Yeoksamdong, Gangnamgu
Tel: (02) 565-5700
Daily 11.30am–3pm, 5.30–8pm.
The very best Cantonese cuisine
with especially good dim sum.

French
La Petite France
135-55 Itaewondong, Yongsangu
Tel: (02) 794-2192
Daily 12–3pm, 6–10.30pm.
A taste of France on the slopes of
Mount Namsan.
Wood and Brick
6, Sinmunro, 1-ga, Jongnogu
Tel: (02) 735-1160
Daily 10am–11pm.
French fare in downtown Seoul at a
reasonable price.

Indian
Taj Mahal
132-2 Itaewondong, Yongsangu
Tel: (02) 749-0316/7
Daily noon–3.30pm, 6–10pm.
Curries, tandoories and all sorts of
spicy fare at reasonable prices.

International
Mein Liebes Alpes
11-14 Daeshindong, Sodaemungu
Tel: (02) 362-0640
Daily 10am–11pm.
Roasts, grills and a stack of other
western-style dishes tastily and
briskly served.
The Nashville
Itaewondong, Yongsangu
Tel: (02) 798-1592
Daily 10am–midnight; closes at
3am on weekends.
There are plenty of fast-food
hamburger joints in Seoul, but
the Nashville beats them all,
hands down; good steaks too,
with movies downstairs or a
sports bar upstairs. Reasonably
priced.
Chalet Swiss
Itaewondong, Yongsangu
Tel: (02) 797-9664
Daily 11am–10.30pm.
Swiss and European Continental; a
favorite with diplomatic types.
Moderate to expensive.
Il Ponte
395, Namdaemunro 5-ga,
Junggu
Tel: (02) 753-7788.
Daily: Lunch: 11.30am– 2.30pm;
Dinner: 6–11pm.
The Hilton's fine Italian restaurant.
Also recommended is the Hilton's
Seasons (French) and Cilantros
(California). Expensive

Italian
La Cantina
B1 Samsung Building, Euljiro 1-ga,
Jeunggu
Tel: (02) 777-2579
Mon–Sat noon–3pm, 5.30–8.30pm;
Sun 5.30–8.30pm.
Smart and friendly, with much of the
atmosphere of an Italian taverna.
Firenze
Grand Inter-Continental Hotel,
159-8 Samsungdon, Gangnam
Tel: (02) 555-5656
Daily: Lunch: 11.30–3pm; Dinner:
6–10.30pm; singing waiters from
7.30–9.30pm.
Good Italian dishes served by
waiters and waitresses who literally
sing while they work. Expensive.

Japanese
Songwon
11-5 Bukchangdong, Jeunggu
Tel: (02) 755-3979
Daily noon–2pm, 6–9.30pm.
Within easy reach of downtown City
Hall, Songwon is extremely popular.
Reservations are essential.

Mexican
Acapulco
358-118 Seogyodong, Mapogu
Tel: (02) 338-1371
Daily 11.30–12am.
Tortillas and all the other spicy food
you can eat.

Northern European
Scandinavian Club
National Medical Center
18-15 Euljiro 6-ga, Junggu
Tel: (02) 2265-9279
Daily noon–2pm, 6–9pm.
Scandinavian patrons make a joke
of this restaurant's location.
However, the food doesn't seem to
stop them coming back repeatedly.

Thai
Thai Orchid
737-24 Hananmdong, Yongsangu
Tel: (02) 792-8836
Daily noon–10.30pm.
Thai eatery that is very popular with
US personnel stationed in Seoul.

Dinner Theater (Korean)
Kayagum Hall
Sheraton Walker Hill Hotel

Drinking Notes

There are at least five kinds of *suljip* (liquor house). The common bar or pub, sometimes called a *hof*, is usually a small, simple cafe, which serves liquor and beer. *Anju* (hors doevres) are served at an additional cost in most places; they are pricey but are nevertheless customarily ordered. The cheapest liquor is *soju* (sweet potato wine). Beer *(maekju)* comes either bottled *(byeong maekju)* or as on draft *(saeng maekju)*.

21 Gwangjangdong, Gwangjingu
Tel: (02) 450-4554
Daily 5.20–7pm, 8.20–10pm.
Exotic shows combining traditional dance with Western-style revues.
Korea House
80-2 Pildong, Junggu
Tel: (02) 2266-9101
April–Nov 7.10–8.10pm;
8.40–9.40pm; Dec–Mar
8.30–9.30pm.
Presents traditional Korean dance performances.
Samcheonggak
Seongbuk 2-dong, Seongbukgu
Tel: (02) 3676-2345
Changing program of Korean traditional music, dance and theater, normally from 8pm.
Sanchon
14 Gwanhundong, Jeongnogu
Tel: (02) 735-0312
Daily 11.30am–9pm.
Performance 8–9pm.
Excellent Korean food all day, and a nightly Korean dance performance.

Restaurant Chains

Even though these restaurants are chains, they offer pretty tasty fare. Mexican food at TGIFs and Chili's. Steaks at all of them, with special mention to Outback Steak House. The best ribs around (though some prefer Korean *galbi* restaurants) are at Tony Roma's.
TGIFs (13 locations)
Bennigans (13 locations)
Chili's (2 locations)
Outback Steak House (25 locations)
Tony Roma's (7 locations)

Nightlife

Koreans love a good drink and a singsong, and so it follows that Seoul's nightlife is pretty lively. From internationally recognized spots like the Hard Rock Café to dedicated jazz bars to hotel discos to off-the-wall techno blast-outs, Seoul provides a pretty fair menu of after-hours entertainment. One point to note is that Korean males can become quite "emphatic" towards the end of the evening, and there is no logical arguing with them. Walk away, briskly, from any trouble.

Nightclubs and Discos

Major Western-style hotels have their own nightclubs and discotheques. Drinks are heavily taxed in hotels.

DANCE

Areno
Hilton Hotel
395 Namdaemunno 5-ga, Jeunggu
Tel: (02) 317-3244
Nightly 6pm–2am.
Gek Cobra
Jonggak Station, subway line 1
Tel: (02) 720-2909
Nix & Nox
Ritz-Carlton
602 Yoksamdong, Gangnamgu
Tel: (02) 3451-8000
Nightly 5.30pm–3am.
JJ Mahoney's
Grand Hyatt Hotel
747-7 Hannamdong, Yongsangu
Tel: (02) 799-8601
Nightly 6pm–2am.
Juliana
Hotel Elle Lui
129 Cheongdamdong, Gangnamgu, Sinchon Station on subway line 2
Tel: (02) 313-3046
Nightly 8pm–2am.

JAZZ

Chonnyondongando
Dongsungdong, Jongnogu
Tel: (02) 743-5555
Mon, Wed 7–11.20pm; Thur 7pm–1.30am; Sat 5.30pm–1.30am; Sun 2.30–11pm.
45th Avenue
Dongsungdong Jongnogu
Tel: (02) 3674-4545
Tues–Sun 7pm–midnight.
Janus
Cheongdamdong, Gannamgu
Tel: (02) 546-9774
Every night 8.30–11pm.
All That Jazz
Itaewondong, Yongsangu
Tel: (02) 795-5701
Nightly 9–11pm.
Just Blues
Sinsadong, Gangnamgu
Tel: (02) 542-4788
Nightly 6pm–2am.

CLUBS

Hongdae-ap literally means "in front of Hongik University" in Sinchon (Hongik University on subway line 2) and refers to the area around the university, which has many popular cafés, bars and clubs. The last Friday of each month is "Club Day", when young Koreans and foreign visitors pack the whole block. You are entitled to one free drink and entrance into all the member clubs on the purchase of an all-round ticket. Call (02) 333-3021 or (010) 2480-9473. Member clubs include **Club Joker Red** (Techno), **Club DD** (Hip-hop), and **Club Evans** (Jazz).

Cabarets

Often located in narrow alleyways in Mugyodong and Myeongdong in Seoul, cabarets are easy to spot: loud band music, neon signs and/or bow-tied doormen attempting to lure passers-by inside. Dance hostesses inside expect a tip for their efforts. Patronize these *jip* with caution or with a good Korean friend. Closing time is midnight. Salons are smarter, more exclusive cabarets.

Bars

Hard Rock Café
Cheongdamdong Gangnamgu
Tel: (02) 547-5671
Mon–Fri noon–2am;
Sat–Sun noon–midnight.
Hunters Tavern
158-9 Samsongdong, Gangnamgu
Tel: (02) 559-7619
Daily 5pm–2am.
Once in a Blue Moon
Cheongdamdong, Gangnamgu
Tel: (02) 549-5490
Daily 5pm–2am.
Goshen
Cheongdamdong, Gangnamgu
Tel: (02) 515-1863
Daily 11am–midnight.
Woodstock
Yeoksamdong Gangnamgu
Tel: (02) 556-9774
Daily 6pm–2am.
Basic on the Stage
Hyehwadong, Jongnogu
Tel: (02) 766-4805
Tel: (02) 3141-6141
Daily 11am–2am.
Mumba
B2, Seoul Finance Building,
Kwanghwamun Station, subway line 5
Tel: (02) 3783-0005

Gambling

Gambling is limited to Jeju-do plus
one venue per province. There are
casinos in the following six hotels.
Sheraton Walker Hill Hotel
San-21, Gwangjangdong,
Singdonggu, Seoul
Tel: (02) 2240-3448
Paradise Incheon
3-2, Hangdong 1-ga, Junggu,
Incheon
Tel: (032) 762-5181
Paradise Beach Hotel
1408-5, Jungdong,
Haeundaegu, Busan
Tel: (051) 742-2110
Shilla Hotel Jeju
3039-3 Saektaldong, Seogwipo
Tel: (051) 738-8822
Cheju KAL Hotel
1691-9, 2-do, 1-dong, Jeju
Tel: (064) 757-8111
Wellich Chosun
Bomun Lake Resort, Gyeongju
Tel: (054) 771-2121

Culture

During the Joseon dynasty, a proper
Confucian gentleman might have
found calm and contentment in an
after-dinner ritual with his pipe,
filling its small brass bowl with
Korean tobacco, and drawing slowly
through the long bamboo stem to
cool the soothing smoke. His
descendants today can seek
diversion in a variety of
establishments offering all manner
of indulgences and female
companionship. These range from
beer halls where the waitress might
share a drink and squeeze one's
hand, to secret salons where the
whiskey flows freely and the
customer's every wish is his
hostess-cum-partner's command.

Somewhere between those
ancient and modern extremes on
the spectrum of hedonistic delights,
there lie a number of common
pleasures available, in startlingly
similar forms, to contemporary
Koreans ranging from day laborers
to tycoons.

When a Korean has been working
or playing (or both) with perhaps
more zeal than wisdom, he is likely
to seek refuge and relief through
one of the few such simple
pleasures that remain amid the
excesses and inconstancies of
urban industrialization. Depending
on his whim, he might well choose
a bathhouse or a barber shop, both
of which abound in every urban
setting, as well as in most sizable
rural communities.

Barber & Massage

A haircut is so much more than
cutting hair in a Korean barber shop
(ibalso). One can easily spend an
hour, and perhaps two, in laid-back
languor as a crew of young ladies

and gentlemen attend to nails,
whiskers, face, ears, muscles,
aches and – not to be forgotten –
hair.

The actual clipping is mere
prologue, a ritual of 10 minutes or
so more aptly termed a "trim", lest
the customer be tempted to wait
too long before his next visit. A
manicure is usually begun just
about the time one's stockinged
feet get comfortably settled on a
cushion placed over the sink, and it
inevitably lasts much longer than
the haircut.

The sequence is not strictly
prescribed, but those interested in
a shave generally get one quite
soon after the haircut. Young ladies
traditionally perform this service,
which is not always limited to the
conventional heavier growths of
whiskers; upper cheeks, noses,
foreheads and even selected parts
of the ear are all fair game for a
well-trained and unrestrained
Korean razor maid.

The next step is often a face
massage *(massaji* in Korean, after
the Japanese rendering of the
English). This can, with luck,
encompass the scalp as well, along
with those chronically
understimulated muscles and
vessels around the base of the
skull. Between soothing
applications of a hot towel, the
young lady in charge might apply a
plastic-like facial pack, peeled off
later like congealed glue, or
perhaps just a simple layer of cold
cream. In either case, as the face is
absorbing allied benefits, the lady
will produce an ear spoon,
preferably made of bamboo, and
carefully begin to excavate hidden
reserves of wax – unless the client
recalls the old doctor's dictum that
only one's elbows are to enter
one's ears. When the delicate
digging is done, each ear is given
an unnerving twirl with a tool
resembling a doll house duster – a
tickling sensation comparable to
hearing kittens' claws on a
blackboard.

By this point, someone has no
doubt already begun a body
massage *(anma* in Korean, from

two Chinese characters roughly meaning "press" and "rub"). This can coincide with other services, and can involve a number of people who come, go, and reappear, according to the needs of other customers. It is not uncommon to have three or four men and women at work in a single curtained cubicle, each kneading a separate extremity. One of them is usually a young man equally well versed in Oriental finger pressure therapy and the orthopedic limitations of the human anatomy – although he occasionally loses his feel for the fine line between stimulation and pain.

Even as a joint effort, a body massage can last half an hour or longer. Ordinarily, it concludes with an extraordinary ritual. First one's wrists, then palms, and then fingers are firmly massaged. Next the young lady gives each finger a sharp, snapping tug, perhaps to realign the knuckles. Finally, she interlocks her fingers with the client's, bends his hand backward, and, while gently running her thumbnails across the taut palm, blows on it ever so softly, telegraphing tingling signals up well past the elbow.

After all this, it's time for a nap, presuming the customer has time. (If he doesn't, he should have postponed his visit until another day.) A towel placed over his eyes softens any harsh visual stimuli, and he is left to dreams and fantasies.

Later on, someone eventually has to mention the code word "shampoo", and the customer knows his respite is nearly over. Not only is the barber chair about to be raised abruptly to the upright position, but that foot-supporting cushion will also be removed from the sink. Within seconds, said groggy gent is roused from his delightful daydreams – not just sitting up, but bent over a basin, head soaked and soapy.

The end comes quickly. A brief towel fluffing is followed by the barber's final touch – the "deurai" (dry) with a comb and hand-held blower – as the client receives a ritual offering: a cigarette and a shot of sweet yogurt drink. Then it's time to button up, straighten up, settle the tab (US$5 to $10) and bid a fond, but hardly final, farewell to tonsorial therapy.

Bathhouse (Mogyoktang)

Just as a visit to the barber shop involves more than a simple haircut, so a call at the bathhouse offers much more than a mere turn in the tub. For the seeker of a slightly more active treatment for weary bones, the bathhouse (mogyoktang) presents a moderate alternative to the passive pleasures of the barber's chair.

At the baths, both men and women are free to set their own schedule, regimen, timing and style. That last choice offers perhaps the widest variety of options, and the images conjured up by the behavior of an ordinary bathhouse's clientele might run the gamut – from scolded puppies to walruses in rut.

There is quite a range of bathhouse types as well, but all offer the same basic accoutrements, focusing on the same essential enjoyment of a steamy, soothing soak. As visitors to Japan may already know, the proper form is to bathe before entering the communal tub, and in Korea too, soap and dirt should be kept out of the bathwater.

One begins by soaping up, shampooing and rinsing down, either by dipping a basin at the edge of the main tub, or under a shower, if there is one. Next should come a leisurely soak in the central tub, where muscles can relax and pores dilate. Then, back on the curb-like lip ringing the tub, it's time to commence some serious scrubbing, again using a basin.

Westerners seem to cling to the illogical conviction that towels should be kept dry, although they only perform their rightful function by getting wet. In the mogyoktang, a hand towel is just the right size, doubling both as an ample

washcloth and as a fig leaf substitute – for modesty's sake – as one moves around. Small red washcloths are available, too – very abrasive, but very popular for doing away with dead and dying skin and stubborn city grit. And for the patron who doesn't savor the strain of a vigorous scrub, attendants are usually on hand to rub, rub, rub with cloths until the customer's skin approaches the hue of that raspy red fabric.

A scrubbing session is by far the best opportunity for a shave. Steam, suds and sweat combine to create the fleeting impression that there is no blade in the razor – an innocent illusion swiftly given the lie if one later slaps on a little aftershave.

All that accounts for the literal "mogyok" (bathing) in mogyoktang, but one is no more restricted to a mere bath in a bathhouse than to only a haircut in a barber shop. Time and the facilities at hand are the only limits, and none but the improvident take towel in hand with less than an hour or two to kill.

Nearly every ordinary bathhouse (daejungtang, or "public bath") offers, in addition to the central tub and showers, an extra-hot tub, a cold tank and, in many cases, a sauna dock as well. These present many alternatives to the basic cycle of bathe, soak, bathe.

The properly heated hot tank greets the bather with a sharp tingling sensation that is easily mistaken for pain, but which gradually mellows into simply stimulating heat. (If the tank is overheated, on the other hand, it turns out to be real pain.) The sauna is often so hot that it hurts to inhale quickly, and persons with abnormal blood pressure or heat sensitivity are advised to exercise appropriate caution.

Alternate visits to the sauna and hot tub, interspersed with breathtaking plunges into the cold tank, can give the pores a healthy workout. A few such rounds, however, can leave one a bit light-headed, not a little enervated, and frankly ready for a short nap. A well-planned bathhouse will have a mezzanine, where those with the time can stretch out and doze off.

The last step in the bathing area is usually a final rinse under the shower – hot or cold, or both. But that is hardly the end. There is more to enjoy out in the dressing room. After all that time in the baths, most patrons seem to feel it a bit abrupt simply to dress and leave. Smokers smoke; thinkers sit and think; trimmers trim (a nail clipper is usually available); and browsers read ads on the walls for products such as soap, ginseng nectar, and "Happiness" – a mysterious compound touted as an aid to a happy married life. Some people simply dry themselves at considerable leisure, perhaps in front of a fan, but better yet, while grabbing one last catnap. (That soggy handtowel, once wrung out, turns out to be quite up to the task.)

Gentlemen can get the same finishing touch they would in a barber shop, while on the ladies' side, bathers can relax one last time under a hair dryer. Eventually though, everyone has to leave. Korean bathhouses, incidentally, close around 8pm, hours earlier than the counterpart *ofuro* in Japan, but they open earlier as well, about 5 or 6am.

Sauna

The man with a little extra cash, and a yearning for a little extra luxury, is likely to patronize a so-called *saunatang*, essentially a plusher version of the *daejungtang*. For perhaps five times the ordinary bathing fee, the customer can spend all day – if he likes – soaking, sweating, napping, snacking or even negotiating business deals over coffee, clad only in a towel or short gown.

One of the oldest and most popular of such establishments in Seoul is in the Sin Sin Hotel, a modest brick complex in the alley beside the Bank of Korea's head office (across a broad intersection from the Sinsegye Department Store). The saunatang in the Shin

Shin's main building provides each guest with his own private section of warm pillow and sheets, dressing gown, adjacent mini-closet and a menu listing every type of refreshment. There is also a spacious lounge with well-padded easy chairs, a television set and a lunch counter.

Those who make it to the Sin Sin's bathing area check their gowns with the young attendants on the way in, and grab fresh towels from a handy pile. Numbered signs mark a seven-step circuit for the uninitiated, beginning with a dip in the main tub or pool (the *ontang*). A small statue of an elephant helps establish the tropical mood.

Next are the two sauna docks – hot and hotter. One can perspire surrounded by the warm tones of golden-grained wood, gazing at quotations on the wall such as "Patience is the skill of having hope".

From the sauna, of course, one could proceed only to the cold tank (*naengtang*), which is appropriately adorned with a statue of a polar bear. A helpful sign notes that there is no further benefit to be gained from remaining in the 18°C water after rinsing off the sweat.

The fourth stop is the hot tub (*yeoltang*), kept at 48°C, which should loosen up the pores again. The *yeoltang* leaves one well prepared for the next stop, the vigorous rubbing away of grit and grime and (hopefully) dead skin by one of a squad of young men.

By this point, one might well feel a bit groggy, in which case Stop No. 6 comes just in the nick of time. It's called *rireksyon* in Korean, a slight muddling of "relaxation", and that's exactly what it entails. At a row of massage tables, more young fellows administer 20 or 30 minute rubdowns, using either cold cream or mentholatum.

The last stop, once again, is the shower, for a final soap and rinse. Stepping out of the bathing area, one promptly receives another fresh (and dry) towel and, moments later, the same, carefully cared for dressing gown. The remainder of

one's time can be spent eating, drinking, reading or watching TV. One can also request the services of a blind masseur, should a few kinks or wrinkles have survived the bathing process. And, of course, one can simply sleep, for a good session in any sort of *mogyoktang* can turn even the most tense or torpid physique into a tingling and squeaky-clean bundle of bait for the sandman.

Nearly every Korean *saunatang* offers comforts and accommodations like those at the Sin Sin, with the little extras (rubdown, scrubbing, etc.) costing, naturally, a little extra. Another establishment in downtown Seoul boasts a cold tank reputedly filled with mineral water piped directly from nearby Namsan (South Mountain); and one might also find such conveniences as a five-minute hourglass in the sauna dock, or a urinal right in the bathing area (to spare customers the indignity of having to relieve themselves over the drains).

Actually, the clientele in the plusher *saunatang* facilities seem more interested in loafing and laying about than in bathing per se, since they probably can afford to bathe in hot running water at home. Thus they embody the core spirit of Korea's modern pleasure principle, as pursued by those fortunate enough to have the means.

To observe the spirit of Korean humanity at large, however, foreign visitors ought to bathe at least once in an ordinary *daejungtang* where everyone can be seen doing his own thing. Europeans sometimes attract a few stares, but they should most certainly feel free to return the compliment.

There are many styles to observe: while one unassuming soul sits modestly facing a wall, another may appear to be drilling for the national splash-and-thrash platoon, exalting in generating frothy waves accompanied by ecstatic grunts and harrumphs to the assembled. Many bathers concentrate on modified calisthenics, such as "push-ups" against the edge of the main tub, or deep knee bends in the cold tank. Some simply fashion a pillow from an overturned basin and a towel, and sack out on the tiled floor.

All in all, the public bathhouse is perhaps the most egalitarian of the institutions to be found amid the considerable Confucian influence in contemporary Korea, stripping customers of all trappings of wealth or power (except perhaps a prodigious stomach), and offering each an identical opportunity to play any role he or she pleases. And that equality does extend generally to the sexes, for while they are strictly segregated in the public facilities, the two remain equal in terms of opportunities for indulgent enjoyment. The sauna remains an exception, with only a handful catering to women. Two of the best women's saunas in Seoul are to be found at the Capital Hotel, which includes a ginseng bath, and the Riverside Hotel.

There are a host of other comforts related to the *mogyoktang*, or at least appealing to the same wholesome hedonism that keeps bathhouses and barber shops in business. At a large *mogyoktang*, for example, one might find a private bathing room upstairs (called a *doktang*) suitable for a couple or a family. Visitors are advised that many establishments which offer massages provide sexual services to male clients. In particular, Turkish baths *(teokitang)*, saunas in all but the super-deluxe hotels and many barber shops will offer such services with a massage. Bath houses and barber shops in main hotels and buildings belonging to large corporations do not provide sexual massage services.

Another facility, the *anma sisulso*, specializes in the services of blind masseurs and masseuses. Those services can often be obtained more conveniently – and more cheaply – by phoning to summon the masseur/masseuse to one's lodging or home. Downtown hotels and *yeogwan* should be able to offer such arrangements, and

some apartment complexes in Seoul have round-the-clock, on-call massage service.

Concerts

National Center for Korean Traditional Performing Arts.
Tel: (02) 580-3380.
Just next to Seoul Art Center, this vast airy venue is the where many of the nation's finest classical musicians of different genres, including Royal Court musicians, practice and teach their art. Regular and special performances are given in its concert halls and also on the outdoor stage. Check the entertainment section of newspapers for engagements.
Sejong Center for the Performing Arts
81-3, Sejongno, Jongnogu
Tel: (02) 399-1114.
Opened in 1978, the Sejong Cultural Center holds foreign and Korean classical and contemporary concerts and dramatic plays.
Seoul Arts Center
Tel: (02) 580-1234
Located at the foot of Mount Umyeonsan in Seochodong, this center is made up of a concert hall, calligraphy hall, gallery, library, opera house and outdoor performance areas.

LG Art Center
Tel: (02) 2005-0114.
Located in the heart of the business district in Gangnam, the Center hosts large-scale classical and modern dance and theatrical performances, as well as a program of concerts.

Theater

NANTA **Theater**. Located in the culturally rich Jeongdong area, this venue is the place to experience the non-verbal theater, NANTA, throughout the year. Tel: (02) 739-8288; www.nanta.co.kr
Korea House. Situated on the slopes of Namsan off Toegyero. Korea House stages free folk dance performances at 3pm on Saturday and Sunday. Art displays decorate

the rooms and Korea-related books are sold in the bookshop. A Korean restaurant overlooks an Oriental garden. Tel: (02) 2266-9101.
Space Center. Housed in an architectural artpiece near the Secret Garden of Jangdok Palace (219, Wonsodong, Jongnogu), the Space Center (tel: 02 763-0771) stages a variety of shows from classical *gayagum* (Korean zither) solos to Dixieland jazz to drama. The Center also publishes a cultural magazine called *Space*.

Other Modern Drama Theaters in Seoul:
Madang Cecil Theater
3–7, Jeongdong, Junggu
Tel: (02) 736-7600.
Minye Theater
1–103, Dongsungdong, Jongnogu
Tel: (02) 744-0686.
National Theater of Korea
San 14–67, Jangchungdong 2-ga, Junggu
Tel: (02) 2280-4114.
Sanoolim Theater
327 Seogyodong, Mapogu
Tel: (02) 334-5915.
Hakjeon Blue
Dongsungdong, Jongnogu
Tel: (02) 763-8233.

Festivals, Holidays and Events

Spring and Fall are the festival seasons but, because they are very profitable events, festivals are popping up all over the place, and you can usually find something going on at any time of the year. The Korean National Tourism Organization website (www.knto.or.kr) has a list of major events, and they will answer your e-mail inquiries.

January
Korea's favorite mountain, Hallasan on Jeju Island, is the center of attention in the mid-winter Hallasan Snowflake Festival. Make a winter climb of the mountain (along with a few thousand others), take part in the snowball contest, and watch some folk performances unique to the island. In January, mild Jeju

Island is probably the best place to be in Korea.

February

One of Korea's two big holidays (the other is *Chuseok*) is the Lunar New Year, known as *Seollal* in Korea (and Chinese New Year most everywhere else). Koreans dress in their *hanbok* and head for their hometown to eat, socialize, do the "deep bows" to their elders, and turn one year older. Travel is almost impossible during this holiday, so it's best just to stay put and wait for it to pass. Based on the lunar calendar, *Seollal* usually falls in February.

March

South of Daegu is the small city of Cheongdo, which hosts an annual Bullfighting Festival in mid-March. Fortunately, these bulls are able to survive their battles with each other (*sans* matador). There's also a bull rodeo, a traditional market, and a beauty contest for female calves.

As if Gyeongju doesn't have enough going for it to attract tourists, there is a Traditional Drink and Cake Festival that begins at the end of March and runs for about a week. The traditional drinks here are alcoholic, and you'll be surprised at the variety of beverages concocted to make life more jovial.

April

The cherry blossoms bloom in early April, presenting impressive displays throughout the country. But the most famous display is in the southeastern port city of Jinhae, which hosts a week of festivities right when the blossoms reach their peak.

In early April, the life of the benevolent Dr. Wang In is celebrated in the southwestern town of Yeongam (Jeollanam Province). Dr. Wang left Korea and settled in Japan several hundred years ago, bringing a little renaissance to Japan as he spread Korea's more advanced culture. At the festival, there is an elaborate memorial rite, some *ssireum*

(Korean-style) wrestling, a few contests for intellects and an exhibition of ancient *Asuka* culture.

May

Buddha's birthday is a national holiday when the celebrations are centered around the temples. Every temple will be decorated for the event, but the larger ones have hundreds of lanterns hanging along the roadways and in the temple grounds (they are lit in the evening), and the faithful line up for the symbolic bathing of the baby Buddha. Jogye-sa in Seoul (and some of the other large temples) has a candlelight parade along with day-long events. Buddha's birthday is based on the lunar calendar, and is usually in May.

On the first Sunday in May, the royal ancestral rites are performed at the Jongmyo Shrine in Seoul. These Confucian rites, in memory of the royal families of the Joseon dynasty, are an elaborate combination of color, ritual, and traditional music and dance. They begin early, and end by midday, but if you're in Seoul you shouldn't miss this event that preserves some of the glory and traditions of old Korea.

On the southwestern island of Jin-do, there is a semi-annual "parting of the sea" that exposes tidal lands between the mainland

and an offshore island. Thousands of Koreans trudge between the two points of land. It has become something of an annual festival, with folk performances, a parade and various contests added to the milieu. The Korean Christian community has dubbed the parting of the seas the Moses Miracle.

June

On the 5th day of the 5th lunar month (early June or late May), the Dano Festival is held in the eastern port city of Gangneung. This is a good opportunity to see traditional shamanistic performances, and mask dance dramas unique to the region.

July

The last week of July and first week of August is vacation season in Korea. Entire companies shut down to allow their employees an annual week off. The crowds at the beaches and in the mountains are unbelievable. And naturally, transportation systems are full-to-bursting at the beginning and end of the holiday season. If you like crowds, come to Korea on August 1st, if not, wait until the short vacation season passes.

August

Geumsan, the center of Korea's ginseng production, is the host of

Cinema

Giant painted billboards of kung fu duels, infernal disasters, love, and despair draw thousands of people to Korea's commercial theaters. Films undergo government censorship and sometimes are edited if too long to allow movie theaters to squeeze in a maximum number of showings. During cold months, underfloor hot water pipes provide some warmth in the theater. Check the entertainment section of *The Korea Times* or *The Korea Herald* for current engagements.

Foreign films are not usually dubbed, but have subtitles in

hangeul, so overseas visitors can enjoy them too. Shows usually run continuously from about 10am each day.

Recently moved into a modern building with high-tech facilities, the Institut Français is a multi-media oasis where visitors can browse through a modern art gallery, sit and view French cultural videos or watch a classic French movie subtitled in English. The Institute shows a variety of films on Friday evenings and offers other cultural programs.

For further information, call tel: (02) 317-8500.

an interesting festival honoring the "elixir of life." Rows of shops sell ginseng and other medicinal herbs (along with bugs and snakes). On the stage, there is ongoing entertainment, and hundreds of food carts ensure that you won't go hungry. There is also the opportunity to go to a ginseng field and harvest your own.

September

Gyeongju hosts a World Culture Expo that begins in September and ends in November. The Expo is held along the touristy shores of Bomun Lake and features folk performances, exhibitions and a general carnival atmosphere. It's an interesting way to kill an afternoon between visits to Gyeongju's historic locations.

The Harvest Moon Festival (Chuseok) is held on the 15th day of the 8th full moon (usually the end of September or early October). Analogous to Thanksgiving in the USA, this is a time for the family to get together, play some traditional games, and

eat until they're ready to pop. This is a three-day holiday in Korea, and a big one. Unless you are invited to someone's home to share in the festivities, this is not a great time to visit Korea. Most shops are closed and transportation is a nightmare.

October

One of Korea's most interesting festivals, the Andong Mask Dance Festival takes place in early October in the city of Andong, and the nearby traditional village of Hahoe. The best dance groups in the country perform folk dance/dramas that have ancient shamanistic roots. Each year, several folk dance groups from other countries are invited to perform for the appreciative audiences.

If you like gimchi, you've got to pay a visit to Gwangju at the end of October. The best of the region's gimchi-makers display their creations inside the display hall, and vendors offer visitors dozens of varieties of gimchis to taste and

purchase. Displays within explain the history and regional variations of this popular dish, and outside are ongoing performances to keep things interesting. There's also a gimchi-making contest for foreigners if you want to show-off or learn how it's done.

December

Christmas is a holiday in Korea and celebrated by a sizable Christian community. Although there are a few Christmas trees, and a few Santa Claus (Santa Grandfather, to Korean children), there is none of the pomp and extravagant gift-giving found in the West. New Year (as opposed to Lunar New Year) is also celebrated but is low-key compared to the West.

Libraries

Royal Asiatic Society (RAS)

The RAS is the Korean chapter of an international British association. Its office is in the Christian Center Building (136-46 Unjidong, Jongnogu, tel: 763-9483) near Jongno 5-ga. There you'll find English translations of most books written locally about Korea and a complete collection of their magazine, Transactions, which contains Korea-related articles that have been written by lecturing members since 1900. Visitors are welcome to sign up for tours conducted by the RAS and by an affiliate, the Korea Art Club.

The National Library of Korea

The Library, located in Banpo, Seochogu, in a nice quiet environment (tel: 590-0542), houses a collection of 5 million volumes including foreign books and over 1,000 periodicals in

foreign languages. Other service facilities such as free PCs and copy machines are available. Foreign visitors may be asked to present IDs. Open 9am–6pm, Nov–Feb closes at 5pm. Tel: 535-4142.

United States Information Service

(USIS; tel: 397-4368) offers a library for public viewing and study. Passport identification is needed. Library hours are 8.30am–5pm weekdays.

UNESCO Library

Back issues of the Korea Journal and the Courier, as well as Korean cultural magazines are available, the latter in English, French, and Spanish. The library is also stocked with other reference publications.

Ewha, Sogang, Yonsei, and other universities also invite foreigners to use their libraries.

Shopping

Where to Shop in Seoul

Places to shop in Seoul include:
Antiques: Janganpyeong, Insadong, Jungang Sijang (Central Market), Itaewon.
Brassware: Itaewon.
Boutique goods: Myeongdong, Idaeap.
Calligraphy paint brushes – Insadong, Gyeonjidong.
Korean costumes: Dongdaemun Sijang, and most other marketplaces.
Korean cushions and blankets: Insadong, marketplaces.
Korean herbal medicine: Jongno 5-ga, Jongno 6-ga, Gyeongdong Sijang.
Name seals (custom-made name seals in stylistic characters carved of hard wood, stone): along the busy streets.
Oriental paper: Insadong, Gyeonjidong .
Silk Brocade: Dongdaemun Sijang (2nd floor), Jongno 2-ga, Myeongdong (Ko Silk Shop).
Custom-tailored men's suits: hotels, Myeongdong.
Sweatsuits and athletic shoes and gear: Itaewon, Namdaemun Sijang.
Topaz, "smoky topaz", amethyst, jade: underground arcades.

Shopping Centers

Major Seoul shopping centers outside central city hotels are:
Hyundai Department Store
456 Apgujeongdong, Gangnamgu
Tel: (02) 547-2233.
Lotte Shopping Center
1, Sogongdong, Junggu
Tel: (02) 771-2500.
Lotte World
40-1, Jamshildong, Songpeagu
Tel: (02) 411-2500.

New Core Shopping Center
70-2, Jamwondong, Socheogu
Tel: (02) 530-5000.
Shinsegae
52-2, Jungmuro 1-ga, Junggu
Tel: (02) 754-1234.

Underground Arcades

Specialty shops can be found in underground shopping malls. Don't let the price tags deter you from bargaining. The larger more centrally located arcades are: Namdaemun Arcade, Myeongdong Arcade, Sogong Arcade, Hoehyeon Arcade, Euljiro Arcade, Lotte Centre 1st Avenue Arcade.

Regional Arts & Crafts

Korea's unique arts and crafts and the towns that traditionally produce the best of particular products are:
Bamboo craft: Damyang
Brassware: Anseong, Gyeonggi-do
Hemp cloth: Hansan, Andong
Lacquerware: Wonju
Oriental paper: Jeonju
Pottery and porcelain: Icheon, Yeoju
Ruchecraft: Ganghwa-do City
Silk: Chuncheon, Ganghwa-do City

Bookstores

Reading material in English or European languages can be tricky to locate in Seoul but there are several places where titles can be regularly found. The major hotels have bookstores that carry periodicals, although they are usually late in coming and are unduly expensive. For the latest issues (also at high prices), the most reliable bookstore is in the basement of the Gyobo Building, a short distance south from the American Embassy on Taepyeongno 2-ga. The Youngpoon Book Store, on Namdaemunro by Jonggak subway station also has a respectable foreign-language selection.

Seoul Selection (tel: 734-9564) is a new attraction for foreign residents and visitors. They publish informative periodicals in English

Markets

Seoul's traditional markets run on for block after block. Anyone who has anything to sell is out there – from the button merchant to the antique dealer to the rice cake *ajumeoni*, including *jige* (A-frame) bicycle and Kiamaster delivery men and haggling shoppers. The distinguishing feature of Korean markets, however, is that shops with the same goods tend to group together, and even set up their goods in the same way. Merchants say they are not hurt by competition caused by the close proximity; instead, the area becomes known for specializing in, say, second-hand books, sinks or antiques. Most things can be found at all the markets.

and hold frequent cultural events. A good selection of books in foreign languages and Korean DVDs with English subtitles is for sale. You can order a drink from the little in-house café and have a read of the books on display.

Used books and magazines can be found in Myeongdong just across from where the Chinese Embassy used to be. There are several small shops here overflowing with books and old magazines which are sold for much less than their original cost. You can also trade in your own used paperbacks or bargain for lower prices, particularly if you purchase several books at a time.

Language

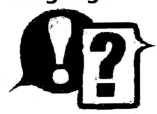

Survival Korean

The romanization of Korean *hangeul* script has recently been revamped: the new system has dispensed with the apostrophe and the breve accent to denote different letters, which makes it easier to understand, and brings romanized Korean fully into the internet age.

As with any language re-think, however, the big disadvantage is that most place names (including street names) in Korea have changed *(see list on page 285)*. Throughout the book we have used the revised system, but some maps and signs within Korea have yet to absorb the new system, and some hotels retain their old names. Everything should be running smoothly by now, but the situation can still be confusing for the visitor.

Basics

Hello/Good morning/Good afternoon/Good evening
Annyeonghasimnikka

Goodbye (said to somebody not departing) *Annyeonghi gyeseyo*
Goodbye (said to somebody who is also departing) *Annyeonghi gaseyo*
Can you speak English? *Yeongeo halsu isseumnikka?*
Thank you *Gamsa hamnida*
Excuse me *Sille hamnida*
I'm sorry *Mian hamnida*
You are welcome *Cheonmaneyo*
Yes *Ne*
No *Anio*
Help! *Saram sallyeo!*
My name is *Je ireumeun…imnida*
I come from *Jeoneun…eseo wasseumnida*

Useful Words

airport *gonghang*
subway *jihacheol*
taxi *taeksi*
Seoul train station *Seoul yeok*
express bus terminal *gosok teominal*
ticket office *maepyoso*
entrance *ipgu*
exit *chulgu*
public bathhouse or private bathroom *mogyoktang*
restroom *hwajangsil*
restaurant *sikdang, eumsikjeom*
tea or coffee house *dabang, chatjip*
bank *unbaeng*
hotel *hotel*
a good Korean inn *joeun yeogwan*
post office *ucheguk*
post box *uchetong*
police station *gyeongchalseo*

Numbers

0	*yeong*	50	*osip*
1	*il/hana*	60	*yuksip*
2	*i/dul*	70	*chilsip*
3	*sam/set*	80	*palsip*
4	*sa/net*	90	*gusip*
5	*o/daseot*	100	*baek*
6	*yuk/yeoseot*	200	*ibaek*
7	*chil/ilgop*	567	*obaek-yuksip-chil*
8	*pal/yeodeol*	1,000	*cheon*
9	*gu/ahop*	2,000	*icheon*
10	*sip/yeol*	4,075	*sacheon-chilsip-o*
11	*sibil*	10,000	*man*
20	*isip*	13,900	*man-samcheon-gubaek*
30	*samsip*	100,000	*simman*
40	*sasip*		

Revised romanization

The following is a summary of the changes to the romanization of hangeul.

K becomes G (Kwangju is now spelled Gwangju)
T becomes D (Taegu = Daegu)
T' becomes T (T'ap-sa = Tap-sa)
P becomes B (Pusan = Busan)
P' becomes P (P'ohang = Pohang)
Sh becomes S (Shilla = Silla)
Ch becomes J (Cheju = Jeju)
Ch' becomes Ch (Ch'angwon = Changwon)

The rule for vowels is that where a breve accent was used on an "ŏ" or "ŭ", this is replaced by "eo" or "eu", so that Chosŏn becomes Joseon, and Ullŭng-do becomes Ulleung-do.

Hyphenation remains optional; in this book we have retained the hyphen in temple and island names, e.g. Bulguk-sa, Jeju-do.

embassy *daesagwan*
International… *gukje…*
…telecommunication office *…(jeonsin) jeonhwaguk*
dry cleaners *setakso*
public telephone *gongjung jeonhwa*
department store *baekhwajeom*
duty free shop *myeonsejeom*
marketplace *sijang*
souvenir shop *ginyumpumjeom*

Useful Questions & Sentences

How far is it from here? *Yeogiseo eulmana meomnikka?*
How long does it take to go there? *Eolmana geollimnikka?*
It takes 30 minutes/1 hour *Samsipbun/hansigan geollimnida*
Please call a taxi for me *Taeksi jom bulleojuseyo*
Just a moment please *Jamkkanman gidaryeojuseyo*
Please go straight *Ttokbaro gaseyo*
Please stop here *Seweojuseyo*
What is this place called? *Yeogiga eodiimnikka?*

Hello (to get the attention of a waiter, sales clerk, etc) *Yeoboseyo*
I will have coffee (or please give me some coffee) *"Coffee" juseyo*
May I have more beer? *Maekju jom deo juseyo?*
May I have the bill? *Gyesanseo juseyo?*
Do you have amethyst? *Jasujeong Isseumnikka?*
Please show me another one *Dareun geot jom boyeojuseyo*
How much does it cost; what is the price? *Eolma immnikka?*
It's too expensive *Neomu bissayo*
Do you understand me? *Ihae hasheosseoyo?*
Please bring me some... *...jom gattajuseyo*
...beer *...maekju*
...cold drinking water *...naengsu*
...hot water (for bathing or drinking) *...tteugeoun mul*
...barley tea *...boricha*
...Korean food *...hansik, hanguk eumsik*
a full course Korean meal *hanjeongsik*
(Something, someone is) good *Josseumnida*
(Something, someone is) bad *Nappeumnida*

Korean Language Schools

Korean language courses are offered at a few institutes in Seoul in two or three-month terms. Student visas can be arranged. Among the prominent schools are:
Language Teaching Research Center
16-17, Daepyongno, 1-ga, Jongdong, Jongnogu
Tel: (02) 737-4641
Yonsei University
Korean Language Institute
Taek 134, Sinchondong, Sodaemungu
Tel: (02) 392-6405
Ewha Womans University
Tel: (02) 3277-3183
Sogang University
Tel: (02) 705-8088

Further Reading

Culture and Religion

A Guide to Korean Cultural Heritage. Korea Overseas Cultural and Information Service, 1998.
Adams, Edward B. *Korea's Golden Age: Cultural Spirit of Silla in Gyeongju*. Seoul International Publishing House, 1991.
Breen, Michael. *The Koreans: Who They Are, What They Are, Where Their Future Lies*. St. Martin's Press, inc., 1999.
Choi, Jae Soon, et al. Hanoak: *Traditional Korean Homes*. Hollym International Corp., 1999.
Covell, Alan Carter. *Folk Art and Magic: Shamanism in Korea*. Hollym Corp., 1986.
Columbia University Press, 1988.
Kendall, Laurel. *The Life and Hard Times of a Korean Shaman: Of Tales and the Telling of Tales*. University of Hawaii Press, 1995.
Korean Buddhism. Korean Buddhist Chogye order, 1995.
Lee, Florence C. *Facts about Ginseng: The Elixir of Life*. Hollym International Corp., 1992.
Lee, Kyonghee. *Korean Culture: Legacies and Lore*. The Korean Herald, 1995. Interesting account of traditional crafts and the people keeping them alive.
Lee, O Young. *Korea in its Creation*. Design House Publishers, Inc., 1994. Poetic writings on everyday artifacts of traditional Korean culture.
Mason, David A. *Spirit of the Mountains: Korea's San Shin and Traditions of Mountain-Worship*. Hollym International Corp., 1999.

Korean Food

Lee, Chun Ja, et al. *The Book of Gimchi*. Korean Overseas and Information Service, 1998.
Millon, Marc & Kim. *Flavours of Korea: With Stories and Recipes from a Korean Grandmother's Kitchen*. Trafalgar Square, 1991.
O'Brien, Betsy. *Let's Eat Korean Food*. Hollym International Corp., 1997.

History and Politics

Alexander, Bevin. *Korea: The First War we Lost*. Hippocrene Books, 1997.
Bird, Isabella. Routledge, 1985. *Korea and Her Neighbours*. Reprint of this thoroughly readable classic first published in 1897.
Choi, Sook Nyul. *The Year of Impossible Goodbyes*. Houghton Mifflin Publishing, 1992. Popular children's book (grade 6+) about the trials and tribulations of a young girl in North Korea at the end of WWII.
Cumings, Bruce. *Korea's Place in the Sun: A Modern History*. W Norton, 1999.
Duus, Peter. *The Abacus and the Sword: The Japanese Penetration of Korea 1895–1910*. University of California Press 1995.
Eberstadt, Nicholas. *The End of North Korea*. American Enterprise Institute for Public Policy Research, 1999.
Hamel, Hendrik. *Hamel's Journal and a Description of the Kingdom of Korea: 1653–1666*. Royal Asiatic Society, Korea Branch, 1998. First in-depth account of Korea by a European.
Haboush, JaHyun Kim (translator). *The Memories of Lady Hyegyong: The Autobiographical Writings of a Crown Princess of Eighteenth-Century Korea*. University of California Press, 1996.
Ilyon; Ha Tae Hung (translator). *Samguk Yusa: Legends and History of the Three Kingdoms of Ancient Korea*. Yonsei University Press, 1972. The first (extant) Korean history.
Kim, Elizabeth. *Ten Thousand Sorrows: The Extraordinary Journey of a Korean War orphan*. Doubleday & Co., Inc., 2000.

Lee, Ki Baik. *A New History of Korea.* Harvard University Press, 1988.

Lone, Stewart. *Korea since 1850.* St. Martin's Press, Inc., 1993.

MacDonald, Callum C. *Korea: The War Before Vietnam.* The Free Press, 1987.

Oberdorfer, Don. *The Two Koreas: A Contemporary History.* Basic Books, 1998.

Yi, Sunshin; translated by Ha, Tae Hung. *Najung Ilgi: War Diary of Admiral Yi Sun Shin.* Yonsei University Press, 1977. Diary of Korea's naval hero of the Japanese invasion of 1597.

Yoon, Inshil Choe (translator). *Yi Junghwans's Daengniji: The Korean Classic for Choosing Settlements.* University of Sydney East Asian Series, Number 12, 1998. A classic 18th-century Korean geography.

Fiction

Carpenter, Frances. *Tales of a Korean Grandmother.* Charles E. Tuttle co., Inc., 1972.

Junghyo, Ahn. *Silver Stallion: A Novel in Korea.* Soho Press, Inc., 1993. A young boy and his mother struggle to survive in their small village recently occupied by UN forces during the Korean war.

O'Rourke, Kevin (translator). *Ten Korean Short Stories.* Yonsei University Press, 1981.

Watkins, Yoko Kawashima. *So Far from the Bamboo Grove.* Morrow, William & Co, 1994. A fictional/biographical account of a young Japanese girl in Korea after World War II, written for a young audience.

Zong, Insob. *Folk Tales from Korea.* Hollym International Corp., 1982.

Other Insight Guides

Over 180 titles in the acclaimed Insight Guides series cover every continent. Titles in the East Asia region include *Japan, Tokyo, China, Beijing, Taiwan* and *Hong Kong*. The entire region is covered in *Insight Guide East Asia.*

There are also over 120 *Insight Pocket Guides*, with an itinerary-based approach designed to assist the traveler with a limited amount of time in a destination. Titles include *Tokyo, Beijing, Canton (Guangzhou), Hong Kong, Macau* and *Tibet*.

Insight Compact Guides offer the traveler a highly portable encyclopedic travel guide packed with carefully cross-referenced text, photographs and maps. Titles include *Beijing, Shanghai* and *Hong Kong*.

Insight Fleximaps combine clear, detailed cartography with essential travel information. The laminated finish makes the maps durable, weatherproof and easy to fold. Titles include *Tokyo, Beijing, Shanghai* and *Hong Kong*.

Feedback

We do our best to ensure the information in our books is as accurate and up-to-date as possible. The books are updated on a regular basis, using local contacts, who painstakingly add, amend and correct as required. However, some mistakes and omissions are inevitable and we are ultimately reliant on our readers to put us in the picture.

We would welcome your feedback on any details related to your experiences using the book "on the road". Maybe we recommended a hotel that you liked (or another that you didn't), as well as interesting new attractions, or facts and figures you have found out about the country itself. The more details you can give us (particularly with regard to addresses, e-mails and telephone numbers), the better.

We will acknowledge all contributions, and we'll offer an Insight Guide to the best letters received.

Please write to us at:
Insight Guides
PO Box 7910
London SE1 1WE
United Kingdom
Or send e-mail to:
insight@apaguide.co.uk

ART & PHOTO CREDITS

AFP 49
AFP/Corbis 172, 173
Art Directors & Trip 134, 187T,
242T, 268
Emil Alfter 128, 140, 222, 251
Heather Angel 18R
Matthew Ashton/Empics 99
Natasha Babaian 95
Paul Barker 48
T. Bognar/Trip 118
Craig J. Brown 4/5, 4BR, 17, 20,
58, 62, 65, 67, 69, 81, 92, 96,
97, 98, 100, 124, 135, 141, 142,
144, 146T, 151, 154T, 157T, 159,
179, 180T, 182, 188, 203, 211,
215T, 220, 221, 223, 223T, 224,
233, 237, 244, 246, 252, 253T,
254, 256, 257, 257T, 258
Tom Coyner 74, 158
Greg Davis 29L, 30, 33, 76, 77,
108/109, 126, 161, 174, 177, 272
Deep-Rooted Tree Publishing
House 145
Mark Downey 57, 116/117, 119
Jean-Leo Dugast/Photobank 226
Alain Evrard 66, 68, 104/105,
194/195
Michael Freeman 131, 149, 270T
From The Voyage of HMS Alceste 31
George Archibald & The
International Crane Foundation 18L
Manfred Gottschalk 106/107
Andreas M. Gross back flap
bottom, back cover centre right,
spine top, 2B, 4BL, 8/9, 52/53,
64, 83, 87R, 102, 140T, 162T,
163, 165T, 166, 167T, 180, 183T,
202T, 205T, 217T, 234, 240, 242,
245, 247
Blaine Harrington back flap top,
back cover centre left, front flap
top, 5B, 6/7, 10/11, 16, 54, 55,
75, 78, 91, 93, 103, 110, 120T,
126T, 129T, 130, 137, 138, 139,
146, 152, 152T, 157, 189T, 190,
190T, 204, 208/209, 210, 213,
214, 218T, 219, 227T, 232, 235,
236, 238, 239, 244T, 259T
D & J Heaton 122
Dong-A Ilbo 255
Hubert D. Vos Collection 34
Volkmar E. Janicke 220T
Catherine Karnow back cover

centre bottom, 2/3, 59, 70, 80,
84, 90, 94, 101, 129, 132, 133,
165, 167, 196, 262/263, 264,
265, 269, 269T, 270
Korea National Tourism
Corporation 1
Lyle Lawson 45, 85, 89, 120R,
153, 154, 160, 231
Tom Le Bas/Apa 123T, 125T,
130T, 132T, 137T, 158T, 169T,
171T, 230T, 232T, 239T, 240T,
255T
Lee Chan-jae Collection 36, 38
Lee Nam Soo 63, 249
Sukje Lim 186
Leonard Lueras back cover centre,
12/13, 14, 39, 61, 71, 79L, 86,
127, 147, 164, 168, 169, 175,
178, 184, 184T, 185, 189, 191,
199, 202, 205, 207, 217, 227,
230, 250, 267, 267T, 271
Melvin P. McGovern Collection
22/23
Barbara Mintz 21
Museum of Yamato Bunkakan,
Nara, Japan, courtesy of A. Yoshida
82
National Museum of Korea 26
Nedra Chung Collection 56
R. Nichols/Trip 123, 144T, 148,
234T
Popperfoto 42
Samuel Moffett Collection 35, 37,
79R
Alastair Scott 47, 120L, 181, 183
Mi Seitelman 19, 171
Norman Sibley 52/53, 60, 215, 241
J. Sweeney/Trip 170
The Center for Korean Studies,

Cartographic Editor **Zoë Goodwin**
Production **Linton Donaldson**
Design Consultants
Carlotta Junger, Graham Mitchener
Picture Research **Hilary Genin,
Natasha Babaian, Susannah Stone**

University of Hawaii 29R
The East West Center, Honolulu 28L
The National Museum of Korea &
The Center for Korean Studies,
University of Hawaii 88
The US Army Archives 40, 41
Topham Picturepoint 25, 44, 46
Bill Wassman front flap bottom, 32,
121, 125, 139T, 142T, 143, 155,
162, 176T, 197, 200L/R, 201,
201T, 206, 207T, 213T, 216, 218,
243, 249T, 253, 259
Werner Forman Archive 24, 27,
28R, 84L, 87L
Stanford Zalburg 43

Picture Spreads

Pages 50/51: *Top row, left to right:*
Craig J. Brown; Craig J. Brown,
Andreas M. Gross, Craig J. Brown.
Centre row: Craig J. Brown, Blaine
Harrington, Craig J. Brown. *Bottom
row:* all photography by Craig J.
Brown.
Pages 72/73: *Top row, left to right:*
Craig J. Brown, Kim Chu-ho, Blaine
Harrington, Blaine Harrington.
Centre row: Craig J. Brown, Craig J.
Brown. *Bottom row:* all photography
by Craig J. Brown.
Pages 192/193: *Top row, left to
right:* Craig J. Brown, Catherine
Karnow, Craig J. Brown, Craig J.
Brown. *Centre row:* Bill Wassman,
Catherine Karnow. *Bottom row:*
Andreas M. Gross, Andreas M.
Gross, Craig J. Brown.
Pages 260/261: *Top row, left to
right:* Taepyongyang (Pacific) Co.,
Craig J. Brown, Taepyongyang
(Pacific) Co. *Centre row:* Professor
An Sonjae; Craig J. Brown. *Bottom
row:* Taepyongyang (Pacific) Co.;
Catherine Karnow, Taepyongyang
(Pacific) Co.,Taepyongyang (Pacific)
Co.

Map Production Colourmap
Scanning Ltd
© 2005 Apa Publications GmbH & Co.
Verlag KG (Singapore branch)

Index

Numbers in italics refer to photographs

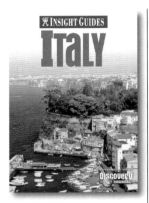

INSIGHT GUIDES

The classic series that puts you in the picture

Alaska
Amazon Wildlife
American Southwest
Amsterdam
Argentina
Arizona & Grand Canyon
Asia's Best Hotels & Resorts
Asia, East
Asia, Southeast
Australia
Austria
Bahamas
Bali
Baltic States
Bangkok
Barbados
Barcelona
Beijing
Belgium
Belize
Berlin
Bermuda
Boston
Brazil
Brittany
Brussels
Buenos Aires
Burgundy
Burma (Myanmar)
Cairo
California
California, Southern
Canada
Caribbean
Caribbean Cruises
Channel Islands
Chicago
Chile
China
Colorado
Continental Europe
Corsica
Costa Rica
Crete
Croatia
Cuba
Cyprus
Czech & Slovak Republic
Delhi, Jaipur & Agra
Denmark

Dominican Rep. & Haiti
Dublin
East African Wildlife
Eastern Europe
Ecuador
Edinburgh
Egypt
England
Finland
Florence
Florida
France
France, Southwest
French Riviera
Gambia & Senegal
Germany
Glasgow
Gran Canaria
Great Britain
Great Gardens of Britain
& Ireland
Great Railway Journeys
of Europe
Greece
Greek Islands
Guatemala, Belize
& Yucatán
Hawaii
Hong Kong
Hungary
Iceland
India
India, South
Indonesia
Ireland
Israel
Istanbul
Italy
Italy, Northern
Italy, Southern
Jamaica
Japan
Jerusalem
Jordan
Kenya
Korea
Laos & Cambodia
Las Vegas
Lisbon
London

Los Angeles
Madeira
Madrid
Malaysia
Mallorca & Ibiza
Malta
Mauritius Réunion
& Seychelles
Mediterranean Cruises
Melbourne
Mexico
Miami
Montreal
Morocco
Moscow
Namibia
Nepal
Netherlands
New England
New Mexico
New Orleans
New York City
New York State
New Zealand
Nile
Normandy
North American &
Alaskan Cruises
Norway
Oman & The UAE
Oxford
Pacific Northwest
Pakistan
Paris
Peru
Philadelphia
Philippines
Poland
Portugal
Prague
Provence
Puerto Rico
Rajasthan

Rio de Janeiro
Rome
Russia
St Petersburg
San Francisco
Sardinia
Scandinavia
Scotland
Seattle
Shanghai
Sicily
Singapore
South Africa
South America
Spain
Spain, Northern
Spain, Southern
Sri Lanka
Sweden
Switzerland
Sydney
Syria & Lebanon
Taiwan
Tanzania & Zanzibar
Tenerife
Texas
Thailand
Tokyo
Trinidad & Tobago
Tunisia
Turkey
Tuscany
Umbria
USA: The New South
USA: On The Road
USA: Western States
US National Parks: West
Venezuela
Venice
Vienna
Vietnam
Wales
Walt Disney World/Orlando

※ INSIGHT GUIDES
The world's largest collection of visual travel guides & maps

Seoul Subway

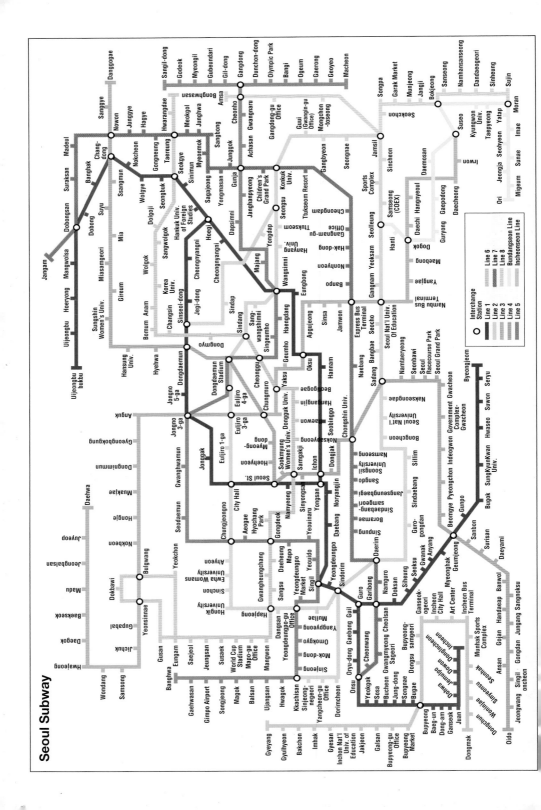